D1626690

The
MAKING
of a
WORLD POWER

WAR AND THE MILITARY REVOLUTION IN SEVENTEENTH-CENTURY ENGLAND

JAMES SCOTT WHEELER

SUTTON PUBLISHING

First published in 1999 by
Sutton Publishing Limited · Phoenix Mill
Thrupp · Stroud · Gloucestershire · GL5 2BU

British Library Cataloguing in Publication Data
A catalogue record for this book is available from the British Library

ISBN 0 7509 2025 4

*To Katie, Sam, Jane and
Brian O'Gorman*

^{TM} ALAN SUTTON™ and SUTTON™ are the
trade marks of Sutton Publishing Limited

Typeset in 10/12 pt New Baskerville.
Typesetting and origination by
Sutton Publishing Limited.
Printed in Great Britain by
MPG, Bodmin, Cornwall.

Contents

Acknowledgements

As in all scholarship, I owe a great deal to many people. My special thanks go to my wife Jane who has worked diligently as a research assistant and cheerleader and to Edith Loe who has been a wonderful common sense editor. I also owe a great deal to Professors Geoffrey Parker, Linda Frey, Jeremy Black, Cliff Rogers, Dennis Showalter, and Brad Gericke for their willingness to read and comment on various portions of this work. The librarians of the Bodleian Library, the Public Record Office, the Pepys Library, the British Library, and the Library of the United States Military Academy have been most helpful and cooperative. Thanks also go to Sarah Moore, a truly superb editor, who has patiently saved me from many of my errors. In spite of the help of these wonderful people, all the errors in this work are mine.

Note: The old style calendar is used throughout this book although the new year is taken to start on 1 January.

Introduction

How did a small, poor, underpopulated nation, which had no regular army and no evident military tradition later than the fifteenth century, whose manufacturing industry was miniscule, whose parliaments prior to 1640 had insisted time and again on the poverty of the taxpaying classes, how did this nation raise, equip, pay and sustain very substantial armies, reaching by 1644 a level of well over 30,000 men on each side, fight two civil wars with considerable skill and sophistication, and emerge in the 1650s as a formidable military power to be reckoned with in the councils of Europe?[1]

How, indeed, did the English state accomplish so much, in such a short time? How did the English governments from 1650 to 1700 sustain and consolidate the gains made in the state's military power during the English civil wars and Interregnum, and, consequently, launch England and the British state on its course as a major world power by 1715?

These questions can only be answered by studying the military, financial, and administrative developments of seventeenth-century England as an integrated history. The explanation for how the English state developed and deployed the armies and fleets that achieved such remarkable success in Britain, Ireland, and the waters surrounding those islands is a military story. England took part in the Military Revolution then ongoing in Western Europe. It did so, however, in a unique fashion because of the obvious geographical situation of the island state. How the English developed the financial and administrative systems and techniques needed to feed and pay the permanent military forces that they organized during their mid-century wars is an equally important question. The answer to this question is essential for an understanding of how the English sustained the military developments of the 1640s and 1650s for the rest of the century.

The forces that made possible the successes achieved by the English during the Elizabethan wars were not maintained when conflict ended in 1604. The government of James I quickly disbanded the fleets and regiments that had fought the Spanish and Irish. Consequently, the first two Stuarts lacked the military resources necessary to support even a very limited foreign policy in the first four decades of the seventeenth century. As a result, England was humiliated time and again by Spain,

France, the United Provinces, and Scotland. These humiliating defeats of the 1620s and 1630s were due to the lack of standing English military forces. The Stuarts' inability to support such forces financially was, in turn, due to their lack of sufficient revenue to pay for the costs of government and war. This failure stemmed from the obsolescence of English financial theories and practices before the 1640s.

Elizabeth I and the first two Stuarts failed to convince their parliaments that the traditional financial notion that the king should be able to fund government from the personal revenues of the Crown during peacetime made it impossible for them to support modern military forces. Consequently, when the Spanish war ended, James I was unable to afford a permanent army or to sustain adequately his small navy. The army was disbanded and the navy allowed to atrophy. During the wars of the 1620s and 1630s, the English parliaments failed to authorize sufficient tax revenue to fund the very expensive forces needed by England to defeat the formidable armies and fleets of her enemies. While English parliaments refused to accept the responsibility for raising the money needed to support modern military forces, the English state remained militarily and diplomatically impotent.

Had this situation continued, it is inconceivable that England would have been able to maintain its control of Ireland, let alone conquer Scotland and defeat the powerful Dutch navy. It is also difficult to imagine how William III would have been able to generate as much military power as he did in 1689. This book seeks to analyse and explain how the English developed the means to sustain the organizational and technical advances made by their army and navy during their mid-century wars. These financial and administrative advances began in the 1640s and 1650s and continued for the next fifty years. They were a direct result of the revolution in military matters that is evident in the development of the New Model Army and the creation of the professional English Navy.

The evidence clearly documents the relationship between military and financial developments in the English state in the second half of the seventeenth century. The English Parliamentarians developed new ways to raise money for their military forces in the 1640s because they faced the choice of doing so or of suffering catastrophic defeat at the hands of the Royalists in the First Civil War. Had they failed to raise enough money to pay their armies, they could not have defeated Charles I. In the 1650s, the Westminster governments found it necessary to retain the standing military forces so that they could conquer Ireland and Scotland and defend the republic's commercial interests abroad. When Charles II was recalled to his father's throne, he continued to maintain a small professional army in his three kingdoms. He and the Cavalier Parliament also agreed to maintain a powerful professional navy. These forces, and especially the navy, found full employment as the King and Parliament led the nation into two more Dutch wars and expanded the overseas empire.

From 1660 to 1688, the taxes and the techniques of financial management developed by the Parliamentarians in the civil wars were continued. By 1688, these new methods of tapping the wealth of a growing commercial economy made it possible for the monarch to sustain a large army and powerful fleet without recourse to additional parliamentary taxes in peacetime. When a period of over twenty years of war began in 1689, the foundations of English military and financial success were well established. In the 1690s, Parliament's final acceptance of its responsibility for the financial affairs of the state made it possible for men like George Downing and Sidney Godolphin to develop the credit mechanisms necessary for a funded national debt. In turn, these fiscal developments enabled the English state to support its continued participation in the Military Revolution and to become a world power.

The first four chapters of this book document when and how England took part in the Military Revolution of early modern Europe. The financial accounts of the navy, army, and Ordnance are summarized to show the trends in the rising costs of modern military forces and to determine when the English state began to maintain permanent and increasingly professional military forces in periods of peace, as well as war. The second half of the book analyses how the English Parliamentarians set in motion a revolution in the state's financial affairs and how this revolution was directly the result and an essential part of the Military Revolution. The role played in English finance by the customs, the excise, and the assessment taxes during the century is looked at closely since these three sources of revenue had become the foundation of English fiscal affairs by the 1650s and continued to be the main sources of state revenue until the late 1790s. Other attempts by the Parliamentarians to avoid levying the costs of war on the taxpaying classes are also examined to demonstrate why regular parliamentary taxation was the only way that the English state could afford the spiralling costs of war.

CHAPTER ONE

The Military Revolution Debate and Seventeenth-century England[1]

England was a second-rate European power in 1605 in spite of her remarkable military achievements in her struggle against Habsburg Spain during the previous twenty years. While her navy had fended off Spanish attacks on England, it had failed to prevent Spanish ground forces from landing in Ireland. Most of the ships that fought against the famous Armada of 1588 were privately owned and hired only for that campaign. Although a permanent naval administration had been established in 1547, and the Crown owned a respectable number of warships, England lacked a peacetime cadre of naval officers and seamen dedicated full time to the profession of arms. A dramatic decline in fighting power and administrative system of the Royal Navy was evident by 1608.[2] A similar trend took place in the affairs of the Ordnance Office, the institution charged with the tasks of providing weapons and munitions to the Elizabethan naval and land forces. The well-oiled Ordnance machine developed during the Spanish war rapidly atrophied as money dried up and experienced administrators retired in the first decade of the seventeenth century.[3]

Early Stuart England also lacked a standing army. No permanent army administrative establishment comparable to the English Admiralty Board or the Ordnance Office had emerged from the Tudor century. Therefore, the Stuarts were forced to employ mercenaries and pressed men to fill the companies and regiments dispatched to fight in their overseas expeditions in the 1620s. To save money, these soldiers were released from royal service as soon as possible upon completion of their specific expedition or campaign. Consequently, for the first forty years of the seventeenth century English fleets and military expeditions remained semi-private affairs. English forces lacked the professional military leadership increasingly employed by the Dutch, Spaniards and Swedes.

The defence of the home islands was left to the militia and a semi-private naval organization, and was never tested. But English overseas military expeditions against Spain and France in the 1620s and Scotland in 1639–40 were abysmal failures, due in part to the lack of trained officers to lead them, and even more to the lack of sufficient money to provide the logistical resources needed to sustain them.[4]

By 1705, this situation had changed dramatically. England's professional navy and army were playing crucial roles in the defeat of Louis XIV's attempt to dominate Western Europe. English forces were operating simultaneously in the Low Countries and Iberia, on the Danube and the North Sea, and in North America. British army and navy personnel, backed by well-established military and financial organizations at home and abroad, allowed the island nation to become a leading European nation state and world power. This remarkable transformation in English power and status was revolutionary.

Warfare reshaped the English state's financial and military organizations in the seventeenth century as England took part in the European Military Revolution. England's participation in a significant number of costly civil and foreign wars forced the English to make fundamental changes to their ideas and practices of warfare and fiscal management. English governments found it necessary to develop permanent professional armed forces in order to surmount the Dutch and French military threats and obstacles to the growth of English political and economic power. These professional military services required immense amounts of money to pay for manpower, logistical material, and armaments. Consequently, the English had to make major changes in their financial and administrative practices and theories to provide the money and material support needed by their greatly expanded permanent military forces. Most of these changes in military organization, finance, and administration were initiated in the rather short period of time from 1639 to 1674, laying the foundation for continued and seemingly self-sustained growth in financial, administrative, and military technologies for the next several centuries.

THE DEBATES ABOUT THE MILITARY REVOLUTION

The evidence concerning the nature of the changes brought about in England as a response to seventeenth-century warfare affects a wider and more important historiographical debate concerning the occurrence and nature of a Military Revolution in early modern Europe. Michael Roberts started this debate with his 1956 article 'The Military Revolution, 1560–1660'.[5] Roberts observed that the period from 1560 to 1660 witnessed 'changes which might not improperly be called a military revolution; and that revolution, when it was accomplished, exercised a profound influence upon the future course of European history. It stands like a great divide separating medieval society from the modern world.' The military developments of that time exerted a lasting influence 'upon society at large', bringing in its train constitutional and social changes.[6]

Roberts believed that this Military Revolution was

> in essence the result of one more attempt to solve the problem of tactics – the problem of how to combine missile weapons with close action; how to unite hitting power, mobility, and defensive strength. And the solution . . . was a return, under the inspiration of Vegetius, Aelian, and Leo the Isaurian, to linear formations. In place of the massive, deep, unwieldy squares of the Spanish *tercio* or the still larger but more irregular blocks of the Swiss column, they relied upon a multiplicity of small units ranged in two or three lines, and so disposed and armed as to permit the full exploitation of all types of weapons. . . . These were fundamental changes; and they were essentially tactical in nature. But they entailed others of much larger implications. . . . [I]t was not only that armies were tending to become permanent, . . . they were rapidly becoming much larger. And this [was] the result of a revolution in strategy, made possible by the revolution in tactics. . . . Battle came again into favour . . . and with it a strategy aiming at battle. . . . The effects of the strategic revolution . . . [were t]he transformation in the scale of war . . . an increase in the authority of the state. . . . Only the state, now, could supply the administrative, technical and financial resources required for large-scale hostilities. . . . This development, and the new style of warfare itself, called for new administrative methods and standards.[7]

Roberts's conclusions are worth quoting at length because he has provided historians with an analytical framework for the understanding of early modern Europe for forty years. It was not seriously challenged until 1976, when Geoffrey Parker published the first significant rejoinder and modification to Roberts's Military Revolution paradigm with his article, 'The Military Revolution, 1560–1660 – A Myth?' Parker modified the concept of an early modern European Military Revolution chronologically by pushing its origins earlier into the late fifteenth century, and geographically by including the sixteenth-century Spanish Army of Flanders in the forefront of the tactical and strategic modernization described by Roberts. Further, he expanded the explanation for the dramatic increase in the size of armies by convincingly pointing out that developments in artillery effectiveness had made medieval curtain-type walls obsolete. This situation, in turn, led to the Italian development of a fortification style less vulnerable to bombardment known as the *trace italienne*, or artillery fortress. As a result, sieges became protracted affairs requiring larger armies to carry them out and, therefore, forcing the dramatic increase in army size observed by Roberts.[8] To sustain the larger permanent forces and fortifications, governments had to revolutionize their financial administrations as well.

Parker's chronological extension of the Military Revolution to the late fifteenth and early sixteenth centuries is amply supported by the evidence. J.R. Hale, in his essay 'Armies, Navies and the Art of War', argues persuasively that 'the forty years between the accession of Charles V in 1519 and the treaty of Cateau–Cambresis in 1559 were more decisive for the evolution of the art of war than any subsequent period.'[9] For Hale, the previous half century had been one of transition, with old and new ideas of war competing, while in the later period 'certain definite breaks with the past were made, and the modes of warfare for two centuries were anticipated'. Like Parker, Hale considers the development of the bastion-fortification, or the *trace italienne*, as one of the most important precipitants of the new age. 'Fortifications were systematized on the basis of the bastioned trace . . . ; no army henceforth dared to take the field without some balance between the three arms, cavalry, infantry, artillery.'[10]

Geoffrey Parker added a valuable extension to the utility of the concept of an early modern European Military Revolution in 1988, with the publication of his book, *The Military Revolution: Military Innovation and the Rise of the West, 1500–1800*. Parker expanded the impact of the concept to the naval sphere by discussing the revolution in naval warfare that took place from roughly 1500 to 1660. He also compares European and non-European military developments in the same period, explaining the reasons for both the rapid collapse of the Pre-Columbian American empires in the sixteenth century and the effective resistance of the Indian, Chinese, and Japanese states to European aggression for several centuries longer.[11]

Not everyone has agreed with the chronological and conceptual parameters of Roberts's or Parker's Military Revolution. For example, Jeremy Black has criticized the concept in several ways. First, he believes that

[a] military revolution is only conceivable against preceding stasis or limited change. Gunpowder clearly brought significant change to fourteenth-century warfare and change continued thereafter at varying rates. But gunpowder did not introduce change to medieval

warfare. . . . An emphasis on the developments and diffusion of gunpowder weaponry in Europe would, however, lead to a stress on the period before that highlighted by Roberts.[12]

Black argues strongly that there were two military revolutions instead of one in early modern Europe and still another at the end of the *ancien régime*. '[T]he revolutionary periods were *c.* 1470–1530, *c.* 1660–*c.* 1720 and (primarily because of the *levee en masse* rather than tactics) 1792–1815.' Black concluded, therefore, that 'Roberts' emphasis on 1560–1660 is incorrect. Equally, though 1660–1720 and 1792–1815 might be periods of fairly dramatic change, the intervening era was not static and unchanging.'[13]

Black also questions the conceptual nature of the Roberts and Parker Military Revolution by pointing out that many of the organizational and technological changes that were part of them, such as the use of artillery or dragoons, were not unique to Europe or to the periods 1430–1660 or 1560–1660. Black maintains that '[t]hese changes have to be distinguished from truly original innovations, such as the flintlock and the socket bayonet, which altered the parameters of conflict'.[14] Further, he points out that many of these 'revolutionary' changes took place over decades and at different rates in different parts of Europe and the world. This pattern of change over a period lasting for decades leads Black to question the use of the word 'revolution' at all.[15]

The debate at this point seems to have produced up to four revolutions in European military affairs from 1430 to 1815. However, this is not the end of the discussion, as Cliff Rogers has entered the lists with two additional military revolutions for our consideration. Rogers argues 'that the focus on the centuries after 1500 obscures the importance of the period in which the most dramatic, most truly revolutionary changes in European military affairs took place'. That period was the Hundred Years' War between France and England, from 1337 to 1453. '[T]wice over the course of the Hundred Years' War new developments revolutionized the conduct of war in Europe. . . . The first was . . . the "Infantry Revolution" [1300–60]. . . . The second, [was] the "Artillery Revolution" [1420–60].'[16]

Rogers understands the logical conceptual implications of his two additional revolutions in the debate. If there were so many military revolutions in early modern Europe, then the paradigm of a single Military Revolution is flawed as a tool for historical understanding. He recognizes, however, the tremendous importance of Parker's 'artillery-fortress' revolution, Roberts's 'administration of war' revolution, and Black's technological and organizational revolutions of the *ancien régime*.

In a brilliant response to the problem of too many early modern military revolutions, Rogers developed an 'alternative paradigm based on the biological concept of "punctuated equilibrium evolution"'. That is, Rogers argues that 'Western military dominance derived from a *series* of sequential military revolutions, each an attempt to reverse a disequilibrium introduced by the previous one, rather than from a single "Military Revolution".'[17] The key to this view is to show that the results of one revolution were both a sharp break with past practice and also that they had profound enduring effects on subsequent history.

The punctuated equilibrium paradigm is a useful concept for understanding the way history seems to have worked over the past five or so millennia. In this model, human affairs, institutions, ideas, etc., have evolved slowly most of the time, but this evolutionary process has been sporadically interrupted and shaped by periods of rapid development. These sporadic and often violent breaks in the equilibrium of an evolving history are what appear to be 'revolutions' to historians.

Rogers's paradigm, however, does not solve the debate swirling around the concept of a Military Revolution in early modern Europe. It misses the point that Roberts, J.R. Hale, Geoffrey Parker, and others are looking at the long course of European history from 'the middle of the second millennium BC' to the era known as the modern period at the end of the second millennium AD.[18] Major 'turning points in the history of mankind', such as the 'scientific revolution of warfare in our own day, . . . may be properly called . . . military revolutions'.[19] To call these turning points periods of punctuated equilibrium is not as useful to our understanding of history as it initially appears. This change underestimates the importance of the few major 'revolutions' in human history which have taken place and qualitatively reshaped subsequent affairs. Roberts's and Parker's Military Revolution is one of these paradigm shifts, on a par with the eleventh-century European urban revolution and the Industrial Revolution of the eighteenth and nineteenth centuries.

There are also problems with Rogers's view that there were two earlier and separate military revolutions in the Renaissance which were of equal importance with the later revolution of Roberts and Parker. First, Rogers's 'artillery-fortress' revolution was technologically, chronologically and geographically part and parcel of Parker's Military Revolution. Parker and Rogers are talking about the same fifteenth- and sixteenth-century interrelated developments in cannon and fortifications that brought about the invention and diffusion of the bastion fortifications.

Rogers's infantry revolution is a much greater problem. The dominance of infantrymen in battle, with a combination of firepower and defensive devices for protection from the charges of heavy cavalry, that Rogers describes in his discussion of the battles of Courtrai (1302), Bannockburn (1314), and Laupen (1339), does not fit his own definition of a revolution. A 'reversal' – Rogers's term – from battlefields dominated by mounted warriors to ones dominated by foot soldiers did not take place in a single lifetime or even in a century, as Rogers said it ought to have to qualify as a 'military revolution'.[20] It is beyond question that infantrymen were being used more intelligently in some fourteenth-century battles than had usually been the case in the previous century. However, infantry, or men-at-arms fighting as infantry as they did at Crecy, Poitiers and Agincourt, played an important role in many battles throughout the medieval period, including Hastings (1066) and the crusader battles of Arsuf and Jaffa (1192). Courtrai and Bannockburn were examples of the proper integration by intelligent commanders of infantry with the other tactical elements available. Good leadership, rather than an enduring tactical system, is the constant in the battles discussed by Cliff Rogers.

The skilful leadership of Edward III and the Black Prince, in the face of inept French generalship, was the key to English tactical successes in the Hundred Years' War. Although the English victories of the Hundred Years' War showed what could be done with the intelligent combination of foot soldiers using a tactical defence and missile weapons on suitable terrain, they did not revolutionize the art of war. More importantly, while infantrymen played a crucial part in a number of fourteenth-century battles, they did not come to dominate the battlefield tactically until the Swiss victories over the Burgundian heavy cavalry at the battles of Grandson, Morat (1476) and Nancy (1477).[21] When not used intelligently as part of what today is known as a 'combined arms team', infantrymen continued to be ridden down by cavalry or torn apart by missile weapons, just as they often had been in the previous two millennia.[22] The English tactical innovations of the Hundred Years' War did not set in motion the political, economic, and social changes that make the Roberts–Parker Military Revolution so important.

Michael Prestwich has recently pointed out that the military reforms and practices of Edward I and Edward III were not a Military Revolution because they did not set in motion the process of continuing, self-sustaining, qualitative fiscal and administrative changes that are the hallmark of the Military Revolution.[23] The significant 'changes of the period 1270 to 1350 were not sustained', owing perhaps in large part to the economic effects of the Black Death. There 'was a striking failure to innovate in the late fourteenth and fifteenth centuries'.[24] In Rogers's paradigm of punctuated equilibrium evolution, the tactical developments of the Hundred Years' War were part of the normal evolutionary process of human affairs.

The ratio of infantry to cavalry varied considerably from 1500 to 1815, as military leaders took into account factors such as terrain, the level of urbanization, and the availability of horses, men and arms.[25] The Spanish, Dutch and Swedes consciously adopted and modified classical models for the solution of the perennial problem of tactics – how to best 'combine missile weapons with close action; how to unite hitting power, mobility, and defensive strength'.[26] Their solutions to these problems were copied by other states attempting to survive in the era of the European Military Revolution. These tactical solutions to a perennial military problem were revolutionary because they set in motion dramatic and lasting changes to the economic, political, and social structures of early modern Europe that have since affected the entire world.

Professor Black's critique of the Roberts–Parker 'Military Revolution' is not as irreconcilable conceptually and chronologically as he contends. Black correctly points out that the year 1660 is not a termination point for major tactical and technical changes in the fiscal–military states that were coming to dominate Europe at that point. Further, he shows how European military techniques were assimilated by the Turks, Russians, Arabs, and other non-West European powers in the seventeenth and eighteenth centuries.[27] However, Roberts and Parker never denied the validity or importance of these points. In fact, Parker, as Black notes in a number of places in his books, expands the Military Revolution to the naval sphere and its implications to the rest of the world, while remaining committed to the Military Revolution paradigm of roughly 1500 to 1660.[28]

The concept of the Military Revolution of early modern Europe, as defined by Roberts and extended by Parker, remains useful and defensible. Many of Black's objections to this concept actually demonstrate its impact on later history. For example, he correctly points out the importance to world history of the tactical, technological, and institutional changes that took place in Europe during the dynamic period of warfare from 1660 to 1815. However, Black is unconvincing in his view that these later changes in warfare, from *c.* 1660 to *c.* 1720, were not the elaboration and diffusion of the Military Revolution of 1500–1660.[29] On the other hand, his recent works on military history convincingly demolish the traditional notion that there was 'an age of limited warfare' in eighteenth-century Europe and for this reason alone are very important to our understanding of the process of seemingly self-sustaining change set in motion by the Military Revolution.[30]

Where does this leave the debate about the Military Revolution in early modern Europe? The debate has clarified the connection of the early modern Military Revolution with the exponential growth in armies, technology, and state power that have taken place in Europe since 1660. It continues to serve as an impetus for further thought and research and has added to our understanding of the process of change.[31] The concept of the Military Revolution in early modern Europe, which is central to this debate, can be fitted into a framework of analysis similar to that used by many economic historians when they deal with the conceptual issues of the Industrial Revolution and the series of changes in human history it has set in motion.

David Landes, in his seminal work *Unbound Prometheus*, deals with an analogous debate about the use of the term 'revolution' in economic history. His conclusions about the conceptual nature of such a revolution are useful to the military history debate. Landes concludes that there was an 'Industrial Revolution' in Europe, from 1750 to 1850, which deserves that title with capitalization. He defends his view by pointing to the long-term sequence of further changes which were set in motion by the qualitative nature of the Industrial Revolution. A paraphrase of his explanation of why the Industrial Revolution is a useful paradigm in economic history is germane to the debate about the Military Revolution in early modern Europe and the major questions raised about it.

Adapting Landes's explanation of the nature of the Industrial Revolution to that of the Military Revolution of early modern Europe points out the wide effects on society of such a truly revolutionary movement. At the heart of the Military Revolution was an interrelated succession of developments in tactics, strategy, technology, and government which changed warfare and the participating states in the relatively short period of time from *c.* 1500 to *c.* 1660. In all of the diversity of these changes, the unity of the movement is apparent: technical, tactical, and strategic innovations exerted pressure on state financial and administrative operations as well as on each other. In this sense, the Military Revolution marked a major turning point in history. In the absence of its qualitative changes, which contributed immensely to the development of the European bureaucratic state, there would have been no guarantee that the quantitative gains would be consolidated. It was the Military Revolution of the sixteenth and seventeenth centuries which initiated a cumulative, self-sustaining advance in military and government technologies whose repercussions have been felt in all aspects of human existence. These advances have in turn provoked and promoted a large complex of economic, social, political, and cultural changes which have influenced the rate and course of military development since 1660.[32]

THE ENGLISH DEBATE

Was England a participant of the European Military Revolution by 1660? John Brewer, in his superb book *The Sinews of Power*, notes that between 1453 and 1689 England ceased to be a major power in Europe and that English military activity consisted largely of naval warfare, civil war, and the occasional overseas expedition. In addition, he contends that England 'was not a major participant in the so-called "Military Revolution" of sixteenth- and seventeenth-century Europe. Only after 1688, when she embarked on the second Hundred Years' War with France, did she again become a major force.'[33] Brewer's views are very important because of the influence *The Sinews of Power* has had on our understanding of war and its relationship to the development of the English state during the late seventeenth and early eighteenth centuries. If he is right, a number of important causal relationships of Roberts's Military Revolution, such as that between tactical developments and the rise of the fiscal state, are reversed in the English case. However, there are some serious problems with Brewer's views about the development of the English state and its participation in the Military Revolution.

One of the problems with Brewer's view is that he confuses the relative status of England as a military power in the sixteenth and seventeenth centuries with whether or not her military, financial, and administrative practices underwent the interrelated changes which are the hallmark of the Military Revolution before 1688. He implies not only that England was often militarily unsuccessful (which is true), but also that she did not exert a major influence on the international wars and politics in the period 1509 to 1688. His second point underestimates the achievements of Elizabethan military forces and diplomacy. His remarks about the timing of the Military Revolution in England are surprising, especially since Brewer acknowledges both the importance of the revolution in naval warfare led by the English Navy in the 1650s and the remarkable performance of the New Model Army in the unification of the British Isles.[34] The absence of a standing army until 1645, and the small size of the English Army in peacetime from 1661 to 1685, may be the main reasons why he discounts the effects of the Military Revolution on the English state and its armed forces before 1688.

Brewer underestimates the impact of Elizabethan military efforts on Western European affairs. While Elizabeth I never possessed large professional military forces in peacetime, her significant wartime military efforts and policies accomplished a great deal more in international affairs than Brewer concedes. The Elizabethans took an active interest and part in European politics and wars in the late sixteenth century. They developed the Royal Navy into the strongest maritime force in the Narrow and North Seas and 'the most powerful battlefleet afloat anywhere in the world'.[35] The English maintained sufficient land forces to retain English suzerainty in Ireland in the face of vigorous Irish efforts to break free. In addition, they influenced the balance of power in Western Europe by committing significant land forces to the Low Countries and France on a long-term basis.[36] During Elizabeth's reign alone, 100,000 Englishmen were levied for English forces serving overseas, and Elizabeth spent three to four times as much money on her land forces as she did on her navy.[37] Most importantly, she and her Dutch and French allies succeeded in their efforts to prevent the Spanish from gaining hegemony over Western Europe.[38] This achievement alone undermines Brewer's conclusion about English impotence in international affairs before 1688.

Elizabeth's long war against Spain brought many of the tactical and technical advances of the Military Revolution to England, even though the island kingdom did not find it necessary to establish a standing professional army until the 1640s.[39] The navy adopted purpose-built warships as the core of the fighting fleet and the Tudors established a permanent Navy Board and naval dockyards to maintain such vessels in peace and war. Army expeditionary forces were armed, organized, and commanded in accordance with the latest continental practice. These military changes were adopted by the English militia as well, keeping England abreast of the technical and theoretical developments taking place in the Dutch, Spanish, and Swedish armies.[40] England was already a participant in the tactical aspects of the Military Revolution, therefore, before her mid-century wars.[41] The military, financial, and administrative practices that were developed during the civil wars and Dutch wars to cope with the requirements of the new model of warfare accelerated the professionalization of England's military forces and of the English state. Most of the military, financial and administrative advances made by the English in the 1640s and 1650s were continued by Charles II after 1660, providing a foundation for later developments.[42]

Brewer minimizes the importance of English military, financial, and administrative innovations made before 1660, and this causes him to conclude that '[t]he emergence of a peculiarly British version of the fiscal-military state, complete with large armies and navies, industrious administrators, high taxes and huge debts, was not the inevitable result of the nation's entry into European war but the unintended consequence of the political crisis which racked the British state after the Glorious Revolution of 1688.'[43] Warfare earlier in the century, and its voracious appetite for money, men and material, was not, in this view, the critical period of the revolutions in government finance and organization which led to the fiscal-military state in Britain. These governmental and financial developments were, instead, the result of the political revolution of 1688. This view turns important elements of both Roberts's and Parker's causality on their heads and supports Black's chronological arguments about the Military Revolution.

Much of the financial side of this argument rests on P.G.M. Dickson's outstanding work in financial history. Dickson, in his book *The Financial Revolution in England*, analyses the remarkable changes English governments made in their long-term credit practices after 1688 and their relationship to the rise of England as a great power in the eighteenth century. He admits that England's amazing string of victories against France between 1689 and 1763 was due to a number of 'extraneous' factors, such as alliances with major continental powers and competent military forces.

> More important even than alliances, however, was the system of public borrowing developed in the first half of the period, which enabled England to spend on war out of all proportion to its tax revenue, and thus to throw into the struggle with France and its allies the decisive margin of ships and men without which the resources previously committed might have been committed in vain.[44]

Dickson's English financial revolution took place after 1688, with the establishment of the Bank of England and the growing acceptance by Parliament of its responsibility for the costs of war and the financial obligations of the government. More recent scholarship by D.C. Chandaman, Henry Roseveare, and Michael Braddick, however, has placed this revolution in fiscal affairs in a longer perspective, from 1640 to 1760.[45] The chronology of the English financial revolution is important to an understanding of the historical relationship of war to the rise of Brewer's fiscal state. Dickson's financial revolution was part of a major shift in financial practice and theory set in motion by the parliamentary wars of the 1640s and 1650s, rather than a sharp break with the past. Its progress was directly linked to the need of successive governments, from 1642 on, to improve all aspects of state financial management. This revolution was one of the interrelated changes that were directly a result of the Military Revolution and the material demands made on the English state by its seventeenth-century wars.

Michael Braddick, in a recent review of the literature on seventeenth-century English military and financial history, concludes that '[t]he 1640s

. . . are important in both naval and army history. It was then that the pressures for change were most intense, and some of the measures taken were of great significance for future military mobilization.'[46] Braddick further notes that the financial and political changes which brought about the 'fiscal-state' were intimately connected with the military changes of the 1640s and 1650s. 'We might say that seventeenth-century England exhibits some of the symptoms of a "military revolution".'[47] While he reminds us not to overstate the significance of the changes before 1688, he observes, 'the discontinuity in revenue totals, army and navy size and the change in the nature of the armed forces in the 1640s and 1650s seem to have been of great significance, and of sufficiently sustained importance, to merit the attention now being paid to them'.[48]

The debate concerning when England and the other Stuart kingdoms experienced the Military Revolution and how this affected their political, economic and military development remains unresolved. This book attempts to resolve it by looking carefully at the effects of seventeenth-century warfare on English military and financial developments. It is useful to review the wars and major military operations of Stuart England briefly before moving on to an analysis of the effects of these on the development of the English Navy, Army, government institutions, and administrative practices.

THE STUART WARS

On the verge of entering the seventeenth century, England was still involved in a long and costly war against Habsburg Spain. Spain was attempting to crush a Dutch revolt in the seventeen provinces of the Habsburg Netherlands. If successful, she would then control the ports facing England across the North Sea. In addition, Philip II, the Spanish monarch until 1598, was attempting to bolster the Catholic League in France in an attempt to crush Protestantism there and eventually in Western Europe. If successful in the Netherlands and France, Philip II would be able to launch the Army of Flanders across the North Sea against the heretical English queen and her semi-piratical subjects. However, because England lay athwart the sea lines of communication from Spain to the Netherlands, her navy and privateers were able to threaten the flow of Spanish forces and money to Spain's main army in the Low Countries, thus preventing a Spanish victory. Elizabeth's deployment of armed forces to the Netherlands and financial aid to the Dutch patriots in the 1580s and 1590s were important contributions to the eventual Spanish defeat.[49] In the early 1590s, she gave similar aid to

Henry IV of France against the Spanish in Brittany. English expeditionary forces served throughout this period in the Low Countries and France, contributing significantly to the Spanish problems of subduing the Dutch and dictating French domestic policies.[50]

In these interrelated wars, the Netherlands and the English Channel were the crucial theatres of operations for the English, even though, after 1594, they were also involved in a major war in Ireland.[51] In 1587–8, because of English financial and military contributions to the Dutch, Philip II made the fateful decision to send the Armada to English waters to neutralize the English and Dutch fleets and to transport the invincible Army of Flanders to England. The English successfully defended themselves from the Spanish Navy (with a fair amount of good fortune), while fighting a long and vicious war of conquest in Ireland. In this way, England played an important part in preventing Spanish domination of Western Europe.

While the English did not develop a permanent professional army in this war, they did raise perhaps as many as 100,000 men for service overseas over twenty years. These men served in armies in Ireland, the Netherlands, and France and in expeditions to the West Indies and Spain.[52] Mountjoy's English army in Ireland numbered over 18,000 men at one point, with thousands of new draftees required to maintain that strength.[53] English garrisons in the Netherlands numbered up to 8,000 men in the 1580s, and another 20,000 soldiers were sent to France in the 1590s. The attrition from disease, desertion and battle in these campaigns was as high as 50 per cent per year, accounting for the large numbers of draftees required to maintain the armies' strength.[54]

These soldiers were, for the most part, infantrymen organized in regiments of 1,000 men each, and armed in the same style as the Dutch and Spanish armies. They cost England nearly £4 million to field and maintain, while the navy cost another £1–1.5 million. These were phenomenal amounts of money, considering that Elizabeth's total annual government revenues were less than £400,000.[55] The garrisons required in Ireland from 1603 to 1614 after the Irish were defeated cost the English Exchequer another £907,488, while the English forces in 'Belgia' required £276,658 in the same period of peace. James I's navy cost another £561,555.[56] However, no serious attempts were made to develop new financial mechanisms to raise the rapidly increasing amounts of money needed for these armed forces, forcing the Crown to sell significant amounts of its land to pay for them in war and peace.[57] Thus, while the Elizabethans and Jacobeans adopted many of the innovations of contemporary continental military practice, they did not carry through the more important financial, administrative, and political changes that constituted the Military Revolution. The absence of the later developments in the face of spiralling costs for war made it impossible for the Stuarts to deploy and sustain effective modern armies and fleets long enough to accomplish national strategic goals.

England emerged financially exhausted from these efforts in 1604, retaining a financial system basically unchanged from that of Henry VIII.[58] While English land forces had adopted the new military practices of the Dutch and Spanish, there was no apparent need to retain a standing army in peace, and the Crown could ill afford one. Consequently, James disbanded his armies as quickly as possible and mothballed most of his fleet. For the next twenty years James paid scant attention to his navy, and even less to the small garrisons in his three kingdoms.

From 1609 to 1620, the Dutch and Spanish maintained a truce, as each prepared for resumption of their struggle. When major warfare broke out again it did so in Bohemia, beginning the European-wide Thirty Years' War.[59] James I attempted to remain uninvolved, even when the Spanish crushed the Protestants at the White Mountain in 1620. However, James did eventually decide to help his deposed son-in-law, the Elector Palatine Frederick V, to regain his patrimony with 2,200 volunteers under Sir Horace Vere. James also sent an army of 12,000 men under the Count of Mansfeld to help the Protestants in 1624. But he could not afford to support his expeditions with money, replacements, or materials. Consequently, Vere's garrisons in the Palatinate were starved out by the Spanish, and Mansfeld's army was quickly destroyed by disease and hunger, returning with fewer than 3,000 men.[60] James I failed miserably in his attempts to influence international relations because he lacked the modern forces or resources needed to sustain modern warfare and diplomacy.[61]

Charles I, nevertheless, carried on the struggle against Spain from his accession in 1625 to 1630. He even expanded the war to include France, but his naval and land forces suffered one disaster after another due to their lack of military expertise and material resources. While Charles received significant subsidies from his first two parliaments, the amounts granted were well below those needed to pay the costs of the navy, let alone to support the army expeditionary forces sent to Spain and France in the late 1620s. Charles was glad to get free of these wars in 1630, having done little more than increase the royal debt and deepen the disillusionment of his subjects.

During these Caroline wars, England's military forces at home and abroad continued to adopt the weapons and organizational technology of the best armies of Europe. However, from 1620 to 1630, royal governments could not afford the resources necessary to sustain their military efforts for any length of time. They also did not seem to conceive of the need to make their naval and land forces permanent and professional until after 1630. By then, Charles I had come to realize that England's diplomatic impotence stemmed from his financial dependence on Parliament and from his lack of a full-time professional navy. His solution to these problems included the levying of a non-parliamentary tax, known as ship-money, and the reorganization and expansion of the Royal Navy from 1634 to 1638. His financial and naval schemes seemed to work, until he found himself at war again in 1639. Then he discovered that his lack of adequate financial resources prevented him from carrying on a war without parliamentary help. So, while the English were abreast of many of the tactical and technological aspects of the continental Military Revolution, they had still failed to undertake the interrelated financial and administrative changes which were essential and integral long-term parts of that process.

The first two Stuarts' failure to solve the related financial and administrative problems of military modernization seems to support Brewer's view that the Military Revolution had not affected England in a fundamental fashion by 1640. Had this pattern of English penury and military impotence continued, it would be hard to refute his view for the period before 1688. However, Charles's unsuccessful wars against the Spanish and French forced him to change the way in which he financially supported and operated his navy, leading to the establishment of a professional navy by 1639. In addition, Charles attempted to modernize his army on the cheap with his 'Exact Militia' programme in the late 1620s. While this programme led to the reorganization and increased proficiency of many county-trained bands, it failed to transform the entire militia because it relied on local taxation for support at a time when England was involved in costly naval wars against France and Spain.[62] In the long run, the progress made in military organization and training in the militia by the Exact Militia programme was important because it enabled Charles and his opponents to begin the civil wars in England, Ireland, and Scotland in 1642 with armies organized in accordance with the latest military standards of the leading continental powers.

THE WARS OF THE MID-CENTURY

England was involved in warfare almost constantly from 1639 to 1674 and the course and outcome of these hostilities reflected and affected the revolution in English military affairs and government in this period. The two Bishops' Wars against Scotland (1639–40) were abysmal failures from the English perspective. While Charles fielded sizeable armies against the Scots in 1639 and 1640, these forces were poorly led conscripts that disintegrated when the Scots advanced. Moreover, the King could not find enough money for his soldiers' pay and sustenance, in part because of his refusal to compromise with Parliament, but also because of the obsolescence of English fiscal theory and the Exchequer procedures used to collect and disburse the revenue that was available.[63] Charles's failure against the Scots was a major part of the reason for the disintegration of Stuart government in the period of 1640 to 1641.[64]

In October 1641, just as Charles and the Long Parliament seemed to be patching up English political affairs, a major rebellion broke out in Ireland, quickly putting English and Scottish settlements and government there in mortal danger. The Irish rebels posed a serious military threat and the resulting war to crush them forced the English to face the military and financial challenges of modern warfare once again. From 1641 to 1652, England fought an expensive and bloody campaign against the rebellion in Ireland, eventually crushing it with Cromwell's conquest. The armies involved in this struggle rose to over 35,000 men on each side, in a kingdom of roughly 1 million people. Before it was over, the war cost at least £6 million and perhaps 600,000 lives, mostly civilians. By its end, a permanent English garrison had been established in Ireland.[65]

Simultaneously to the Irish war, the King and the Long Parliament fought two bloody civil wars in the 1640s, with military casualties as high as 80,000 men.[66] Armies on both sides exceeded 60,000 men and required the complete reorganization of English financial and logistical resources to sustain them. When the Second Civil War ended in 1648, the English standing army had a strength of 40,000 men, not counting the thousands more in the garrisons scattered throughout the nation, and its annual cost was close to £1 million (compared to total annual state revenue of roughly £600,000 in the 1630s).[67]

The Westminster governments fought two more wars against Scotland soon thereafter (1648 and 1650–2), winning both and incorporating Scotland and Ireland into a unitary state garrisoned by English regular army units. At the same time, the Commonwealth's Navy cleared British waters of Royalists, North African pirates, and French privateers. These civil and foreign wars had little effect on European affairs except that they were the crucibles in which England's new professional army and navy were hardened.[68] By 1653, the English Army exceeded 50,000 professional soldiers deployed in Ireland, England, and Scotland and the Navy consisted of over 200 warships manned by as many as 30,000 sailors.[69]

The sustained efforts by the English military forces in these wars was possible because of the revolution in finance and administration that was initiated by John Pym in 1643 and carried through by the Commonwealth and Protectorate. England adopted 'Dutch finance' with the new excise tax in 1643. Traditional theories of taxation were abandoned as the excise came to tax all classes of society and the assessment taxed income and property.[70] All subsequent English governments have continued excise taxes as a mainstay of state finance. Charles I's experiment with a ship-money tax on the entire nation was adopted and expanded with the assessment of 1645, a tax which eventually evolved into the Land Tax of 1693.

Militarily, the English no longer just copied continental practices. By 1656, their army had set a new standard for professionalism and was sought as an ally by both the French and Spanish monarchs. Equally important, their navy was to set the standards of performance and professionalism for the other European naval powers to follow for the next two centuries.

In 1652, England again ventured into a war against a major European power. The First Dutch War (1652–4), was a strictly naval affair, but was none the less extremely bloody and expensive, costing nearly £1 million in 1653 alone. It resulted in a clear English victory and was followed by some major gunboat diplomacy against France and a naval war against Spain (1656–60), both of which were successful displays of England's new prominence as a major naval power. English administrators developed techniques of government short-term credit that allowed the Commonwealth to provide the immense amounts of money needed to support its rapidly expanding navy.[71]

Ultimately, Cromwell's Protectorate government over-extended itself financially by engaging in a major naval war against Spain while reducing taxation in England below the level needed to maintain its credit operations. This situation led to near-bankruptcy, greatly facilitating the restoration of the Stuart monarchy. However, neither the professional navy nor the army was disbanded in 1660/1. Charles II maintained a fleet with a peacetime strength of 60 to 80 warships and a force of 4,000 professional soldiers in or near London, 2,754 regulars in Scotland, 7,500 men in Ireland, several thousand more in 28 garrisons about England and 1,000 troops in Dunkirk.[72] These forces, along with English brigades of roughly 3,000 men each in French and Dutch employ, allowed England to keep abreast of continental tactical and technical developments after 1660.

Equally importantly, the changes in financial and administrative practices and the change in the theory of the king 'living of his own' made between 1640 and 1672 were largely retained. The direct collection of the excise and customs, which had been practised in the 1640s and 1650s, resumed in the 1670s and 1680s, after an interlude of tax farming. The parliamentary oversight of government financial affairs by committees, which was first introduced in the civil wars, continued with the rise of the Treasury.

The changes in English fiscal theory can be seen in the difference between the kings' attitudes to the Forced Loan of 1626 and the Stop of the Exchequer of 1672. In the first case Charles I expropriated his subjects' money through the illegal practice of a forced loan, a loan which was not repaid.[73] In the case of the Stop of the Exchequer of 1672, when Charles II ordered a suspension in the repayment of the short-term loans of a number of goldsmith-bankers, 'there was, . . . no attempt by Charles to repudiate this huge debt'.[74] Instead, the Crown and Parliament recognized the debt as a state obligation, and the bankers received interest and eventual repayment over the next thirty years. The parliaments of the 1670s and late 1690s accepted responsibility for the debt, and it was Parliament which largely made good on the interest and principal.

Charles II fought a Second Dutch War (1665–7) and a Third (1672–4), each of which was inconclusive militarily, although they demonstrated the limits of Stuart financial theory and practice when Parliament provided too little money to sustain the fleet. In the Second Dutch War the Royal Navy showed that it had successfully amalgamated the experienced naval commanders of the Cromwellian period with the gentlemen naval officers of the Restoration.[75] Most English tactical weaknesses in this conflict stemmed more from the confused leadership at the top, than from tactical or technical weaknesses in the fleet. The Third Dutch War was tactically an English victory, but the Dutch outmanoeuvred the English strategically, giving the English time to begin to realize that they faced a new and far more dangerous threat from the growing power of France.[76]

THE GROWTH OF BRITISH MILITARY POWER, 1674–97

The period from 1674 to 1688 is often seen as one of relative peace for England and, therefore, not a period of significant military developments. However, in 1678 England sent a well-equipped and capable expeditionary force of over 17,000 men to the Netherlands to serve with the Dutch and Spanish in a short and inconclusive war against France. Professional Spanish, Dutch and French officers accepted these troops as 'just another regular army'. This acceptance by continental professionals shows that the English Army had come a long way in terms of technical competence from its performance in the abortive expeditions of the 1620s.[77] Large naval deployments to the Mediterranean were also made every year in this period, as England fought a series of wars against the pirate states of Tripoli, Algiers, and Sallee. These military operations on land and sea account for the continued high level of English military expenditure that we see in chapters three and four.[78]

In the intermittent periods of peace between 1654 and 1688 the English also sent major expeditions to the Caribbean and Baltic region. The army regiments and naval squadrons which took part came from the standing professional land and sea forces that were maintained in England, Ireland, and Scotland. By 1687, the English Army numbered over 20,000 men in England alone, and the Navy included 173 major warships manned by thousands of sailors, making England a major military power before the Glorious Revolution.[79] While her peacetime professional army was small when compared to that of either France or Austria, it was capable of rapid expansion. On the other hand, the Royal Navy was one of the two largest in Europe and was led by a comparatively large cadre of battle-tested officers.

None the less, considerable difficulties in English government finance, especially in the long-term credit operations so important to war finance, continued to plague English military operations. These difficulties stemmed from the conflict of political philosophies between the Stuarts and their parliaments about sovereignty and about who was responsible for the costs of war and government. These issues were not completely resolved until the Glorious Revolution, allowing the Military Revolution to continue in Britain in the eighteenth century.[80]

William III's accession to the English throne in 1689, and the political resolution of the Glorious Revolution, harnessed English power to his coalition against the powerful forces of France under Louis XIV. Beginning in 1689, England fought major land and sea wars around the British Isles (1689–92), the Netherlands (1689–97), and the Mediterranean region (1689–97). The growth in the size of the Royal Navy and Army was spectacular. English military costs exceeded anything previously experienced (at least £19.5 million for the navy and £15 million for the army in these eight years).[81] However, the qualitative changes in the English military establishments and many of those in English financial and administrative institutions that made success possible occurred before 1688. The improvements made after 1689 derived from these earlier developments and made possible the continued quantitative growth of the English military forces over the next century of struggle against France.

The next three chapters analyse the development of the English Navy and Army during these seventeenth-century wars. The tactical improvements characteristic of the Military Revolution were evident in the organization of English expeditionary forces and militia by 1600, and starkly clear with the establishment of a standing professional army. Even then, the creators of the New Model Army did not intend for that army to become permanent. The English Navy, on the other hand, had started to become a professional force in the 1630s, with the full-time officer cadre of the ship-money fleets of Charles I. The wars of the three decades after 1640 forced Parliament to adopt these forces as its own. In turn, Westminster governments found it necessary to develop radically new financial and administrative methods to pay and support its fleets. Concurrently, English naval leaders developed a professional ethos complete with articles of war and standing instructions for the fleet.

By 1688, James II had built further upon these developments, providing, ironically, his usurper William III with the administrative, financial, and military institutions necessary for the succeeding twenty years of war against France. England's success in these wars made the island nation of 6 million people a world power known as Great Britain after 1707. British naval dominance for the next two centuries had profound impact on the economic, political and cultural development of the world.

CHAPTER TWO

Prelude to Power: the English Navy, 1509–1648

The Tudor monarchs founded the modern English Navy. Although building on the sporadic traditions of the royal fleets of the fifteenth century, Henry VIII established, by the 1540s, the first permanent administrative establishment on shore to outfit and sustain the king's purpose-built warships at sea.[1] The Royal Navy and its shore establishment continued to grow and develop under Edward VI, Mary, and Elizabeth I, reaching its first peak of glory in its operations against Spain from 1585 to 1603. Allowed to atrophy as an instrument of war by James I, the navy was reformed and reinvigorated by Charles I and his republican and royal successors, as the island nation recognized that its political independence and economic well-being was intimately tied to the defensive and offensive power of its fleets. An analysis of the growth and development of the English Navy and its operations in the sixteenth and seventeenth centuries demonstrates that revolutionary administrative, tactical, and strategic changes took place in naval affairs in the period from 1635 to 1674. These changes were due to the need for English governments to meet the demands of civil and foreign wars. As a result, the English developed the large permanent and professional navy that made England a major European power by 1654, and a world power by 1700.

The most important developments required to make England a first-rate naval power occurred in the 1640s and 1650s in response to near constant warfare. During those turbulent years the English Navy grew dramatically and developed new tactical and strategic practices which allowed it to meet ever-growing naval challenges in British and Mediterranean waters. As a result, the financial, administrative and logistical procedures needed to support far-flung naval operations underwent revolutionary changes from those used before 1640. These changes are evident and measurable in the seventeenth-century naval records. This chapter and the next analyse the changes the English made in their naval administrative and financial techniques in the seventeenth century, showing how the financial, logistical, and military demands of civil and foreign wars forced them to develop the sinews of naval power.[2]

THE TUDOR INHERITANCE

The achievements of seventeenth-century English naval administrators were built on a well-laid foundation and tradition of success. Henry VIII had inherited 7 warships in 1509. He added 82 ships to the Royal Navy in his reign (47 built and 35 purchased or captured), leaving his successor with a fleet of more than 40 major warships.[3] Henry also inherited the naval dockyards at Portsmouth, Woolwich, and Deptford, and established a permanent naval installation near Chatham, on the Medway. The first two Tudors built some of the most technologically advanced warships of their day, incorporating increasingly heavy cannon firepower in sailing ships designed for open ocean voyages and capable of sustaining heavy bombardment.[4] Henry VIII used the navy successfully as his first line of defence against the French and Spanish, and as an offensive instrument against Scotland in the 1540s.[5]

Henry VIII's continuous need to maintain fleets in the 1540s forced him to establish England's first permanent naval administrative body, known as the Council for Maritime Causes. This body began the process of institutionalizing the management of the financial and logistical affairs of the fleet. The Lord Admiral headed the council, which included the principal administrative officers of the navy (the Treasurer, the Clerk Comptroller, the Keeper of the Storehouse, and the Surveyor or Clerk of the Ships, the Surveyor and Rigger, and the Master of Ordnance).[6] Once the council was in place, most naval payments were made through the first Navy Treasurer, William Gonson. By 1557, the government provided a regular, or 'ordinary', annual revenue for the navy's support.[7] The fleet itself was not professional in the Tudor century, since most ships were laid up in peace, and there was no full-time officer corps dedicated solely to the naval service of the state. However, permanent shipyards and a Navy Board had come into existence as 'the expansion of the navy [by Henry and later Mary and Elizabeth] inevitably produced an expansion of bureaucracy'.[8] Elizabeth formalized the duties of the Navy Board in writing, as the fleet expanded in her long war against Spain.

While the later Tudors' regular use of the navy forced the further development of increasingly bureaucratic bodies ashore to take care of the logistical, financial, and administrative needs of the fleet, these changes did not force Elizabeth to create or pay for a professional officer corps or a large peacetime establishment at sea before 1585. Even in wartime, Elizabeth was notorious for not feeding her crews properly and for not paying them after the ships returned to port. Elizabeth earned her reputation for tight-fistedness the old-fashioned way – by doing everything as cheaply as possible. She reduced the 'ordinary' budget of the navy from £13,000 to £6,000 by 1564, in spite of the effects of rapid price-inflation on the purchasing power of this money.[9] She had no other real choice, since she correctly focused her military efforts and expenditures on the critical land wars going on in France and the Netherlands, especially after 1585.[10] However, she continued her father's investment in naval technology and her navy's success in 1588 was, in part, the result of 'a relatively heavy investment by the state in its navy'.[11] Elizabeth I did more with less than any English monarch perhaps, but she failed to modernize English financial thinking about who should pay for government in war and peace (and she failed to create a permanent professional navy). While she kept her military costs as low as possible, she found, as Table 2.1 (below) shows, that the Spanish war required unprecedented sums for the support of the Royal Navy.

Elizabethan naval costs jumped from an annual average of £25,000 in the peacetime years (1566–85) to £87,000 in the war years (1585–1603). The amounts in this table do not include the money invested by Elizabeth and her subjects in the semi-private operations such as the Cadiz expedition of 1596, which alone cost an additional £78,000.[12] Elizabeth also discharged the majority of the crewmen of the thirty-four royal ships whenever she could and relied on hired merchant vessels to serve as additional warships during times of immediate danger. While this saved money, it made it impossible for the traditions of a professional cadre of navy personnel to develop in her reign. Figure 2.1 shows the sharp increase in naval expenditures during the Spanish war.

Shortages of money caused most of the logistical problems of the Elizabethan navy, in spite of the 240 per cent increase in expenditures for the navy in the twenty-year period after 1585. The ordinary charges of the fleet were set between £5,000 and £12,000 per year, a range well below

Table 2.1: Naval Expenditures and Total Exchequer Issues, 1566–1605[13]

Period	Exchequer (£)	Average per annum (£)	Naval expenditure per annum (£)	Naval expenditure as % of whole
1566–70	787,160	157,000	27,497	18
1571–5	896,023	179,204	26,699	15
1576–80	c. 710,000	142,000	26,194	18
1581–5	c. 950,000	190,000	21,718	11
1586–90	1,763,019	352,603	84,387	24
1591–5	1,674,085	334,817	63,179	19
1596–1600	2,205,938	441,187	127,322	29
1601–5	2,268,692	453,738	77,080	17

the amount needed to sustain the force in the dangerous times of the 1570s and 1580s, and barely enough to keep the royal ships maintained and guarded in harbour. The 'extraordinary' naval expenses of the Spanish war forced Elizabeth to sell large blocks of Crown property, in spite of significant amounts of taxation voted by her parliaments. But these large parliamentary grants did not prevent her government from falling deeply into debt. At the end of her reign, Elizabeth's government attempted to solve part of this chronic financial problem by proposing to levy a ship-money tax on the inland counties to help pay for the fixed ordinary charge of the navy. This logical step was abandoned in the face of strong parliamentary opposition.[14] How to pay for an increasingly expensive and sophisticated navy remained one of England's biggest problems throughout the next century. Only after Englishmen fundamentally changed their notions about government and taxation, and Parliament assumed responsibility for both, would the modern English state emerge. These changes were a long way off and would only take place under the pressures of war in the seventeenth century.

The cost of putting ships to sea and maintaining them grew dramatically in the late sixteenth century. Part of the increase was due to the high inflation of the period; for example, the cost of feeding one sailor for one day at sea increased from $2d$ in 1512 to $7d$ in 1588 (a 250 per cent increase).[15] Costs increased also because of the expenses of technological changes, such as the double planking of hulls and the use

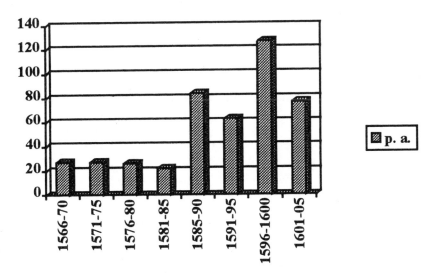

Figure 2.1: Average Annual Naval Expenditures, 1566–1605 (£000s)

of increasing numbers of heavy bronze guns in broadsides. Growth in ship and crew sizes further added to the spiralling costs. The results of these cost factors can be seen from the only Navy Treasurer's account still in existence from Henry's reign. This record indicates that £41,000 was spent on the war fleet in 1546/7, while Elizabeth's 1588 fleet cost between £90,000 and £112,000, and the 1596 expedition to Cadiz cost a total of £172,260.[16] In Henry VIII's and Elizabeth's reigns the war fleet was comprised of roughly thirty royal ships, but the royal ships were larger and more expensive in 1588, and the number of heavily armed merchant ships hired to serve with the royal fleet had increased.

These financial facts should not be allowed to mask the point that the Elizabethan navy was a smashing success strategically. Adequate administrative structures were developed and enough money was found to build and get the fighting ships to sea in critical periods. The Tudor Navy Board functioned well enough under the able administrative leadership of the Navy Treasurer, Sir John Hawkins. The results were properly built ships and adequately supplied fleets. Only two of Elizabeth's royal warships were captured by the Spanish, and none of the ships built in the state's dockyards foundered at sea (while Spain lost most of two armadas to weather damage in the 1590s).[17] England remained independent and Protestant. English money, troops, and ships helped the Dutch United Provinces win their independence from Spain. The Spanish and French could only wish for such results from their efforts.

JACOBEAN NEGLECT

The need for large annual fleets ceased with the accession of James I and the end of the Spanish war in 1604. The Navy Board continued to oversee the royal dockyards and to maintain the thirty warships kept on the navy rolls. These vessels spent most of the time laid up in port, minded only by ship keepers, without a cadre of officers and seamen to man them in war. The decline in the Royal Navy's power presented no immediate danger to England as her former continental foes were busy with the struggles culminating in the outbreak of the Thirty Years' War. James did not purposely decide to run down the navy; he simply treated it like most other parts of his government, allowing neglect, peculation, and lack of supervision to rot the fleet. A succession of inefficient Surveyors of Victuals, a corrupt Navy Treasurer (Sir Robert Mansell), and continuing price-inflation crippled efforts to maintain the force properly. The superannuated Lord Admiral, the Earl of Nottingham, who had commanded the fleet successfully in 1588, failed to display the energy or the administrative skill needed to ensure that the most was made of the

£57,000 spent, on average, annually on the navy from 1605 to 1619.[18] In this period, naval administrative efficiency reached its nadir, although the Navy remained at a strength of roughly thirty ships.

The neglect of the Jacobean navy was so obvious that even James's Council could see the need for reform of its administration. Several attempts were made to correct the situation, with the Council ordering two commissions to investigate corruption. The first, in 1608/9, produced a report that the Lord Admiral and principal officers of the Navy Board were able to ignore. The second commission of inquiry, in 1618, however, proved far more successful.[19] In 1619, all principal officers except the new Navy Treasurer, Sir William Russell, were suspended, the Board's powers entrusted to a commission, and the Duke of Buckingham made Lord Admiral.[20] The Admiralty Commission corrected some abuses and carried out a ten-vessel building programme to replace the oldest warships. However, most fundamental inefficiencies and abuses, such as using fees and perquisites instead of adequate salaries to pay officials, and the practice of treating navy offices as private, inheritable property, continued.[21]

During the period from 1604 to 1624, James's government provided too little financial support to meet his navy's needs for maintenance and new construction in a time of continuing price-inflation and costly technological development. Although the government spent an annual average of £68,000 on the navy from 1620 to 1624, this was not enough to pay for current operations, new construction, and munitions.[22] A look at the annual average naval expenditures from 1600 to 1624 indicates that the amount of money spent on the maintenance of a fleet of roughly thirty ships may have increased sufficiently to cover inflation for the maintenance costs, but it did not cover the costs of new construction to replace worn-out vessels or to pay for sustained operations of more than a small number of warships on the summer or winter guards.

Table 2.2: Jacobean Naval Expenditures and Exchequer Cash Issues, 1600–24[23]

Period	Exchequer (£)	Exchequer cash issues per annum	Naval expenditure per annum (£)	Naval expenditure as % of whole
1600–4	2,366,444	473,288	82,733	17
1605–9	2,574,959	514,991	52,948	10
1610–14	2,931,725	586,345	66,496	11
1615–19	2,112,393	422,478	51,830	12
1620–4	1,869,831	373,966	68,589	18

The first five years of the seventeenth century were war years. Annual average naval costs of £82,000 were very close to the average of £91,000 spent annually in the previous fifteen years of war by Elizabeth's government. During peacetime from 1605 to 1624, the annual average naval expenditures fell to just under £60,000, reflecting the facts that the fleet was laid up in port for most of this time and that little new ship construction took place.

James I's annual naval expenditures were significantly larger than those of the years of Elizabethan peace before 1585 (£25,527 per year). Jacobean increases in peacetime expenditures came close to matching the price-inflation of roughly 150 to 200 per cent from 1575 to 1620, but were inadequate to pay for technical modernization of the ships and replacement of worn-out vessels.[24] Making naval financial matters worse, James's naval administration lacked a treasurer like Hawkins who was committed to the honest management of expenditures. Instead the fleet suffered the financial depredations of the dishonest Robert Mansell, Navy Treasurer from 1604 to 1618.[25] Even if James's government provided enough money to maintain the ships in roughly the manner Elizabeth had from 1562 to 1587, it certainly provided too little to develop the type of professional navy that the Dutch and Spaniards had started to deploy in the early 1600s.[26]

The Jacobean state could have afforded a properly maintained navy, but James chose not to spend enough of his income and personal time for that purpose. Total annual Exchequer receipts during this period of general peace ran from £400,000 to £700,000, amounts considerably higher than the £395,000 per year during Elizabeth's wartime administration.[27] Figure 2.2 shows how small a percentage of total Jacobean Exchequer expenditures were made to support the naval forces.

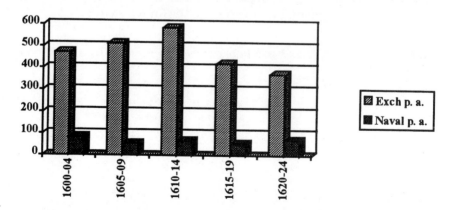

Figure 2.2: Naval and Exchequer Expenditures, 1600–24 (£000s)

During the period from 1586 to 1600, Elizabeth's Exchequer had issued over £91,000 per year in cash for the navy's support, while Elizabeth accumulated £400,000 in Crown debt even after selling large amounts of Crown lands.[28] James lacked the foreign threats faced by Elizabeth and was able to spend more of his revenue on other favourite pursuits.[29] While neglecting his navy, James accumulated debts of over £900,000 by 1620, in spite of a growth in revenue which exceeded the rate of inflation.

Financial and administrative problems continued to plague the Royal Navy into the reign of Charles I. Seamen's wages remained unchanged from 1603 until 1630. Crews could not be filled through voluntary enlistments during the Spanish and French wars, forcing the government to resort to the press-gang, while still leaving the King's ships badly undermanned. The allowance for victualling remained below the costs of the purchase and preparation of food, a situation that financially ruined three victuallers in a row.[30] The Ordnance Office, which provided guns and munitions for the fleet, was consistently asked to do too much with too few personnel and too little money, resulting in disorder and slow delivery of armaments when naval warfare resumed in 1624.[31]

The financial shortfall underlying the navy's administrative problems was part of the larger political, strategic and financial crisis facing Stuart England in the mid-1620s.

> With the advent of the Thirty Years' War the long naval revolution of early-modern times moved up a gear. Changes in the size, fire-power and numbers of warships . . . gathered pace once more. The race for sea power became urgent as Spain . . . on the one hand and the United Provinces on the other, . . . fought for control of the narrow seas and the vital sea-link between Spain and Dunkirk. . . . England lost her lead. . . . The sinews of state power, dependent as they were on taxation and the voluntary collaboration of the landed and commercial élites which largely owned and managed the realm, could not sustain re-armament on the scale required to wage successful war in the 1620s.[32]

CAROLINE DISASTERS

Charles I inherited these strategic and financial problems. His political and religious views made the very difficult challenges seemingly insoluble through the traditional parliamentary system, leading to the military and naval disasters of the 1620s and the rebellions of the three Stuart kingdoms from 1637 to 1642.[33] The Royal Navy played an important part in the Caroline drama before 1640. Realizing the need for an effective battle fleet to support his diplomacy, Charles provided the peacetime financial resources to sustain a full-time cadre of professional officers and senior seamen for the navy for the first time in English history. In the process, however, Charles worsened his domestic political situation dramatically.[34]

In 1625, Charles boldly attempted to face the strategic threat posed by Spain. England sent a force of over eighty-five ships to Cadiz that year in hopes of repeating the financial exploits of the Elizabethans. Only twelve of these ships were royal warships, since the King's vessels were either committed elsewhere or unfit for service.[35] The Cadiz expedition was a disaster, although the English initially were able to seize an undefended bridgehead. Few professional naval or army officers existed in England to command the operation competently, and the ill-trained and poorly led sailors and soldiers got drunk on Spanish wine and disintegrated into a militarily ineffective mob.[36] The King was unable to pay the crews and troops when they returned to England, in spite of the expenditure of £163,968 in 1625 by Sir William Russell, who had replaced Mansell as Navy Treasurer in 1618.[37] The reforms made under the panel of navy commissioners, from 1618 to 1623, had not addressed the problems of how to create a professional naval officer corps since that was an idea unknown at the time. When England needed experienced professionals to train and lead her inexperienced soldiers and seamen in 1625, they were not available.

Charles next decided to face a threat posed by France to English interest in the Narrow Seas, widening his war without adequate military or financial resources. In 1627, Buckingham led an expedition against the Isle of Rhe to help the Huguenots besieged there by Louis XIII's army. The results were predictable. The English army and fleet were improperly victualled, poorly armed, and untrained. England had no leaders capable of conducting amphibious warfare, while the French possibly were better off in all categories.[38] Other equally fruitless naval expeditions in 1627 and 1628 impoverished the Crown while destroying much of the faith Englishmen had in their King. The sight of starving English sailors on the returning ships, combined with the effects that mutinous sailors and soldiers had on the property of people living near the ports, confirmed that English naval administration was on the verge of collapsing.[39] Lack of sufficient money for war and military operations conducted without the benefit of professional naval officers and administrators were the root causes of what was truly the 'low water mark of English seamanship' and naval operations.[40]

Anyone who served in the King's naval administration in the late 1620s faced a potentially disastrous financial situation as well. For example, the Surveyor of Victuals from 1612 to 1630, Sir Allen Apsley, was bankrupted by his efforts to feed the fleet. At the beginning of 1628, he owed £170,338 to the contractors who sold him the food and drink for the fleets of 1625 to 1627. Due to the reduction of naval operations in 1628, he was able to pay off £17,000 of this debt, while providing £72,000 worth of victuals to the navy.[41] In 1629, Apsley ended the year owing his suppliers £189,694. He petitioned for payment from the Crown in 1629, claiming that he had sold or mortgaged his property to the sum of £100,000. He died in 1630 with the government owing him and fifteen other contractors £202,588.[42]

Sir Sampson Darrell became the Surveyor of Victuals in 1630. He carefully avoided Apsley's situation by advancing only £3,242 of his own money in 1630, and by repaying himself for this advance from the money provided to him by the Exchequer during 1634. In 1635, his widow had to pay £3,282 to the Navy Treasurer, since Darrell had come out financially ahead of the navy in his victualling efforts.[43] His successor, Sir John Crane, served from 1635 to December 1642, when he fled to Oxford. He too was careful not to advance large sums to the navy's victualling effort. After seven years in office, he owed the government £1,121, while owing suppliers only £177. Darrell was Surveyor during a period of little naval activity.[44] Crane, on the other hand, was providing victuals during the era of the ship-money fleets and the two Bishops' Wars. His ability to contract for supplies without incurring personal debt was possible because of the much larger amounts of money provided for the navy by the ship-money tax, and because the attitude towards the principal naval offices clearly began to shift in 1635. The incumbents were ceasing to treat their offices as personal possessions and the obligations of these offices were just beginning to be considered state obligations.[45]

Crane was the last Surveyor of Victuals to serve independently of the control of the Navy Treasurer. Beginning in 1643, the Navy Treasurer received all funds for the service and paid a contractor or a consortium of contractors who undertook the task of providing victuals for the Parliamentarian Navy. The Restoration government revived the Surveyor of Victuals office in 1660, but the money for victuals was provided by the Navy Treasurer from the funds he received from the Exchequer. In a number of years between 1643 and 1700, the treasurer dealt directly with victual contractors, rather than through a surveyor.[46] The new procedure for managing victualling money may have improved efficiency and lessened the chances for fraud, since there was now only one responsible financial agent. The subordination of the victualling operation to the Navy Board and Navy Treasurer was a major move in the right direction to a centralized naval administration. While this change did not improve the quality of the food put on the ships, it made it much more likely that there would be sufficient supplies as long as there was money provided to the navy to pay for it.

The years of peace, from 1630 to 1634, allowed Charles I to diminish his naval efforts and expenditures. The figures in Table 2.3, which lists the net combined amounts spent for support of the navy by the Navy Treasurers, the Ordnance Office, and the Surveyors of Victuals from 1625 to 1644, show this trend. These totals are of the money actually paid, and not for the real cost of the fleet in many of these years. For example, the July 1629 estimate of the Navy Board for the charge of the entire naval establishment and operations for 1629/30 was £139,726, while the amounts spent in either 1629 or 1630 were considerably less.[47] Many sailors and merchants who supplied goods and services were not paid, accumulating more debt for the king and generating more ill will towards him.

Annual average naval spending during the wartime years from 1625 to 1629 exceeded £170,000 and constituted over one-quarter of total state expenditures. Little positive results were achieved by the navy in the French and Spanish wars because of the lack of a professional service and because too little money was provided to the fleet to pay and sustain the ships' crews year round. Had England's enemies not been distracted by the Thirty Years' War and their internal strife, the results might have been even more painful to the English. Peace, from 1630 to 1634, allowed a significant decrease in expenditures (to £77,000 per annum); however, starting in 1635, Charles's efforts to develop a professional navy with which to face a threatening international

Table 2.3: Caroline Naval Expenditures and Exchequer Issues, 1625–40[48]

Period	Exchequer (£)	Exchequer cash issues per annum	Naval expenditure per annum (£)	Naval expenditure as % of whole
1625–9	3,356,683	671,336	174,396	26
1630–4	2,155,890	431,178	77,959	18
1635–9[49]	3,809,505	761,901	209,395	27
1640[50]	899,518	899,518	246,474	27

situation increased naval costs above those of the earlier war years, while the Bishops' Wars forced expenditures for the navy and Ordnance Office to over £246,000 in 1640.[51]

Threats to English commerce in the North Sea, the Channel, and the Irish Sea from the French, Dutch, privateers, and North African pirates increased significantly in the 1630s, causing Charles to search for a way to finance adequate summer and winter guards to protect English merchant ships. Charles's new standing navy cost roughly three times as much money as his peacetime navy had from 1630 to 1634. However, the King's political conflicts with his parliaments in the 1620s prevented him from convening a parliament in the 1630s to address the need for a significant increase in taxes to support the navy in peacetime. Had he done so, his parliaments probably would not have provided sufficient taxes every year to pay for the navy, even if the King had granted redress of grievances before asking for supply. The poor results achieved by the fleets fitted out in the 1620s would have discouraged such a course. More importantly, the assumption by many Englishmen that the King should and could pay for the peacetime military needs of the realm out of his ordinary revenue would have prevented parliamentary approval of large peacetime levies. This view of taxation and fiscal responsibility was very slow to die. By 1635, Charles had debts totalling £1,173,198, with an annual budget shortfall of £50,000 to £100,000.[52] These assumptions about government spending and obligations did not change completely to a recognition that the state's debts were Parliament's until the 1690s.[53]

In 1634, Charles and his advisers looked for a way to fund the navy without parliamentary assistance. This was not a new problem. Their eventual solution of levying ship-money on the entire nation was not new either. Ship-money was a charge levied by royal writ on the ports of the coastal counties with the explicit purpose of providing ships, or money for the hire of ships, for service in the Royal Navy. Traditionally, ship-money was levied only when there was a threat to England by foreign naval forces. The Tudors levied ship-money on a number of occasions during their wars, but they restricted its burden to the coastal counties. However, when Elizabeth I faced increased financial problems late in her Spanish war, her Council had considered extending ship-money to the inland counties.[54] James and his advisers had also talked about collecting the levy in peacetime. In those cases, though, the government felt the political cost of extending ship-money would be too high. Charles had a different understanding of taxation and royal power, and a far less sensitive political touch than his predecessors.

In 1634, Charles I, while already collecting the customs without parliamentary approval, decided to collect ship-money in peacetime from the coastal counties that had traditionally paid it when called upon to do so in war.[55] The advantages of a levy of ship-money over a parliamentary subsidy were significant. Parliamentary subsidies had come to produce a stereotyped amount of money with little relation to the changes in wealth or inflation, and over the years had decreased in real and notional value.[56] Ship-money totals could be set by the government based on the need for money to face the current threat, and then apportioned to the counties as a quota for collection by the sheriffs. The annual amounts levied could be changed by the monarch to fit his economic need. Charles's success with ship-money, from 1635 to 1639, proved its great potential as a predictable source of tax revenue. For this reason, ship-money became the model for the assessments later levied by the Parliamentarians during the First Civil War.[57]

The first ship-money writs, levying taxes only on the coastal counties traditionally assessed, went out in October 1634, for collection in the following year. The King promised that the money would be used to equip and support the summer and winter guards needed to defend the coasts and commerce of the realm from the privateers and pirates operating openly in English waters. The need for such protection was clear, with merchants reporting that hundreds of their ships had been seized in the previous few years.[58] The 1634 rate was set at £104,688 worth of ships to be provided by the various ports and counties. The size of the ships called for was intentionally larger than any English vessels except those found in London, with the plan being to commute the provision of ships for money. In this fashion, a cash receipt of £84,594 was expected, along with vessels from London with an annual rental cost of £20,688.[59]

The Sheriffs, who were the collectors of ship-money, paid their receipts to the Navy Treasurer, rather than to the Exchequer. Charles hoped, in this fashion, to separate ship-money from his peacetime revenue, emphasizing that it was for a specific and traditionally condoned defensive purpose. The Navy Treasurer, Sir William Russell, maintained two sets of records and made two declared accounts for each of the years in which ship-money was collected. In this way, the notion was supported that ship-money was solely for its stated purpose and not to pay for the King's ordinary government. The first year's levy was an unqualified success, with £83,571 collected in 1635.[60] Russell received an additional £85,247 from the Exchequer for the ordinary support of the navy that year, enabling him to provide £168,631 for the fleet and new construction, a peacetime record. The Ordnance Office received another £26,376 from the Exchequer in 1635, most of which was spent for naval ordnance and munitions. These amounts were more than had been provided for the navy in any wartime year in the past century except for the years 1625–8 (see Table 2.2).

In the summer of 1635, the first annual peacetime summer guard of 34 ships and 4,130 men was sent out to cruise English waters under the command of the Earl of Lindsey.[61] The fleet did not accomplish much in the way of tactical victories initially, with the ships too slow and large to catch the swift corsairs of Dunkirk and North Africa.

The following year Charles took the next logical step and extended ship-money to the inland counties and towns. The basic premise of this extension was that the entire realm benefited from the protection of the fleet and so the entire realm should share the financial burden of defence. Seven of the twelve justices of the Common Pleas agreed with this line of reasoning and with the idea that the King had the right and power to determine when the realm was endangered sufficiently to require defence.[62] The 1635 ship-money levy totalled £199,700, to be collected in 1636. The amount was apportioned to the counties, with county rates varying from £1,000 for Rutland to £12,000 for Yorkshire.[63] London's share fell to £10,500 and was to be paid in cash.[64] The declared accounts of Sir William Russell provide the following information about the collection of ship-money (below). The rate of collection from 1635 to 1638 was high, especially compared to the uncertain returns of a parliamentary subsidy. Charles spent nearly 90 per cent of the receipts for the direct support of the navy, and only £23,323 of the ship-money went into the Exchequer to repay money borrowed the year before from the Exchequer for the fleet.[65]

Englishmen had good reason to fear the imposition of ship-money in peacetime and its extension to the inland counties. When ship-money

Table 2.4: Ship-money Received, 1635–40[66]

Year	Assessed (£)	Received (£)	%
1635	84,594	83,571	98.7
1636	199,700	195,164	97.7
1637	196,400	189,493	96.4
1638	196,400	178,662	90.9
1639	69,750	55,808	80.0
1640	210,400	47,915	22.8
Total	957,244	750,613	78.4

receipts are added to the ordinary revenues received in the Exchequer in the period 1635 to 1640, it becomes clear that Charles I had the potential to become independent of future parliaments if he kept England out of war. Because ship-money rates could be set by the King, based on his appraisal of the money needed to meet the threats to the nation, they provided an easily expanded income for the Crown. With ship-money, Charles I's total revenue in the peacetime year of 1636 was over £780,000, and his expenditure for the support of the navy was £276,686.[67] Part of the remainder of his revenue possibly could have been used to pay a standing army.

Charles's attempts to improve and properly fund his navy paid off, at least in military terms. In 1637, Captain William Rainsborough successfully blockaded the Moroccan pirate base of Sallee for five months, forcing the Sallee rovers to cease their attacks on English commerce for some time.[68] The full-time employment of the ship-money fleet was the beginning of England's professional navy. The maintenance of regular summer and winter guards provided the year-round duties needed to develop a corps of professional officers and crews. Charles I's ship-money fleets helped to restore 'England's reputation as an ally worth gaining and an enemy worth appeasing.'[69]

Charles spent more money on the navy in the period from 1635 to 1639 than he received from ship-money. He maintained forty-two ships in 1635, most owned by the state, and he employed over 5,700 men on active duty.[70] He sent out sizeable summer guards in 1637 and 1638, while building seven warships to replace vessels constructed before 1600.[71] Charles spent a lot of money on new ships, especially on the *Sovereign of the Seas* (£41,642), the first warship mounting three decks of guns and carrying over ninety large cannon.[72] He deployed a small regular winter guard from October to March, ensuring British waters were protected all year round. Charles's steady deployment of naval squadrons did not stop privateers or pirates completely, but it did provide the opportunity for a professional cadre of officers and sailors to develop, making the English navy a permanent service for the first time in its history. The problems Charles could not solve were how to feed the sailors properly while at sea, and how to pay the fleet when war broke out against the Scots in 1639.[73] Although Charles could afford a peacetime professional navy, he received too little income from ship-money to retire his debts of over £1 million, and he certainly could not afford the enormous additional costs of a land war against Scotland. Naval expenditures fell in the period from 1640 to 1644, as the lion's share of government pay-outs were made for the support of armies engaged in the Bishops' Wars and the First Civil War.

The existence of an effective fleet in the late 1630s seemed to give Charles the idea that he could affect continental affairs without the costs associated with putting an army into Germany or the Low Countries. The ship-money fleets gave him some leverage with the Spanish and French because they both sought English naval help to prevent the other from using the Channel and North Sea as a supply route or operational area. The ship-money fleets gave England sufficient force to serve as a balance among these two powers and the Dutch, but not enough to control the Narrow Seas. Charles misused this strategic opportunity by demanding too much for too little (the return of the Palatinate to his nephew without an English commitment to war). Spain and France saw through Charles's weaknesses and duplicity, as he courted both powers simultaneously.[74] The Scottish revolt of 1638 showed the European powers that they had little to fear from the English, even before Tromp's destruction of a Spanish fleet in English waters in 1639 confirmed the underlying financial weaknesses of Charles's foreign policy.

Charles decreased the ship-money rate to £69,700 in 1639, just as he needed his navy to help in his campaign against Scotland. He was unable to set out a summer guard for the Channel that year, as his expenditures on the navy fell to £167,535, including ordnance costs. Ship-money receipts provided £55,000 of this amount. The regular revenues of the Exchequer proved too little and were collected too slowly to pay for the army the King raised for the invasion of Scotland and for a fleet powerful enough to protect English territorial waters from the Dutch. This situation led directly to England's humiliation when the Dutch attacked a Spanish fleet in English territorial waters and elicited no English response.

The King's chief advisers, Thomas Wentworth, the Earl of Stafford and William Laud, Archbishop of Canterbury, advised him to launch a three-pronged invasion of Scotland in the summer of 1639. Two of these attacks – one by an army moving along the east coast by sea from Newcastle to Leith and the other by a force transported from northern Ireland to south-western Scotland – required the navy to play a prominent part.[75] None of the main thrusts of the plan were carried out successfully, as the King's armies disintegrated without a battle due to lack of pay, food, and adequate leadership.[76] The breakdown of the royal forces left Charles further in debt to soldiers, seamen, and suppliers, forcing him to sign a peace with the Scots and to call an English Parliament. The military leadership needed to carry out these moves may have been available, but the money and logistical structures needed to support them were absent. The biggest cause of the King's financial problems was a lack of credit. This was caused by his previous debts, his failure to enlist Parliament's support for his Scottish war, and because no financial mechanism existed for the Crown to borrow the ever-larger amounts of money needed to support modern armies and navies.

Charles and his Council again decided to send out ship-money writs for the collection of £210,400 in 1640, knowing that part of the money could be spent on the army they planned to raise to renew the Scottish war. The low levels to which the King's esteem and power had fallen by 1640 were shown by the refusal of the taxpayers to pay more than £47,915 of the ship-money assessed.[77] The attempt to collect ship-money as the Short Parliament met in April made it more difficult to get that body to grant financial supply. The King's demand of supply before redress of grievances made it impossible, leading Charles to dissolve Parliament rather than submit.

The débâcle of the Second Bishops' War in the summer of 1640, followed by the revolution carried forward by the Long Parliament in 1641, brought no major changes to naval administration, while the need for an effective fleet remained. The navy received at most £251,681 in 1640 and 1641.[78] This was too little to pay the new debts of 1639 and 1640 and the costs of maintaining a fleet of some forty warships.[79] The navy's debt to its suppliers and contractors in early 1641 alone was £36,937, with a total accumulated debt of over £100,000 for the years 1642 and 1643.[80]

THE PARLIAMENTARIAN NAVY

Charles's greatest contribution to England in his reign thus far had been the creation of a professional naval officer corps paid for by the unparliamentary collection of ship-money and customs, a development not really noticed by contemporaries. Based on the results of Charles's naval efforts, little of the future greatness of English sea power could be foreseen. The performance of the navy in the 1640s showed more positive results, prompting one historian recently to conclude that Warwick and the Parliamentarian Navy may have 'contributed as much to parliament's ultimate victory as any land commander'.[81] When the First Civil War began in 1642, the navy's officer corps and crews joined the parliamentary side, allowing Parliament to cut the Royalists off from continental help while protecting English commerce and thus ensuring the continued collection of the customs.[82]

The Long Parliament understood the importance of the navy and entrusted the position of Lord Admiral to the Earl of Warwick, a competent seaman and leader. By 1643, newly created parliamentary committees of the Admiralty and of the navy worked closely with Warwick to determine naval strategy and to approve the expenditure of funds for the navy's support. The Puritan Parliamentarian Sir Henry Vane became the Navy Treasurer, remaining the sole financial agent for the navy and receiving instructions concerning financial policy from the Committee of the Navy. The professional administrators who had worked with the ship-money fleets continued to manage the naval dockyards and to oversee victualling and ship maintenance.[83] The essential structures of naval administration were thus set for the future.

The Lord Admiral was responsible for the overall management of naval affairs, to include the command and strategic direction of the fleet. The parliamentary Committee of the Admiralty provided guidance concerning policy and strategy to the Lord Admiral. When the Self-Denying Ordinance of 1645 forced the Earl of Warwick to resign the Lord Admiral's office, this committee of Lords and Commons assumed the responsibilities of the Lord Admiral, appointing William Batten to command the fleet at sea. This system worked well enough until the political crisis between the parliamentary Presbyterians and Independents in 1648. Then, when the Independents tried to foist Thomas Rainsborough on to the fleet as commander, a mutiny erupted on eleven ships in the Downs, leading to the establishment of a small Royalist navy in Holland, where these ships defected to the Prince of Wales. During this mutiny, the Long Parliament brought Warwick back to serve as Lord Admiral. He quickly established order in the remainder of the fleet. Warwick served without distinction in this position until the end of the Second Civil War and the execution of the King.[84]

The Commissioners of the Navy, also known as Navy Commissioners, directed the daily administration of the fleet and the dockyards. They performed the responsibilities of the former Surveyor of Victuals and the Surveyor of Ships. Although increasingly overworked as the fleet expanded, the Navy Commissioners carried out their routine work efficiently. They provided estimates of the cost of the fleets and its administration for coming years, contracted with merchants and manufacturers for food, drink, rations, and clothes, and communicated with ship captains concerning the supply and maintenance of their ships at sea and in port.[85] The Navy Commissioners were professional administrators who had learned their skills in private commercial ventures and in the service of Charles's navy in the 1630s. These men were, in the words of Oppenheim, 'prompt, capable, honest and energetic, sparing themselves neither in purse nor person', although it must be remembered that these terms are relative.[86] They were appointed to these salaried positions because of their extensive maritime or commercial experience and loyalty to the parliamentary cause.[87] They were the most important agents in naval maintenance, logistics, and finance in the 1640s.

The Parliamentarian Navy performed effectively in the 1640s. Its summer fleet deployments grew from thirty ships in 1642, to over sixty

Table 2.5: Naval Expenditure, 1 January 1642–31 December 1647[88]

Period	Amount (£)	Monthly average (£)
1 Jan– 31 Dec 1642	201,761	16,813
1 Jan–7 Aug 1643	230,047	31,730
8 Aug 1643–12 May 1645	519,948	24,468
13 May 1645–31 Dec 1646	408,658	20,956
1 Jan–31 Dec 1647	192,258	16,021
Total	1,552,672	
Annual average, 1 Jan 1642– 31 Dec 1647	258,778	

ships in 1648. The number of purpose-built warships owned by the government in the fleet expanded from thirty to forty-five ships in this same period.[89] Parliamentarian naval squadrons steadily improved in their ability to cut off English Royalists from Irish reinforcements in the 1640s, while supplying army garrisons in coastal towns that were cut off by the Royalists during the First Civil War.[90] During the civil wars, the costs of the navy grew dramatically, even though naval operations were secondary to those of the armies. Table 2.5 (above) lists the amounts spent by the Navy Treasurer during the civil wars, including pay, victuals, maintenance, and munitions.

The civil wars caused dramatic increases in the amounts spent by English governments for their navy. The average monthly expenditures for the navy of £23,756 nearly equalled the peacetime annual average of Elizabeth's reign and nearly half of the average *yearly* expenditure in James's reign. Parliament spent nearly twice as much per year as Charles I had from 1625 through 1639 (£153,000), even though Charles had been involved in naval wars in four of those years. Table 2.5 understates Parliamentarian naval expenditure because it lists only the amounts spent in cash each year by the Navy Treasurer: the navy accumulated another £175,562 in debt for supplies, goods, and services used during this period by the fleet, bringing the annual average to £305,294.[91]

The ships on which this money was spent were considerably more effective than Tudor or Jacobean vessels. Frigates built along the lines of the fastest and most modern vessels in Europe became the main fighting machines of the fleet. A ship-building programme was initiated in 1646 to add nine frigates to the force, giving the navy the ability to catch the most capable privateer or Royalist ship.[92] The officer corps begun by Charles I continued to develop, and the navy's shore establishment became better managed and more professional under the Navy Commissioners. The improvement in the technical expertise of the officers which had begun in the ship-money fleets continued, providing England with one of the best navies in the world by 1649.[93]

These developments, and the ship-building programme initiated in 1646 to expand the fleet, were largely paid for with customs receipts. The customs commissioners provided over £1.1 million to the Navy Treasurer from August 1643 to May 1649, or 74 per cent of the cash disbursed for support of the navy by the treasurer. Excise receipts provided another 12.8 per cent of the money spent by the treasurer, and the net proceeds from the sale of prize goods and ships provided 2 per cent. Profits from the sale of Royalist property and fines for delinquents were insignificant sources of revenue for naval finance in the 1640s, providing only £32,000 to the Navy Treasurer (2 per cent of the total).[94]

As the Parliamentarian Navy grew in the 1640s, an increasing percentage of the ships sent out in the summer and winter guards were vessels owned by the government. At the same time, the number of merchant ships hired to serve in the fleets steadily decreased. A process of functional specialization is clearly evident in these statistics. To put this into a wider perspective, the fleet sent to Cadiz in 1625 consisted of 85 ships, with 12 (14 per cent) owned by the Crown, and the summer guard of 1642 consisted of 30 ships, with 12 state ships (40 per cent).[95] The 1643 summer guard of 63 ships included 34 state-owned warships (53 per cent), while the fleets of 1647 and 1648 included 43 navy warships out of a total of 60 vessels (72 per cent of the total).[96] The officer corps needed to command these vessels increased accordingly, further separating the fighting navy from the merchant marine traditions. The creation of a group of officers whose primary purpose was the service of the state's navy in this period was a major step in the professionalization of England's navy.[97] This professionalization of the service continued into the Commonwealth period, with 70 per cent of the fleet deployed being owned by the government in 1651/2, and virtually the entire fleet of 85 to 200 warships in the period 1653/4.[98]

The growth of the Parliamentarian Navy was not inevitable. At the end of the First Civil War, in 1646, the Long Parliament hoped to reduce the fleet as well as the army. Had Charles I come to an agreement with his opponents, the navy might have returned to its Jacobean condition, although perhaps better trained. It is true that the need of the growing commercial and fishing fleets of the nation for protection from pirates and corsairs remained undiminished. Charles I had been correct in his appreciation of the need for the routine deployment of naval forces for defensive purposes in peacetime. A government increasingly dependent on the London merchant community for taxes and loans could not have ignored this situation. In fact, the Long Parliament continued to deploy summer guards of over sixty ships in both 1646 and 1647, but its reluctance to finance these forces adequately increased the navy's debt.[99] In any case, renewal of civil war and the outbreak of a third war against Scotland in 1648 forced the Westminster government to recognize the continued requirement for a large navy. The need for a navy would become even clearer in the 1650s.

THE RESULTS

The English Navy had come a long way administratively and technically since the Henrician foundation of a Council for Marine Causes in the 1540s. Permanent dockyards and logistical facilities had been established and expanded by 1600. State-owned, purpose-built warships had come to dominate the ranks of the fleet in 1648. Professional financial and administrative staffs had been created. Annual estimates of financial and logistical needs for the sustenance of the navy were routinely developed and, after 1642, given to the House of Commons for its consideration in budgeting. A cadre of professional officers, serving the state year round, had come into existence. While the navy had only forty-five warships in 1648, up from thirty in 1603, the potential for expansion was clear, as a number of new ships had been built during the civil wars.

The Achilles heel of naval administration and operations remained its shaky financial base. Further, the techniques needed to deploy fleets at sea for extended periods of time, far from England, had not yet been fully developed. These weaknesses and the lack of technical and tactical expertise were to be addressed and mastered in a systematic fashion in the period 1649 to 1660, as the republican Commonwealth and Protectorate faced numerous foreign and domestic military threats.

CHAPTER THREE

The Naval Revolution

By executing Charles I in January 1649, the leaders of the New Model Army and the parliamentary Rump made continued warfare inevitable. Royalists in Ireland were moving to eliminate the last Protestant strongholds there, while the Scots looked on the English regicides with hatred and were negotiating with Charles II for his return to Scotland as king. Monarchical and Catholic France and Spain condemned the King's murder and freely opened their ports to Royalist privateers preying on English commerce. During the next eleven years, the republic's wars against Royalists, the Irish, the Scots, and the Spaniards imposed unprecedented demands on the English state and its navy. The exigent need to meet these demands compelled the Commonwealth government to revolutionize its naval administration and operations and to continue the taxes developed by the Parliamentarians during the civil wars.

THE COMMONWEALTH NAVY

The Commonwealth, established after the execution of Charles I in early 1649, inherited a professional navy of roughly forty-five warships. The navy went right to work to chase down a small Royalist fleet under Prince Rupert and to maintain sea control in British waters.[1] The Commonwealth's executive body, the Council of State, assumed the duties of the Lord Admiral and appointed three army officers as 'Generals at Sea' to command the naval squadrons. The Council of State created a Committee for the Affairs of the Admiralty and Navy (also known as the Admiralty Committee) to develop naval policy and strategy with the three Generals at Sea. The Navy Commissioners continued to operate the administrative and logistical system in the naval dockyards, while expanding the logistical support provided to the fleet through agents in other major ports.[2] The Council of State's Admiralty Committee directed the Navy Commissioners and the Navy Treasurer in their administrative and financial duties, providing a coherent hierarchical structure for the conduct and support of naval operations.[3]

The small Royalist fleet commanded by Prince Rupert was the most dangerous threat to English commerce and logistical communications in British waters. The Commonwealth Navy hounded Rupert's fleet from British waters in 1649, chased it to Portugal in 1650, and then to its destruction in the Mediterranean in 1651. Professional naval officers commanded squadrons operating against privateers in the Mediterranean, Caribbean, Irish, and North Seas, as well as in the Atlantic and the Channel.[4] These squadrons protected the army's supply lines to Ireland and Scotland during Cromwell's conquests of those kingdoms between 1649 and 1651. Also, for the first time in history, they protected English commerce successfully from pirates in British waters and the Mediterranean.[5] The navy expanded from forty-five warships in 1649 to seventy-two in 1650, as England maintained fleets in the Downs, the Irish Sea, and off Portugal simultaneously.[6] To provide enough ships for these operations, the Commonwealth spent over £42,000 for the construction of ten frigates in 1650, in addition to six frigates built in 1649.[7]

The growth in fleet size and operations required major expansion of the navy's logistical system. General at Sea Robert Blake's sustained deployment off Portugal for most of 1650 forced the Navy Commissioners to expand their logistical activities to supply his fleet with food from England. While water was Blake's biggest logistical problem, requiring the use of Vigo and other Spanish ports for its replenishment, most of his fleet's food and munitions were shipped to him from Portsmouth aboard chartered merchant vessels.[8] These supplied Blake's fleet at sea, allowing him to maintain a close blockade of Lisbon for over six months. When Blake's squadron returned to England in 1651, General at Sea William Penn arrived off Portugal with another squadron to continue the English presence in those waters. These naval deployments were a far cry from the 1625 Cadiz expedition! Such extended long-range operations were possible only because of the radical changes made in English naval finance and administration by the Commonwealth: and they would have been impossible without the professional officers and crews that efficiently operated the Commonwealth's new frigates.

In the early 1650s, the separate parliamentary Committee of the Navy continued to deal with many of the financial and logistical aspects of naval administration, providing warrants for payment and instructions to the Navy Treasurer. However, after 1649, the Admiralty Committee of the Council of State maintained the executive branch's daily control of naval administration while also dealing with naval policy and strategy.[9] The membership and functions of the different committees in the 1650s were not completely distinct, as a number of men served on several committees simultaneously. For example, Sir Henry Vane served as the Navy Treasurer until December 1650 while also serving as a member of the Committee of the Admiralty and the parliamentary navy committee. In addition he was an active member of the Council of State. Vane was one of the most important English politicians and naval administrators in the Commonwealth period. His multiple committee memberships, however, were not unique.[10] The parliamentary navy committee and the Admiralty Committee of the Council of State often dealt with similar categories of business. Increasingly, however, the Navy Commissioners served full-time in their administrative jobs and transacted most of the fleet's administrative and logistical business with the commanders. They had become the heart of naval administration, although a number of parliamentary politicians continued to serve in administrative capacities below the executive or legislative policy-making level as well.

The costs of the Commonwealth Navy exploded from 1649 to 1651 due to the deployment of Blake and Penn to Iberian waters and the Commonwealth's need to maintain squadrons in the Irish Sea and on the Scottish coasts in support of army operations. This trend continued when the First Dutch War of 1652 to 1654 drove expenses higher, to levels never before imagined. Table 3.1 indicates these trends by listing the cash provided to the Navy Treasurer from January 1648 to July 1660.

The Commonwealth and Protectorate governments were at war for most of their existence. The navy played an increasingly important role

Table 3.1: Cost of the Navy, 1 January 1648–7 July 1660[11]

Period	Amount (£)	Monthly average (£)
1 Jan 1648–12 May 1649	316,596	19,787
13 May 1649–31 Dec 1650	782,060	41,161
1 Jan–31 Dec 1651	347,572	28,964
1 Jan–31 Dec 1652	531,361	44,280
1 Jan–31 Dec 1653	1,335,100	111,258
1 Jan–31 Dec 1654	1,101,844	91,820
1 Jan–31 Dec 1655	580,241	48,353
1 Jan–31 Dec 1656	732,486	61,040
1 Jan–31 Dec 1657	572,748	47,729
1 Jan 1658–7 Jul 1660	1,101,319	36,108
Total	7,401,327	
Annual average, 1 Jan 1648– 7 Jul 1660	592,000	

in these wars, which demanded a dramatic increase in its cost, size, and administrative operations. The First Dutch War, a largely seaborne conflict, forced annual expenditures for the navy to over £1 million per year in 1653 and 1654. The Spanish war from 1655 to 1660 cost less, but the fleet was used as a diplomatic tool in the late 1650s in the Baltic and Mediterranean regions as well, keeping its costs high. The sums in Table 3.1 understate the total spent for the navy's support and operation because another £850,595 in net debt to contractors, seamen, and suppliers was accumulated by July 1660. This amount brought the total cost of the navy to £8.25 million in this period (an annual average of over £660,119). Price-inflation accounted for only a part of the increased costs (real prices rose, at most, 300 per cent from 1560). Seamen's wages and the cost of feeding sailors, however, increased less than 200 per cent from 1560 to 1650 and the rise in prices ended in the early 1650s.[12]

Annual average naval expenditures in the Interregnum were more than ten times those for the navy in the heroic years of 1585–94, due in part to the increased size of the fleet (200 state-owned vessels in 1654, fewer than 35 in 1588), and in large measure to the greatly increased tempo of operations. While Elizabethan fleets had been sent out for short periods of time to accomplish defined tasks, the fleets of the Interregnum governments operated at sea for long periods and served thousands of miles from the home islands. The Commonwealth ended the use of merchant vessels as warships, as warships became more heavily armed and specialized.[13]

The requirements of modern naval warfare drove the revolutionary changes which occurred in English naval administration and finance. During the First Dutch War, the navy grew to over 200 warships, requiring 30,000 seamen as crew and thousands more workers to maintain them.[14] This 200 per cent increase in fleet size in two years swamped the Navy Commissioners with work as they attempted to provide the munitions, rigging and food needed to support such a force. The most troublesome challenge they faced was procuring enough properly preserved supplies for the sailors, especially since there were too few seasoned barrels available in which to pack food and drink when the surge in demand took place in late 1652. Shortages of cash and the reliance on an uncoordinated group of victual contractors for rations also prevented the commissioners from fully meeting the logistical needs of the fleet in the summer and autumn of 1652, contributing directly to the defeat of Robert Blake's fleet by the Dutch at the Battle of Dungeness in November. This defeat made the deficiencies in finance and administration crystal clear.

THE NAVAL CRISIS OF 1652–3

The naval crisis of 1652 was a major turning point in English history. The breakdown in the naval logistical system forced Oliver Cromwell and a number of the other leading members of the Council of State to serve on a super-commission to spur along the Navy Commissioners' work. Even more importantly, the Rump raised the assessment tax from £90,000 to £120,000 per month and allocated an additional £1 million from the assessment which was formerly reserved for the exclusive support of the army to the navy over the next three years.[15] Once sufficient money was available, the logistical problems could be faced, enabling the fleet quickly to recover from Blake's stinging defeat. To support this turn-about, the naval administration was reorganized.

From the start of the civil wars, the Navy Commissioners rather than a Surveyor of Victuals had conducted the contracting procedures used to provide food to the navy. Until 1652, this method of victualling met the demands of a forty-ship fleet. However, the five-fold increase in the navy from 1649 to 1653 changed the logistical problem. In response, the commissioners turned to a consortium of victuallers to provide food to the fleet in 1653 while also greatly expanding the logistical infrastructure in the dockyards to handle the massive amounts of comestibles needed to feed 30,000 men at sea in 1654.[16] A consortium of contractors, led by Thomas Alderne, processed and preserved the food and purchased the beer needed on the ships. The system had a consistently poor record in the quality of the victuals provided. Yet, no operations were cancelled or battles lost after 1652 due to the poor quality or shortage of provisions. During the summer of 1653, provisions were sent in a steady stream of merchant ships, used as under-way replenishment ships, to the main fleet of over 100 vessels operating off Holland.[17] This logistical system allowed the English to strangle Dutch commerce with a close blockade of the Netherlands' coast, forcing the Dutch to fight a series of large fleet actions at a disastrous disadvantage in the summer of 1653.[18]

Seven major fleet engagements took place in British waters and the North Sea during the First Dutch War. While none was decisive in terms of bringing the end of the war closer, five were clear English victories, resulting in the capture or destruction of dozens of Dutch warships. These victories gave England control of the North Sea and English Channel, allowing English ships to capture over 1,250 Dutch merchant vessels by 1654.[19] While the Commonwealth's navy was decisively beaten out of the Mediterranean by the Dutch, its success in the North Sea was conclusive.

The battles were bloody for both sides and the task of refitting the battered ships after each engagement was tremendously challenging. The English began the work in 1653 with their much improved logistical organization backed by the full financial power of the republic. By July 1653, the use of hired merchant ships to serve as major combatants had ended. Robert Blake, George Monck, and the professional naval officers had established a tradition of victory which would always be harkened to in future wars. Behind these warriors was a reorganized administrative system that had ably coped with unprecedented demands for the men, material, and munitions needed for victory. The essential lubricant of this system was the dramatically increased flow of money extracted from English taxpayers by the excise and assessment receipts.

The Navy Commissioners oversaw the construction of thirty frigates (at a cost of £300,000) in 1653 and 1654. These ships were to remain the core of the Royal Navy into the 1660s. The navy's expanded construction and logistical activities required a major increase in the size of the dockyards. New bake ovens, slaughter houses, and rope works were built, as the navy became the largest single employer of labour in the country.[20] The commissioners organized hospitals in Dover and Southampton for the care of the many sailors and soldiers wounded in the large and bloody fleet actions.[21] Seamen's wages were raised and pensions were provided for those maimed in action and for widows.[22] The army sent 2,000 soldiers to serve in the fleet, helping the recruiting effort needed to add 14,000 men to the navy in one year.

Blake and the special Navy Commissioners of 1652 and 1653 also made major operational and tactical changes that affected the organization of the fighting force for the next two centuries. The main battlefleet was organized into three squadrons: the Red, Blue, and White. Blake and Monck issued standardized 'Fighting Instructions' to the captains, describing what to do when battle was joined. (The use of such standardized tactics is a major characteristic of modern military organizations.) George Monck joined Robert Blake and Richard Deane in 1653 to serve as the third General at Sea, providing aggressive military leadership to the force. The Generals at Sea exercised unquestioned authority in tactical matters.[23] The Ordnance Office was subordinated to the Navy Commissioners and the Generals at Sea after 1651, streamlining the provision of munitions to the warships and facilitating the arming of the thirty new frigates.[24] All but the last of these reforms were continued after the Restoration.

England's navy became the envy of Europe and brought Oliver Cromwell, the Lord Protector, official recognition from all European Crowned heads by 1654. Clarendon correctly observed the difference this made in the European diplomatic situation, and the enhanced security for Britain that it provided.[25]

To achieve all of this, vast sums of money needed to be generated in a short period. Naval costs were paid for primarily through taxation, contrary to the belief of the eminent naval historian Paul Kennedy, who observed that 'the greater part of the funds for the Commonwealth Navy came out of sequestered Royalist lands'.[26] Only £32,000 was received by the Navy Treasurer from the proceeds of Royalists' fines or land sales from August 1642 to May 1649: another £31,897 was given to the Navy Treasurer by the commissioners as proceeds of the sale of prize goods, for a total of 4 per cent of the treasurer's receipts.[27] A total of 86 per cent of the money spent in the period ending in 1649 came directly from the excise and customs commissioners to the Navy Treasurer. The Commonwealth and Protectorate governments continued to rely primarily on taxation for the financial support of the navy from 1649 to 1660. Table 3.2 (below) lists the sources of money received by the Navy Treasurers from May 1649 to July 1660, clearly indicating that taxes provided most of the cash.

The three regular sources of taxation (customs, excise, and assessment) directly provided 40 per cent of the money received by the Navy Treasurer. From November 1654 to July 1660, the Exchequer provided another 41.8 per cent of the money given to the Treasurer. The Exchequer, in turn, received over 82 per cent of its revenue in this period (£4 million of the total £4.89 million in Exchequer receipts) from taxes and fees such as excise, customs, probate of wills, and the new building

Table 3.2: Sources of Money for the Navy, 13 May 1649–7 July 1660[28]

Source	Amount (£)	%
Exchequer	3,300,859	41.8
Customs	1,318,903	16.7
Assessment	1,105,590	14.0
Excise	733,089	9.3
Fines and sales	506,341	6.4
Loans, gifts, etc.	406,812	5.2
Prize goods	286,857	3.6
Col Barkstead	234,000	3.0
Total	7,892,451	

tax.[29] Another 7.6 per cent of Exchequer receipts came from the sale of enemy ships and goods taken at sea, to include £254,759 worth of silver captured from the Spanish in 1656.[30] Receipts from Royalist and church land sales, composition fines, and sequestrations provided £376,311 in cash to the Exchequer, for 7.7 per cent of total receipts, confirming H.J. Habakkuk's point that most of the proceeds of land sales in the Interregnum were used to retire old debt rather than to provide ready cash for current operations.[31]

Improvements in short-term credit methods were some of the most important developments made in naval financial management in the period from 1649 to 1660. English naval administrators developed an effective way to anticipate revenue and to borrow large amounts of money, well ahead of the development of the order system of the 1660s and 1670s, and long before the national debt was established in the 1690s. Each year the Navy Commissioners spent more money than the Navy Treasurer received in cash. They did this by contracting for ship construction, munitions, food, etc., without making immediate payment. This was not new procedure; what was new was that these debts were carefully accounted for as public and that in the following two or three years most of such debts were repaid 'in course'.[32] Undoubtedly suppliers raised prices to include the carrying costs involved in this deferred payment plan, but they continued to advance goods and services before their previous bills were paid off. This system had not existed in the 1620s, forcing the fleet to limp home from its abortive operations against Cadiz and Rhe and preventing Charles I from equipping the fleet for future expeditions.

One way in which this deficit financing was facilitated can be seen in the provisions for deferred payment written into the contract by the navy victuallers in 1652.

We can supply 12,000 men for one month if we can have present pay of what is already due, *viz.* £23,859 3*s* 8*d*. The balance, *viz.* £15,845 0*s* 8*d* could be paid by monthly instalments between now and March [1653]. What is now under proposal being £11,900 to be paid in six equal payments, at the rate of 8½*d* a man per day. Authority should be given for taking up ships to carry the provisions to the General of the fleet, and the receipts of the shipmasters for the provisions should be our sufficient discharge, in passing our accounts.[33]

The increase in the number of sailors to be fed required the provision of larger food-processing facilities in the dockyards. Money and credit

Table 3.3: Victuallers' Accounts as Percentage of Navy Debt, 1650–60[34]

Period to	New debt (£)	Owed victuallers (£)	%
Dec 1650	116,471	24,640	21.2
Dec 1651	112,289	67,926	60.5
Dec 1652	189,329	148,743	78.6
Dec 1653	287,501	191,223	66.5
Dec 1654	328,308	195,989	59.7
Dec 1655	64,424	Unknown	
Dec 1656	259,593	193,300	74.5
Dec 1657	252,966	189,485	74.9
Dec 1660	421,356	329,829	78.3

remained the crux of logistical matters. The largest single item for which the navy owed money in each accounting period was the provision of food and drink. As a result, the victuallers demanded and received a 12.5 per cent increase in the amount of money allowed to them for each sailor they fed.

A large percentage of the money advanced by the victuallers was paid off in the succeeding accounting periods. Consequently, the victuallers were willing to advance more money with the added incentive of receiving the 12.5 per cent premium. The successful logistical operations of the Navy Commissioners depended on this system of debt management, since tax revenues lagged well behind the immediate financial needs of the fleet. In this way the navy accumulated debt of £128,995 by December 1650, and £506,637 by December 1656, when more than half of that year's total debt was owed for services and goods provided in just that year. This change in financial management is reflected in a change in the format of the declared accounts. At the end of each account the Navy Treasurer listed the individuals to whom money was 'depending', the date of the warrant that authorized this payment for their services or goods, and the amount. The treasurer continued these entries in subsequent accounts until they were paid off.

Suppliers still were willing to advance over £250,000 in goods and services to the navy in 1656 because, from January 1650 through December 1656, the Navy Treasurer had paid off £1,000,925 in old debt, maintaining the navy's credit.[35] To make this system work, warrants listing the service or goods provided, and the amount to be paid by the Navy

Treasurer for them, were issued by the Admiralty Committee or the Navy Commissioners. These warrants could be assigned or sold by the original lender, serving as credit instruments in much the same manner as Exchequer 'Sol tallies' were to in the 1660s and beyond.[36] When the Navy Treasurer paid off the advance, the warrant was endorsed by him and the holder of this credit instrument.[37]

This system worked as long as sufficient tax revenue was collected by the government to pay off significant portions of old debt. When Oliver Cromwell and his Council cut taxes dramatically in 1657, not enough money was provided to the Navy Treasurer, Richard Hutchinson, to retire old debt and to provide enough cash for current fleet operations. As a result, naval debt soared from £506,637 to £1,058,826 between January 1657 and July 1660. The Navy Treasurer paid off only £123,775 in old debt in the last two and a half years of the Interregnum.[38] Because the retirement of old debt had slowed, suppliers and contractors were demanding cash on delivery for food and supplies by early 1659. Such a situation could have been avoided only if the Protectorate had remained at peace after 1654, or had continued to levy higher taxes on the nation. The political crisis of 1659, when Parliament and the army could not agree on the size of the army or how to pay for the large navy and army, might have been avoided had the Protectorate done so.

None the less, the point is often missed that the navy remained effective in the period from 1658 to 1660, as the Navy Treasurer spent £1,101,318 in cash while accumulating an additional £343,788 in debt for naval operations and pay.[39] Officially, the English government did not default on its debts before or after the Restoration, although the evidence is not clear on whether all of the 1650s debt was paid off by later governments.[40] While the navy played a minor role in the coups of 1659 and 1660, and a major role in the restoration of Charles II, English squadrons remained active in the Baltic, North, and Irish Seas, protecting an English expeditionary force in Flanders and the commerce of the home islands.[41] Smaller flotillas operated in the Caribbean and Mediterranean as well, requiring a total of 140 major warships on active duty in 1660.[42]

The power and success of the English Navy in the 1650s is undisputed, although the fleet suffered some notable setbacks in the Mediterranean and Asian waters. Whether a revolution in naval operations, administration, and finance had taken place, however, is still under debate. Richard Harding, in his work *The Evolution of the Sailing Navy*, and John Brewer, in *The Sinews of Power*, maintain that the success and the fine performance of the Cromwellian navy did not mark a Military Revolution at sea for England. Harding points out the contributions of the Tudor and Caroline navies, but concludes that only at the highest level of the state was there a revolution in the 1640s and 1650s. Paradoxically, he goes on to note that 'between 1649 and 1660 the shape, organization and function of the modern Royal Navy was consolidated. . . . It is perhaps this period that was most crucial for the evolution of the Royal Navy.'[43] Brewer clearly believes that England 'was not a major participant in the so-called "Military Revolution" of sixteenth- and seventeenth-century Europe'.[44] If one considers naval developments to be outside military matters, as Brewer seems to, he might be on strong ground. However, this is an exclusion that ignores the most important aspects of the Military Revolution in early modern Europe: its effects on the development of state finance and administration.

Jeremy Black, in his book *European Warfare, 1660–1815*, points to the period after 1660 as one of revolutionary change. However, he is not dogmatic about this, nor does he exclude naval affairs from the Military Revolution. In fact, Black discusses the tremendous advances made by the Dutch and English in naval warfare from 1639 to 1660 as part of a military/naval revolution that took place from 1660 to 1720, leaving the door open concerning England's participation in the Military Revolution of the seventeenth century.[45]

Jan Glete, in his *Navies and Nations*, and Geoffrey Parker, in *The Military Revolution*, are much more positive about the revolutionary nature of English naval history in the 1640s and 1650s. Glete notes that 'the starting point for the great naval race in Western Europe was the [English] civil war', and that this was not a temporary effort by the English. He further sees a process of modernization at work in the growth of the English and other Western navies in which 'the overwhelming importance of war, armament and the creation of permanent military and naval institutions' were central characteristics.[46] Parker observes a 'revolution in naval affairs', culminating in Commonwealth England which, by 1656, produced 'a high-seas fleet capable of operating at long range, on a permanent basis, as an ocean-going force: it was arguably the first in European history'.[47]

The evidence we have looked at so far in this chapter and in chapter two supports the conclusion that a naval revolution occurred in England in the mid-seventeenth century. The English built on the Tudor tradition, but their naval administration, finance, logistics, and tactics changed dramatically in the 1640s and 1650s. The magnitude of the changes is easy to see when looking at the financial data and the growth in the fleet. The professionalization of the naval officer corps and of the administrative services is equally clear and important. A transition took place from the use of politicians in key financial or administrative posts, such as Sir Henry Vane as Navy Treasurer, to the employment of professionals in these posts, such as Richard Hutchinson. In the 1650s, Navy Commissioners such as John Hollond and Phineas Pett became full-time administrators. Men like George Downing in the Exchequer and Samuel Pepys in the navy administration carried this tradition into the Restoration. The first set of standing fighting instructions for the tactical employment of the fleet that were developed in the First Dutch War (1652–4) remained the standard for English naval practice through the Napoleonic wars.[48] These developments continued after the Restoration in 1660, marking them as the beginning of the modern English navy and not as just harbingers of future naval methods and greatness.

The Commonwealth's navy, under the command of Edward Montague, joined the army in facilitating the return of Charles II in May 1660.[49] Charles was quick to promise payment of all of the sailors' arrears in pay, securing their immediate loyalty, and to install his brother James, Duke of York, as Lord High Admiral.

THE RESTORATION NAVY

Charles II inherited one of the strongest navies in Europe. In 1661, he maintained a peacetime fleet of sixty-six warships on active service, manned by over 8,000 sailors, to defend his kingdom's far-flung possessions and commerce. At least another sixty warships were kept in storage for use in conflict.[50] Charles II's brother James served as Lord High Admiral, while the tactical command of the squadrons remained in the hands of veteran admirals such as George Monck, Edward Montague, and William Batten. The administrative improvements of the 1650s were continued, especially the work of the commissioners in the state dockyards managing victualling, construction, and ship maintenance.[51] Although a number of politically radical officers were removed from the navy in 1661, a large percentage of the flag officers, captains and masters were kept, and even more were recalled to duty in 1664.[52] The professionalization of the officer corps continued, with a formal officer education programme instituted in 1662 for the training of young gentlemen, leading to a competitive certification and oral examination by 1670.[53] Such a system allowed the Royal Navy to merge experience-hardened sea captains with aristocratic gentlemen, both of whom had a vocation for the naval service.

England continued to need a strong navy in the 1660s, as Colbert and Louis XIV expanded the French battlefleet from twenty-five ships in 1661 to eighty-one in 1671, and the Dutch expanded their challenge to the growing English commerce and empire. The Second Dutch War in 1665–7 and a third in 1672–4 put the English Navy to the test, finding it not always up to the task because too little money was provided to maintain the ships in fighting trim. While the tactical results of the battles at sea were a draw, the English were humiliated by the Dutch destruction of a number of laid-up ships in the Medway in 1667. These challenges and wars forced the English to sustain the dramatic increases that had taken place in the size, cost, and administrative complexity of the navy during the Interregnum.[54] Table 3.4 (below) lists the expenditures made by the Navy Treasurers for the support of the navy, to include victualling costs and new debt accrued for services and commodities, from 6 July 1660 to 31 January 1680.

The separate Ordnance Office spent an additional £2 million for the purchase of cannon and munitions for the fleet and army from July 1660 to April 1680.[55] Most of the Ordnance Office expenditures were for the support of naval operations. Consequently, total naval expenditures exceeded £12.8 million (£643,000 annual average). Charles II's governments spent nearly the same amount on the navy, on the average, from 1660 through 1680 as the Commonwealth and Protectorate governments had spent in the 1650s (£692,000 per year, including new debt). During this period real prices declined slowly.[56]

It is somewhat amazing that Charles II's ministers could find so much money to spend on the fleet, since Parliament still operated with the impression that the King should live of his own. Parliament's unwillingness to finance adequately the ordinary operation of the government and English armed forces after the Restoration remained the most important reason for the nation's governmental insolvency. While

Table 3.4: Navy Treasurers' Expenditures, 7 July 1660–31 January 1680[57]

Period	Amount (£)	Average per annum (£)
7 Jul 1660–31 Dec 1664	1,814,653	403,256
1 Jan 1665–31 Dec 1669	3,916,130	783,226
1 Jan 1670–31 Dec 1674	2,616,852	523,370
1 Jan 1675–31 Jan 1680	2,470,022	494,004
Total	10,817,657	
Annual average, 7 Jul 1660– 31 Jan 1680		551,921

methods of debt management and government finance had developed remarkably during the Interregnum and Restoration, the attitudes and theories of fiscal responsibility on the part of the nation's representatives in times of peace were still semi-medieval. Only the Commonwealth government of 1652 to 1654 had raised adequate tax revenue to support its navy, and that was due primarily to the obvious threat to London's commerce by the Dutch fleet.

The Cavalier Parliament did settle an ordinary annual income of £1.2 million on the King in 1660. This permanent revenue was to be raised on the receipts of the customs and the excise. Unfortunately, these revenues were unpredictable, depending as they did on the rate of economic activity in the nation. In 1662, the ordinary revenue was well below £1 million, forcing Parliament to impose a hearth tax designed to raise another £300,000 per year.[58] This tax brought in only £87,000 in its first year and never more than £200,000 before 1678. As a result, a poor financial situation got worse, even before war with the Dutch broke out in 1665.

Navy short-term debt grew from about £50,000 in 1661, to at least £299,000 in June 1667. Most of this debt was carried in the form of tallies or bills imprested on tax receipts due into the Exchequer which had been allocated to the navy's financial support. The greatest increase was the £180,109 in debt accumulated during the First Dutch War from 1665 to 1667. Only £102,070 in old debt was cleared by 1668.[59] Tallies of over £1 million, anticipating the ordinary revenue of the customs, excise and hearth tax, also had been issued by the government by 1665. These immense obligations of future revenue for all practical purposes made it impossible to raise additional sums on the credit of the ordinary revenue when the Dutch war began. Although Parliament responded by granting direct taxes worth over £1 million per year in the period of 1665 to 1667, the net debt continued to increase.[60]

However, from 1665 to 1667, a major improvement was made in the methods of deferred payment used during the Interregnum. George Downing, Secretary to the Treasury Board from 1667 to 1671, and an Exchequer Teller in the 1650s, advocated the use of a 'credit order' system to solve the perennial problem caused by the time lag between tax authorization by the legislature and its collection in the country.[61] In 1665, the Exchequer issued written repayment orders payable in the sequence in which written and secured only by the receipts of the extraordinary war taxes granted by Parliament.[62] This system of order payments supported the credit needed to get the 130 warships of the fleet ready for sea. This system worked well, and was carried a step further in 1667.

It was in these circumstances . . . that the Treasury Commissioners embarked on the most important financial experiment of the period by deciding to apply to the ordinary revenue the technique of raising credit upon Orders, registered and repayable 'in course', which had been introduced, with parliamentary backing, in 1665 as an expedient of extraordinary war finance. The essence of the Order system was an attempt to reach down for government loans beyond the . . . moneyed interests to the . . . small investors by offering them, in contrast to the haphazard repayment methods of the [Exchequer] tally, . . . guaranteed means of repayment with interest at the Exchequer from the yield of strictly reserved funds.[63]

This system allowed Charles II's government to stave off bankruptcy for four more years and might have become the basis for a national debt and national bank in the 1670s if Parliament had funded the government adequately. As W.A. Shaw observed, if Downing's experiment had succeeded,

the Exchequer would have become a national bank. . . . Thus was evolved the method of paying 'in course' which was subsequently, under William III, made the basis of the scheme for working Exchequer bills. Had Charles's experiment not been interrupted by the Stop of the Exchequer in 1672, it is possible – even likely – that the Exchequer would have evolved something like the later Exchequer bill much earlier than 1696. As it was, the experiment was a modified success. Money began to come from the public by way of loan on the Additional Aid in January 1665–6.[64]

However, any state's credit system is only as good as its lenders' faith in the government's ability to repay its obligations, with interest. Thus, public faith was based on the extraction of adequate tax revenue by Parliament.

Parliament, however, reduced the level of extraordinary direct taxation to £800,000 per year from 1667 to 1669, and then to less than £100,000 in 1670 and 1671, just as the effects of a naval war, plague, and the London fire devastated economic activity and, therefore, the yields of the customs and excise.[65] Not surprisingly, the Exchequer Order system was abused by the cash-starved government. The Exchequer issued far more orders than could be paid off by the steadily decreasing revenues. While the Exchequer issued the Navy

Treasurer over £1.7 million in money, tallies, and orders for the support of the fleet in 1667 alone, much of the navy had to be demobilized because insufficient money was available to repair and rearm the ships and to pay and feed the crews. This situation led directly to the humiliation on the Medway in 1667, when the Dutch sailed into the Thames and up the Medway, where they burned or captured a number of warships. This naval disaster was the lowest point in modern English naval history since 1625, and was brought on by Parliament's failure to provide adequate revenue to the government to defend the nation against her greatest commercial rival. The Stop of the Exchequer, in 1672, capped off this dismal period in English financial and political history.

By July 1673, the navy's financial situation had dramatically worsened, with naval short-term debt standing at £661,107, reflecting the general financial crisis that brought on the Stop of the Exchequer. Charles's financial problems in the 1660s and 1670s were caused by the Restoration Parliament's failure to give him adequate ordinary revenues to pay the state's debts in 1660, and by his desire to maintain a large fleet in both peacetime and war.[66] However, Charles still found £9.6 million to spend on the maintenance of an active fleet varying in size from 60 warships and 8,000 men in 1662 to over 130 warships and 23,000 sailors in the Second Dutch War.[67] The maintenance of such a large fleet in peace and war continued the process of professionalization already evident in the 1650s.

The consolidation, during the 1660s, of earlier professional and administrative advances were due in large part to the keen interest taken in the navy by James, Duke of York and Lord High Admiral, and the practical experience of administrators and commanders like William Batten, Samuel Pepys, Peter Pett, and William Penn. The Commonwealth's use of salaries in combination with fixed fees to pay the commissioners, officers and the treasurer continued. Offices were held at the King's pleasure instead of 'for life', as before 1635.[68] The amount of work transacted by the Navy Commissioners expanded nearly twenty-fold from the First Dutch War to the Second, forcing further elaboration of the bureaucracy.[69] The Admiralty Board and its agents in the dockyards and ports responded well to the wartime challenges in the 1660s, in spite of their financial difficulties. The fleet held its own in battle against a powerful Dutch navy until the débâcle of the Medway. The inconclusive results of the battles in the Second Dutch War, and the Royal Navy's poor tactical performance in the Third Dutch War had more to do with poor decisions by senior commanders, and lack of cooperation with England's French ally, than with any major failures in

Table 3.5: Navy Expenditures, 1 February 1680–31 December 1699[70]

Period	Amount (£)	Average per annum (£)
1 Feb 1680–31 Dec 1684	2,561,748	521,740
1 Jan 1685–4 Apr 1689	1,807,351	425,259
5 Apr 1689–31 Mar 1694	6,730,686	1,346,137
1 Apr 1694–31 Dec 1699	10,902,507	1,896,031
Total	22,002,292	
Annual average, 1 Feb 1680–31 Dec 1699		1,100,114

administrative or logistical practice.[71] The inability of the naval administration to provision and arm the fleet in 1667 was due to the government's general fiscal crisis.

After 1674, Charles II gave up his attempt to maintain the navy on or near a wartime footing during peacetime. None the less, English squadrons remained active in the Caribbean, the western Mediterranean, and the Channel, protecting commerce, attacking North African pirate-states, and serving as a valuable diplomatic tool for the King. As a result, during the fifteen years of peace after 1674, high expenditures in support of the navy continued, as Tables 3.4 and 3.5 indicate.

The Ordnance Office received an additional £597,793 from the Exchequer from April 1680 to September 1688, bringing total annual naval costs to £584,000. While the annual average expenditure of £584,000 in the peacetime years from 1680 to 1688 was below the annual average of £643,000 spent in the period from 1660 to 1680, it was a significant amount. Clearly, the English spent enough on their navy in peacetime to maintain its professional officer corps and to keep an adequate battlefleet afloat to preserve England's place as a major naval power.[72] Navy debt continued to grow, reaching £1,521,284 in June 1681.[73] But this debt was largely in the form of Exchequer tallies and 'navy bills' that were secured for payment by future revenues earmarked for the navy's support. These tallies or bills were issued to men such as the banker Edward Backwell (owed £66,492 from 1667), the victual contractor Denis Gauden and his partners (owed £638,524), and the overseas agent in Leghorn, Sir Thomas Clutterbuck (owed £103,553).[74]

The Exchequer paid interest of at least 10 per cent on these short-term credit instruments until they were retired by payments from the

Exchequer 'in course'. A large discount market developed for them in London. The Navy Treasurers made significant profits by holding the interest-bearing Exchequer tallies for as long as possible, and by receiving kickbacks from men like the Goldsmith banker Backwell, for selecting them to hold the tallies as well.[75] Parliament backed these tallies and bills, and even paid some interest on the £1.3 million in short-term debt affected by the Stop of the Exchequer in 1672, making the market in tallies and bills most lucrative.[76] These abuses continued into the eighteenth century and a chronic temporal gap in the redemption of these financial instruments was evident well into the War of the Spanish Succession.[77]

Changes in accounting practices in the declared accounts by the Navy Treasurers in this period reflected an evolution in assumptions about navy debt that had taken place between 1630 and 1680. For example, when Sir Edward Seymour's tenure as treasurer ended in 1681, the £1.5 million in debt secured on the Exchequer in the form of tallies and navy bills was no longer carried forward to the succeeding treasurer's account as the new treasurer's debt. Instead, they were governmental debt in the wider sense.

From June 1681 to April 1689, the Navy Treasurer, Lord Falkland, carried new and accumulating debt in the same manner as that developed in the 1650s, paying off older debts while maintaining significant amounts of tallies 'in hand', reaping the interest paid on them. His accounts' 'debt' never exceeded £282,000, and was reduced to £139,470 at the end of his 1689 account.[78] He counted the debt as paid when the tallies cleared the Exchequer. Most of this short-term debt, or amounts 'depending', were for bills or tallies imprested in the Exchequer, rather than for cash owed by the treasurer to contractors or lenders. By carrying this debt in the form of Exchequer revenue anticipation instruments, the navy debt was being transferred to the state. The recognition of this transition is shown by the fact that the Navy Treasurer ceased to carry these debts as owed by the navy after 1689. Instead, he listed them as tallies, orders and bills imprested on the Exchequer for the navy – a subtle but important difference.[79]

The navy's financial situation clearly improved after 1682, as shown by Falkland's ability to reduce outstanding bills and tallies to less than £140,000. This improvement reflected the dramatic improvement in the English economy and the Crown's finances, as the commercial expansion of the 1680s increased the customs and excise revenues.[80] It also reflected the reduction in naval expenditures made possible by a decade of peace.

CONSOLIDATION OF THE REVOLUTIONS

The Glorious Revolution of 1688 changed naval administration and finance slightly, if at all.[81] The navy followed its leaders politically, switching allegiance to William and Mary once it was clear the rest of the nation was doing so.[82] There is disagreement as to whether the English Navy would have fought the Dutch fleet, if winds and circumstances had allowed. The fleet certainly was sufficiently strong and well enough supported to have given a credible, and perhaps decisive performance. Although James II had decreased naval expenditures from 1685 to 1688, he retained a peacetime fleet of over eighty warships in commission in 1688, supported by an experienced and effective administration. When William III called on this force to fight the French, its administration responded well, putting over 173 warships to sea in 1690, and 323 major combatants out in 1695.[83] For the next twenty years, the Royal Navy played a crucial role in a world war against France.

Naval costs soared as war resumed in 1689. England needed a fleet that could simultaneously fight and win the big battles against the French battlefleet, with its large battleships or 'first rates' of over 100 guns each, and protect English commerce from the fast frigates of Dunkirk, Brest, and Toulon. It eventually succeeded in both tasks, ensuring that the English state could tap its commercial wealth to provide over £42 million for its navy and army in the decade from 1689 to 1700.[84] The navy received between £17 and £19 million in this period. Clearly, the creation of the concept of a funded and long-term national debt in the mid-1690s was crucial to the island empire's long-term ability to continue to spend so much money without suffering the breakdowns or bankruptcies that plagued France and Spain. C.D. Chandaman and Henry Roseveare correctly conclude that this 'financial revolution' was a long time in the making, and the developments made in naval finance from 1650 on were an important part of that process.[85]

As changes were made in financial methods, more money was available for the navy. There was also a great deal of money available to line the pockets of those entrusted with its disbursement. Table 3.6 summarizes the Navy Treasurer's receipts, expenditures and balances of cash and imprested (or obligated) bills and tallies from 1689 to 1699. The amounts listed as depending at the end of each account included money owed ('imprested') to merchants, victuallers and seamen for services and material provided for the navy. There were also considerable sums of Exchequer tallies and navy bills held by the treasurer, Sir Edward Russell. The declared accounts do not identify how much of the total amount depending was in each category.

Table 3.6: Navy Treasurers' Balances Depending, 1689–99, beginning 4 April 1689[86]

Period ending	Received (£)	Disbursed (£)	Remaining (£)
1 Apr 1690	757,591	232,123	525,467
31 Mar 1691	1,305,253	556,241	1,274,478
31 Mar 1692	1,260,727	817,268	1,717,937
31 Mar 1693	1,991,634	907,627	2,801,943
31 Mar 1694	1,415,481	1,023,631	3,189,193
31 Mar 1695	2,362,824	1,123,803	4,428,214
31 Mar 1696	2,355,370	2,684,784	4,098,503
25 Dec 1696	524,375	893,781	3,729,396
31 Dec 1697	2,995,701	1,220,276	5,504,821
31 Dec 1698	1,014,677	2,847,025	3,672,472
17 Nov 1699	1,107,499	2,954,251	1,824,719
31 Dec 1699	55,804	772,276	713,936

Russell's final account indicates that £713,936 remained imprested or obligated to various people for services and supplies provided to the navy. The two accounts for 1699 are the only two declared examples of Russell's which indicate how much of the remaining amount was imprested and how much was held by the Navy Treasurer. In the account ending 17 November 1699, Russell indicated that £394,311 of imprested in bills for past services were outstanding, and that £1,430,408 in current tallies and bills were in the treasurer's hands.[87] Most of these Exchequer tallies and bills paid interest. It was to the treasurer's benefit to retain these and their interest in his hands as long as possible. In this manner, the Navy Treasurer had an opportunity to make profits on his account beyond anything we have seen in these records before. Sir Edward Russell routinely held interest-bearing tallies and bills totalling between £3 and £5 million.[88] At the official rate of 6 per cent interest, this could have generated hundreds of thousands of pounds profit for him. Eventually, most of these tallies were used to provide money to maintain the navy and to pay for the construction of new ships. No serious attempts were made to recover Russell's windfall profits, although the auditor of the first two of his accounts noted at the foot of the account that Russell should be held accountable for this interest. There is no evidence that he was ever brought to account.[89] In Russell's final account £709,128 was imprested, and £4,807 remained in the treasurer's hands, indicating that he settled most of his account and that the millions in bills and tallies used in the 1690s were eventually paid off.

The Exchequer assumed the liability for navy debt by issuing tallies or bills for its payment. As these tallies were cleared in the Exchequer, for payment of services to the navy or for wages, the Navy Treasurer was credited with their discharge.[90] The ability to use Exchequer bills as credit mechanisms for the support of the navy, and to consider them as secured by future Exchequer receipts was possible only because Parliament assumed responsibility for these obligations and allocated specific taxation for their ultimate settlement in the 1690s. The growing use of Exchequer and navy bills was one of the main benefits of the creation of the Bank of England and a funded national debt in the 1690s. When the bank was founded, this outcome was not so certain.

The creation of the Bank of England in 1694 was one of a number of desperate attempts by the English government to solve its perennial problems of credit for the Royal Army and Navy in wartime.[91] Even if Parliament could have provided enough money from taxation to pay for the eight years of war from 1689, cash from this taxation would not have come in quickly enough to meet the immediate cash needs of the military forces. During the seventeenth century, English governments had found ways to borrow short-term money or to receive advances of supplies and services on contract in anticipation of tax revenues; but they had never developed ways to convert this short-term debt into long-term securities.[92] The various methods of short-term revenue anticipation always depended on the state's ability to pay the debt off, and that in turn depended on Parliament's willingness to tax the nation's wealth. Parliament's gradual assumption of responsibility for the nation's defence and, therefore, the financing of the state's administration, received its strongest boosts in the 1640s, 1650s, 1660s, and in the 1690s. During those turbulent years, the ruling and moneyed classes began to identify their interests with those of the government, and to experiment with ways to manage those affairs. This identification of interests provided the true security for the long-term credit instruments increasingly used after 1695.

Ironically, the Restoration Parliament's attempt to give Charles II sufficient 'permanent' revenue to run his government without parliamentary extraordinary taxation would have set back the political gains of the 1640s had the permanent revenue met the King's ordinary financial needs. Fortunately, it did not, making it necessary for Charles to rely on parliamentary financial action in peacetime, in turn causing Parliament to continue its regular interest in the state's financial affairs and administration. This situation was nearly undone by the growth in the King's normal revenues in the years of peace from 1680 to 1688. In fact, the political crisis of 1688 was caused in part by James II's ability to manage his financial affairs and simultaneously support large professional military forces in peacetime without parliamentary help. This situation left the ruling élites little choice but revolution if they did not want to accept James's religious and political policies.

The settlement of 1689 recognized the financial and political lessons of the previous fifty years. Henceforth, Parliament assumed responsibility for the state's financial obligations, providing annual appropriations, while accepting that the costs of the state's army, navy, and foreign policy were its own. The short-term debt mechanisms developed from 1640 to 1689 were now firmly based on these assumptions. The 'Publick Faith', a termed used regularly by the Long Parliament in the 1640s, came to mean Parliament's acceptance of responsibility for all public debt. This made possible the establishment of a funded national debt.

Warfare from 1639 to 1674 forced the state to develop a large permanent navy. The growth of the English navy, with its full-time cadre of officers and men and professional administration, was intimately connected with the larger revolutions of war and state finance that took place in England from 1640 to 1695.[93] Table 3.7 illustrates the stages of the navy's part in the financial revolution by summarizing the trend of English naval expenditures during the century. These figures undoubtedly understate expenditures for a variety of reasons, but based as they are upon the declared accounts of the Navy Treasurers and the Exchequer records, they show the clear trend.

The steady growth in naval costs was caused by the need to fight a long series of naval wars. Figure 3.1 shows the dramatic increase in annual

Table 3.7: Annual Average Navy Expenditure, 1 January 1600–31 December 1699

Period	Total (£)	Average per annum (£)
1600–24	1,357,098	54,000
1625–44	2,777,014	138,000
1643–7	1,526,473	305,000
1648–60	8,251,497	660,000
1660–80	12,868,003	643,000
1680–99	22,048,913	1,102,000
Total	48,828,998	
Annual average, 1600–99		488,000

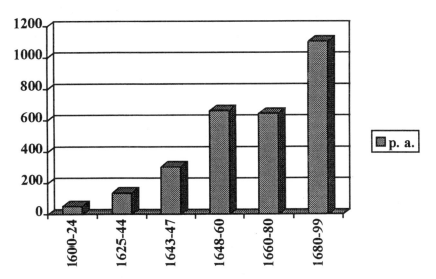

Figure 3.1: Annual Average Naval Costs, 1600–99 (£000s)

average naval costs during the seventeenth century. Military costs spiralled, mostly because of increased operations and the tactical and technical requirements of the Military Revolution rather than price-inflation. In fact, inflation ceased to be a major factor in the 1650s as prices stabilized.[94] The battlefleets deployed in the wars of the century grew from 30 to over 200 state-owned warships by 1660 and nearly 400 in 1695. The warships grew larger as well, from 40 to over 100 guns, and from roughly 600 to 1,200 tons each for the first-rate vessels. The administrative and logistical system that supported this naval force grew to be the largest single employer of labour in Britain, and the largest regular consumer of state financial resources. The impact on world history of these military developments has obviously been immense and requires no belabouring or elaboration. The rise of England to naval mastery in the world by 1700 was due to her successful transition through the intimately interconnected seventeenth-century Military Revolution and financial revolution.

CHAPTER FOUR

The Creation of the English Standing Army

English armies earned a prominent place in the military history of Western Europe hundreds of years before Cromwell's soldiers drove the Spanish infantry 'at push of pike' from the field at the Battle of the Dunes. But the modern professional English army had existed for only thirteen years at that point, and its official origins were not recognized for another three years.[1] One of the most obvious impacts that the civil and foreign wars of the 1640s had on England was the impetus they gave for the formation of a standing English Army and the permanent financial and administrative organizations needed to sustain it. Parliament's creation of the New Model Army in 1645 was the beginning of the modern English Army. The continuation after 1660 of the standing army and the new taxes used to sustain the 'New Model' provide clear evidence of England's active participation in the Military Revolution.

THE ELIZABETHAN ARMY

The British wars of the mid-seventeenth century and the general European Military Revolution of the preceding 100 years or so brought about the creation of a permanent army in England. The changes in warfare and the structure of armed forces that were evident, especially in the Spanish and Dutch armies, in the late sixteenth century had already greatly influenced the organization of English armed forces before James I ascended the English throne in 1603. The thousands of English troops sent by Elizabeth I to serve in the Netherlands in 1685 were organized in companies and regiments and armed with pikes and muskets comparable to the organization and equipment of the Spanish army they copied and fought.[2] These innovations did not create a standing English army because the island nation did not need such a military force once the wars of the late sixteenth century ended. Consequently, these Elizabethan military developments did not bring about the changes in state financial and administrative theory and practice that would have made possible the maintenance of a permanent army in England.

During the Elizabethan wars, local militia units increasingly were organized and armed along the same lines as the regiments sent overseas. The English militia mobilization of 1588, in the face of a possible Spanish invasion, showed the obsolescence of English military armament as well as the seriousness of the Tudor government's attempts to put its land forces into a state of readiness more akin to that of the Royal Navy. The Queen's Council made efforts to improve the arms and organization of selected militia units and to continue the modernization of key coastal defences that had been started fifty years earlier by Henry VIII. Yet, these efforts to improve the land forces in England flagged once the navy and Atlantic storms had eased the threat of Spanish invasion. Thus neither the Tudor nor Jacobean governments felt it necessary to establish a professional army. Further, even if Elizabeth I or James I had wanted to establish a standing army, given the prevailing sentiment of the nation's political élites it was very unlikely that a permanent force would have been supported financially by parliamentary taxes in the first half of the seventeenth century. Therefore, English governments could not afford to maintain an army of any size in peace.

Overseas, however, a different story of English military prowess emerged. Elizabeth committed significant numbers of soldiers to the continent to support the Dutch (from 1585 to 1603) and the French (from 1589 to 1593) against the Spanish. These soldiers performed remarkably well, especially after they had survived their first year of campaigning and learned their trade. Elizabeth's expeditions provided critical help to her allies, diverted the Spanish from their designs against England, and gave many English soldiers, such as the Vere brothers, the opportunity to practise the latest military techniques.[3] At the same time, Elizabeth's government faced an even more dangerous threat from a Spanish-supported rebellion in Ireland.

From 1595 to 1603, eight years of unrelenting warfare in Ireland against Ulster clansmen under the Earl of Tyronne forced the English to increase dramatically their military efforts on land. While maintaining the steady commitment of English troops and money to the Netherlands, Elizabeth sent her largest army to Ireland. The troops were organized and armed in the continental fashion, giving them battlefield superiority over the Irish who, as a result, adopted the elusive tactics of the guerrilla.[4] In order to win the long Irish war, the English had to develop an effective logistical system to support the Earl of Mountjoy's methodical, sustained, and brutal destruction of the Ulster hinterland – a strategy designed to destroy the enemy's logistical and manpower base.

Before Mountjoy finally defeated the Irish and their Spanish allies in Munster, the English had spent at least £1.8 million on the Irish war and had established a system capable of supplying Mountjoy's army with a large percentage of its logistical requirements from England.[5] Once peace returned, the English retained a few garrisons in Ireland, but nothing that could be called a standing army was left on foot. Instead, the English government turned to plantation schemes to maintain control over the Irish and bring 'civilization' to Ulster.

Elizabethan overseas expeditions always retained an *ad hoc* quality due to the amateur nature of their commanders and the absence of a fixed commissariat and honestly run pay system.[6] As a result, the wastage of manpower was appalling in these expeditions, with often half of the poor souls sent overseas from England killed by the effects of disease and malnutrition rather than by enemy action. These problems persisted throughout the Spanish war, in spite of the fact that Elizabeth spent roughly £4 million on her land campaigns in addition to the £1.5 million she spent on her naval operations against Spain's strategic communications.[7] None the less, English continental military operations were part of a strategy that was successful in its goal of keeping the Habsburgs from dominating the coasts of the Netherlands and France. By 1598, Philip II of Spain had to admit the futility of his attempts to crush the Dutch, overawe the English, and dictate French domestic politics. The English thereby won their first war to maintain the balance of power in Western Europe.[8]

JACOBEAN PEACE

Peace with Spain allowed James I's government quickly to dismantle the English armies abroad, and to ignore the poor state of readiness of its militia at home. However, a practical legacy of the long struggle against Spain was a reservoir of English officers and soldiers who had trained in the latest skills of the military art. Many of these men continued to serve in Dutch, Swedish, French, and Spanish armies from 1604 to 1638, ultimately giving the Stuart kingdoms ready access to experienced practitioners of modern military methods, without the creation of a standing army in England.

James I enjoyed a reign remarkably free from foreign dangers. This situation allowed him to indulge his penchants for religious philosophy and human pleasure, while largely ignoring his military establishments. England's militia forces provided the nation with her main home defence and police force and served as a reservoir of manpower for foreign operations in the 1620s. Many historians note that the weaknesses of the Elizabethan militia went largely unreformed by James,[9] while the Royal Navy reached its all-time low point. However, in spite of these trends, a great deal of quiet change took place in the organization and armament of the militia during the reign of the first two Stuarts, especially in the period after 1612.

From 1612 to 1638, many of the recent tactical and technological lessons of the European Military Revolution reached Britain and Ireland. Historians have often observed that British mercenaries – especially Scotsmen – serving in the armies of Sweden, France, and the United Provinces provided the British armies of the 1640s with a professional cadre, trained in the latest Dutch or Swedish tactics and organization. In addition, English arms-makers also profited from the demand for arms on the continent, thereby transferring modern military technology to England. These observations are valid. Additionally, the English and Scots equipped and organized their militias in accordance with the latest practices available, while numerous military manuals occupied the book-shelves of Scottish and English gentry.[10] The role of the British militias in the transmission of many of the technical and tactical aspects of the Military Revolution should not be underestimated.

The quality of English militia units in the early seventeenth century varied dramatically from county to county because of the different interests and leadership abilities of each county's Lord Lieutenant and his Deputy Lieutenants. The Crown charged these men with the responsibility for maintaining the militia. They served as the unsalaried administrative link between the King's Council and the local communities in military affairs. The Lord Lieutenants and their deputies raised the money needed to equip the local militia companies and ensured that the necessary musters and training occurred. Consequently, militia units were competent only in those counties where the lieutenancy felt the need for a well-ordered force. Lacking any sustained push from the Westminster government to maintain readiness or training, a number of Jacobean militia units atrophied. In roughly half of the counties no muster returns were made in many of the years from 1604 to 1624, although in some counties a sizeable and reasonably well-armed militia continued to exist.[11]

While James I did not spend much money or time on militia reform, he did spend a great deal more on military operations in the first ten years of his reign than is realized by most historians. While the amount of money spent on the military forces of England dropped dramatically in 1604 from the amounts spent by Elizabeth during the Spanish war, the nation was not completely disarmed on land, as the figures in

Table 4.1: Land Forces Costs as Part of Government Expenditure, 1600–24[12]

Years[13]	Total (£)	Land forces (£)	%
1600–4	2,336,444	1,293,658	55.4
1605–9	2,574,959	484,903	18.8
1610–14	2,931,725	455,556	15.5
1615–19[14]	2,112,393	157,601	7.4
1620–4	1,869,831	235,590	12.5
Total	11,825,352	2,627,308	

Table 4.1 indicate. This table, based on F.C. Dietz's 'The Receipts and Issues of the Exchequer during the Reigns of James I and Charles I', compares the amounts of cash issued by the Exchequer for garrisons, guards, military operations, and ordnance supplies and arms to the totals issued by the Exchequer for all purposes in each period. Since it is probable that not all of the King's revenue went through the course of the Exchequer, these figures may omit some of James's spending on his land forces. Additionally, most of the cost for the militia and trained bands was borne by the county and hundred governments. However, this data does indicate the trends in Jacobean spending.

The account for the last year of Elizabeth's war against Spain, ending in September 1603, provides an illuminating statistic. Fifty-three per cent of the £440,840 issued by the Exchequer during that accounting year was issued for the support of land forces and the expenses of the Ordnance Office, and only 13 per cent for the navy. The forces in Ireland consumed £185,948, the navy £70,577, while the Ordnance Office received £12,347.[15] In 1604, the only year of James's reign in which England was still at war, 36 per cent of issues were for the armies and ordnance, compared with 12 per cent for the navy. The garrisons and forces in Ireland remained the largest single military expenditure until 1614, receiving between £30,000 and £70,000 per year. The Exchequer also issued significant amounts for the support of military operations in 'Belgia' until 1615, with an average of £22,103 provided annually for them. Garrisons in England received an average of £4,000 per year for the twenty-one years between 1603 and 1624 for which Dietz has data.[16]

James's government spent significant amounts of money on its land forces, thereby allowing a number of Englishmen to continue in the military profession in a period when no English professional army existed. Further, the evidence shows that whenever England was involved in a land war either on the continent or in Ireland, as in 1603, the lion's share of the issues of the Exchequer was spent to support the land forces rather than the navy. James's government was able to decrease steadily the amounts and proportion of Exchequer issues provided for naval and land forces from 1603 to 1618. The increase in the percentage of issues provided to the forces, which is evident from 1621 to 1624, was actually caused by a large decline in total Exchequer cash receipts and issues due to a trade depression rather than just to the increase in Exchequer issues for the forces on the continent.[17] The annual average amount spent for land forces fell steadily from £258,000 (1600–4) to £96,000 (1605–9), to £91,000 (1610–14), to £47,000 in the last period.

CAROLINE EFFORTS AT REFORM

The accession of Charles I brought a marked increase in activity in the English militia and in the number of overseas military expeditions. For the first time since Elizabeth's Spanish war, regular mustering of militia took place in nearly every county, especially from 1625 to 1629. In 1626, the King's Council arranged for experienced English officers and non-commissioned officers with service in continental armies to come to England and spend up to a year training local militia companies in the rudiments of drill and tactics.[18] Local English leaders were exposed to current military practices in Charles's attempts to create 'the Perfect Militia'. The value of such training varied greatly from county to county since the presence or absence of enthusiasm for the militia differed so from area to area.[19] The burden of paying for this training fell on the ratepayers of the counties. Consequently, it was not continued in many counties after 1628, especially as more and more local money was spent caring for the sick and wounded soldiers returning from Charles's disastrous overseas expeditions.

Reforms made to the militia in the late 1620s were important to the long-term development of a professional army in England because the trained bands, as selected units of the militia were called, provided examples for Englishmen of military forces organized and equipped along modern lines. These local companies became a school of arms for a number of the junior officers and non-commissioned officers of the armies of the 1640s.[20] During the early part of the reign of Charles I all of the infantry of the trained bands received muskets and pikes and obsolete weapons such as the bow and the bill were removed from the armories and replaced by gunpowder weapons.[21] Charles's government encouraged the maintenance and improvement of the trained bands while spending little money from the King's Exchequer for that purpose. These improvements in some of the counties' trained bands did not produce a professional army, nor even a proficient army for home defence, since most militia units refused to serve outside their county. Certainly, these units were ill-trained and inexperienced, given the little time and money spent on their drill and arms practice, but they were units that could provide the nucleus for a modern army. For example, by 1642 the six regiments of the trained bands of London were well equipped with muskets and pikes and quite well drilled. When called upon to save the Parliamentarian cause, in 1642 and again in 1643, they proved their worth by demonstrating a reasonable level of competence in defensive situations.[22]

Caroline improvements in the militia were not accompanied by similar efforts to better the manner in which overseas expeditions were carried out. When Charles I went to war against Spain and France in the 1620s, men were available in the trained bands to defend the southern and eastern coasts from possible invasion, though by law and custom militia units could not be pressed into service for the overseas expeditions. The absence of a professional English Army made itself painfully apparent in the disastrous expeditions to Cadiz (1625) and the Isle of Rhe (1627). Both of these operations were conducted by an army made up of pressed men with little or no military training, and commanded by company and regimental officers with little if any combat experience and often no practice with their new units.[23] Similar problems had been evident in the Elizabethan expeditions to Ireland and France, but those deployments had continued long enough for English soldiers to develop their military and logistical skills. Because Charles could not harness the long-term financial support of his nation in the 1620s, he was unable to maintain his army long enough for its officers and men to become technically or tactically competent.[24]

When Charles I chose to rule without parliaments, beginning in 1629, he slackened noticeably his attempts to reform the militia into an effective and deployable fighting force. Many Lord Lieutenants relaxed their efforts to muster, train, and arm the local forces when the King's Council lost interest in the state of the trained bands.[25] Regular musters and limited training were carried on only in London and about half of the counties, most notably in those in the north and along the southern coast.[26]

During this period, anyone desiring a military career had to serve in continental armies, as many future leaders of the Royalist, Parliamentarian, and Scottish armies did. Militia training and reform continued, as noted, in a number of counties, but the limitations of the utility of the trained bands outside their county also continued. Charles spent no money on the trained bands during his personal rule, even when he had available the additional revenues of ship-money. So, the condition of the county militias depended on the concern of local leaders for county defence. In this situation, it is not surprising that the better-regulated units were found in the counties most exposed to foreign danger.

When Charles called upon the northern trained bands for the invasion of Scotland during the First Bishops' War, in 1639, he got an effective response by 6,000 militiamen from the northern counties, organized into regiments armed with pike and musket in accord with modern European military practice.[27] However, since the militias of the rest of the country could not be ordered to the north without a great deal of political difficulty, most of his soldiers were men without militia experience whom county authorities pressed to fill quotas assigned to them by the King's Council. Had Charles been able to afford to pay and supply these units for a longer period than he did, he might have been able to shape them into an effective fighting force. Further, had he used militia officers to command his regiments, rather than appointing untrained courtiers and nobles, he would at least have had more effective company and regimental commanders and better-disciplined units. As it was, Charles's lack of resolution and inept leadership in the face of a seemingly more powerful Scottish army, and, most of all, his lack of ready money to pay his troops spelt failure for the 1639 campaign.[28]

The distinctly superior performance of the Scottish Army over the English in 1639/40 shows what might have been accomplished in the 1620s and 1630s had Charles effectively enlisted the support of the nation through the proper use of parliaments. The Scots relied upon the amalgamation of local militiamen into regiments with a large cadre of mercenary professionals who had returned from service in the Dutch and Swedish armies.[29] These veterans led an army united by religion and organized and equipped for modern warfare. They proved able to outmarch and outmanoeuvre the King's army in the Second Bishops' War, beginning the English Revolution by forcing Charles to call the Long Parliament.

Only after his military situation had deteriorated beyond hope in the Second Bishops' War of 1640, did Charles again call on the trained bands of the northern counties, having until then relied on untrained levies of pressed men. In addition, the King's financial situation was even worse during the Second Bishops' War since he was trying to raise a larger army than in 1639 without adequate financial resources. Only an English parliament could have provided the taxation required to raise the amounts

Table 4.2: Land Forces Costs as Part of Government Expenditure, 1625–40[30]

Years	Total (£)	Land forces (£)	%
1625–9	2,576,385	730,324	28.3
1630–4	2,155,890	197,192	9.1
1635–9[31]	3,106,807	337,419	10.9
1640	899,519	517,723	57.6
Total	8,738,601	1,782,658	20.4

of money needed to pay for the operations of a large army. Charles was unwilling, however, to make the kind of concessions that the Short Parliament demanded in exchange for this money in the spring of 1640.

While Charles I's naval and military operations were always plagued by inadequate financial resources, his government did increase the proportion of royal revenue spent on the military forces from that of his father's reign, as Table 4.2 indicates. The amounts listed under Land Forces are for the cash issued for the field units, the garrisons, and the Ordnance Office. They exclude the money issued to the Navy Treasurer.

Table 4.2 understates total Caroline military costs. Additional money for 'coat and conduct' for the troops marching to the north in 1639 and 1640 was paid by the counties which had been ordered to levy, clothe, and dispatch the men pressed for service with the field army. The amounts above also do not include the costs of free quarter and the financial losses from looting suffered by the areas through which these soldiers marched since these costs were not reimbursed by the Westminster government. The table provides a clear idea of trends in royal expenditures in this period. The English government spent an annual average of £146,064 for its land forces during the war years of the late 1620s. During the 1630s, Charles spent an annual average of £53,461 on land forces and garrisons, and in the six months of the Second Bishops' War he spent £517,723.

The Exchequer provided more money for the land forces (£730,324) in the period from 1625 to 1629, than for the navy (£675,666). The combined issues for all military purposes exceeded 54 per cent of all Exchequer issues in that period. During the years of peace, from 1630 to 1639, the land forces received roughly 10 per cent of issues, while the navy received 34 per cent. One could argue that Charles spent his ship-money in the wrong place (on the navy), and instead should have created a standing army. Of course, it would have required the wildest imagination to anticipate the Scottish Revolution and the two Bishops' Wars. The political and financial costs of a standing army would have been far higher than were those of the ship-money fleets. During the war year of 1640, the land forces consumed 60 per cent of Exchequer issues and 57 per cent of all issues including ship-money. These large expenditures were completely inadequate to meet the financial needs of supporting roughly 25,000 men in England and another 11,000 in Ireland.[32]

The reason for the large amounts required for the maintenance of an army is easy to see. The King's Council of War estimated that an army of 30,000 men, the number initially planned for in 1639, would cost £935,000 per year. The King raised at least 15,000 men in the First Bishops' War. Their pay for six months would have been about £450,000.[33] The Exchequer was able to provide half of this amount (£128,700) to William Uvedale, Treasurer at War from 20 March 1639 to 16 February 1640, and only £15,000 to Francis Vernon, the paymaster of the amphibious force, numbering an additional 4,000 soldiers, led by the Marquis of Hamilton.[34] As a result, Charles found his army beset with all the difficulties caused by a shortage of money.

The Royal Army's financial situation was worse in the 1640 campaign, even though the Exchequer provided another £352,360 to Uvedale and £5,860 to Vernon for their respective forces.[35] These sums exclude the £90,964 provided to the Ordnance Office that year for the purchase of munitions and the deployment of the train of artillery.[36] While the King's navy could defer paying its seamen, as long as it fed them at sea, his army had to provide its soldiers with a large portion of their pay or face desertion, mutiny, and looting by hungry men. In the summer of 1640, the King's army disintegrated as sufficient pay failed to appear at the critical moment. And yet this force received a greater proportion of its expected pay than future Royalist and Parliamentarian armies would in the 1640s, indicating that its disintegration had far more to do with poor leadership by Charles, his generals, and his inexperienced regimental commanders. Many of these failures might have been avoided had he been able to use the existing trained bands more effectively.

During the Scottish crisis and Bishops' Wars, Sir Thomas Wentworth, Lord Lieutenant of Ireland organized and maintained another army in Ireland. This force of 9,000 foot and 1,000 horse was raised in 1639 for the three-pronged invasion of Scotland that Charles planned; however, it was not deployed before the King lost his nerve. The Irish army was paid for by Irish subsidies and a £50,000 grant from the English Exchequer.[37]

While the King partially disbanded this army in late 1640, roughly 3,000 of its soldiers were retained in garrisons, later becoming the nucleus for the Royalist Army under the Marquis of Ormond in 1642.[38] Throughout the 1640s the financial needs of all armies operating in Ireland went largely unsatisfied, as England and Scotland turned their attention to their own civil wars.[39]

THE CIVIL WARS

In 1640, the Scots' humiliating defeat of Charles's army at Newburn ended the Second Bishops' War in a single day. The Royal Army was disbanded, the Scots occupied the north of England, and Charles called for Parliament to meet in November. Future Stuarts would never forget the price Charles I paid for the lack of a professional army cadre and sufficient funds. Parliament, on the other hand, never forgot the danger that a professional army in the hands of someone like Charles I (or James II) held for parliamentary power. Meanwhile, the need for military forces quickly emerged, as the Ulster Catholics revolted against English rule in October 1641. The need for an army expeditionary force to crush the Irish rebellion led directly to the final confrontation between Charles I and the Long Parliament, as the latter clearly saw that it could not entrust the command of the militia or of a field army to the man who had attempted to seize five of its members by armed force in January 1642. As a result, in March, the Long Parliament seized control of the militia and reserved to itself the right to appoint the commanders for the expedition needed to suppress the Catholic rebellion in Ireland.[40]

When Charles erected his standard at Nottingham in August, civil war was unavoidable. The first challenge facing both parties was how to raise and equip an army to win the struggle. The King, remembering the difficulties of dealing with the county militias in the Bishops' Wars, used Commissions of Array to raise forces. By this feudal recruiting device he called on nobles and gentry to organize infantry and cavalry units on his behalf, at their expense. In this manner he had mustered at least ten cavalry and nineteen infantry regiments by the Battle of Edgehill in October 1642.[41] To recruit these forces, the King's leading supporters mustered the trained bands in those counties not under parliamentary control, based on the authority of the King's commission. Where the sentiment seemed Royalist, the militia was used for local defence. In a number of cases the trained bands, due to their uncertain loyalty and limited deployability, were asked to 'loan' their weapons to the King, and then dismissed. These weapons and the many more that the Queen procured in the Netherlands, Denmark, and France, armed the newly formed Royalist regiments. Having fled London, the King lacked the cash to pay his troops himself. Only the proceeds from the pawning of the Crown jewels and the generous financial support of nobles such as the Earl of Worcester and the latter's son Lord Herbert, who alone provided over £100,000 in July, enabled Charles to field his forces in 1642.[42]

Charles's army was generally organized in the Swedish manner due to the influence of officers such as Prince Rupert and Lord Goring, who had served in the Swedish forces in Germany. Because most Royalist regiments were raised by militarily inexperienced aristocrats, who paid for the initial costs of the units, Charles was unable to rationalize and consolidate his foot and horse regiments as the attrition of battles, disease, and desertion reduced them in strength, in many cases to company size.[43] However, casualties among officers and the hardships of campaigning forced the faint-hearted and unlucky out, allowing professional soldiers with continental experience progressively to assume command of most Royalist regiments and all of the King's regional armies by 1644.[44] As a result, the Royalist armies proved tenacious and competent foes on the battlefield, forcing the Long Parliament to match them with a remodelled army of its own by 1645.

The greatest weakness of the Royalist military effort was not financial or logistical, although it was never overly strong in these attributes.[45] The Royalists created a reasonably effective financial system in 1643, allowing them to support their armies in the north, Midlands, and the west. This system relied on a small customs revenue, a trickle of money from an excise, loans and gifts from supporters, and local levies and assessments.[46] Too few Royalist financial records survive to allow even a ballpark guess to be made as to the total amounts raised through these means. The amounts were substantial. For example, the Queen raised £180,000 in the Netherlands and the Earl of Worcester provided at least another £318,000. The Royalist Treasurer at War, John Ashburnham, received £180,768 from November 1642 to October 1643 from the Oxford Exchequer, and the universities contributed £25,000.[47] Local assessments for the support of garrisons sustained the Royalist regiments in many counties during the first two winters of the war, and the King's men regularly took free quarter. Royalist financial administration, however, was poorly organized, with multiple treasurers and treasuries, and it lacked central audit procedures.[48] Ultimately, these administrative deficiencies were not corrected, as the Royalists failed to consolidate and rationalize their financial system in a manner similar to that pursued by the Parliamentarians.[49]

Royalist financial and administrative failings reflected the single greatest Royalist weakness, and the most important cause of the King's defeat. The King's war effort suffered severely from a disorganized and disunited command structure, presided over by a secretive and double-dealing King, who came to see himself as a great strategist.[50] Lack of an effective command structure and policy-making apparatus prevented the Royalists from developing and pursuing consistent strategic and operational plans, thus throwing away their early tactical superiority and successes in the first two years of the war.[51] The administrative changes needed in this case were not forthcoming probably because the King's approach to war remained eclectic and personal. Such an approach to war worked well enough in Elizabethan England, where the military challenges, and most repercussions of inadequate administration, were felt overseas. The Royalists' inability or unwillingness to correct this situation in 1643 and 1644, however, gave the Parliamentarians time to get their military and political acts together.

Parliament, by seizing control of the militia in friendly areas, had ready to hand a military structure around which to build its army in 1642. Like the King, the Long Parliament called on prominent supporters to form the eighty troops of horse and twenty regiments of infantry that initially composed its main force. The militia units, except for the London trained bands, were in too great a disarray from the Bishops' War to provide the regiments for a field army and local units refused to march from their home counties for long periods of time. However, militia units were mustered and assigned local garrison duties. At these musters aspiring commanders invited recruits to join them in the companies and regiments forming to join the field army. When an area was directly threatened by Royalist incursions, the militia often helped the Parliamentarian field forces. Once the threat to their locality subsided, the trained bands returned home.

The regiments of Parliament's main army in 1642, commanded by the veteran soldier Robert Devereaux, Earl of Essex, were raised on a regional basis and usually led by the local leaders who formed them. Parliament provided the money to equip and pay these units for the most part, leading to a greater uniformity in organization and arms and giving Parliament greater control over its regiments.[52] As in the case of the Royalist forces, a number of English and Scottish veterans of continental armies served as officers in Essex's army, and a number of officers, non-commissioned officers, and soldiers had some experience of drill from service in the Stuart militia. These men were given too little time for training the raw volunteers before the first major encounter at the Battle of Edgehill. That the regiments could be deployed at all on that field and used tactically, albeit with little skill, argues for a certain level of knowledge of arms and drill that likely came from militia experience.[53]

The indecisive Battle of Edgehill spurred both sides to raise more troops and seek external allies. The Royalist forces secured the west and north of the country for the King, while Parliamentarian armies held the south and east. The widening of the civil war and the garrisoning of most of the British Isles caused a massive expansion of military forces. However, individual field armies in Ireland and Britain during the 1640s seldom numbered over 15,000 men on each side in the major battles. This fact may have prevented some historians from realizing that the British kingdoms experienced one of the major characteristics of the Military Revolution in this period – the rapid increase in the size of standing armies and a noticeable change in the 'military participation ratio'.[54]

During the 1640s, at least 60,000 men were raised by each side in England and the Covenanters in Scotland raised another 20,000 to face the 5,000 men fielded by their opponents. In addition, a total of between 60,000 and 70,000 soldiers were raised and maintained in Ireland by the warring factions.[55] These numbers do not include the militia units that often served for short stints of duty. Roughly 200,000 soldiers were engaged in the field armies of three nations with a total population of perhaps 9 million in the mid-1640s.[56] The rapid proliferation of garrisons in towns and fortresses and the steady improvements in military architecture clearly illustrate Parker's conclusion that there was a connection between the growth in army size and the technical changes in artillery and fortifications in the Military Revolution.[57]

Most of the soldiers in the British Isles served in garrisons during the civil wars. In Ireland alone, over 400 small fortifications required between 10 and 200 soldiers each to hold. Consequently, while Cromwell had over 16,000 men in his army in Ireland in late 1649, he could muster fewer than 5,000 for field duty in Munster and another 4,000 men in a subsidiary force in Ulster. This diminution of strength was caused partially by the effects of sickness, but Cromwell's letters make it clear that he steadily had to detach small units to hold strong points that were strategically important. He maintained larger garrisons in Dublin and the other major towns that he captured.[58]

Prolonged warfare forced a shift in the nature of the military forces involved in the British civil wars. As the gentry and gentlemen who had recruited the original regiments were killed in the short violent campaigns or disillusioned by the dreary garrison duty that characterized much of their service, professional soldiers took over the units and raised or reorganized the forces that fought in 1644 and 1645. Some of these professionals, such as Prince Rupert, George Monck, the Earl of Essex, and Philip Skippon had learned their skills in the standing armies on the continent. Others, like Oliver Cromwell, John Lambert, and Richard Deane acquired their professional skills and vocation in the First Civil War.[59] The Scottish armies in England and Ireland began active operations with a much stronger professional element of continental veterans than their English counterparts. However, in 1650 the Scots purged their army of many of these leaders because they did not display an active enthusiasm for the Covenanter cause. This purge greatly facilitated Cromwell's destruction of the Scottish army at the Battle of Dunbar.[60] By 1652, standing armies, led by experienced officers and non-commissioned officers, were the norm throughout Britain and Ireland. While their strength decreased after 1656, such military forces have continued to exist in England, Scotland, and Ireland to this day.

THE NEW MODEL AND WAR FINANCE

When the Long Parliament created the New Model Army in the spring of 1645, it was the clearest sign that the professionalization of the English Army had begun. During the first two years of the English Civil War, Parliament had relied on a decentralized military organization and an *ad hoc* financial structure.[61] The main army commanded by the Earl of Essex was joined by armies raised in 1643 to defend different regional associations of parliamentary-controlled counties from local and national Royalist forces. William Waller commanded an army in the southern counties, Lord Ferdinando Fairfax commanded the Northern Army in Yorkshire, and the Earl of Manchester commanded the army of the Eastern Association. When these armies cooperated with one another, and with the Scottish Army that entered the First Civil War on Parliament's behalf in September 1643, they could muster a decided numerical superiority over the Royalists on the battlefield. In this manner the Scots and English brought 28,000 men together to defeat the outnumbered Royalist armies of Prince Rupert and the Earl of Newcastle at Marston Moor in June 1644. More generally, however, the Parliamentarian armies failed to cooperate, allowing the main Royalist army to defeat Waller's Western Army at Cropredy Bridge and Essex's army at Lostwithiel in the late summer of that year.[62]

Parliament's military confusion was accompanied by a similarly disunited and confused executive and command structure in Westminster in 1643 and 1644. Even with the creation of the Committee of Both Kingdoms to coordinate Anglo–Scottish strategy and operations in January 1644 the anti-Royalist forces lacked the unity and the resolve needed to defeat the King. The rout of Waller's and Essex's forces, and the unwillingness of the Earls of Manchester and Essex aggressively to prosecute the war against the King, helped provoke a political crisis in London in the autumn of 1644. Parliament ended this crisis by passing a series of ordinances, from February to April 1645, that amalgamated the armies of Essex, Waller, and Manchester into a New Model Army. These parliamentary acts denied military employment to Members of Parliament without special parliamentary approval, and reorganized the financial system needed to support a successful war effort.[63] As a result, the Long Parliament created England's professional army and provided the government with the financial resources needed to fund an effective logistical operation in its support.

The New Model Army Ordinance of February 1645 dramatically altered the financial situation of the Parliamentarian armies by including a provision for a monthly assessment to raise a steady stream of parliamentary revenue. This assessment was a direct response by the Long Parliament to the financial demands imposed by the need to maintain a standing army. Parliament continued the monthly assessment with only a brief interlude until 1661.[64] The revenue from this tax and the excise taxes, which the Long Parliament had first instituted in 1643, allowed Westminster governments to spend unprecedented sums on their military forces and, in the process, to create the traditions of a professional standing army. Table 4.3 lists the amounts of money spent by the Westminster government on its main field armies from August 1642 to February 1660. The Treasurers at War and Army Paymaster accounted to Parliament for these expenditures in their declared accounts. Several committees of the House of Commons received regular reports on the status of the army accounts and issued orders for how the tax receipts were to be spent. This continuous parliamentary oversight and active participation in the routine affairs of the army during the 1640s was a major departure from past practice and a clear precedent for the future parliamentary involvement in administrative details which W.A. Shaw thought was so revolutionary in the 1690s.[65] The money disbursed by the Treasurers at War came from a number of sources, with the monthly assessment providing the majority. The habit of raising the largest portion of the money needed for the army in wartime from direct taxes such as the assessment or land taxes continued into the next century.[66]

From March 1645 to February 1660, the Westminster governments provided four times as much money to their armies as had been spent by

Table 4.3: Expenditures on the Main Armies, 1 August 1642–2 February 1660

Period	Total (£)	Monthly (£)	Per annum (£)
Aug 1642–Mar 1645[67]	1,105,826	35,671	428,061
Mar 1645–Dec 1651[68]	7,323,718	90,416	1,084,995
Jan 1652–Jul 1653[69]	1,472,738	77,512	930,150
Jul 1653–Feb 1660[70]	5,214,021	66,000	792,003
Total	15,116,303		
Monthly average		71,982	
Annual average, Aug 1642–Feb 1660			863,788

the King on English land forces in all of the years from 1603 to 1640 (£3.6 million).[71] The parliamentary armies cost nearly twice as much from 1642 to 1660 as the navy (£15.1 million to £8.8 million).[72] Parliament's naval and land forces received over £23.8 million for their support from the treasuries of the central government. The Parliamentarians used at least another £1.5 million in debentures to settle soldiers' arrears of pay. These debentures were secured by the proceeds of the sale of land in the period from 1649 to 1653.[73] When the republican government collapsed in 1660, the English state owed members of its army and navy at least another £1.5 million for their pay.[74] At least £27 million was spent in cash and debt for the Westminster government's land forces in an eighteen-year period by the central government. The majority of this money was raised through taxation.[75]

Parliament probably spent a great deal more on its forces from August 1642 to March 1645 than is shown in Table 4.3. The amounts listed for this period are for Essex's and Waller's armies only and exclude the money raised and spent in the Eastern Association and the Northern Association for the support of Manchester's and Lord Ferdinando Fairfax's armies respectively.[76] The amounts in the table for the periods after March 1645 are much closer to the total spent because the Long Parliament centralized its assessment collections and disbursements in that year, directing that the assessments should be paid to the Treasurers at War in London's Guildhall.[77] By assigning control of the receipt and issue of the monthly assessment to London financiers, Parliament reassured its creditors in London that the money raised by the assessment would be spent for the support of the army.[78] This greatly increased the government's ability to raise loans and to contract for munitions, etc., in anticipation of tax revenue.[79] Parliament's practice of identifying specific taxes as security to service and repay government loans facilitated its credit operations and set the precedent for such methods after 1660.

Table 4.3 does not include the money spent by county committees for the maintenance of local garrisons and for the costs incurred by citizens as the armies took free quarter.[80] When the soldiers' accounts were audited and settled by the parliamentary Committee for Taking the Accounts of the Soldiers, deductions were made from the soldiers' pay arrears for free quarter.[81] Publicans and householders who had received tickets from the armies for the free quarter taken by the soldiers in the 1640s received reimbursement from money deducted from the soldiers' pay or by amounts deducted from the house owners' future taxes.[82]

During the First Civil War the Parliamentarians worked out the problems of how to raise enough money to pay their armies with a fair amount of regularity by levying and collecting excise and assessment taxes. These were the major sources of revenue for the armies, although they were supplemented significantly by the proceeds of sequestration fines and land sales. Parliament's armies achieved a tremendous operational advantage from this financial success because it allowed them to sustain their soldiers on extended campaigns, while the Royalist forces disintegrated due to lack of pay, clothes, and arms.[83] Parliament's steady supply of money ensured the provision of munitions, clothes and rations to its soldiers.

MILITARY ADMINISTRATION

The Parliamentarians developed a reasonably well-organized system of contracting and purchase to procure and transport the thousands of weapons and sets of clothing and the tons of food and ammunition consumed by their forces. This was accomplished by the hard work and skill of numerous administrators who, with efficiency and fair honesty, handled the money, contracted for the supplies, mustered and paid the soldiers, and maintained detailed records of these financial and logistical transactions. The immense volume of the records of these actions, catalogued in the Public Record Office as State Papers 28, provides ample evidence that the system worked. The military success of the Parliamentarian armies speaks for itself and is a stark contrast to the abysmal military, financial, and logistical failures of Charles I's expeditions of the late 1620s and the Bishops' Wars.

Remarkably, this rational organization of military administration escaped the notice of Martin Van Creveld, who implies in his book, *Supplying War, Logistics from Wallenstein to Patton*, that administrators in the seventeenth century lacked the sophisticated conceptual and mathematical skills needed to operate a sustained financial and logistical system.[84] This view grows naturally out of his failure to study the British wars from 1639 to 1700. Van Creveld's confusion over this matter makes it worthwhile for us to look in greater detail at how the English developed their financial and logistical practices in the 1640s.

The army's logistical and administrative system evolved dramatically from 1642 to 1645. The financial expedients used to raise and manage money at the beginning of the First Civil War gave way to a system of settled taxes collected and disbursed by competent administrators. The men who managed Parliament's finances after 1644 were experienced London financiers and merchants. The bulk of their remuneration came from their salaries rather than from the traditional fees and poundage rates.[85] Had they continued to take the traditional poundage rate from the millions of pounds they handled, the Westminster government would have lost significant amounts of money, undermining its ability to field and support the New Model Army.

Superficially, the pay system of the army looked very similar to that of the Elizabethan forces in Ireland. The Treasurers at War provided the money for the soldiers' pay to the regimental commanders on the authority of warrants issued to the treasurers by the Lord General or his designated agents.[86] To ensure that the correct amount of pay was provided to the units, regiments were required to muster monthly, with a muster master or his representative present to verify the count of soldiers.[87] In contrast to the practice of the Elizabethan armies, 'dead pays' were not allowed.[88] Each soldier in the company was listed by name on a monthly muster or list. These documents were used to determine the amount of money to be issued to the companies. Company commanders no longer routinely made a profit from the handling of their men's pay, nor did they receive pay for vacant positions in their companies. Although it is certain that fraud was still practised by some commanders, in many cases the officers used their own money to loan to their men to help them survive the times when their pay was not forthcoming. This may help explain, as much as any other reason, the remarkable cohesion of the New Model Army.[89]

Regimental accounts were maintained and periodically audited. Each regiment and field army had financial agents who looked after its affairs and ensured that the muster data was transmitted to the treasurers so that the proper amount of money could be provided[90] The Treasurers at War shipped the money in carts to the units where the paymasters paid the soldiers with coins. Before a soldier's final pay was determined, the paymasters made deductions for the clothes and food provided by the government 'as pay' to that soldier.[91] When the men were paid regularly, they purchased their own food and paid for their billets. When they were not paid regularly, Parliament authorized the taking of free quarter, and regimental quartermasters issued tickets to the innkeepers or home owners who provided quarters.[92] These actions to protect property rights certainly reflected the notion of the commanders, such as Cromwell, that the forces were England's army, and not mere mercenaries.

Contractors provided food, munitions, arms, and clothes to the army. Parliament's Committee of the Army issued most of the warrants authorizing these purchases. These warrants were endorsed by regimental commissary officers and quartermasters when they received the supplies. Contractors could then use the warrant as a bill to present to the Treasurers at War in the London Guildhall for payment.[93] The Treasurers at War retained the warrants to substantiate their accounts of disbursements or 'discharges' in their declared accounts.[94] These methods of military administration and accounting survived the Interregnum and remained in use well into the next century.

Money remained the essential lubricant of this administrative system. If it was not provided on a regular basis in sufficient amounts, the system ground to a halt. When this happened in the period from November 1646 to early 1649, soldiers' pay fell into arrears and the amounts the state owed to contractors soared until they refused to provide further supplies on credit. This was the low point in the New Model Army's history, until the government collapse in early 1660. However, these periods of financial distress should not be allowed to mask the fact that, beginning in the 1640s, English armies have been among the most regularly paid and well-supplied forces in Europe.

When the New Model Army won the Battle of Naseby in July 1645, crushing the main Royalist Army, and then captured all of the King's remaining garrisons in England by the summer of 1646, it appeared to many Englishmen that they could dismiss most of their army and send the residue to Ireland to crush the Catholic rebellion. The treasuries in London were empty in late 1646, however, because many taxpayers had refused to pay their assessments after it had become clear that Charles had been defeated.[95] This situation gave the Long Parliament a serious financial problem because English armies totalling over 60,000 men and a Scottish Army of roughly 20,000 men were garrisoned about England, while additional British forces of over 25,000 men in Ireland looked to Westminster for support.[96] The opponents of the New Model Army, who were a majority of the Commons, resolved in February 1647 to disband all but 6,400 cavalrymen and dragoons in England and to pay arrears only to those soldiers who enlisted in the thirteen regiments of horse and foot going to Ireland.[97] But the New Model Army's soldiers refused to be disbanded on the terms proposed by the Presbyterian-dominated Parliament, and eventually seized London in August 1647.[98] This, the first of three English Army coups, meant that for the first time in history an English government was forced to maintain a standing army in England during peacetime.

The Cromwellian conquests of Ireland and Scotland, in the period from 1649 to 1652, required the maintenance of occupation forces in those nations throughout the 1650s. The forces in England, Ireland, and Scotland, numbering between 30,000 and 50,000 men, were joined by expeditionary forces sent to the Caribbean and France totalling another 3,000 to 6,000 men. As a consequence of these wars and occupations, substantial military expenditures continued throughout the 1650s, as Table 4.3 indicates.[99] In March 1659, 23 cavalry regiments and 34 infantry regiments, totalling 44,650 officers and men, were supported by the Westminster government. Their annual cost exceeded £1 million.[100] Annual English revenue totalled an estimated £1,868,717, while current expenses for the army, navy, and civil government were estimated to be between £2.2 million and £2.8 million per year.[101] This widening gap between revenue and expenses came about because of Cromwell's decision to reduce the assessment from £60,000 per month in 1656 to £35,000 per month in 1657. By February 1660, total state debt exceeded £2 million, with revenues decreasing and expenditures increasing.[102] This miserable financial situation had a lot to do with the collapse of both the Protectorate and the Second Commonwealth. Only a parliamentary system that was representative of the élites of society could tap enough of the nation's wealth to balance the state's accounts and pay its armed forces on a long-term basis.

THE RESTORATION ARMY

The restoration of the monarchy in 1660 came about in part because of a desire to do away with the large standing army in England and the powerful Commonwealth Navy, as well as to end the political chaos in London. But the state owed the Cromwellian soldiers substantial amounts for their arrears and consequently, the Restoration Parliament continued the excise and assessment taxes, in addition to the hereditary grants of the customs, into the 1660s. The debts, caused mainly by the wars of the 1650s, forced the English to maintain the major features of the financial revolution that had commenced in 1643. The Convention Parliament's first order of business was to secure the new regime and to pay off and disband the army.

It is unclear how much of the soldiers' and sailors' arrears Parliament actually paid off in the period from 1660 to 1662. The Restoration Parliament appointed James Nelthorpe and John Lawson to serve as special Treasurers at War for disbanding the army. Their accounts indicate that they disbursed at least £762,946 to the soldiers who were disbanded. Most of this money came from a monthly assessment of £70,000 and a poll tax.[103] Tax collectors paid these sums directly to the treasurers and therefore this money did not pass through the Exchequer. However, the treasurers for the disbandment provided the Exchequer with their declared accounts. The soldiers' arrears were roughly £835,000 in the autumn of 1660, so the amounts paid to the soldiers by Nelthorpe and Lawson came reasonably close to settling the debt.[104] The disbandment of the regiments in England progressed smoothly under the supervision of George Monck until, by December 1660, only one regiment of infantry and one of cavalry remained.[105] The majority of the forces in Scotland and Ireland were disbanded as well, although the King permanently retained over 10,000 soldiers on the establishments of the three Stuart kingdoms and an additional seven regiments of infantry in Dunkirk.[106]

Charles II never intended to disband fully the forces he inherited in 1660. General Monck, Duke of Albemarle thereafter, retained his regiment of infantry in November 1660. The King ordered him to raise another regiment of foot and two cavalry regiments in January 1661. These four regiments, along with the twenty-eight small garrisons throughout the country, became the first English standing army in peacetime if one accepts John Childs's argument that the Interregnum was a time of war.[107] In any case, over half of the soldiers in the four guards regiments in 1661 had seen regular service in English units in the 1650s, and it was no accident that Albemarle, the former Cromwellian commander of Scotland, gave them the red coats of the Commonwealth's army. Charles also retained 66 companies of infantry and 30 troops of cavalry, drawn from the Cromwellian army, in Ireland, and nearly 3,000 more former New Model soldiers in Scotland.[108]

Restoration governments continued to use the administrative and financial systems developed during the civil wars and Interregnum to support the Royal Army. The paymasters of the forces, such as Sir Stephen Fox from 1661 to 1687, received most of the money to pay and sustain the King's guards and garrisons from the Exchequer. The Exchequer provided additional money to special paymasters for overseas operations such as the Dunkirk garrison in 1661/2 and the army expedition to France in 1677/8. The paymasters disbursed the money on the authority of warrants issued by the King and by the Lord General.

Table 4.4: Costs of the English Army, 1 January 1661–31 December 1687[109]

Period	Total (£)	Per annum (£)
Jan 1661–Sep 1667	1,230,375	188,000
Sep 1667–Sep 1672	1,039,670	207,000
Sep 1672–Dec 1677	2,123,973	405,000
Jan 1678–Dec 1682	2,109,620	421,000
Jan 1683–Dec 1687	2,256,195	451,000
Total	8,759,833	
Annual average, Jan 1661– Dec 1687		324,000

The paymasters' accounts provide an idea of the magnitude of the cost of the English army from the Restoration in 1660 to the Glorious Revolution of 1688.

Charles II maintained a professional army in England and Dunkirk in 1660 at a cost of roughly £188,000 per year. By continental standards this army of fewer than 10,000 soldiers was puny. But it did not remain small for long. The need to send 17,000 soldiers to France in 1677 and then to pay for their disbandment in 1678 cost the English Exchequer £1.5 million.[110] Figure 4.1 makes this trend even clearer.

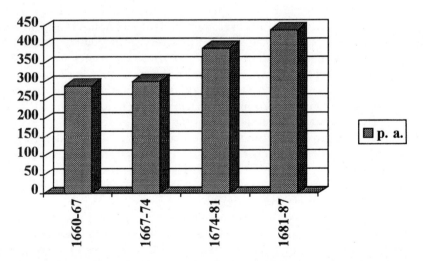

Figure 4.1: Annual Average Army Costs, 1660–87 (£000s)

The King's retention of a professional army required his government to develop permanent military installations in London. Barracks and stables were erected in St James's Park, in Whitehall, and at the Horse Guards for the guards regiments. In addition, Charles spent a great deal of money on fortifications and billets in the Tower, at Chatham, Hull, and other strategic points in which garrisons were maintained.[111]

The Army Paymasters' accounts omit a significant portion of the expenditures of Charles II and James II on military forces from 1660 to 1688. The Irish Exchequer paid the 7,500 soldiers in the Irish establishment, just as the Scottish Exchequer paid the 2,700 men in Scotland.[112] The English Exchequer also issued money to paymasters in Tangiers and Dunkirk for garrisons maintained in those outposts. For comparison purposes with the data in Tables 4.1 and 4.2, Table 4.5 lists the amounts issued by the Exchequer from Michaelmas 1660 to Michaelmas 1688 for the land forces in England, Dunkirk, Tangiers, and the Netherlands.

The percentage of total Exchequer issues that were made for the support of field regiments and garrisons grew steadily under Charles II and James II, even though there were no major land wars during this period and only two major expeditions to the continent during the Second Dutch War and the war against France in 1678. Internal revolts were minor affairs in this period as well, except for Monmouth's rebellion in 1685. Inflation does not account for the increase of military costs in this period since inflation had peaked in about 1650, and prices fell slowly from then to the end of the century.[113] The largest

Table 4.5: Army Expenditure as Part of Total State Expenditures, Michaelmas 1660–Michaelmas 1688[114]

Period	Total (£)	Military (£)	%	Per annum (£)
M 1660–M 1667	11,056,438	2,043,049	18.5	291,000
M 1667–M 1674	13,360,935	2,110,431	15.8	301,000
M 1674–M 1681	12,214,543	2,734,452	22.4	390,000
M 1681–M 1688	10,860,024	3,088,096	28.4	441,000
Total	47,491,940	9,976,028	21.0	
Annual average, M 1660–M 1688				356,000

M = Michaelmas

expenditures made in support of the army took place in the years of peace from 1686 to 1688, when James steadily increased his standing force. In these years, Exchequer issues for the army totalled £1,897,877 and averaged £632,625 per year, while expenditures averaged £610,883 for the army in England.[115] These amounts exceeded those spent in any other three-year period of the century except in the war years from 1642 to 1660. James II spent none of this money in anticipation of William's invasion.

Charles II and James II spent another £2,450,911 on the munitions, arms, and equipment provided to the army and navy by the Ordnance Office from 1660 to 1688 (over £87,000 per year), along with another £14 million issued to the navy.[116] These sums omit the £146,260 per year required from the Irish Exchequer to pay the twelve regiments of the King's Irish Army.[117] The Irish units and the garrison in Scotland served as excellent reservoirs of troops for overseas expeditions to Tangiers, Bombay, Barbados, and the Netherlands.[118]

English professional soldiers also served in Anglo-Dutch and French brigades during the Restoration period. These units were manned by English, Irish, and Scottish soldiers and paid by the Dutch and French governments. These soldiers were available to the King of England for recall to form the cadre of a large British army when needed. For example, the French Brigade provided a significant proportion of the company and field-grade officers of the twelve new regiments raised to serve against Louis XIV in 1678.[119] These regiments were part of an expeditionary force of over 17,000 men that was sent to aid the Dutch in 1678. While they saw little action, they seem to have been well supported logistically from England and respected by the professional officers of the French, Spanish and Dutch armies.[120] When this short war ended, Parliament took an active interest in the affairs of this army and provided £1,552,000 for its support and disbandment.[121]

Although Parliament succeeded in forcing Charles II to disband the regiments of the 1678 expedition, Charles and his brother James II maintained professional armies in each of their three kingdoms. In these armies and in the brigades in foreign service, future British military professionals such as John Churchill, Duke of Marlborough, learned their profession. In 1685, James II had little difficulty raising a force of over 20,000 soldiers to crush Monmouth's rebellion. He kept most of this army on duty thereafter. From 1683 to 1688, the English Army paymasters disbursed £2.25 million just for the army in England. By 1688, James had as many as 40,000 men under arms in England alone. His failure to use this force against his son-in-law had nothing to do with inadequacies on the army's part, but a great deal to do with his lack of nerve.

Much of James's army later served in the forces of William III in Ireland and the Low Countries. These troops acquitted themselves well, reflecting the tradition of the redcoats of the New Model Army. Their success in battle during the wars of the 1690s and the 1700s rested on the financial and administrative foundations laid down in the civil wars and Interregnum. Parliament took the same direct interest in military and government affairs that had been evident during the Long Parliament, although methods of management and theories of who was responsible for the state's financial obligations and policies continued to evolve. The firm and final assumption by Parliament for the financial obligations of the state in the 1690s consolidated the financial revolution set in motion by Parliament's need to support prolonged warfare in the 1640s. As a result, the full financial potential of the British Isles could be tapped.

A MILITARY REVOLUTION?

Clearly, England took part in the Military Revolution in the mid-seventeenth century, well before 1689. The creation of standing armies in the 1640s was directly connected to the professional English army that was officially founded in 1661. The administrative, logistical, and financial methods and bureaucracies needed to pay and maintain these forces were adapted, with significant expansion and improvement, from those in use from 1645 to 1660. Regular and honest musters of units, periodic audits of individual and unit financial accounts, and warrant-based record keeping allowed the English to develop methods to account for and forecast military expenditures. Large standing forces received regular pay for the first time in peacetime in the 1650s, and continued to do so after 1660.

English military costs skyrocketed again in the period from 1689 to 1700, as England became an important member in the Grand Alliance to stop the French advance into the Netherlands. All of the financial and military tricks and skills the English possessed were needed to survive this struggle with the Sun King. The results were often in doubt. Had England not already passed through the Military Revolution, she would have failed her first test as a world power. Table 4.6 provides a look at the quantum leap in the costs of modern warfare incurred by the English for the support of their armies and the forces they subsidized in the Nine Years' War (also known as the War of the League of Augsburg).

Table 4.6: Exchequer Issues for the Land Forces, 5 November 1688–September 1700[122]

Period	Amount (£)	Average per annum (£)
Nov 1688–M 1691	5,200,022	1,733,000
M 1691–M 1697	13,319,741	2,219,956
M 1697–M 1700	2,719,955	906,651
Total	21,239,718	
Annual average, Nov 1688– M 1700		1,769,974

M = Michaelmas

The War of the League of Augsburg forced Parliament to authorize military and naval forces nearly twice as large as those that had been maintained by the Commonwealth and Protectorate governments and costing twice as much per year to maintain. The English state employed as many as 87,000 men in its land forces during the 1690s. The declared accounts of the paymasters of the army indicate that they received over £18 million from the Exchequer to pay and sustain these troops, including over £4.7 million in army bills.[123] English armies served in Ireland, the Netherlands, North America, and the Caribbean islands. The Williamite conquest of Ireland from 1689 to 1697 cost the Exchequer over £4.9 million, of which £1.4 million was still owing to contractors for supplies and services in 1700.[124] A large portion of the forces employed were British troops, continuing the standing army tradition begun in 1645. William III also hired a significant number of foreign soldiers – Dutch, Danes, and Bavarians. The paymasters of the army issued £1.7 million to the foreign units serving with William's armies in Ireland and the Low Countries.

While there clearly was a major jump in the cost of war in the 1690s, the forces raised in Ireland and Britain in the 1640s and the 1690s are comparable in size if the forces raised in Ireland, Scotland, and England by all parties during the 1640s are considered as a single body: well over 120,000 men served in the Irish, Scottish and English armies of 1649/50. The human cost of war in the two periods was also of the same relative magnitude. Charles Carlton has recently concluded that total English military casualties in the 1640s comprised 3.6 per cent of the total English population, a figure which is greater than the 2.6 per cent of the total population of the United Kingdom killed in the First World War.[125]

So, in terms of financial cost, size of forces, and casualties, the mid-century wars proved to be a watershed in English military affairs. The changes evident in William's wars are quantitative not qualitative.

In March 1699 the English state still owed the officers and men of its army more than £1.5 million for their pay accrued during the War of the League of Augsburg. As late as 1705, the state still owed these soldiers over £1 million.[126] Although the English experimented with a number of new ways to borrow money in the 1690s, they still had not solved the problem of how to keep their army's pay current. In order to cut costs in 1697, Parliament ordered the rapid reduction of the army to fewer than 15,000 men in England and 1,250 in the West Indies. However, William III transferred many of the regiments on active duty in 1697 to the Irish establishment. Also, for the first time, the state retained a large proportion of its military officers on half pay in peacetime, preserving the cadre of the professional army begun in the 1640s.[127] Renewed warfare against France soon made it necessary for Parliament to agree to the army's expansion again.[128]

From 1645 on, the English maintained a standing army whose costs in peace and war steadily increased as the state found it necessary to fight to protect its interests and expand its opportunities. The need for this army, along with the navy discussed in the previous chapter, forced a revolution to take place in the ways in which English governments raised and managed money. This financial revolution, like the Military Revolution, started in the 1640s and continued to change the way the English state did business into the eighteenth century.

The modern English Army came into existence in response to extended periods of warfare during the seventeenth century. Well before 1640, the English had adapted their militia to many of the organizational and tactical lessons of modern military practice learned from their observation of the Dutch and Swedish armies. But this process of modernizing the militia did not create a standing army. Parliament's decision to fight a prolonged civil war and then to conquer Ireland and Scotland made it necessary to create the English professional army. The cost of supporting that army on extended military campaigns forced the Parliamentarians to develop new administrative practices to supply the army with arms, food, and equipment. To pay for all of this material and the soldiers who used it, the English developed ways to finance war from the collection and the anticipation of the receipts of permanent new taxes. These taxes, and especially the excise and assessment, continued to be the most important source of English revenue to the end of the eighteenth century.[129] How the English worked through the challenges of providing adequate financial resources for their navy and their new standing army in the half century after 1640 is the subject of the next four chapters.

CHAPTER FIVE

The Financial Crisis of the Long Parliament

The increased scale and cost of warfare, and the resultant steady expansion of professional military forces that was evident in England during the Military Revolution forced a fundamental change in English financial theory and practice. The fault line of this seismic change was in the 1640s. Before that decade, traditional financial ideals and methods continued to dominate English fiscal practice. These ideals and practices were not easily abandoned, and vestigial remains of them continued into the 1660s and 1670s. None the less, by 1660 much of the fiscal apparatus of a modern state was clearly in place, although significant changes continued in response to the rising naval costs of the Dutch wars. This chapter discusses a number of the fiscal expedients which the Long Parliament used in its efforts to solve the financial problems of how to raise money for the support of the navy and the New Model Army. The failure of most of these methods to provide sustained support for the Parliamentarian fleets and armies forced the Westminster government to develop new forms of taxation known as the excise and assessment. These taxes became the financial mainstay of the English state until the end of the eighteenth century.

The Long Parliament's painful shift to new fiscal methods and ideas in English state finance was a product of its need to finance very expensive civil and foreign wars. Representative governments have tried an amazing variety of schemes to avoid enacting the taxes necessary to support their state's military forces and government. The Long Parliament was no exception. In early Stuart England the men who dominated the parliamentary ranks still accepted the Tudor notion of government financial theory that the 'king should live of his own'.[1] However, the exponential rise in the costs of English armies and fleets that took place in the seventeenth century, coupled with the general price-inflation which had eroded the value of the Crown's traditional ordinary revenues, made it increasingly difficult for English parliaments to avoid facing their financial responsibilities. The Long Parliament's desire to dictate foreign policy and the domestic religious settlement to the King in 1641 made it impossible for it to ignore the fiscal reality that the King's traditional revenues were no longer sufficient to pay for the costs of government and the defence of the realm.

The obsolescence of the idea that the King should fund the cost of England's peacetime government from the receipts of the tonnage and poundage, feudal dues, and the revenue of the Crown lands was not abandoned until the 1640s. In that turbulent decade Parliament instituted permanent and predictable taxes which could be used to pay for the military expenses of the state and to service the additional costs and debts incurred in wartime. However, the members of the Long Parliament tried nearly every financial scheme they could devise to avoid enacting the permanent taxation needed to support their military forces and policies. These expedients were unsuccessful, just as earlier fund-raising expedients had proven inadequate to cover the growing costs of warfare from 1624 to 1640.

GOVERNMENT FINANCE IN EARLY STUART ENGLAND

The Tudor and first two Stuart monarchs had long faced the difficult task of paying for increasingly expensive military forces during a period of time when the real value of royal revenues was declining.[2] The spiralling growth in the costs of English fleets and armies was most visible in Elizabeth's long Spanish war (1585–1604), in the Stuart wars against Spain and France (1624–30), in the British civil and foreign wars of the mid-century, and finally in William III's war against Louis XIV (1689–97). Wartime expenses outran what was then called the 'ordinary' revenues of the monarch in each of these periods. Consequently, 'extraordinary' revenues had to be sought from Parliament to support the military forces. Just the fact that there were these two categories of revenue and expenditure in the English state's financial system until the late seventeenth century shows the strong grip older notions of royal finance had on the minds of Members of Parliaments. In 1640, ordinary revenue was the income of the royal demesne and the customs (or tonnage and poundage). Extraordinary income came from temporary direct taxes, usually in the form of subsidies or aids, that Parliament granted to the king in times of extraordinary state activity such as a war.[3]

Elizabeth I had barely made financial ends meet during her wars through the sale of Crown property, careful management of her ordinary revenues, and by successfully asking her parliaments for a remarkable number of subsidies. Even with these efforts, forced loans, and the sale of £372,000 worth of land, Elizabeth's government fell progressively deeper into debt, owing its creditors over £422,000 by 1603.[4] This debt was due primarily to the costs of the Spanish and Irish wars which had forced expenditures to rise from £164,000 per year in 1580 to £274,000 per year in the 1590s. At the same time, a noticeable decline occurred in the value of parliamentary subsidies.[5] Elizabeth and her ministers managed their financial situation ably, but they failed to develop new sources of revenue and new credit mechanisms that would allow the government to function without the sale of capital assets and the accumulation of unfunded short-term debt.

James I failed to recoup the Crown's financial fortunes during his generally peaceful reign. Instead, he spent lavishly on his court, his favourites and a large family, running a steady annual deficit of £50,000 in the balance of his ordinary revenues.[6] As a result, royal debt soared to £735,000 by 1606, while the Exchequer issue of £366,790 in cash that year exceeded ordinary cash receipts by £51,831. The Lord Treasurer, the Earl of Salisbury, reduced the accumulated debt to £280,000 by 1610, using parliamentary subsidies and the proceeds of the sale of Crown lands totalling over £400,000.[7] However, these extraordinary taxes and actions were seen as a one-time solution to the government's financial distress, not as an augmentation to the King's ordinary income, and they were not accompanied by retrenchment in royal expenditures. For example, the annual cost of the royal family grew from £26,284 in 1603 to £237,042 in 1610. Consequently, the net deficit on ordinary revenue in this period was £334,332 and only the sale of royal property reduced the total debt.[8]

To make matters worse, Jacobean deficits were met with inadequate borrowing techniques which reduced the Crown's credit while irritating the politically important classes of the nation. Feudal aids, non-parliamentary impositions on imports and exports, sale of noble titles, and forced loans were some of the devices that accompanied the use of unsecured short-term loans and the deferral of payment of Crown debts for goods and services to cover annual deficits. The 'Great Contract', negotiated but never concluded between the King and Parliament in 1610, was an attempt to exchange many of the anachronistic and politically inexpedient traditional revenues for the grant of perpetual parliamentary taxes of over £200,000 annually to meet the extraordinary and ordinary accounts' deficits. The Great Contract floundered when the Parliament of 1610 refused to provide such a large increase in income. As a result, Crown debt continued to rise from £280,000 in 1610 to £900,000 in 1618.[9] Table 5.1 provides an idea of the trend of the cash receipts and issues of the Exchequer from 1603 to 1640. These figures include the revenue and expenditure of ship-money from 1635 to 1640.

Table 5.1: Government Cash Receipts and Issues, 1603–40[10]

Period	Receipts (£)	Issues (£)
1603–5	1,319,234	1,296,198
1606–10	2,775,666	2,768,361
1611–15	2,813,786	2,586,130
1616–20	1,834,362	2,183,445
1621–5	2,166,988	2,336,400
1626–30	3,140,241	3,213,311
1631–5	2,285,313	2,133,598
1636–40	3,541,981	3,530,729
Total	19,877,571	20,048,172

During the first eighteen years of his reign, James I's government failed to live within its income. The royal family cost over £2.6 million (29.7 per cent of expenditures), while less than £2.5 million (28.6 per cent of expenditures) was provided to the Ordnance Office, the navy and the army combined. Two of the worst features of Jacobean fiscal management were that £935,074 (10.5 per cent of receipts) of the royal revenue came from forced and voluntary loans and £762,602 (8.6 per cent of receipts) was raised through the sale of Crown property, seriously depleting the King's demesne. Ordinary sources of revenue, such as the customs and the income from royal manors, provided only £2.7 million (30.5 per cent) and £738,000 (8.4 per cent) of the royal receipts respectively.[11] Not only could the monarch could no longer live from his own income in wartime, but he could no longer balance the royal budget in peacetime without taking extraordinary fiscal measures which eroded the future income of the government. For example, increasing amounts of the revenue were encumbered through the process of 'tally anticipations'. These were book transfers in which tallies were issued to a Crown creditor or disbursing officer for a sum due to the Crown from a revenue source in the future. When the sum was collected, it was paid directly to the holder of the tally, rather than to the Exchequer.[12] In this manner, the government could borrow money or pay for services with anticipated revenue. The problem with this was that in future years these receipts could not be used to pay for unexpected expenses such as war. Further, these tallies were not easily assignable to other persons or purposes. Therefore, their redemption could not be deferred in times of crisis without major loss in government credit. When England again went to war in the 1620s, things got considerably worse, since provision had not been made by the King or Parliament for adequate taxes to solve the state's endemic fiscal crisis.

The Stuart fiscal crisis became clearly evident when James attempted to provide military aid to his son-in-law Frederick V of the Palatinate against the triumphant Spanish army. James went to war without having adequate revenues for the purpose. As a result of the King's lack of money, his foreign policy was ineffective. By the time of the official declaration of war against Spain in 1624, Crown debt had already soared to £1 million, before the mobilization of English forces even started.[13] Much of this money was owed to merchants who had provided goods and services to the Crown and the armed forces. The remainder was due for loans made to the government through the Exchequer. Parliament had approved £1.2 million in subsidies from 1603 to 1620, and it provided another £203,810 in grants for the war effort by 1625. However, Exchequer cash disbursements for military costs totalled £608,998 in this five-year period, easily consuming the subsidies provided after 1620. In spite of these large outlays, the forces sent to Germany received only a portion of the money necessary for their pay, sustenance, and munitions. The results were the failure to reinforce Vere's garrisons in the Palatinate in 1621 and the disaster which later struck Mansfeld's army in Germany as thousands of his English soldiers starved and died of disease.

CAROLINE FINANCES

Charles I inherited this abysmal financial situation and worsened it through his and his Parliaments' unwillingness to work together in the war effort.[14] While parliamentary subsidies raised an additional £549,961, from 1626 to 1630, the total government cash expenditures of £3.2 million outran Exchequer receipts of £3.1 million. Worse, loans and land sales provided 22.1 per cent of these receipts, while additional large sums were owed to the soldiers and sailors for their pay. By 1628, the English government no longer could provide enough money to mobilize effective land and sea forces to continue the war. Only the involvement of England's enemies in the Thirty Years' War saved the nation from more military disasters than those suffered by English forces at Cadiz and Rhe. Peace was concluded with France and Spain by 1630, giving Charles the chance to recoup his financial situation.

Charles I made some important improvements in the state's financial situation after 1630. He spent less money annually on the royal family than his father had,[15] but his revenues from Crown lands and recusant fines were considerably less as well. The steady sale of Crown lands by Elizabeth I, James I, and Charles I had reduced the monarch's capital assets, in turn reducing future ordinary income. After 1630, Charles received no new parliamentary subsidies. Consequently, average annual government revenue declined to £457,000 in the first five years of the 1630s, from an annual average of £628,000 in the 1620s, while annual expenses fell to £426,719, leaving little to pay off the large accrued debt. Royal revenue increasingly depended on the continuation of the customs due to the declining demesne rents and the absence of parliamentary subsidies. But Parliament had refused to grant the customs to Charles for life as had traditionally been done in other reigns, forcing him to collect the duties and add new impositions without parliamentary approval. Even though the customs revenue grew dramatically from £197,080 in 1631 to £535,746 in 1640 (62 per cent of the 1640 Exchequer receipts), the accumulated political costs of these actions were extraordinarily high by 1640.

Charles's increases in the customs and his imposition of the non-parliamentary ship-money tax from 1635 to 1640, improved the government's financial position, although both moves were major political mistakes. These tax increases quite possibly could have ensured government solvency had England remained at peace. Ship-money provided 19 per cent of total government receipts from 1635 to 1640, allowing Charles to develop the first truly permanent professional navy in English history. Later, the Long Parliament recognized the utility of Charles's ship-money as a tax on all counties when it adopted the ship-money rating and quota procedures as the basis for the weekly and later the monthly assessments in 1643 and 1645.[16] These later assessment taxes were to become the linchpin of parliamentary finance in the civil wars and Interregnum, providing most of the support for the New Model Army.[17] The assessment remained an important part of English state revenue into the 1690s, and the basis for the land tax of the next century.[18] However, these developments occurred only after the Parliamentarians tried every seemingly less painful approach to raise money to fund state operations.

Charles's eleven years of personal rule ended in 1640 because he decided to ask Parliament for the additional taxation needed to raise the large amounts of money required to support another war against the Scots. He failed to get the money he requested because the Short Parliament refused to grant extraordinary revenue before he redressed its numerous grievances. Significantly, most of these grievances were related to the financial actions of the government (forced loans, coat-and-conduct money, ship-money, and the collection of the customs without parliamentary approval).[19] Consequently, the king dismissed the Short Parliament and attempted to field a large army against the Scots without parliamentary help. He failed miserably, due in large part to insufficient funds.[20] After the military débâcle of the Second Bishops' War, Charles called another Parliament because the Scots refused to withdraw their army from northern England until he paid its costs of £850 per day. The Long Parliament imposed a revolutionary settlement on the King, forcing him to accept the principle of parliamentary control of taxation and oversight of the selection of his chief officers of state.

Then, as a political settlement seemed possible in 1641, a major uprising of Irish Catholics in Ulster threatened to expel the English and Scottish colonists from Ireland. The need to field an army to crush the Irish rebellion brought the struggle of King and Parliament to a new crisis over the issue of military command. Parliament feared that if Charles were given command of an army to crush the rebellion, he would use it on his domestic opponents, undoing the gains in parliamentary power. A growing mutual distrust between the King and a majority of the members of the Long Parliament over this issue and over religion drove the nation to civil war in the summer of 1642.[21]

The First Civil War began when Parliament resolved, on 12 July 1642, 'that an army shall be forthwith raised, for the safety of the king's person, the defence of both Houses of Parliament, and of those who have obeyed their orders and commands; and for the preservation of the true religion, the laws, liberties, and peace of the kingdom'.[22] This army, to consist initially of 24,000 infantry and 5,000 cavalry and to be commanded by the Earl of Essex, was to defend London from the growing Royalist tide in the west and north. It was one thing for the Long Parliament to pass such a bold resolution to raise an army; quite another for it to find the men, arms, and the approximately £695,000 needed to raise and support it for one year.[23] For the first time, Parliament had to accept full responsibility for the nation's financial needs and face the consequences of the predictable results if it provided inadequate financial resources for the support of the nation's foreign policy and military forces. For John Pym and those in the Long Parliament favouring a military solution, providing adequate financial support for Parliament's army became a matter of life or death.

Parliamentary leaders did not see the full implications of the situation at the time. For example, in March 1642 they attempted to pay for the conquest of Ireland through the anticipated confiscation and sale of Catholic-owned lands in Ireland rather than by increasing taxes in England. This expedient raised only a little over £300,000 of the £1 million expected from it in the next five years.[24] Only their experiences over the next three years of civil war forced the Parliamentarians to face the fundamental problem of English government finance: steady taxes were needed to provide the predictable revenue required to maintain the state's credit in wartime and to pay for the costs of warfare since the Crown could no longer live of its own. Further, it was becoming clear that the traditional division between ordinary and extraordinary revenues and expenditures had to end. Although it took a number of years for Englishmen to fully assimilate these facts into their thinking about financial affairs, the Long Parliament's control of its war effort during the English civil wars provided a massive shift in this direction.

During the next two years the Parliamentarians tried an amazing array of methods other than major tax reform to raise money for the support of their land and sea forces. Many of these extraordinary and *ad hoc* fiscal expedients failed or proved inadequate. Some raised money in irregular, unpredictable spurts. Two of them produced the excise and assessment taxes. These two taxes, along with the customs, eventually became the three great pillars of public finance, but only after a great deal of experimentation and development had taken place. Ultimately, the unreliability of the *ad hoc* attempts to raise money for the wars forced the Parliamentarians to realize that only regular and predictable revenues could produce the money needed for victory.[25]

THE FAILURE OF *AD HOC* FINANCE, 1642 TO 1645

The Long Parliament moved swiftly in 1642 to secure its position in London and its control of the navy, which had declared its loyalty to the Westminster government.[26] London was the commercial and financial heart of the kingdom and the main administrative offices of the customs, the only regular tax then levied, were maintained in London. However, the customs receipts were committed to the support of the navy, and the outbreak of the civil war meant that the fleets would grow as the navy isolated the Royalists from foreign support, protected English commerce, and escorted Parliamentarian reinforcements and supplies to besieged ports such as Plymouth and Hull.[27] The annual costs of the fleets rose from £41,604 in 1642 to £320,569 in 1643, swallowing the entire revenue of the customs (£165,000 in 1643), and leaving a debt of at least £110,000 by the end of 1643.[28] With the customs revenue fully committed, John Pym and the other revolutionaries had to look elsewhere for money to support the Parliamentarian armies.

Parliament decided not to use the traditional royal Exchequer as a central treasury for its financial management.[29] This was partially explained by Parliament's earlier decision to have the customs receipts paid directly to the Navy Treasurer, bypassing the Exchequer and thereby greatly reducing the Exchequer's cash receipts available to the King. Also, since a large proportion of the Exchequer's receipts were anticipated by tallies to pay the debts and the pensions of the favourites of the King, by shutting down the Exchequer, the Parliamentarians struck a major blow at the King's supporters.[30] Finally, much of the traditional Crown revenue was no longer available to the Exchequer because the Royalists controlled the regions from which this revenue was drawn, cutting the annual receipts of the Exchequer to roughly £79,000 by 1643.[31]

Borrowing was the first expedient used to raise money for the Parliamentarian forces. In June 1642, Parliament called for the advance of horses, plate, money, and arms by its supporters.[32] The results were impressive: advances generated a large portion of the money and equipment needed to arm and mount the newly raised soldiers. However, this was a source that quickly dried up as the war continued.[33] A delegation from the House of Commons also approached the Common Council of London to request a loan of £100,000 in June. The Council granted the loan, requiring in return a pledge by Members of Parliament of their personal property as collateral.[34] In July 1642, the Long Parliament ordered another £100,000 to be borrowed from the money being raised for the English and Scottish troops in Ireland by the Adventurers for Irish land.[35] This was a start towards raising the money needed to sustain an army in England of 20,000 men. However, this fiscal tactic was only a one-time expedient because the Westminster government remained committed to support another 20,000 Protestant troops operating against the Catholic rebellion in Ireland.[36]

Then, as the King raised his army in August, the Long Parliament found it necessary to increase its force under the command of the Earl of Essex to 29,000 men.[37] The parliamentary commitment to support this force made the use of voluntary loans an inadequate financial option, especially after the inconclusive encounters between the opposing armies at Edgehill (October) and Turnham Green (November 1642). Consequently, the Parliamentarians began to organize their war effort for the long haul by imposing the first parliamentary tax without royal approval, on 29 November. This ordinance assessed a fine of not more than one-twentieth of the value of the estates of those in London, Westminster and Southwark who had refused earlier to voluntarily loan plate, horses, or money for the cause. Parliament quickly extended this punitive tax to those parts of England under its control, while also appointing county committees with sweeping powers to oversee the collection of supplies and loans for its forces.[38]

In November, Parliament established the Committee for the Advance of Money to systematize the process of seeking loans from the London livery companies and individuals and to find other sources of revenue. This committee, which met and maintained its treasury in Haberdashers' Hall, was the model for all succeeding fiscal committees, operating with clerks, a registrar, legal counsel, and a treasury.[39] Nevertheless, the committee could only raise limited amounts of money through voluntary contributions and, therefore, it soon moved into the business of forced loans.

One of the basic problems of parliamentary finance in 1642 was that no one knew for sure how much money was needed for the forces in England since no one knew how long these troops would need to be maintained. Loans, secured by Irish land or individual property, might have sufficed if the war had ended in the autumn of 1642. Such loans tapped too little of the wealth of the nation to support a long war and, more importantly, were insufficient to pay for forces that cost £1 million in the first year of the war.[40] After the first rush of enthusiasm for the cause ebbed, the only loans of any size raised by the Westminster government were secured by the anticipated receipts from the sale of property and the anticipated income of the parliamentary taxes.

Parliament did not give up trying to penalize those who refused to support the cause willingly. In May 1643, another parliamentary ordinance, requiring forced contributions, used the principle of the fifth and twentieth parts of pre-war subsidies to assess non-contributors. This ordinance stipulated that one-fifth of the value of movable property and one-twentieth of that of fixed property of those people taxed as non-contributors was to be paid. The Committee for Advance managed the collection of this Fifth and Twentieth part tax. M.A.E. Green, in her preface to *The Calendar of the Proceedings of the Committee for the Advance of Money*, indicates that £1,418,299 was levied on the Fifth and Twentieth part ordinance in 1643, but only £260,306 of this amount was collected in the accounting year ending in March 1644.[41] No record exists beyond this estimate for the national receipts of this tax, although John Weaver, treasurer of the Eastern Association, indicated that he received £87,340 from it alone by 1650.[42] Resistance to permanent parliamentary taxation was strong in early 1643, and the Long Parliament dared push people only so far. As the war intensified and the military forces grew larger, Parliament turned to the creation of regional associations to recruit and pay for the armies defending the different regions from the Royalists, hoping that the sense of immediate local danger would make taxation more palatable.

The creation of regional associations of counties began in December 1642 and continued as a method of organizing Parliament's war effort and its finances for the next three years.[43] The associations were allowed to assess taxes on income and property and to use the proceeds for the support of local defence forces and garrisons. The most famous of these organizations was the Eastern Association which supported an army commanded by the Earl of Manchester. The regional associations raised large amounts of money and supplies of which few complete totals have survived.[44] However, even the Eastern Association, the strongest and best organized, only raised enough money in 1643 and 1644 to pay its regional forces for 260 days per year.[45] Several of the regional associations did a reasonably good job of raising armies to defend themselves, but they did not raise the soldiers or the money needed to support the main Parliamentarian Army, which received pay for less than 175 days in 1644. Further, the associations dissipated the Long Parliament's military and financial power, a problem only rectified with the creation of the New Model Army in 1645.[46]

While regional forces defended the associations, Essex's army continued to defend London and to attempt to bring the King's main army to battle. Parliament was unable to support this army adequately in 1642, and so, in February 1643, it passed a weekly assessment which levied a tax on all counties of England for its support. This weekly assessment had major long-term implications, but as a weekly tax it proved inadequate for the support of the main war effort in its first two years, producing not much more than £129,819 by March 1645.[47] Consequently, beginning in March 1643, Parliament decided to make Royalists pay for the war through the confiscation, or sequestration, of their rents and incomes.

The sequestration process was operated by county committees authorized to seize Royalists' properties and to collect their rents and income for use by the Westminster government.[48] A parliamentary Sequestrations Committee was established in London with only limited control over the sequestration activities of the county committees. Only a small part of sequestration fines and rents were received in London. The records of the amounts raised in the counties and spent there on local defence and administration are incomplete. Those sequestration receipts that the county committees sent to London were deposited in a treasury managed by Richard Waring and Michael Herring at Goldsmiths' Hall.[49] These fines and rents of sequestered estates of the 'delinquents', as the Royalists were known, raised a total of at least £377,535 between 1643 to 1655.[50] The sequestration treasurers' accounts do not list the separate amounts received in individual years, and it is reasonable to believe that until Parliamentarian armies were finally winning the First Civil War in 1645, only a small proportion of the total sequestration revenue could be collected. The revenue and rents of episcopal and royal lands were also sequestered in 1643, but the amounts raised from them were not large enough to cover the costs of the armies, with the rents of royal property bringing in only £45,237 from September 1643 to September 1644 for example.[51]

Sequestrations receipts and various loans were unpredictable. The former required military victories and the occupation of Royalist territory by Parliamentarian troops, and this did not happen until 1645. Such victories depended on people's willingness to advance credit to the Westminster government to pay for its armies, and this depended on the existence of faith in the Long Parliament's ability and willingness to repay its obligations. The forced loan levied on the treasury of the Irish Adventurers did little to maintain such faith. By early 1643, London aldermen and the Common Council required each loan to the Westminster government to be accompanied by financial concessions. These concessions included the demand that Londoners could nominate the customs commissioners and the army Treasurers at War and that the receipts of sequestrations and contributions were to be paid into treasuries in the Guildhall and the halls of the city's other liveried companies. The management of these treasuries and the collection of these revenues was profitable and, more importantly, gave City financiers and merchants who advanced money to the Long Parliament an added sense of security. This explains in large part why so many different treasuries were used to collect revenue in the 1640s. It also helps to explain why the Exchequer was not used as a central treasury for most tax receipts after 1641.[52]

Parliament, in addition to forming a number of committees to raise money, formed an executive committee in May 1642 to try to coordinate its war efforts and financial expenditures. Within several months this Committee of Defence evolved into the Committee of Safety. It was the first of the great executive-administrative committees to serve the parliamentary cause, with twenty-two Commons' and twenty three Lords' members serving on it from July 1642 to December 1643. The committee directed military operations, approved money to be spent on the armies of Essex, Sir William Waller, and Lord Fairfax, and attempted to conduct foreign relations.[53] John Pym dominated the work of the Committee of Safety, using it to negotiate loans in London, raise troops for the armies, and to negotiate with the Scots for the alliance of September 1643. The committee, however, proved unable to regulate adequately the financial affairs of the Westminster government because it lacked a permanent secretariat, established accounting procedures, and clearly defined authority over the revenue committees and treasuries. Consequently, the amounts of money it authorized for the armies greatly exceeded the revenue, creating a large, undetermined, and unsecured debt. In the autumn of 1643, the committee disappeared as the Long Parliament assumed the executive functions carried out by the Committee of Safety. The lack of a clearly defined and powerful central executive made financial management very difficult throughout the 1640s, as the Long Parliament continued to struggle to get a firm grip on its financial affairs.

Parliament's financial situation worsened in mid-1643, as its war effort continued with little success.[54] Essex's army melted away as his soldiers were seldom paid and provisions were too often not supplied. Essex's successful efforts to recruit his army to 19,000 men in April 1643 were undone as its strength fell to less than 9,000 men by July.[55] Parliament created at least two other main field armies – Waller's and the Earl of Manchester's – without providing sufficient money to support them. If these armies totalled only 30,000 men, and Firth estimates them at twice that strength, they would have cost well over £780,000 per year for pay alone.[56] This amount excludes the costs of arms, ammunition, and horses.

THE FISCAL CRISIS OF 1643/4

Some way had to be found to provide a predictable flow of money to support these forces if the Parliamentarian cause was to survive. Customs receipts remained committed to the support of the navy, although the customs raised too little to pay for the fleet's growing costs. Consequently, John Pym had to create the excise and the assessment taxes to provide sufficient revenue to fund the war effort. The excise system was established in July 1643 and quickly became heavily obligated by loans raised in anticipation of tax receipts.[57] By securing loans with anticipated excise revenue, Parliament raised over £249,000 for its armies between September 1643 and September 1644, and another £156,000 by September 1645.[58] Excise taxes could not provide, however, the millions needed for a long war and the assessment system took at least two years to establish and regulate. The development of the three main parliamentary revenues is discussed in detail in the next three chapters because they became the backbone of English government finance for the next fifty years. As they developed, the Parliamentarians faced a financial crisis in 1643 and 1644 that could only be met with further fiscal expedients, since these three regular revenues were not in place and functioning smoothly yet.

A major boost to the Parliamentarian cause was the Scots' entry into the civil war against the King. In September 1643, the Scots committed themselves to a Solemn League and Covenant with the Westminster government and promised to provide a 20,000-man army for operations in northern England. The English Parliament promised to pay this army £100,000 when it entered England, and £30,000 per month thereafter for its support. An already woefully inadequate government revenue was now committed to provide financial support for Scottish and English armies in Ireland and England, necessitating new revenue sources.

The next logical step from sequestering the rent of the property of Royalists, bishops, and the King was to sell those lands. In the autumn of 1643, the House of Commons formed a Committee for Scottish Affairs to meet regularly in Goldsmiths' Hall and to find ways to pay the Scottish Army. This committee became increasingly active in 1644 as Scottish forces moved into England. The Committee for Scottish Affairs soon absorbed the weak Sequestrations Committee, becoming known as the Committee for Compounding. The London merchants Michael Herring and Richard Warner were its treasurers.[59] The additional requirement to pay the Scottish Army in the north made it essential for the Westminster government to find better ways to provide a steady flow of money. As a result, the House of Commons ordered 'the Committee at Goldsmiths' Hall' to consider selling the estates of leading delinquents and to use the proceeds to support the forces.

The Committee for Compounding at that point hit upon another less drastic method to raise money.[60] Royalist delinquents were to be allowed to 'compound', or pay one-time composition fines as a penalty for their previous support of the King. Once they had compounded for their delinquency, their rents and income were no longer sequestered by the state. The process of compounding required the delinquent to come to London, declare his guilt, and pay a one-time fine of one-sixth of the value of his estate for his delinquency. This process brought the money to the London treasury instead of to the county Sequestrations Committees and it allowed former Royalists to return to loyalty to the parliamentary state. It was a brilliant financial stroke, if not entirely successful politically.

Additional money could now be raised for the Parliamentarian armies. Their successes in 1644 and 1645 led to a greater flow of compositions, providing greater revenue. M.A.E. Green concluded that the process of compounding by Royalists provided £1,304,957 to the Westminster governments over the eight years ending in 1652. The declared account of treasurers Herring and Warner place the amount they received from compounding at £1,285,204 for the period 16 October 1643 to 16 June 1653. Herring and Warner also listed the receipts from sequestration fines as £377,535, for a total receipt of £1.66 million.[61] This money was not paid in at the steady rate of £180,000 per year. The warrants issued by the Committee for Compounding for expenditure of composition receipts show that not much more than £3,000 was raised and spent in 1643, £65,000 in 1644, and £44,000 in 1645. The largest amounts were received and disbursed in 1646 and 1647, when over £200,000 in payments were authorized by the committee's warrants and paid by the treasurers. These amounts in no way made up for the arrears in the soldiers' pay, although they did make it possible to encourage the Scots to work actively with Manchester's army in Yorkshire. Ultimately, the Long Parliament had to look elsewhere to find the money needed to win the First Civil War.

During 1644, the Westminster and Edinburgh governments enjoyed a clear military advantage over the King, but were decidedly inferior in terms of strategic coordination of their forces. The King was the undisputed commander of the Royalist armies, while his enemies suffered from a fractured command structure due to their use of regional forces and several field armies. The Parliamentarians and Scots created a joint body in January 1644, known as the Committee of Both Kingdoms, to coordinate political policy.

The Committee of Both Kingdoms, also known as the Derby House Committee after its place of meeting, worked unsuccessfully to synchronize operations in Ireland, as well as in the north and south of England. A great deal of the problem was that the English Parliamentarians lacked a unified military command structure, making their armies vulnerable to defeat in detail by the Royalists. In addition, the English dissipated their financial strength with their regional tax authorities and decentralized sequestration process. As a result, the allies' victory of Marston Moor could not be exploited because of the inability, or at least unwillingness, of the coalition armies to work together against the King's main army. The poor command relationships that existed between the parliamentary commanders, along with a continuing severe money shortage, allowed the Royalists to recoup their situation in 1644 with victories against the armies of William Waller (June) and the Earl of Essex (August).[62] The Parliamentarians' political, military and financial prospects were bleak in the autumn of 1644, in spite of the victory of Marston Moor and their quantitative advantages in manpower and resources.

By the autumn it seemed as if the war effort against the king had become completely unravelled. After his humiliation at Cropredy Bridge, Sir William Waller's army had disintegrated, and he had retired to London; the Earl of Essex had been compelled to surrender [Parliament's main field army] at Lostwithiel; and in

October the Earl of Manchester had failed to stop the relief of Donnington Castle by a Royalist force half the size of his own. This dismal record of failure had its natural consequence: discord and discontent within the armies, in Parliament, and in London, as people cast about for someone to blame. Wide cracks disfigured the fragile facade of parliamentary unity.[63]

Parliament's financial situation was desperate. Armies numbering nearly 70,000 men were receiving much less than half of the pay due to them, forcing the soldiers to take free quarter. Military operations were difficult to execute because of shortages of food and munitions.[64] The total amounts due to soldiers for their pay arrears cannot be determined exactly, but they had to be enormous by early 1645. English forces totalling 60,000 men would have cost over £1.7 million per year to sustain and pay. The Scottish Army in northern England required an additional £360,000 per year and the anti-Catholic armies in Ireland needed at least an additional £525,000 annually.[65] The Scottish and English forces in England alone cost over £2 million, while parliamentary revenues, excluding the customs, probably did not exceed £1 million per year from January 1643 to December 1644.[66] England had yet to perfect the financial methods needed to support the costs of modern warfare.

Parliament did not adequately address its command and financial problems until the beginning of 1645, when it passed several ordinances that revolutionized the English military and financial structures. These ordinances were a direct response to the requirements of modern warfare. If the Long Parliament had failed to pass them, it is likely that the civil war would have had a dramatically different outcome.

THE NEW MODELLED FINANCES

Parliament's passage of the New Model Army Ordinance, on 17 February 1645, went a long way towards uniting its military command structure by appointing Sir Thomas Fairfax as the Lord General and commander of Parliament's main army. The New Model Army Ordinance established the professional standing army in England and began the reform of the assessment taxes that would eventually provide enough money to adequately, if not completely, pay the Long Parliament's armed forces.[67] The use of the same ordinance for the creation of the standing army and the regular source of income to support it illustrates the direct connection between the financial and military demands of the Military Revolution in civil war England.

The New Model Ordinance consolidated the weekly assessments into a monthly tax designed to raise £53,436 per month. This tax was levied only on the seventeen counties completely within Parliament's control. The money was to be paid into a central treasury maintained by the Treasurers at War in London's Guildhall rather than diverted to pay local forces. The ordinance authorized those counties not yet completely in Parliament's control and the existing regional associations to continue raising local assessments to pay for local defence.[68] On 21 February, an ordinance levied another monthly assessment of £21,121 on the same counties 'towards the Maintenance of the Scottish Army. . . .';[69] and on 31 March 1645, the Committee for Compounding received permission from Parliament to allow delinquents to come safely to London to ask to be allowed to compound for their opposition to the Westminster government, eliminating the need to prosecute delinquents before they compounded for sequestrations.[70]

The military and financial fruits of these measures followed swiftly. Parliament quickly negotiated an £80,000 loan from the City secured by the anticipated receipts of the monthly assessment. In the measure securing this loan, Parliament named eight London merchants as Treasurers at War to collect and disburse the receipts of two assessments from the Guildhall, assuring the City of additional control of the revenue and security for its loan.[71] These Treasurers at War became an important link in the financial system, receiving Parliament's largest revenue and accounting for its disbursement over the next fifteen years (see chapter eight for a full account of the assessment system). The loan, totalling £83,610, was raised by subscription, providing the money needed to pay for the arms, munitions, and horses to allow Fairfax to put the New Model Army into the field.[72] Collection of the monthly assessment in the counties was backed by armed force if necessary. As a result, the New Model monthly assessment provided the parliamentary government with £475,278 in the next year, while the assessment for the support of the Scottish Army brought in another £162,727.[73] Parliament also extended the excise in January 1645, allowing additional money to be borrowed in anticipation of excise receipts. Although the excise, assessments and compositions did not bring in enough money to pay Parliament's forces fully in 1645 and 1646, they provided enough to support the New Model and Scottish armies during the campaign of 1645, making possible the decisive victory over the King at Naseby in June.

Parliament's political crisis was ameliorated with the passage of the Self-Denying Ordinance on 3 April 1645, and another on 1 April giving Sir Thomas Fairfax full powers as Commander in Chief over all parliamentary forces.[74] Due to the Self-Denying Ordinance, the Earls of

Essex and Manchester resigned from their commands, allowing their armies to be disbanded and most of their soldiers incorporated into Fairfax's New Model Army. These changes removed the influence of the peace party within the Long Parliament from direction of military operations, allowing a much more vigorous prosecution of the war. The Committee of Both Kingdoms coordinated the operations of Fairfax's and the Scots' armies more effectively as well in 1645, as its members learned to trust Fairfax and his Lieutenant General of Horse, Oliver Cromwell, with the tactical decisions. The combination of these political, financial, and military changes marked a revolution in the conduct of English warfare, resulting in the defeat of the King and the eventual unification of England, Scotland, and Ireland. The harvest of these fruits, however, took another six years of very expensive warfare to gather, requiring further drastic financial expedients by the Westminster government.

THE SALE OF PROPERTY

The surrender of the King to the Scots in May 1646, and the capitulation of his capital of Oxford in June, essentially ended the First Civil War. Parliament then hoped to focus its attention on the conquest of Ireland. However, the financial obligations and continuing burdens did not disappear with victory over the King. By the end of 1646, the arrears of pay of the soldiers of Fairfax's army alone exceeded £1 million.[75] The return of peace in England brought a clamour to end the heavy taxation and to disband the army. The most pressing financial problem facing the Long Parliament was how to pay off and disband most of its forces while sending a large portion of it to Ireland to crush the Catholic rebellion. These challenging tasks became even more difficult when the House of Commons failed to renew the monthly assessment for the New Model's support after October 1646, and many English taxpayers refused to pay the full amounts already assessed. For these reasons, the arrears of the soldiers and the money owed to contractors for supplies and services reached £3 million by late 1648.[76]

Parliament attempted to provide money for the conquest of Ireland and to deal with the army's arrears and its other debts by selling the episcopal lands. Bishoprics were abolished in October 1646, and ordinances authorizing and regulating their sale were passed over the next six months.[77] Also, in October 1646, the Long Parliament negotiated a loan of £200,000 in the City to pay for the forces being sent to reinforce the Protestant garrisons in Ireland and to help pay off the Scottish Army.

Londoners quickly subscribed the full amount of this loan, probably because it was secured by the anticipated proceeds of the sale of the episcopal lands and because the money raised in this manner was rapidly spent for its stated purposes.[78] Unfortunately, the sale of episcopal lands took twelve years to complete, thus making only a small dent in the immense debts of the Westminster government in 1647–8.[79]

A process called 'doubling' was used in these sales. By this scheme, anyone who had loaned money to the Westminster government before could advance the same amount again, thereby doubling the debt. In return, the lender received the right to use this doubled amount to purchase that value of church lands. In this manner the lender received a doubled debt secured by tangible assets that he then could use or sell.[80] From 1647 to 1655, roughly £676,000 in old and new debt was retired through the sale of the episcopal lands, with only £17,501 of this amount raised in ready cash.[81] Loans raised on anticipated revenue from the sale of bishops' lands allowed the English to pay the Scots the £200,000 they had demanded before they would surrender the King to the English Parliament and depart England. However, the proceeds of the sale of episcopal lands did not reduce the arrears of soldiers of the New Model Army because so little cash was realized.[82]

To make things worse for parliamentary finances in 1647, a bitter political, religious and financial struggle broke out between the army and the Long Parliament. A parliamentary majority, strongly supported by the Presbyterian and crypto-Royalist majority in London's government, attempted to disband the New Model Army without having reached a settlement with the King about the political and religious nature of the English state. Further, this Presbyterian majority attempted to disband the army without providing adequate security for its pay arrears and without passing an act of indemnity and oblivion for the soldiers forgiving them for acts they had committed during and since the civil war.[83]

The House of Commons ordered the New Model Army to disband in May 1647, while offering to pay the soldiers only six weeks of their arrears. At that time, Fairfax's cavalry regiments were forty-three weeks behind in their pay and the infantry were eighteen weeks behind in theirs.[84] In response, the army's General Council asked for a comprehensive act of indemnity, visible security for the soldiers' arrears, only voluntary enlistments for service in Ireland, and financial provision for soldiers' widows and orphans. The controversy escalated until open armed conflict was avoided only by the complete capitulation by Parliament and the City Common Council and the occupation of London by the army in August.[85] These military moves did not solve the financial problems of the army. London remained over £60,000 behind in its assessment payments and there were violent demonstrations against the collection of the excise in Smithfield, where the Excise House was pulled down.[86]

Parliament, purged of the eleven leading members of the Presbyterian faction in August, renewed the monthly assessment of £60,000 in October 1647.[87] The monthly assessment, which had first been enacted in 1645 and continued to November 1646, had not been successfully collected since mid-1646. Therefore, the Commons promised that if the past six months were paid by 15 January, it would forgive the taxpayers three of the next nine months' assessments. Further, Parliament appointed General Receivers for the assessment in each county in an effort to prevent the diversion of the revenue at the local level.[88] These measures had little immediate effect, although they facilitated future collection of assessments when the political and military situations stabilized. The use of military force to support the assessment collections in the country, and the quartering of army troops in London, did more in the short run to aid tax collection.

Fairfax and the army's high command made significant reductions in the size of the forces in late 1647 and early 1648. In September, Fairfax sent 8,900 soldiers to Ireland to reinforce the Parliamentary garrisons there. These men were given two months of their pay arrears and one month's pay in advance, and promised debentures secured by future land sales as security for the remainder of their pay arrears.[89] In January and February, Fairfax radically reduced the strength and structure of the New Model in England, cutting it to 24,000 men, while eliminating politically unreliable regiments and retaining only those units that had remained loyal and disciplined during the crisis of the previous summer. The explosive problem of back-pay was taken care of by issuing debentures to all soldiers for their arrears, after each of their pay accounts were taken and deductions made for free quarter.[90] The northern and western armies were also disbanded in 1647, with only their best regiments absorbed into the New Model.[91] When this was done, 'the military high command had reshaped the parliamentary army into a leaner, more politically homogeneous and less costly body of men'.[92]

England's military costs still exceeded its revenues in early 1648. The financial support of the 24,000-man New Model and the garrisons maintained throughout England easily consumed the £60,000 per month that the monthly assessment could provide.[93] The excise was heavily encumbered with loans made for the support of the army in the civil war, and the navy cost far more than the customs receipts provided. The Westminster government was committed to a costly war in Ireland where it maintained 26,000 men at an annual cost of £293,768 for pay alone.[94] A separate £21,000 monthly assessment for Ireland did not cover the costs of the Irish war. Before these serious financial problems could be addressed by the army command or Parliament, the Second Civil War erupted, postponing their settlement and the conquest of Ireland for another year.

COMMONWEALTH FINANCE

The victory of the New Model Army in the Second Civil War was a spectacular vindication of the military value of a standing professional army. Cromwell and Fairfax crushed numerically superior enemies in England, capping their achievements with the complete defeat of the Scots' army at Preston in August 1648.[95] The tactical excellence and cohesion of the New Model Army made these victories possible, in spite of a major fleet mutiny on behalf of Charles I and the continuing drain of the war in Ireland. After completing the military victory in England, the victorious Independents and their army purged the Long Parliament (Pride's Purge), creating 'the Rump' which, in turn, tried and executed the King (January 1649) and proclaimed England as a Commonwealth ruled by the House of Commons alone (March 1649). In March and April 1649, the Rump attempted to solve the arrears and debt problems inherited from the Westminster governments of 1642 to 1648. Simultaneously, the republican government had to find ways to pay an army in England of over 44,000 men, with a monthly cost of £120,000.[96]

The Rump Parliament established an effective executive, known as the Council of State, giving it the power to

> order and direct all the militias and forces both by sea . . . and land, of England and Ireland, and the Dominions for preserving the peace and safety thereof. . . . To raise and arm such forces as you judge necessary. . . . To use all good ways and means for the reducing of Ireland . . . and all other parts and places belonging to the Commonwealth of England not yet reduced.[97]

The Council of State needed unprecedented amounts of money to accomplish these tasks. Consequently, the Rump increased the monthly assessment to £90,000 per month, achieving with it alone a tax rate 'of something like eighteen pre-war parliamentary subsidies a year!'[98] But the army was still owed over £1.4 million in pay arrears in 1649, and the state's other creditors were owed at least another £1.7 million. The customs, excise, and assessment taxes could not sustain the current forces and secure the debt in such a way that the government could negotiate further loans and advances in anticipation of taxes. This situation became clear in April and May, when the London Common Council refused to loan the Council of State the £120,000 needed to send Cromwell's 12,000 men to Ireland with an adequate war chest. In addition, Cromwell's expeditionary force needed £106,676 for its pay from April to July, and another £100,028 in cash to pay the two months in arrears promised to the soldiers who had volunteered for service in Ireland.[99] Lacking adequate long-term credit mechanisms, the Commonwealth had to resort to the further sale of capital assets to establish its credit and carry on its war in Ireland.

By 1649 the proceeds of the sale of episcopal lands had reached at least £285,000, with another £177,330 worth of debt retired in 1649 through the doubling process. The total of debt reduced and new money advanced on doubling for the former bishops' lands eventually reached £676,000.[100] In April and June 1649, Parliament resolved to sell the cathedral chapter lands as well, using the same method of doubling used in the sale of the bishops' lands.[101] Over the next eight years, the sale of the dean and chapter property allowed the Westminster governments to retire another £1.17 million in debt.[102] Most of the property was sold or contracted for by September 1650. Only £503,179 of the total sale proceeds was received in cash, with the remainder paid off in previous debt that was doubled for in exchange for the lands sold.[103] These sales of church property did nothing to redeem the huge pile of soldiers' pay debentures then outstanding, but they did go a long way towards bolstering the government's short-term credit with victuallers and arms makers.

Cromwell's campaign in Ireland could not commence until the soldiers received concrete satisfaction for their arrears. Therefore, on 4 and 16 July 1649, Parliament voted to sell the former royal family's personal goods and lands and to use the proceeds to redeem the soldiers' debentures.[104] The legislation allowed the Crown lands to be completely paid for with the soldiers' debentures and gave soldiers a special opportunity, after the tenants currently on the land, to purchase the property. The soldiers were expected to pay a minimum of thirteen years' purchase for the lands, one of the highest rates for any lands sold by the government during the Interregnum.[105] Practically the entire £1,464,409 worth of Crown lands sold was paid for with debentures, according to the declared account of John Dethicke, treasurer for the sale.[106] H.J. Habakkuk claims that £84,763 in cash was received as well, although Dethicke's account does not seem to support this conclusion.[107] The key point is that the government paid off at least £1.4 million of the soldiers' arrears, clearing it of that much debt.

The royal family's personal possessions were sold for an additional £134,383 over a nine-year period, beginning in 1649. The cash raised in these sales was used to pay the King's creditors for debts from the early and mid-1640s, as well as to help pay for the navy's current expenses.[108] Little of this money reached the army.

The Irish war continued well into 1652, and the republic became involved in another war with Scotland in the summer of 1650.[109] Consequently, the Commonwealth found itself maintaining over 35,000 men in Ireland and at least that many again in both Scotland and England. Simultaneously the navy grew in response to the need to support these theatres of operation and to protect English commerce.[110] To pay for these operations, the Rump authorized the sale of the fee farm rents in March 1650 and raised the assessment to £120,000 monthly in November.[111] In the long term the assessment brought in more money than land sales, but the sale of the fee farm rents allowed the Commonwealth to pay off another £816,484 of short-term debt.[112]

The treasurers paid most of the cash received from the fee farm rents' sales to the Navy Treasurer (£100,000) and the army's Treasurers at War (£317,396).[113] The cash raised in this manner was invaluable to the financial and logistical support provided from England for Cromwell's campaign in Scotland which culminated in the final battle against Royalism at Worcester in September 1651.[114] The remainder of the proceeds of these land sales retired state debt of roughly £400,000. With the sale of the fee farm rents, the Commonwealth had sold the last major block of royal or church property available to it.

However, the Royalist uprisings in conjunction with the Second Civil War in 1648, and the Scottish invasion of England in the summer of 1651, gave the Rump one last major source of property to confiscate and sell. Parliament had in place the legislation and administrative apparatus to sell the property of Royalists who had failed previously to compound and of the Royalists who joined in the risings of 1648 and 1651. This machinery was set in full motion.

The Commonwealth's sale of the estates of Royalists brought in £1,224,916 in cash and retired debt in 1651 and 1652. The treasurers for the sales received £604,934 in cash through the process of doubling and £15,048 in cash from sales, with the remainder in paid-off debt. The cash raised in this manner provided £619,926 to the Treasurer of the Navy, the army's Treasurers at War, and others involved in direct support of England's military operations.[115] These receipts, along with the £95,237 realized by a separate sale of the late King's houses, were the last of the money raised through sales, forcing the Commonwealth and Protectorate governments in the future to rely on the regular revenues of the customs, excise and assessment. The way in which the Commonwealth sold these properties by doubling and through debentures prompted Habakkuk to conclude that 'the Long Parliament had repaid its debts on terms so unfavourable to its original creditors – at such a heavy discount – that it irreparably damaged the ability of its successor [the Protectorate] to raise fresh loans'.[116] The English governments needed to develop new ways to anticipate tax receipts, especially in wartime.

WAR PROFITS

English governments had another source of wartime revenue that is often overlooked. The proceeds from ships and goods taken at sea from enemies as prizes and sold in English ports provided a net profit of at least £695,931 that the Westminster governments used to support their military efforts in the 1640s and 1650s.[117] A large percentage of this money was spent for the maintenance of the navy and for the support of sick and maimed seamen and their families. Prize goods receipts were very helpful during the First Dutch War (1652–4), but they were unpredictable, since they depended on a victorious navy operating against another country that had a substantial merchant marine to prey on. During the Spanish war from 1655 to 1660, this was not the case, although £256,759 was received by the revived Exchequer from Blake's capture of part of the Spanish West Indies' treasure fleet.[118] Although prize goods' proceeds and the government's share of captured treasure produced a great deal of money, they, like all of the other expedients used during the Interregnum, were too unpredictable to be used as sources of money for the sustained support of a modern military power.

THE MAGNITUDE OF *AD HOC* FINANCE

Considerable amounts of money, other than those raised with the excise, customs and assessment, were collected by the Parliamentarian governments and the Protectorate from 1642 to 1660. Table 5.2 lists most of the sources and amounts of these more irregular receipts, but it omits the money levied and raised on the local level through county assessments, by free quarter, and organized looting. It also omits the value of the gifts given under the Parliament's Ordinance for the Donation of Plate, Money and Horses in the first two years of the First Civil War. The totals in the table include both the cash and the amount of

Table 5.2: Special Sources of State Revenue, 1642–60[119]

Source	Amount (£)
Money raised from Irish Adventurers	306,718
Profits of royal lands, 1643–4	45,756
Profits of episcopal land, 1646–56	64,677
Delinquent fines of Fifth and Twentieth 1643–4	260,306
Compositions with delinquents 1644–57	1,304,957
Fines and rents of delinquents 1643–56	377,533
Sale of episcopal lands 1649–59	675,603
Sale of dean and chapter lands 1649–57	1,170,000
Sale of King's personal goods 1649–58	134,383
Sale of royal houses	95,237
Sale of Crown lands 1649–58	1,464,409
Sale of fee farm rents 1650–5	816,484
Sale of forfeited Royalists' estates 1651–2	1,224,916
Prize goods receipts 1642–60	695,931
Spanish bullion, 1657–9	254,759
Irish revenues, collected by the English	1,942,546
Sale of Irish lands to pay the English Army	1,113,273
Sale of royal forests	733
Total	11,948,221

debt retired by the doubling process, since this debt represented money owed for pay and logistical services provided to English military forces.

By previous standards of English government revenue, these sums were immense, causing many historians to incorrectly conclude that the Westminster governments' military efforts were supported predominantly by such irregular and generally one-time financial sources. This was not the case. The customs, excise, and monthly assessment raised well over £22 million from 1643 to 1660, and the Irish revenues listed above were from the Irish customs, excise and assessment.[120] Local weekly assessments levied from 1642 to 1645 raised further large amounts that cannot be determined. The significance of the sources discussed in this chapter was that they provided large blocks of money at critical times in the military struggles of the 1640s and 1650s that the English state used to redeem the short-term debt of the revolutionary governments and partially to restore public credit.

After 1651, when most of these sources of money were exhausted, English governments had to rely mainly on regular taxation for the financial support of their military and naval operations and they had to develop short-term credit practices based on these regular tax revenues. The Commonwealth and Protectorate governments fought nearly continuous warfare in the 1650s, driving annual government expenditures to record levels. Remarkably, the Westminster governments managed their finances in such a way that, until at least 1656, they could raise substantial amounts of money through advances on parliamentary taxes. These advances were paid off within a reasonably short period of time, with interest. Consequently, the soldiers, seamen, suppliers and merchants involved trusted the government to pay its obligations.

The regular taxes – customs, excise and assessment – became the bedrock of English finance after 1650. English governments could no longer resort to the sale of capital assets and fines. Consequently, they were forced to continue these taxes into the Restoration period, even in peacetime. These parliamentary taxes provided, henceforth, the ordinary revenue of the English state. As the next three chapters will show, England's position as a major European power by 1652 rested on the financial resources extracted by these taxes. The methods of revenue anticipation and government debt devised from 1650 to 1700 also relied primarily on the receipts of the regular revenues for their security, making it clear that the essential foundations of the English financial revolution were laid by the Parliamentarians in the 1640s.

CHAPTER SIX

The Customs

Tonnage and poundage, more commonly known as the customs, was the cornerstone of English government peacetime revenue in the sixteenth and early seventeenth centuries. It was the largest single source of money for the ordinary expenditures of the monarch, that is the money spent to maintain the royal household and to pay for the routine operation of the government. Parliament normally granted the customs to the monarch for the duration of his reign and, in return, expected the ruler to live of his own, or pay his own way, from the revenues of Crown lands, the profits of justice, the hereditary fees and fines, and the customs. This fiscal tradition remained the prevailing belief of the English taxpaying classes well into the seventeenth century in spite of the fact that most monarchs after Henry VII found it impossible to make ends meet from these resources.[1]

Michael Braddick and C.D. Chandaman have provided superb accounts of the place of the customs in the evolving English financial system in the sixteenth and seventeenth centuries.[2] This chapter reviews some of the same material, but its main purpose is to illustrate how the English state's need to pay for its wars in the mid-seventeenth century directly affected many of the changes in customs' administration and the fiscal theory and traditions that governed its organization and collection. The English civil wars and the Anglo-Dutch wars forced the English state to rapidly expand its navy, in turn leading Parliament to increase the customs and to assume responsibility for its administration. Consequently, the customs, which was mainly a prerogative tax before 1640, became a parliamentary tax in the 1640s and remained so at the Restoration of 1660. From then on, the customs became a major source of parliamentary revenue and a very important tool in Parliament's attempts to affect the commercial policy of the English empire. In fact, Michael Braddick correctly points out that the 'enforcement of the Navigation Acts rested largely on the customs service (with help from excise officers, and the army and navy)'.[3]

ELIZABETHAN CUSTOMS ADMINISTRATION

The customs became the mainstay of English state finance in the sixteenth century, as the other ordinary revenues of the Crown fell well below the levels needed to fund Elizabeth's wars. Because of the rapidly growing costs of warfare, Elizabeth turned increasingly to extraordinary taxes, such as subsidies, to raise money to support her armies and fleets. Her parliaments granted a number of subsidies, but they proved to be of decreasing value to a state belaboured by continuous warfare after 1585. The monetary values of parliamentary subsidies steadily declined during the late sixteenth and early seventeenth centuries for two main reasons. Firstly, local tax assessors underrated their own wealth and that of their neighbours, pushing the notional yield down. Secondly, price-inflation steadily eroded the real value of the fixed subsidies while raising prices by as much as 300 per cent from 1500 to 1600, increasing the effective cost of government.[4] To fill the gap between increasing expenses and the declining value of subsidies granted periodically by their parliaments, Tudor and Stuart monarchs sold significant amounts of royal lands to pay for the costs of war, further undermining the ordinary income derived from the royal demesne in future years.[5]

Up to 1640, the customs was one of the few sources of royal income which could be adjusted to tax new commodities and to respond to the growing financial needs of the state without parliamentary approval. Consequently, the customs increased in importance to the monarchy because of continuing price-inflation, the decreasing value of subsidies, and the increasing costs of war. The monarchs regularly expanded customs receipts by issuing new books of rates to reflect inflation, allowing them to tap the increasing commercial wealth of the country without calling for parliamentary help.[6] In addition, Tudor and Stuart administrators did all they could to increase customs receipts through varying reforms and modifications of customs management and collection.[7]

During the sixteenth century, Tudor administrators made significant changes to the administration of the decentralized customs inherited from earlier times. These changes paralleled the consolidation process evident in the naval and ordnance administrative reforms made under Henry VIII and Elizabeth I.[8] By 1558, the customs administration in the port of London had been consolidated, and a revised Book of Rates issued reflecting the changes in monetary value and the introduction of new commodities in English commerce. Early in Elizabeth's reign, Lord Treasurer Winchester imposed direct Crown supervision over the collection of the customs in an attempt to limit corruption.[9] Winchester's efforts to reorganize and centralize the customs collection in the outports and London did not eliminate corruption, but they did make it easier for the government later to farm out, or lease, the collection of portions of the customs to merchants who were willing to pay large cash advances for the privilege of collecting the revenue.[10] Farming the collection of the customs offered a way for the government to receive a predictable income from the customs at the beginning of the accounting year. This predictable income had the additional advantage of making it easier to raise loans to support government operations.

In 1570, Thomas Smyth secured the farm of most of the London customs. He quickly established more efficient means for the supervision of the collection of duties, increasing the receipts of the London customs from £11,599 in 1570 to £25,486 in 1584.[11] Smyth retained the services of the personnel who had been employed in the collection of the London customs before he leased the farm, while also imposing central supervision and audit procedures. He made quarterly payments to the Exchequer, in addition to a large 'fine' paid in advance of assuming his administration. He collected more from the customs duties than he paid in his rent of the farm. In addition, he was able to use the 'running cash' balances maintained in his hands between his quarterly payments as capital in his business as a banker.[12] Smyth's farm of the London customs and similar farms of the outports proved successful until the mid-1580s. Then, in 1588, the government's need for money dramatically increased at the same time as the risks involved with the collection of the customs grew significantly due to the Spanish war's disruption of commerce with the Netherlands.

The financial demands of prolonged warfare ended this period of Elizabethan revenue farming. There had been grumbling before 1585 that the customs farmers were making exorbitant profits as the volume and value of commerce and tax rates increased. Suggestions had been made by political allies of Lord Burghley that the Crown could reap much greater rewards for the ordinary revenue if the customs collections were directly administered. The expansion of English military involvement in the Netherlands into a naval war against Spain in 1588 tipped the scales in favour of those advocating direct collection in hopes of reaping greater profits for the government.[13]

Burghley, one of Elizabeth's greatest ministers, took great pains to reap the largest returns possible for the state from the government's direct customs administration and collection. He had the number of taxable items increased while expanding the warehouses and wharves of the collectors in London and the major outports. These measures helped to increase the customs receipts paid to the Exchequer to over £100,000 per year. However, upon Burghley's death in 1598, the pressures to return to farming increased due in large part to the government's need to borrow large amounts of cash in anticipation of future tax receipts, and perhaps also in response to complaints about the extortion and corruption of poorly-paid local customs officials.[14]

JACOBEAN ADMINISTRATION

James I continued Elizabeth's practice of increasing the customs with 'impositions'. Technically these were additional customs duties charged at the discretion of the monarch for the purpose of protecting and encouraging English commerce and manufacturing or in recognition of a new item of commerce. Royal use of new impositions was challenged in the Bate's Case, in 1606, and found to be a constitutional use of the royal prerogative, further increasing the fiscal importance of the customs to the Crown.[15] New impositions provided a steady increase in the value of the customs revenue in the seventeenth century.

The need for a predictable customs revenue became the paramount concern of the government in the early seventeenth century. The customs receipts paid into the Exchequer had fluctuated between £120,000 in 1595 and £87,000 in 1600, rising again to £114,000 in 1603.[16] In response, the Queen's government resorted to two additional impositions and to the granting of a series of farms of some of the smaller branches of the customs.[17] These small farms were unsatisfactory from a financial and an administrative perspective. It was too difficult to monitor them for honest practice and the loans that the tax farmers could advance to the government were too small to meet the wartime needs of the state for cash. In response, the government took steps to complete the Elizabethan centralization of the customs branches while reaping the financial rewards of a farm by creating the 'Great Farm of the Customs', in late 1604.[18]

James's government leased this single tax farm of all branches of the customs for seven years to a consortium of London merchant bankers led by William Garway and Francis Jones.[19] Under the administration of the Great Farm, the consortium retained the previous agents and sub-officials of the customs offices in the major English seaports. The tax farmers reaped the benefits of the updated Book of Rates of November 1604, while improving customs administration and unifying the receipts, thereby making them much easier to account for and audit. They also regulated the fees that could be charged to merchants by subordinate customs officials and increased the salaries and fees of the collectors, hoping to replace bribes and extortion with reasonable fees.[20]

James I established the Great Farm most of all so that its farmers could provide his government with the large cash advances needed to repay part of the Crown's inherited wartime debts, while still providing significant amounts of money for the current expenses of his court and administration.[21] The Great Farm was a success from James's perspective. The farmers paid all administrative costs of the customs plus a fixed rent of £112,400 per year (increased to £120,000 in 1607).[22] Within several years they were making loans to the King secured by up to two full years of their customs rent. In this way, the customs farmers became the single greatest source of credit for the English government until the 1640s.

But there was a limit to how much in loans James could squeeze from the tax farmers and to how much the customs could be expanded. The customs provided enough money to the Exchequer to support the navy in peacetime, if the King chose to spend this portion of his ordinary revenue on the fleet's support. James I, however, spent only a part of customs receipts on the navy and his total expenses greatly exceeded his ordinary income for a variety of reasons. Consequently, his debts totalled £829,000 by 1621, in spite of efforts made to reduce the debt through land sales and retrenchment.[23]

Frequent recourse to new impositions, forced loans, and to the more careful cultivation of feudal dues and the sale of noble titles increased royal income. But impositions were a form of extra-parliamentary taxation which soon led to parliamentary criticism because James I used these additional revenues for the support of his household, rather than for the purposes of maritime defence and the encouragement of English economic activity.[24] James also levied forced loans in 1604/5, 1611/12, and 1617. These were only partially and tardily repaid.[25] King and subjects clashed in Parliament over the royal collection of the feudal dues related to purveyance and wardships in this period as well. These dues were unpredictable in amount and consequently seen as capricious by the subjects and inadequate by the monarch. The Parliament of 1610 and James nearly reached a compromise by which the former would provide fixed annual subsidies of £100,000 in return for the King's abolition of the feudal dues. Unfortunately, both parties felt they were giving up too much and James I dissolved Parliament before the final provisions were enacted in law.[26] James's later parliaments failed to resolve the questions of impositions and feudal dues and these issues blended into the larger constitutional and religious questions of the 1620s and 1630s.

The dispute over impositions illustrated a larger question of Stuart England's government finance. Was the monarch to live of his own ordinary revenue during peacetime and only to resort to additional taxation in times of war or threat of war? Until 1585, Elizabeth I had successfully financed her peacetime government from her ordinary revenues from the royal lands and the tonnage and poundage granted to her at the beginning of her reign. During the long Spanish war, her parliaments had granted a large number of subsidies, but Elizabeth had still been forced to sell significant amounts of Crown lands to cover the gap that developed between her ordinary and extraordinary revenues and her wartime expenditures. This situation had come about primarily because Tudor parliaments routinely granted too little revenue to cover the rising costs of modern war in an age of spiralling inflation.

James I's government had higher peacetime costs than Elizabeth's because he had a family to support, a more expense lifestyle, and because of the effects of steady inflation on the value of the customs and the fixed revenues from the diminished royal demesne. Additionally, in times of war the value of parliamentary subsidies to the Crown had not been adjusted for inflation and, in fact, had fallen in notional value as well. The Stuart kings faced the question of how a modern monarch was to conduct government without fundamental changes in the theories of government finance. The evolution of the administration of the customs in the 1640s and 1650s was to be part of the transition from the older theories of taxation and finance, where the monarch lived of his own in peacetime, to those of the modern state in which the ruler routinely tapped the wealth of all classes in peace and war to fund state activities. This evolution of government financial theory took long strides forward during the mid-century wars and is evident in the history of the customs from 1640 to 1660.

CAROLINE CUSTOMS

At the accession of Charles I in 1625, his first Parliament granted the King the customs for only one year in an attempt to retain the ability to consider the question of impositions before granting the customs to him for life.[27] Charles allowed this financial grant to fail and, 'relying on the long prescription of the Crown, continued to levy tonnage and poundage without a parliamentary grant'.[28] However, Charles had inherited his father's debts and found himself involved in major maritime wars with Spain and France from 1625 to 1630. As a result of these wars and the inadequate financial backing received from the Caroline parliaments royal debt spiralled to over £1.1 million in 1635, even though annual revenue exceeded £600,000.[29]

The customs was one of the few portions of his revenue that the King could increase to meet his growing obligations through the prerogative power to adjust the Book of Rates and by the use of new impositions, since the judges had found the increase of impositions to be within the royal prerogative. Table 6.1 lists the receipts of all branches of the customs from 1603 to 1640 and compares them to the net proceeds of the parliamentary subsidies granted in the same period. Customs receipts became a steadily more important part of the revenue and exceeded the receipts from parliamentary subsidies consistently after 1605.

Table 6.1: Customs and Subsidies Receipts as a Percentage of Total Exchequer Receipts, 1603–40 [30]

Period	Customs (£)	% of Total	Subsidies (£)	% of Total
1603–5	291,260	22.1	429,507	32.6
1606–10	619,804	22.3	519,045	18.7
1611–15	1,024,032	36.4	174,624	6.2
1616–20	816,853	44.5	79,679	4.3
1621–5	1,043,083	51.8	203,810	10.1
1626–30	1,129,380	36.0	549,961	17.5
1631–5	1,088,881	49.5	155,822	7.1
1636–40	1,781,277	62.0	78,552	2.7

In addition to the total of £19.8 million in cash paid into the Exchequer from all revenue sources in these thirty-eight years, £2 million worth of Exchequer tallies were issued in anticipation of future revenue. A large portion of these tallies anticipated customs receipts. This use of tallies was a form of short-term credit. Exchequer tallies circulated in a manner similar to bills of credit and were discounted based on the number of tallies in circulation and the amount of revenue anticipated. The use of tallies as credit instruments had developed over the previous century. A form of tally, known as the Sol tally, eventually became, in the 1660s, a form of negotiable currency.[31] During the reign of Charles I, the use of tallies by the government mushroomed, with £500,000 worth issued in each of the periods from 1626 to 1630 and from 1635 to 1640.[32] Unredeemed tallies constituted a large portion of the Crown's short-term debt.

Charles I continued to expand the customs revenue through new impositions and a new Book of Rates, while also farming much of its collection to a syndicate of prominent London merchants. Under the provisions of the lease, the King granted the customs collectors the entire revenue of the customs in exchange for a fixed payment. This method of administration guaranteed Charles an annual revenue of £150,000 from the Great Farm alone, while providing him with a large cash advance at the beginning of the accounting period with which to operate his government. He also received the increased revenue from new impositions that were often not included in the Great Farm. This explains why his average annual income from customs receipts exceeded £200,000 from 1626 to 1640. Unfortunately for Charles, the lack of parliamentary approval of the customs weakened his ability to use the anticipated revenues of the customs as security for large loans from those London merchants who were not connected with the customs farm. This situation narrowed the sources of credit for the government drastically in the late 1630s. Charles never resolved this problem satisfactorily. In addition, the customs farmers feared eventual parliamentary reprisals in the future if they collected the customs too aggressively or if they advanced too much money to Charles.[33] This fear proved well founded.

The customs system functioned fairly effectively during the 1630s in spite of these difficulties. The new Book of Rates of 1635 raised the level for the taxation of imported and exported goods. The lease of the customs farm brought the King £150,000 per year from 1635 to 1638 and £172,000 in 1638/9.[34] In 1638, the farm of the customs was sufficiently attractive to cause two London merchant syndicates to compete for its possession. These groups eventually joined to manage the customs farm in 1639. By that time, as Charles faced the Scots in the First Bishops' War, the customs farmers had become the King's only source of large loans, advancing over £250,000 to the King for his war against the Scots. These men were still in control of the customs when the Long Parliament met in 1641.[35]

The customs was one of Charles's largest sources of income during his eleven years of personal rule and the farmers advanced large amounts of money to him.[36] They speedily regretted this service when the Long Parliament fined them £150,000 as a punishment for their financial support of the King. Thereafter no financier would support Charles without careful reflection on the costs of such an act.[37] The execution of Strafford was a more dramatic signal of the Long Parliament's resolve to rule the kingdom and its ability to punish supporters of the King. With such financial and judicial punishments, Parliament earned the fear and respect of the London merchant and financial community. Most importantly, the 'calling of the Long Parliament saw the beginnings of parliamentary control of government borrowing and marks an obvious break in the history of the relations between the government and the money markets'.[38]

PARLIAMENTARY ADMINISTRATION

The Long Parliament ended the farming of the customs as one of its first acts in 1641, placing the operation of the customs system into commission.[39] Under a commission, a group of leading London merchants became customs commissioners, taking charge of the administration of the customs in return for fixed salaries and fees. The entire revenue collected, minus the costs of administration and the fees and salaries of the commissioners and customs officials, belonged to the state. All expenditures by the commissioners had to be approved either by parliamentary acts or the warrants of the parliamentary Committee of the Navy and Customs. Parliamentary acts and ordinances modified the details of customs collection and administration in the 1640s. Direct collection of most of the branches of the customs continued through the 1650s, even though a few smaller branches were again put out to farm. A subcommittee of the republican Council of State assumed most of the customs oversight functions of the parliamentary Committee of the Navy and Customs in 1649.

The potential financial gain of direct customs administration by the state was obvious. As revenues grew, the majority of the gain went to the government, rather than to the tax farmers, as it would have in a fixed farm. Further, since the commissioners were merchant bankers, they could still be expected to advance loans in anticipation of customs receipts, while collection remained under government control.

The customs continued to provide the majority of the financial support for the navy in the 1640s. This financial support went a long way to ensure the loyalty of the fleet, giving the Parliamentarians the means to prevent Charles from receiving much foreign support during the civil wars and to protect English commerce from privateers and pirates. The accounts of the commissioners of the customs for the period from 1642 to 1660 reflect the nature of the support provided to the parliamentary cause and illustrate the close connection between political and military developments and government financial operations. Parliament made personnel and administrative changes in response to the evolving situation of its wars against the King and later in its wars against the Dutch and Spanish. Throughout this period, the customs provided a reliable flow of revenue to the English state for the support of its growing navy. Changes made in customs administration also illustrate important revision in government financial theory.

On 12 July 1642, shortly after the Long Parliament resolved to raise an army 'for the safety of the King's person, the defence of both Houses of Parliament, . . . and for the preservation of the true religion, the laws, the liberties, and the peace of the kingdom', a bill concerning the tonnage and poundage was introduced. The Commons passed this bill on 28 July and the Lords agreed to it on 1 August.[40] Parliament ordered the customs to be collected without the royal assent and stipulated that its revenue was to be used for the support of the navy. This ordinance further made it clear that the navy was already over £200,000 in debt to its sailors and suppliers and had an obligation to support fifty-five ships for the defence of English commerce and the conquest of Ireland. A new Book of Rates that had previously been prepared by Parliament, but not consented to by the King, was put into use, and the collection of the customs revenues that had been made since the last customs act was legalized.[41]

Most of the personnel of the customs bureaucracy accepted these changes in the management of the system in 1642. The major Customs House was in London, and London continued to provide up to two-thirds of the revenue. The customs personnel in most of the outports of the realm continued to serve loyally as well, allowing the Long Parliament to tap the wealth of most of England's incoming and outgoing commerce. The procedures of the previous regime were continued, as customs officials maintained port books listing the arrival and departure of each ship and the tax status of its cargo to ensure that goods did not escape taxation.[42] Parliamentary ordinances required all merchants to 'make due entry of all such goods and merchandizes as they shall . . . export or import. . . . The Customers, Comptrollers, Searchers, and other officers' of the customs were to 'carefully attend their several charges and make due seizure, as forfeited, of all such goods and merchandise as shall not be entered according to the intent of the said statute.'[43]

Under the farming of the customs, the farmers had kept the gross receipts collected in this fashion, having already paid the Crown for the rights of the farm at the beginning of the period. Under the direct management of the parliamentary commissioners, the customs collectors remitted the entire revenue to the central Customs House in London and then the commissioners paid most of the net proceeds to the Navy Treasurer for the support of the fleet, having deducted administrative costs and salaries. Parliament granted a 15 per cent interest rebate on the amount paid 'over and above all other allowances made in the said bill or book of rates' to merchants who willingly complied with the customs ordinance. Evidently, Parliament was still uneasy in 1642 about the legality or acceptability of its ordinances and, therefore, provided financial incentives to merchants willing to comply. Parliament deleted these provisions from later customs ordinances as it asserted its sovereignty more confidently.[44]

The Long Parliament exercised much greater oversight of the routine operations of the customs than any parliament had done before. This was achieved by the creation of a permanent parliamentary Committee of the Customs and Navy (also known as the Committee of the Navy) and by strengthening the accounting procedures of the customs. The London collectors were required to prepare a true account of the complete customs' receipts and expenses monthly for the examination of William Toames, Surveyor General in the London Customs House. Mr Toames was to make an account for the use of the House of Common's

Committee of the Customs and Navy to refer to when that committee appropriated money for the support of the navy.[45] These provisions gave the Commons the ability to play an active role in the administration of the state's finances and they marked a revolutionary step in the role of Parliament in the mundane operations of English government.

The merchant community reacted favourably to the customs ordinance, according to Giles Greene, a London merchant and a member of the Committee of the Navy.[46] The House of Commons was undoubtedly pleased to hear that there would be no widespread resistance to the collection of the customs and proceeded to define the lines of authority for the expenditure of the customs revenue. The Committee of the Navy and Customs was to approve the various expenditures of the customs commissioners, since the greatest recipient of the customs revenue continued to be the navy. Sir Henry Vane, the Navy Treasurer, was to receive the money from the customs commissioners and to account for its expenditure.[47]

The 1642 commissioners of the customs, also known as collectors of the customs, were the London merchants Sir John Jacob, Sir Job Harby, and Sir Joseph Nulles. These men had definite Royalist sympathies and at least John Jacob had been disabled from sitting in the House of Commons because he was a monopolist.[48] Although it seems anomalous that the Long Parliament allowed Royalists to continue in office in 1642, there were sound political and financial reasons for it to do so. Parliament, while believing in the legitimacy of its cause, did not foresee the lengths to which it would have to carry the struggle against Charles. Hence, it seemed of little consequence if Londoners with Royalist sympathies retained their positions. These men had raised large sums of money for the government on short notice in the past, advancing the money to the government in anticipation of later customs revenue. This was a financial operation advantageous to both the state and the customs commissioners in 1642. The former received the cash needed to support the navy and the latter received 8 per cent interest on their advance plus the fees and salaries involved in the operation of the customs. As the struggle against the King intensified, however, this symbiotic relationship came under increasing strain.

The breakdown in the relationship between the Long Parliament and commissioners Jacob, Harby, and Nulles began in early August 1642, when Parliament asked the commissioners to advance £4,500 to pay for the costs of moving munitions from Hull to London for the use of Essex's army.[49] The customs commissioners evidently made this loan, but there was increasing friction between them and the staunchly Parliamentarian Sir Henry Vane and a number of London merchants. Parliament soon had to promulgate 'orders for the better regulating [of] the customs' and to order the Committee of the Navy to adjudicate disputes between the merchants and the customs collectors.[50] None the less, disputes continued and the collectors managed to alienate the Common's Committee of the Navy. In September, the Committee of the Navy achieved a notable permanence with the appointment of Thomas Smith as a full-time secretary. In October, Henry Vane reported from the committee that persons of 'especial trust, confidence, skill, and knowledge' should be added to the commission of the customs. As a result, Sir Giles Greene was made a collector of the customs.[51] The final breakdown in relations between the Long Parliament and the customs commissioners came in December, when the latter refused to advance £20,000 to the Navy Treasurer. In retaliation, the Long Parliament removed Jacob, Harby, and Nulles and appointed new commissioners.[52]

Giles Greene and the Committee of the Navy turned to a group of London aldermen and merchants who were sympathetic to the parliamentary cause to serve as customs commissioners for a total salary of £10,000 per year. These were aldermen Thomas Andrews, John Foulke, and Richard Chambers, and merchants William Berkeley, Francis Allen, Stephen Estwicke, James Russell, and Maurice Thomson.[53] Their appointment represented Parliament's determination to pursue to great lengths its struggle to make the King recognize that it was his true and proper 'adviser'. Most of the new customs commissioners were Puritans of an Independent inclination. Many of them had been imprisoned for refusing to pay ship-money and the non-parliamentary customs, or to loan money to the King for the Bishops' Wars.[54] They demanded parliamentary indemnity for their future performance of duty, a guarantee that they would not be put out of office before any money owed to them was repaid, and the promise that a new customs ordinance would be passed granting them 8 per cent interest for all money they advanced. Parliament accepted these terms and passed a new customs ordinance on 21 January 1643.[55]

The new customs collectors were ceremoniously installed in London's Customs House on 23 January 1643. They quickly loaned £20,000 to Henry Vane for the navy and set about reorganizing the customs system.[56] The commissioners had the power to appoint and remove deputy collectors in London and the outports as they saw fit, and to appoint their own secretary. Further, they could remove 'for just cause' searchers, waiters, tidesmen, noon-tenders, and watchmen and replace them with men of their choosing.[57] The January customs ordinance continued the current Book of Rates in force from 1 March 1643 to 25 March 1644 and required that a monthly account of the customs be provided to the

Table 6.2: The Customs, 16 January–25 December 1643[58]

Item	Amount (£)	%
Revenue of customs	165,691	100
Expenditures: a. Navy	145,000	85.0
b. Salaries of customs	16,379	9.6
c. Repayments	6,467	3.7
d. Incident costs	1,090	0.6
e. Interest payments	1,040	0.6
f. Special payments	263	0.1
g. Total	170,239	
h. Owed to customs	19,600	

Committee of the Navy. The House of Commons also ordered the accounts of the former commissioners audited and the arrears of customs still due assigned to the new commissioners as security for the money they advanced to Vane for the fleet.[59] The recently ousted commissioners of the customs owed at least £32,000 in 1643. One of the former customs farmers, Sir Nicholas Crispe, owed another £16,341, while the sub-collector of Dover, Anthony Percival owed £6,524. Crispe fled to Oxford and the Commons hailed Percival before the bar of the House and, after he claimed he could not pay, sequestered his estate.[60]

The customs functioned relatively smoothly under the new commissioners. Their account for the period from 16 January to 25 December 1643 provides data for an evaluation of the size of the revenue and the efficiency of its collection and administration. The customs receipts for a period of a little less than a year were £165,691, a sum which compares favourably with the income in similar periods of time before 1643. Nearly 10 per cent of the money that should have been paid by merchants was not paid on time. Administrative fees, costs, and interest for advances made by the commissioners to the navy totalled £18,500, or 10.8 per cent of receipts, but the commissioners advanced an additional £45,000 to the treasurer in 1643, solving in a very practical way the governmental problem of revenue anticipation.[61] These advances were secured by the future customs receipts and provided the cash essential for the operation of the navy. This was an effective way to anticipate revenue and was similar to the advance by farmers of the customs at the start of their term. When the farming of the customs was resumed in 1661, a similar advance of the rent of the farm was made. However, in this later farm, the revenue in excess of the fee for the farm and the collectors' cost and profit was paid to the government, making the farming of revenue much less lucrative to the farmers.[62] Parliamentary oversight of the regular operations of the customs and a constant review of its revenue after 1642 marked an important change in the role of Parliament in English governmental finance.

The Long Parliament's control of the customs system, provided by the commissioners, greatly aided its war effort on land as well as financing that at sea. Parliament used the customs revenues of Hull and Plymouth to transfer cash from London to the army garrisons in those besieged towns in 1643.[63] To do this, the local customs collectors paid the army garrisons and the Treasurers at War in London repaid the customs commissioners there an equal amount. Otherwise, with only a minor exception, the customs revenue was used only to support the navy. The minor exception was a short-term loan of customs money to the Treasurers at War that was repaid within four days.[64]

During 1643 and 1644 the customs commissioners worked in close harmony with Parliamentarian leaders. They served as both the administrators of a major branch of the state's income and as its leading creditors. Consequently, on 1 May 1643, when the commissioners reported that merchants' payments of the customs were £24,000 in arrears, the House of Commons authorized the sale of the ships and goods of those merchants who were delinquent in their customs duties.[65] The relationship between the custom commissioners and the navy was very close also because the majority of the customs receipts went to the navy and the Common's Committee of the Navy oversaw the operations of both the navy and the customs. Parliamentary ordinances routinely secured loans raised for the navy's support with anticipated customs revenue.[66] This harmony lasted until the autumn of 1644, and the official position of the commissioners – Andrews, Foulke, et al. – continued unchanged until February 1645.

During the fourteen-month period from 25 December 1643 to 24 February 1645, the customs was one of the English state's most dependable and regularly collected revenues. Merchants accepted the customs because they had traditionally paid it and because the government obviously spent its revenue on a fleet that protected their commerce. The customs commissioners' declared account for this period indicates the importance to the government of the direct collection of the customs in terms of an enhanced revenue. The last farm of the customs for the year 1639 had raised £175,000, whereas the customs receipts for these fourteen months was £241,000.

Table 6.3: The Customs, 26 December 1643–24 February 1645 [67]

	Item	Amount (£)	%
Income	a. Arrears	15,052	5.9
	b. Revenue	225,822	89.2
	c. Loans	12,228	4.8
	d. Total	253,102	
Expenditure	a. Navy	151,462	59.8
	b. Salaries	22,018	8.7
	c. Previous Comrs	19,600	7.7
	d. Repayments	15,384	6.1
	e. Special payments	5,543	2.2
	f. Interest	3,186	1.3
	g. Incidentals	2,042	0.8
	h. Total	219,235	
Unaccounted for		33,867	13.3

The customs commissioners provided only £151,462 (59 per cent) of their disbursements to the immediate support of the navy in 1644 and another £19,600 to repay the previous commissioners for money they had loaned the state. However, they loaned £91,000 in cash for the operation of the fleet during this period as well, an amount that is listed as the principal on which the interest for advances was paid.[68] Thus, the customs commissioners provided £242,462 to the navy, but they also made a large profit. Salaries, incidental costs for items like paper, coal, and candles, and interest at 8 per cent on advances earned the commissioners £27,246. A further £33,866 remained unaccounted for at the end of the account. Possibly this last amount was money owed to the customs by merchants in this period, but the declared account is unclear on this matter. The decrease in the percentage of the customs receipts provided to the navy (from 85 to 59 per cent) and the slight increase in the cost of administration (10.2 to 11 per cent) masked the fact that the Long Parliament was able to secure large loans for the fleet in anticipation of future customs receipts.

There is evidence in the Journals of the House of Commons which indicates, however, that the customs commissioners repaid themselves for part of the loans they had made to the Navy Treasurer with the £33,866 not accounted for in this declared account. The Committee of the Navy did not appreciate the diversion of the customs revenue which this entailed. Disagreement came to a head on 15 October 1644, when the Commons ordered the commissioners to begin paying all customs received after 15 September to Sir Henry Vane weekly, and to do so regularly henceforth.[69] Four days later the Commons ordered the commissioners to forego repayment for the loans they had made to the Westminster government, expecting them instead only to receive the 8 per cent interest due on those loans. Simultaneously, the House ordered the Committee of the Navy to 'examine the miscarriages of the customs' and asked the customs commissioners to advance another £12,000 for the navy.[70] Parliament was using threats of investigation to bring the customs commissioners to heel and to extract another loan. These efforts were partially successful, as the commissioners did advance another £8,000, but this process undercut the relationship between creditor and debtor.[71]

Shortly after this confrontation, the Committee of the Navy concluded that a customs revenue which provided only £150,000 per year was inadequate for the long-term needs of the navy. Even though the customs commissioners had advanced an additional £91,000 for the navy by November, their growing reluctance to advance more money was logical since the receipts upon which such advances were secured were too small to carry more debt. Further, the navy committee estimated the cost of the fleet for the upcoming summer to be £208,000.[72] Consequently, in January 1645, Parliament decided to order the customs commissioners to advance another £23,596 to pay off the money owed for the hire of merchant ships for the navy in 1644. This request brought on the final confrontation with the customs commissioners.[73]

Parliament saw clearly that the net customs revenue to the state must be increased and that none of it could be diverted to repay previous loans during wartime. The House of Commons met in Grand Committee on 25 January and decided that the present commissioners must forgo all loan repayment or be replaced. On 12 February 1645, Mr Foulke, on behalf of the commissioners, refused to provide another £70,000 advance for the next customs period. The House declared this answer unsatisfactory and notified the commissioners that they would be replaced.[74] Parliament promised Foulke and the other commissioners eventual repayment for their loans and salaries due to 25 March 1645, ending their service on 24 February.

Andrews, Foulke and the other commissioners relinquished their positions in the customs because the costs and risks of operating it had grown greater than the profits. Their cash advances to the government had become too large for them to expect reasonably prompt repayment. Additionally, the payment of current revenue to the Navy Treasurer removed one of the more lucrative advantages of administering the state's revenues by denying the commissioners the short-term use of government funds for their own financial operations. In effect, the Long Parliament had ended most of the advantages enjoyed by the former farmers of the customs while still expecting the commissioners to provide large cash advances. The commissioners logically resisted additional demands for loans unless they were given the ability to repay these loans out of future revenue. When they did so, Parliament replaced them.

The Long Parliament made these changes in the methods of financial administration because of the rising costs of an expanding navy and because of the plans in early 1645 to create and support the New Model Army. The absence of a credit system that could sustain the armed forces in the long periods of time during which expenditures outran income had forced the Long Parliament and the customs commissioners to this impasse. The old commissioners parted on good terms and another group of London financiers took over the customs, hoping to make a profit.

Daniel Avery, Richard Bateman, Charles Lloyd, Christopher Packe, and Walter Boothby became the new commissioners and collectors of the customs on 25 February 1645.[75] The new commissioners had not been aldermen before 1642, although Avery and Packe later achieved that status. Bateman was an East India Company member and had been associated with the Royalist Nicholas Crispe in the contested mayoral election of 1642. Packe was the most notable of the group and his zeal for the Parliamentarian, Commonwealth, and Protectorate causes carried him successfully through the political storms of the Interregnum.[76]

The Westminster government secured a £50,000 loan from the new customs commissioners on 5 March and increased the expected revenue of the customs by allowing the importation and taxation of Levantine currants.[77] Parliament passed ordinances that allowed the commissioners to search warehouses and merchants' stores for goods being smuggled in or out of England, fixing their term in office until 24 March 1646, and allowing them 8 per cent interest on all sums advanced or loaned to the state. The increase in income and these steps to cut down smuggling had some positive effects on the revenue, helping to make it profitable for the new commissioners to remain in office until 21 July 1649.

Parliament installed the new commissioners during the same period of time that it passed the New Model Army and Self-Denying Ordinances. The settlement of the customs in such a way as to defer repayment of the commissioners' loans was accompanied by the passage of the monthly assessment ordinance which significantly increased total government income. These actions demonstrated the Parliamentarians' increased resolve to win their struggle with the King and their recognition that this task would be hard and expensive. Although the navy cost considerably less than the army in the 1640s, the fleet became an increasingly expensive force whose financial needs quickly exceeded the revenue of the customs and whose debt grew dramatically. This growth in naval debt was funded successfully by the anticipated revenues of the customs until at least 1648.

Avery and his colleagues served as commissioners until July 1649. Their accounts (below) show a significant increase in customs revenues. This increase was due to the expansion of the number of goods taxed and to an evident growth in English commerce after the end of the First Civil War in early 1646.

The political controversy between the Independent and Presbyterian factions of the Parliamentarian cause in late 1647 and the Second Civil War in 1648 diminished the receipts of the customs. While the gross receipts dropped 22 per cent in 1648, the net proceeds provided to the navy dropped a dramatic 56 per cent. The revolt in the fleet and the defection of eleven warships in mid-1648 exposed London's shipping to greater attacks from pirates and Royalist privateers, especially when the Prince of Wales briefly blockaded the Thames estuary in August. The steep fall in customs receipts provided to the navy took place primarily

Table 6.4: The Customs, 25 February 1645–21 July 1649[78]

Period	Receipts(£)	to Navy (£)	%
25 Feb–25 Dec 1645	192,867	188,836	97
25 Dec 1645–25 Dec 1646	276,844	201,809	72
25 Dec 1646–25 Dec 1647	262,785	225,617	85
25 Dec 1647–25 Dec 1648	203,055	98,629	49
25 Dec 1648–21 July 1649	158,127	68,852	43
Total	1,093,678	783,743	72

Owed to commissioners	110,089
Repayments for re-exports	51,386
Salaries	50,412
Judges' salaries	24,750
In hand at end	24,241
Interest for loans	20,349
Paid to next commissioners	10,807
Incidental costs	9,964
Paid to Fauconberge	3,626
Total accounted for	1,089,367

because the sub-collectors in the major outports either failed to collect or failed to forward £110,000 in customs receipts to the London office. This amount remained due, but unaccounted for, at the end of the declared account of the customs commissioners in July 1649.[79] The customs commissioners' declared accounts and contemporary documents make no mention of the reasons for this discrepancy, although it possibly is due to an accounting error or it is evidence of a tax revolt. The main point, however, is that a significant reduction in the amount of cash provided to the fleet brought on a major crisis in naval and financial administration for the Commonwealth government in mid-1649.

Avery and his partners certainly made a profit from their work with the customs while providing significant financial help to the Parliamentarian cause. They reduced the total cost of administration to under 10 per cent of receipts due to the use of a fixed salary system rather than a poundage payment system. During their time in office the accountants paid themselves over £20,000 in interest and another £50,000 for customs salaries and collection expenses. They controlled roughly £20,000 in cash at any one time, allowing them to undertake short-term banking operations with state money. At the same time, they paid customs receipts regularly to the Navy Treasurer. At the end of their tenure of office they also had £24,000 in cash, but they paid only £13,521 of this to the succeeding customs commissioners.[80]

The political turmoil from early 1648 to mid-1649 caused a drop in all state revenues, leading to a financial crisis for the Commonwealth government in the summer of 1649. Avery, Bateman, *et al.* were closely associated with the traditional merchant community and the Common Council of London. The failure of the Presbyterian or moderate faction of the Long Parliament to disband the New Model Army in 1647, and the resultant expulsion from the House of Commons of the leading eleven members of that faction at the insistence of the army, was the precursor of Pride's Purge in late 1648.[81] Together these climactic events marked the break-up of the London-dominated Presbyterian majority in the House of Commons. These political setbacks for the Londoners undermined the willingness of the customs commissioners to collect aggressively the customs, making it necessary for the newly purged House of Commons, called the Rump, and the Council of State to replace these commissioners on 22 July 1649.

REPUBLICAN ADMINISTRATION

The Rump Parliament selected Colonel Edmund Harvey, Robert Tichborne, Mark Hildesley, and Daniel Taylor as the new customs commissioners.

Harvey had served as a judge at the King's trial, was a member of Draper's Hall, and a Member of Parliament for Wiltshire. He had supported the army in the constitutional crisis of 1647/8, and voted with the Independents against accommodation with Charles I. He brought his brother-in-law Henry Langham with him as cashier-general in the London customs office.[82] Little information is available about Taylor and Hildesley. Tichborne served as Lord Mayor of London, was a regicide, and eventually, according to Thurloe, served as one of 'Cromwell's creatures'.[83] The army and Independents not only defeated the Royalists but also much of London's established merchant and financial community, as the appointment of these 'new men' shows. The political changes affected the administration of all of the state's revenue systems, and the charges and counter-charges of peculation made by the various factions of the Long Parliament and the financial and merchant leaders of London who operated these systems led Gerald Aylmer to conclude that the financial affairs of the Interregnum were a tangled skein.[84] We shall attempt to untangle that skein.

Harvey and his associates operated the customs from 22 July 1649 to 25 March 1656. Their accounts tell a great deal about the financial success of the Interregnum governments.

Table 6.5: The Customs, 22 July 1649–25 March 1656[85]

Period	Receipts(£)	to Navy(£)[86]	%
22 Jul 1649–24 Jun 1650	296,147	203,455	69
25 Jun 1650–24 Jun 1651	320,504	308,231	96
25 Jun 1651–24 Jun 1652	331,888	242,260	73
25 Jun 1652–24 Jun 1653	311,819	202,936	65
25 Jun 1653–24 Jun 1654	418,022	314,685	75
25 Jun 1654–29 Sep 1655	501,570	345,509	69
30 Sep 1655–25 Mar 1656	162,152	177,132	100
Total	2,342,102	1,794,208	77

Owed to commissioners	108,030
Salaries and incidentals	266,538
Repayments for re-exports	66,786
Judges' salaries	45,202
Poor relief and captives	38,125
Interest on loans	16,859
In hand at end	326
Unaccounted for	6,028

Customs receipts grew dramatically in the period from 22 July 1649 to 25 March 1656 compared to the previous five years (see Table 6.4). Rates were not raised. Instead, receipts increased because the Commonwealth's navy established its naval dominance in British waters by the end of 1649, thereby providing English commerce with effective protection from pirates, Royalists, and privateers. Additionally, peace in England, Ireland, and Scotland increased domestic commercial activity in general, spurring on imports and exports. Parliament facilitated this growth of customs revenue by establishing new requirements for having the accounts audited regularly and for receipts to be paid promptly to the Treasurer of the Navy and, after July 1654, to the Exchequer. These actions reduced the amount of 'running cash' in the hands of the customs commissioners.[87]

These administrative and military accomplishments undoubtedly facilitated the increase of economic activity and trade just as continental markets began to recover from the Thirty Years' War. Further measures such as the Navigation Act of 1651 also may have increased English trade, while England's startling victory over the Dutch in the First Dutch War of 1652 to 1654 greatly increased her role as an entrepôt and commercial power.

The salaries of the new commissioners and of the collectors, searchers, and other customs officials in London and the outports were nearly £200,000, with the cost of incidentals and office expenses adding another £67,000 to the total administrative costs. This was 11.4 per cent of the gross receipts. At the same time, the commissioners provided £1,794,208 to the navy (76.6 per cent of their receipts). These administrative costs and the seemingly small percentage of revenue provided to the fleet prompted a number of people like Thurloe to propose that the customs again be farmed. These men hoped that a customs farm would reduce the chances for fraud, although they never explained how that was to be done.[88] Certainly the costs of administration were high, but not out of line with previous years' costs. The reason only 76 per cent of the revenue reached the navy was because other government costs such as judges' salaries and money for the relief of the poor were also paid for with customs receipts. Farming the customs would not have ended the need to pay for such things. None the less, the Protectorate government attempted to farm the customs in June 1657, but this attempt collapsed because the would-be farmers backed out.[89]

The belief that chances for fraud would lessen with a customs farm is difficult to evaluate. Certainly fraud existed. Harvey and his brother-in-law Langham were accused of embezzling £54,000 from the customs in 1655.[90] The customs commissioners had opportunities to skim the revenue and to disguise it as money owed to the London office by the outport collectors. These sums were carried forward to the next account and could have been obscured during the six years in which Harvey and the others managed the customs. However, farming would not have eliminated this opportunity for peculation and may, instead, have moved the accounts further from the scrutiny of parliamentary auditors. Twice during the period the commissioners were asked for a complete accounting and they eventually paid an additional £146,000 to the Navy Treasurer.[91] At the end of the period, in 1656, the commissioners owed only £8,047 to the state. They paid £7,720 of this and were forgiven the remaining £327.[92]

During their tenure as commissioners, two other significant developments took place. Firstly, the costs of the navy consistently exceeded the revenue of the customs by hundreds of thousands of pounds per year. Secondly, in 1654, Parliament revived the Exchequer and ordered all major revenues of the state except the assessment to be paid into it. This second change separated the customs from the Committee of the Navy and made it easier for the government to provide money for the navy or army from various revenues. This was a break from the tradition that each revenue was to be committed to a fixed government activity and was a step towards a truly modern concept of state finance in which revenues would be consolidated and expenditures paid out of the general revenue fund, rather than out of designated revenues. The Exchequer also exercised audit control over the customs, ensuring more frequent and professional account reviews and possibly making it more difficult for the customs commissioners to skim the receipts.

The Protectorate government replaced Harvey and his co-commissioners in 1656. The probable cause of their removal was that they were suspected of fraud, but political factors also played a role in their replacement. For example, the men who took over from them were closely identified with John Thurloe, whose star was rising in the Protectorate, and Lord Broghill, who had done a great deal for Cromwell in Ireland between 1649 and 1650, when he brought most of the Munster gentry over to Cromwell's side; the new commissioners were also affiliated closely with a major faction of the Protector's Council and these, rather than evidence of great administrative ability or probity, were probably the main reasons they were selected.

The new commissioners assumed control of the customs on 26 March 1656. The most prominent among them was Edward Horseman, a member of the Nominated Parliament, a salaried member of the Army Committee, a teller of the revived Exchequer.[93] Horseman was a former

army captain whose fortune had been made by the turmoil of the
Interregnum and his close association with Oliver Cromwell. George
Foxcraft was a bureaucratic pluralist, serving as a commissioner for
sequestrations, prize goods, the excise, and the customs. Aylmer labelled
Foxcraft as a man 'less than honourable', but provides no evidence for
this appraisal.[94] Upton was a haberdasher and related to both John Pym
and John Thurloe. By 1650, he had served as a commissioner and
treasurer for the sale of prize goods, as one of the victual contractors for
the navy, and as a member of the Rump's Committee for Irish and
Scottish Affairs.[95] Upton was a committed Cromwellian who managed to
weather the fall of Richard Cromwell and eventually became a customs
commissioner again under Charles II. Finally, Saltonstall was a client of
Lord Broghill and a customs commissioner in Scotland in 1655.[96]

No significant organizational or administrative changes were made to
the customs system during the 1650s, indicating that the desire for
administrative reform was not a motive for the change of commissioners
or the return to partial farming of the revenue. The large increase in
customs receipts in this period was due to improved trade rather than to
increased rates or better administration.[97] Table 6.6 summarizes the
declared accounts of the customs commissioners for the period 25 March
1656 to 29 September 1659.

Table 6.6: The Customs, 25 March 1656–29 September 1659[98]

Period	Gross receipts (£)	Net receipts (£)
26 Mar 1656–25 Mar 1657	386,383	310,630
26 Mar 1657–25 Mar 1658	381,439	282,000
26 Mar 1658–29 Sep 1659	667,940	486,294
Total	1,435,762	1,078,924
Customs' salaries	114,257	
Repayment on re-exports	70,076	
Poor relief and captives	58,022	
Judges' salaries	56,235	
Incidentals	41,245	
Interest and loans repayment	11,097	
Owed by outport collectors	5,573	
Paid to Exchequer in Mar 1658	5,515	
Cash in hand at end	11	
Unaccounted for	4,728	

The net receipt in the table is the amount paid into the Exchequer by the customs commissioners. The costs of administration declined slightly from 11.4 per cent in the previous period to 10.8 per cent in this period. Annual salaries for all customs officials and workers increased from less than £12,000 in the mid-1640s to over £31,000 per year in the period from 1649 to September 1659 (see Tables 6.4, 6.5, and 6.6). These increases in annual customs receipts may have been due in part to the larger and more reliable salaries paid to the customs officials in London and the outports, as well as to the return to regular Exchequer audits. The customs receipts paid into the Exchequer were much smaller than the amounts disbursed from the Exchequer for the support of the navy from 1656 to 1659, indicating again that the concept of dedicating revenue to some particular branch of government expenditure was giving way to a system that consolidated all revenue and then disbursed money to wherever the need was greatest. The customs commissioners continued to pay judges' salaries and for things like captives' ransoms directly out of their receipts.

The Protectorate's customs commissioners declared their accounts annually to Exchequer auditors, and they paid any surplus running cash into the Exchequer at the end of each accounting period.[99] Consequently, at the end of their tenure, in 1659, the commissioners owed just £11. No accusations of peculation or fraud were made against them in contemporary documents. The largest arrears owed by sub-collectors was £7,855 (1659), and the largest surplus was £5,573 in the same year. The dramatic decrease in the amounts owed to the central customs office by the outport collectors indicates that the scrutiny of the Exchequer may have kept others besides the customs commissioners honest. In some ways, the customs system of the late 1650s approached the modern ideal of bureaucratic efficiency and honesty, although this point can be pushed too far.

The collapse of the government in Westminster in the autumn of 1659, along with the return of military rule, ended Horseman's and his associates' control of the customs. There is a chronological gap in the declared accounts from September 1659 (E351/659) to 24 July 1660 (E351/660), reflecting the turmoil before the Restoration. The men who assumed control of the customs in 1660 were John Wolstenholme, John Harrison, Nicholas Crispe, and Jacob Harby.[100] Most of these London merchants had served as customs farmers before 1641 and all of them, with the possible exception of Shaw, were active Royalists in 1642.[101]

THE RESTORATION CUSTOMS

The return of these Royalists to customs administration reflected the direct connection between the political situation and the management of the customs. On the one hand, these men did not improve the customs' efficiency or increase the percentage of gross revenue paid into the Exchequer. On the other, they changed few of the subordinate officers and continued to use fixed fees or salaries to pay the customs officials working for them, keeping the administrative costs at roughly 10 per cent (£77,133) of the gross revenue of £836,529 that was collected from July 1660 to 29 September 1662. The increase in average annual receipts from £378,000 in the previous three-year period to £386,000 indicates the permanence of at least some of the changes made to customs accounting procedures during the Interregnum, as well as the continued economic prosperity of England.[102] Annual audits and the frequent deposit of large running cash balances into the Exchequer continued, with the result that the commissioners held only £11,117 in cash and were owed only £10,183 by outport collectors.

The civil wars and the wars of the Interregnum forced the English Parliament to raise customs rates and to establish regular parliamentary supervision over the government's direct collection of the customs. The manner in which these changes took place fundamentally altered the place of the customs in the English financial system. In 1640 the customs had been one of several prerogative revenues that made up the ordinary income of the monarch. Its management was a royal concern and parliamentary oversight or inspection was unconstitutional. By 1660 the customs had become a tax granted to the monarch for life and only increased through parliamentary action. Parliament was intimately involved in the management and accounts of the customs and its receipts were seen as part of the 'fund of credit' for the government rather than the monarch. After 1660, English governments increasingly used assignment tallies to anticipate Exchequer receipts. These tallies were often secured by the customs revenue and served as both a means of government credit and as negotiable or transferable bills, presaging the greatly increased use of Exchequer bills in the 1690s. The administrative personnel involved with the collection of the customs also became a recognizable state-bureaucracy, especially after the permanent return to direct collection in 1671.

These changes had clear impact on the net revenue of the customs. From 1642 to 1660, annual average customs receipts had exceeded £293,000. By 1664, annual revenue was running at a predictable £310,000, an amount close to the £308,000 provided annually by the customs to the Protectorate from 1656 to 1659. Increases in the rates and in the number of goods taxed, along with an increase in English commerce in the 1670s and 1680s, maintained the customs as one of the most important peacetime sources of money for the English government, as Table 6.7 illustrates.

Table 6.7: Net Customs Receipts and Total Government Receipts, 1660–1700[103]

Period	Total (£)	Customs (£)	%	Customs average per annum (£)
Jul 1660–Ms 1664	5,208,842	1,346,797	25.8	269,359
Ms 1664–Ms 1669	9,251,201	1,550,817	16.8	310,163
Ms 1669–Ms 1674	9,005,725	2,433,992	27.0	486,798
Ms 1674–Ms 1679	8,261,103	2,883,907	34.9	576,781
Ms 1679–Ms 1684	7,286,176	2,845,797	39.0	569,159
Ms 1684–Ms 1688	7,701,732	3,472,165	45.1	868,041
Nov 1688–M 1691	8,613,190	1,919,514	22.3	639,838
M 1691–M 1695	19,643,620	3,335,538	16.9	833,884
M 1695–M 1700	24,301,914	5,742,898	23.6	1,148,579

M = Michaelmas

Ms = Midsummer

During the long period of peace from 1674 to 1688 customs receipts made up over 39 per cent of the total state revenue. Conversely, in periods of intensive warfare, such as from 1664 to 1667 and 1689 to 1697, customs receipts declined as a component of total revenue, but the annual average amounts of money raised by the customs did not decline. In part, this was a result of increased rates and expansion of taxable items. Most of all, it reflected the fact that the navy was able to protect commerce in most of the wars of the late seventeenth century. During the two wars in which the navy was least successful in its mission of commerce protection the customs made up the smallest percentage of total income (from 1664 to 1667 and from 1691 to 1695).

When partial farming of the customs revenue was resumed in 1662, the Westminster government, and especially its Treasury, maintained a much closer interest in the business of the farmers, reducing the farmers' ability to reap overly large profits.[104] These measures increased annual gross customs receipts from £172,000 in 1639 to over £386,000 in 1662, with an annual average gross revenue in the period from 1662 to 1671 of £338,361.[105] Salaries or fixed fees for the payment of customs officials were used increasingly instead of variable fees. The gross revenue came to be thought of as belonging to the state rather than to the commissioners or farmers. In 1662, when farming of the entire customs was resumed, the farmers were expected to pay excess receipts to the Exchequer, whereas before 1640 they had been allowed to keep them as profits.

The greater government interest in the routine affairs of the customs administration, and Parliament's belief that the farmers' cash balances beyond a reasonable profit were not the property of the farmers, undermined the attractiveness of the customs farm. In the 1660s, the Second Dutch War and the sharp decline in English commerce connected with the war, the plague and the London fire, further eroded the opportunities for tax farmers to make large profits. It is no wonder that the government had difficulty finding men willing to continue to provide the large cash advances demanded at the start of the lease, since many of the profitable practices of earlier tax farming had been eliminated previously. In 1671, the farm proved especially unattractive to prospective farmers in the face of the governmental fiscal crisis that was leading to the Stop of the Exchequer. Therefore, the government resumed direct collection of the customs, never to surrender it again. The average annual gross revenue jumped from £338,361 to £637,745 with the return to direct collection. Part of this increase was due to higher rates on wine and to a steady improvement of commerce after 1674. These increased customs receipts certainly helped to convince Englishmen that direct collection and commissioner management was the best option for gathering the customs.

The administration of the oldest regular source of English tax revenue evolved steadily from the 1540s to the 1650s. The need to finance extended wars greatly affected customs administration, with the most important changes coming during the long Elizabethan wars (from 1585 to 1604) and the wars of the Interregnum (from 1639 to 1660). Periods of war seemed especially to have made farming of the revenue unattractive for potential farmers. Warfare greatly increased the government's need for large cash advances and adversely affected commerce and, therefore, customs revenue. These conditions made the customs receipts very unpredictable. At these junctures, the state found it necessary to resume direct collection.

A process of professionalization is also evident in the historical record of customs administration from 1540 to 1671. Direct collection of the tax by permanent government employees was tried in the 1590s and resumed in the 1640s. In the intervening periods, when the customs revenue was farmed, the existing customs personnel in the ports were retained by the farmers, providing bureaucratic continuity. Over the same period, customs officials depended less and less on variable fees (or on bribes from merchants) and more on salaries or fixed fees for their remuneration, approaching modern notions of civil service probity. The money being collected was increasingly seen as the state's, not the king's or the tax farmers', and Parliament showed an increasing interest in the routine of administration. The patterns of customs administration that had developed by 1660 continued in many respects to the late eighteenth century, when the impact of long wars again forced major changes.[106]

The customs remained a major source of money for English governments into the eighteenth century and the largest of the regular peacetime revenues. For example, gross receipts of the customs averaged £637,945 annually from 1671 to 1688, while the total revenue of the state was well over £1.6 million per year.[107] Parliament controlled its expansion by passing legislation to increase rates and adding new items for taxation. After 1688, the last vestige of the notion that the customs belonged solely to the king was ended when Parliament no longer granted even a portion of the customs to the monarch for life. It was then that the concept of ordinary revenue was finally replaced with the Civil List for the maintenance of the monarch's household and family, and all revenue was put under parliamentary control.[108]

Parliament adopted two new taxes during the 1640s to support its incredibly expensive war effort: the excise and the assessment. The Long Parliament adopted the excise because the customs revenue was absorbed by naval costs and because the various fiscal expedients that were tried in 1642 and 1643 had failed to raise the steady stream of money needed to pay for the Parliamentarian armies. The next chapter documents the development and importance of the excise to England's Military Revolution.

CHAPTER SEVEN

The Excise

The Long Parliament's adoption of an excise tax to support its armies in 1643 was one of the most revolutionary steps ever taken in English fiscal management. The excise was a parliamentary tax from inception. The legislature's oversight was maintained throughout the civil wars and Interregnum, and continued after the Restoration. The excise became an enduring part of the state's regular revenue, even though originally only intended for use as a wartime levy.[1] Today its descendant is known as the value added tax. The adoption of such a regressive consumption tax, which rated many items of daily life, overturned the Elizabethan ideal that the working poor and indigent should not be taxed. The excise gave Parliament the means to levy new impositions on any item of inland consumption it desired, providing the state with tremendous financial elasticity in peace and war. Perhaps one of the greatest ironies of the English civil wars is that a political revolution caused in part by the fiscal exactions of Charles I brought into existence two taxes – the excise and assessment – that allowed the parliamentary state to extract unprecedentedly large sums of money from Englishmen on a permanent basis.[2]

The excise was the second largest regular source of revenue for the Long Parliament during the civil wars and one of the most important enduring legacies of the wars of the Interregnum.[3] The excise was a consumption tax levied initially on beer, liquor, ale, and a number of imported goods considered luxury or non-essential. Parliament intended to use its proceeds to provide the money needed to support the Parliamentarian armies commanded by the Earl of Essex and William Waller.[4] It became a tax on a wide range of commodities, to include meat and fish until 1647, and after the Interregnum remained a major source of government revenue.[5] The development of an excise system in English towns and villages brought 'the state' to the English people in a way they had never experienced before. The intrusiveness of excisemen was unavoidable as they went about their business of taxing the consumables of everyday life. The excise, born of the need to support modern armies in the 1640s, provided a revenue system that could be expanded to meet the financial needs of the state as those demands increased dramatically during the next century.[6]

The early history of the excise supports the observation that the

period between the meeting of the Long Parliament and the Treaty of Utrecht [1713] is of great importance in English financial history. It marks the transition between two very different systems of finance, those of the early seventeenth and of the eighteenth century, and it is one of the few formative periods in English tax policy and opinion.[7]

THE ESTABLISHMENT OF THE EXCISE

Parliament adopted such a regressive consumption tax very reluctantly, largely because of its fear of popular resistance. The relentless pressures brought by the enormous costs of war and the continued intransigence of the King made such a step necessary. As early as May 1643, a formal proposal was made in the House of Commons for an excise. This idea was one of several advanced to find ways to raise money to support Parliamentarian military forces. The Royalists' victories at the Battles of Adwalton Moor and Roundway Down in the spring and summer made it clear to most Parliamentarians that the King was not about to accept a negotiated peace as long as he believed he could crush the rebellion.[8] The pressing need to reinforce and sustain the armies forced the great parliamentary war leader John Pym to propose to the Commons the first bill for a 'tax on commodities' to reach the floor for debate. The Commons referred the excise bill to the Committee of Sequestrations, 'to consider of some way for the better putting in execution the [existing] ordinances [for] weekly assessments; for sequestrations; and for the Twentieth part', in hopes that the imposition of an excise tax could be avoided.[9]

Meanwhile, Parliament created a Committee of Accounts to oversee and enforce the various ordinances for raising money already in force and another committee to 'determine how to regularly pay the army'. The latter committee adopted a procedure to account for the issue of money by use of warrants which, when signed by a certain number of committee members, could become authorization for the expenditure of money and provide documents suitable for the tracking of money spent to support the forces.[10] While these were major steps forward in fiscal practice, by allowing the legislature routinely to oversee the financial bureaucracies and government expenditures, they did not solve the immediate fiscal problem of how to support the Parliamentarian armies. The basic problem was the same one faced by Charles I's government in the late 1620s and in 1639/40: there was insufficient revenue available to pay and support the armed forces needed in wartime.[11]

In late June 1643, as the Royalist armies continued to make progress against the inadequately supported parliamentary forces, John Pym again presented an 'ordinance for the speedy raising and levying of monies . . . on the several commodities'. However, only further military defeats and the fall of Bristol to Prince Rupert's Royalist army in July enabled Pym to get the first excise ordinance enacted.[12] The importance of the excise is apparent: without it, the Parliamentarian armies would have remained unpaid and incapable of preventing a Royalist victory. With an excise, Parliament still had to resolve that

> the arrears of the army shall be accounted as a debt of the kingdom. . . . That an ordinance shall be prepared to enable my Lord General to take free quarter for his army upon his march, for two months, if the war shall so long continue, upon giving tickets, which this House will take care shall be satisfied and defalked out of the soldiers' pay.[13]

The money raised from weekly assessments, loans, and sequestrations had proven inadequate to cover the costs of war. They were collected irregularly at best in 1643, forcing Parliamentarian armies to take free quarter while in the field. Parliament enacted the first excise ordinance hoping to end this situation and to provide adequate financial resources to sustain the armies needed to defeat the Royalists.

On 22 July 1643, the House of Lords passed Pym's excise ordinance to pay 'for the maintenance of the forces raised for the defence of the King and Parliament . . . and towards the payment of the debts of the Commonwealth for which the public faith is, or shall be given'.[14] The excise ordinance taxed tobacco, wine, cider, beer, ale, raisins, currants, figs, sugar, playing cards, thread, and silk. It established an excise office in London and provided for the appointment of eight commissioners to govern the system. The first commissioners of the excise included three London aldermen (John Towse, Thomas Foot, and John Kendrick), a sheriff of London (John Langham), and four prominent London merchants (Simon Edmonds, John Lamot, Edward Claxton, and Thomas Cullen). Langham served as treasurer. The excise ordinance forbade him to issue any money without 'an order of both Houses of Parliament, unless it be for . . . payment of wages' and rents of the commissioners and officers of the excise.[15] The excise commissioners answered to the orders and warrants of a committee of the Lords and Commons appointed to oversee the advance of money and were to submit their accounts quarterly to 'one or more auditors' appointed by and from the Members of Parliament.[16] This ordinance was annulled and replaced with a similar ordinance which slightly lowered the excise rates on 8 September 1643.[17]

The men selected as the first excise commissioners reflected the close connection of the parliamentary war party with London merchants and financiers during the First Civil War. Alderman Towse died in 1645. Aldermen Foot and Kendrick supported the parliamentary Independents and the army against the Presbyterians and City during the political crises of 1647. These commissioners accommodated themselves to the Commonwealth and Protectorate governments and, consequently, served as Lord Mayors in 1649/50 (Foot) and 1651/2 (Kendrick). Foot and Kendrick continued their active roles as excise commissioners until 1655 and 1650 respectively, maintaining good relations with Oliver Cromwell.[18] Aldermen Langham and Cullen, on the other hand, supported the Presbyterian majority in the Long Parliament in 1647 and were imprisoned in September 1647 for their opposition to the army. Parliament subsequently removed them from the excise commission in late 1647 and replaced them with new commissioners in 1650.[19]

The first excise commissioners had become aldermen only in the early 1640s. They had not previously managed government financial affairs and their operation of the excise was their entrance into that lucrative arena. The excise was the least popular tax of the Long Parliament. This may explain why its management was not sought aggressively by the wealthier merchant-financiers, giving these 'new men' their opportunity. The excise was also the most difficult tax to collect, due to its decentralized nature as a consumption tax. It remained an unpopular and difficult tax to collect and became the most bureaucratic of the major revenue systems used during the civil wars and Interregnum.[20]

The eight commissioners established the London excise office 'with several registers, collectors, clerks, and other subordinate officers as the eight commissioners . . . nominated and appointed'.[21] They set up offices in the major towns of the kingdom staffed with sub-commissioners and collectors. These officials remitted their receipts and accounts to the London office of the excise treasurer (also a commission appointee). The excise offices were to be open 'in the week days . . . for the entering and registering of the names and the surnames . . . of the sellers, buyers, and makers of all and every commodities' listed in the excise schedule, and for the 'receiving of all monies as shall be due upon the sale or making of the same'. The first buyer usually made the payments and was allowed up to eight months to complete payment, with interest at 12 per cent per annum, at the discretion of the treasurer. When a buyer purchased a taxable commodity, an entry was made in an account book at the excise office and the purchaser received a ticket showing that he had paid the tax.[22] The treasurer made quarterly reports to Parliament about the receipts and handled disbursements from the London office.

Pym's initial ordinance enabled the commissioners to place a lien on the goods of any merchant or shopkeeper who failed to pay the excise and to collect four times the value of the commodity in question. The ordinance allowed the commissioners to sell the commodity if the merchant failed to pay his fine and to keep the proceeds. If they could not seize goods, or get the fine, then the commissioners could have the evader imprisoned 'until he pays the penalty by him forfeited'. Excise collectors and sub-commissioners were given the power to call on the trained bands or other military forces for aid and assistance in these actions.[23]

Excise commissioners were initially paid a salary, the amount of which was removed from the copy of the first two ordinances. They were to provide fit and reasonable wages for the collectors, clerks, and officers, with parliamentary approval. Eventually the costs of administering the system reached 9 or 10 per cent of the gross receipt and the Long Parliament changed the salary system into a fee system based on a poundage rate of 6d for each pound collected.[24] Most likely this was done because Parliament believed that greater revenue would be gathered from the excise taxes if the collectors were paid based on the amount they collected, rather than with a fixed salary. In some ways the excise system of the 1640s resembled a tax farm, but there were some important differences. Although the commissioners received a poundage rate rather than a salary, they did not pay a fixed rent for their offices. Further, the profits of the commissioners were limited by the poundage rate of 2.5 per cent of receipts plus collection expenses.

Anticipated excise revenue soon became the security for large amounts of money borrowed in London for the pay, supply, and recruitment of parliamentary forces. However, before the excise system could become fully operational, the Long Parliament had to pass another ordinance to clarify the administrative details and alter the excise rates on a number of goods. Passed on 8 September 1643, this second ordinance allowed 'for the better and more speedy advancement of this work and the more easy payment of the said charge'.[25] It required the commissioners to regularly audit the accounts of the excise collectors from around the country and to submit their central London accounts to parliamentary auditors. Merchants were to submit bills of entry to the excise officers before they landed goods in the seaports, and sheriffs and constables in local parishes were required to assist the unpopular excisemen.[26] This ordinance reduced excise rates on many items, further indicating that a fair amount of resistance to the tax existed. These modifications seemed to have eased the difficulties of collection. By early October, the first £8,000 for support of Essex's army was obligated on the anticipated excise receipts.[27]

Oliver Cromwell, Lieutenant-General of Horse in the New Model Army, 1645, and conqueror of Ireland and Scotland, 1649–51. (National Maritime Museum)

Charles I, executed in 1649 after his failed attempt to defeat the parliamentary cause in the English Civil Wars. (National Maritime Museum)

Edward Montagu, General at Sea and later Earl of Sandwich, 1650s and 1660s. One of the major English naval commanders in the Second Dutch War. (National Maritime Museum)

George Monck, parliamentary commander in Ireland and Scotland and a General at Sea in the First Dutch War. One of an emerging professional military élite. (National Maritime Museum)

Richard Deane, an artillery commander in the New Model Army in the 1640s and General at Sea in the victorious Commonwealth Navy in the First Dutch War. (National Maritime Museum)

Battle of Lowestoft 1665 *by Van de Velde. The battle was fought on 3 June between the Royal Navy*

and the Dutch fleet – an English victory that was not exploited because of poor English leadership.
(National Maritime Museum)

The English Ship London *by Van de Velde, 1660? (above) and* The English Ship Neptune *by Van de Velde, 1685 (below). These two vessels are separated in age by four decades but clearly show the continuity of warship design between 1650 and 1690. (National Maritime Museum)*

Robert Blake, leading English General at Sea from 1649 to 1657. He was responsible for developing line ahead tactics and died while returning from a long voyage to Mediterranean and Iberian waters. (National Maritime Museum)

Parliamentarian commanders left to right: Sir Thomas Fairfax, Lord Fairfax, Major-General Skippon, Lieutenant-General Cromwell, Robert Essex, the Earl of Warwick, Alexander Leslie and the Earl of Manchester. These men defeated Charles I and established the standing army in England. Cromwell and Fairfax emerged as the most powerful and influential of these revolutionaries. The army they created conquered three kingdoms in ten years. (Ashmolean Museum, Oxford)

Robert Devereux, Earl of Essex, Lord General of the main Parliamentarian Army from 1642 to 1644. He was commander of the Parliamentarian forces at the Battle of Edgehill in 1642.

Battle of Marston Moor, *2 July 1644 by James Ward, the first major Parliamentarian victory in northern England against the Royalists. (The Cromwell Museum, Huntingdon)*

Pikemen of the New Model Army, illustrating forms of military drill associated with the Military Revolution. (Courtesy of Graham Edwards)

Sir Thomas Fairfax, Lord General and creator of the New Model Army in 1645 and victor in the English Civil Wars. (Courtauld Institute of Art)

THE GROUNDS OF
MILITARY DISCIPLINE:
Or, Certain brief Rules for the Exercifing of a Company or Squadron.

Obferved by all.

IN March, in Motion, troop or ftand,
Obferve both Leader and right hand,
With filence note in what degree
You in the Body, placed be:
That fo you may without more trouble
Know where to ftand, and when to double.

Diſtance.

True diftance keep in files, in ranks
Open clofe to the front, reare, flanks,
Backward, forward, to the right, left, or either,
Backward and forward both together.
To the right, left, outward or in,
According to directions given.
To order, clofe, open, double,
Diftance, diftance, double, double:
For this alone prevents diftraction,
And giveth luftre to the action.

Facings.

Face to the right, or to the left, both wayes to the
Inward, outward, and as you were: (reare,
To the front, reare, flanks, and peradventure
To every Angle, and to the Center.

Doubling.

To bring more hands in the front to fight,
Double Ranks unto the right,
Or left, or both, if need require,
Direct divifionall or Intire:
By doubling files accordingly,
Your flanks will ftrengthened be thereby.
Halfe files and bringers up likewife
To the front may double, none denies.
Nor would it very ftrange appear
For th'front half files or double the reare :
The one half Ranks to double the other,
Thereby to ftrengthen one the other.

But left I fhould feem troublefome
To Countermarch, next I come.

Which though they many feem to be,
Are all included in thefe three :
Maintaining, gaining, loofing ground,
And feverall wayes to each is found;
By which their proper motions guided,
In files, in ranks, in both divided.

Counter-march.

Wheel your battell e're you fight,
For better advantage to the right,
Or left, or round about
To either Angle, or where you doubt,
Your Enemie will firft oppofe you,
And therefore unto their Foot clofe you.
Divifionall wheeling I have feen
In fundrie places practis'd been,
To alter either form or figure,
By wheeling feverall wayes together.
And had I time to ftand upon't,
I'de wheele my wings into the front.
By wheeling flanks into the reare,
They'le foon reduce them as they were.
Befides it feems a pretty thing
To wheel front, and reare to either wing:
Wheele both wings to the reare and front;
Face to the reare, and having don't,
Clofe your Devifions; even your Ranks,
Wheel front and reare into both flanks :
And thus much know, caufe, note I'le fmother,
The one wheeling doth reduce the other.

Wheeling.

One thing more and I have done,
Let files rank by Converfion :
To th'Right, to th'Left, to both, and then
Ranks by Converfion fill again:
Troop for the Colours, march, prepare for fight,
Behave your felves like men, and fo goodnight.

Converfion and Inverfion.

The fumme of all that hath been fpoken may be comprifed thus.

Open, clofe, face, double, countermarch, wheel, charge, retire:
Invert, Convert, Reduce, Trope, March, Make readie, Fire.

FINIS.

The Grounds of Military Discipline, an example of the standardization and centralization of the standing armies of the Military Revolution. (Thomason Tract, British Library)

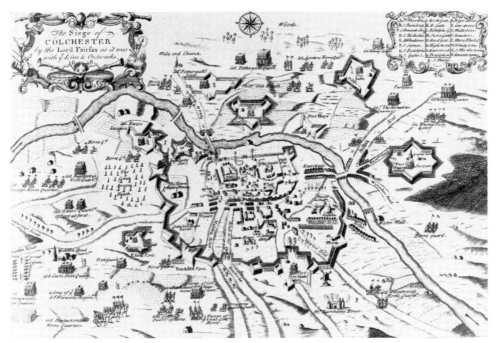

The Parliamentarian siege of Colchester, 1648, an example of the application of modern siege methods and defensive works to the English theatre of operations during the Military Revolution. (Ashmolean Museum, Oxford)

Battle of Dunbar, 1650, Oliver Cromwell's most stunning victory over the Scottish Army and the beginning of the end of Scottish independence for the next ten years. (Ashmolean Museum, Oxford)

The Rump Parliament, an experiment in republicanism and the result of the second army coup in English history. (Mansell Collection)

John Pym, architect of victory, the
Parliamentarian who created the tax system
that sustained the modern English, and later
British, state.

Sir Henry Vane (1613–62) by Robert Walker.
Vane was a Parliamentarian, member of the
Council of State and Navy Treasurer, 1642–50.
(The Cromwell Museum, Huntingdon)

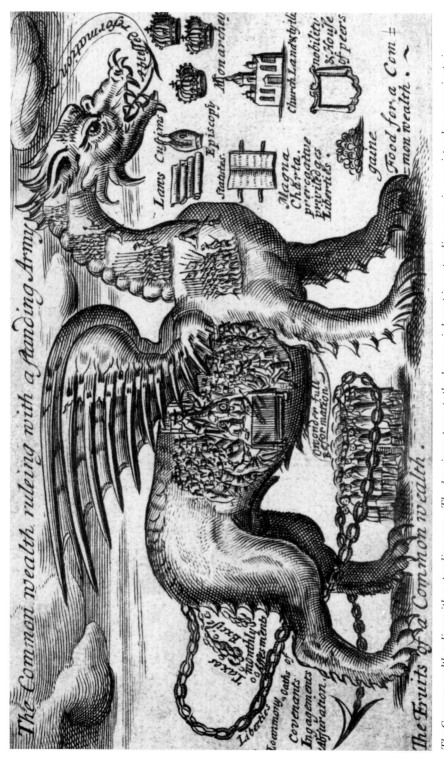

The Commonwealth ruling with a standing army. The drawing represents the dangers inherent in a standing army in a society where sovereignty is uncertain. (Ashmolean Museum, Oxford)

The Long Parliament used the excise to secure loans or advances totalling over £249,000 for the support of the army and navy during the year from September 1643 to September 1644.[28] Most of these advances required direct repayment by the excise commissioners 'in due course'. The anticipated excise receipts rapidly became a major prop of the short-term credit system of the parliamentary state. The Parliamentarians negotiated the first two loans secured by the excise shortly after the Parliamentarian forces lifted the siege of Gloucester. By then it had become clear to creditors that the Parliamentarians were in the war for the long term.[29]

All loans secured on the excise, except for one of £30,000, were for the support of the army and paid 8 per cent interest per year. Some examples of loans include the £20,000 borrowed for recruitment of new soldiers to fill the gaps in the ranks caused by the defeat of Roundway Down and the withdrawal of the London trained bands after the relief of Gloucester.[30] Another £10,000 was borrowed to pay Waller's army in November, and £1,000 was earmarked to pay and supply Plymouth's garrison.[31] From September 1644 to September 1645, the Long Parliament encumbered the excise with further obligations totalling at least £156,000 for the support of its armies, and a further £281,000 in the following year to September 1646. These sums probably do not include all of the loans made on the security of the excise, since the declared accounts of the excise commissioners for the period before September 1647 are missing.[32] None the less, the available data indicates that at least £686,000 was provided in loans or advances secured by the excise for the support of the Parliamentarian armies in the first three years of its existence. The excise provided the Long Parliament with a major revenue on which to secure the large loans required to make its war effort possible.

However, excise receipts probably did not reach the £228,000 needed each year to repay these obligations. A report made to the House of Commons in January 1647 concerning the condition of the excise indicated that the charges made on it, and as yet unpaid, totalled £398,211. An additional £400,000 in advances were secured on it in December 1646 to pay the Scottish army to leave England.[33] The annual gross revenue of the excise only exceeded £300,000 in the more settled years after 1654. The revenue for the period from 1647 to 1650, for which we have declared accounts, did not exceed £287,000 per year.[34] If the Long Parliament had used the excise solely to pay the £20,444 per month to Essex's army that it had originally obligated it for, the account balance of the excise might have remained even. Parliament did not do so. Additionally, the interest alone paid on the excise obligations cost £64,000 per year from September 1647 to September 1650.[35]

The large sums secured by the excise receipts show how important the tax was to war finance in the 1640s. They are also evidence for the existence of an increasingly successful system of short-term credit management used by the Westminster governments to sustain their forces. The repayment with interest of most of the money secured on the excise in these years often goes unnoticed since £230,000 in loans were still secured on it in 1660. However, this sum was not an unmanageable debt load for a revenue with receipts exceeding that much each year. These lessons were not lost on the Restoration Parliament when it settled the King's revenue in 1660.

The Long Parliament added alum, copperas, hats, and domestic silk to the tax rolls in July 1644, and beef, mutton, and veal in January and August 1645. These latter levies on necessities were exceedingly unpopular and probably would not have been collected were it not for the vested financial interest of the London financiers and merchants who had advanced so much money to the parliamentary cause. As it was, armed force had to be resorted to for the protection of the excise collectors on several occasions.

Parliament continued to improve and better regulate the audit procedures of the excise during the civil wars. In September 1645, the House of Commons appointed a comptroller 'to keep accounts of all entries, receipts, . . . within the office . . . [and to ensure] that no person . . . shall be discharged of any duty belonging to the office of the excise before the same be signed by the said [comptroller] Thomas Fauconberge or his deputies'.[36] Thomas Fauconberge served as Parliament's permanent overseer of the daily accounting of the excise, with a salary of £500 per year. He reported regularly to William Bond, the 'sole auditor of all excise and new imposts', concerning the excise accounts.[37] The Parliamentarians attempted to avoid unnecessary collection costs and to prevent garrison commanders from seizing local excise receipts before they could be transmitted to London. Unfortunately, this last goal was not met, as the excise accounts list £12,949 as taken by soldiers in 1647.[38]

Parliament continued to encumber the excise with more debt than the revenue could support, in spite of the increase in the number of goods taxed. In addition, the political turmoil of the spring and summer of 1647, caused by the struggle between the Presbyterians and the New Model Army, adversely affected the collection of the excise as it did those of the customs and assessment. By August 1647 the excise could no longer be used to secure additional loans, making it impossible for the

Long Parliament to pay the arrears of the army before its disbandment. Therefore the constitutional crisis deepened.[39] When the parliamentary Presbyterians and their allies on the London Common Council attempted to disband the regiments piecemeal, the excise could not provide the collateral for loans to pay the soldiers. Therefore, Parliament's attempts to assert civil control over the army collapsed. Had sufficient money been available to the government in mid-1647, the political and administrative history of England would have been radically different.[40]

The Long Parliament lost control of its army when it could no longer pay it or pay off its arrears and disband it. This situation had developed over many months. After the January 1647 report concerning the heavily encumbered state of the excise revenue, the Parliamentarians attempted to borrow another £30,000 for soldiers' pay from the London Common Council, but it was forced to resolve not to borrow further on the collateral of the excise until its revenues were cleared of other obligations.[41] The Common Council refused Parliament's request in May for a £200,000 loan to provide funds to disband the army. At the same time, the receipts of the excise declined. In spite of its promise not to do so, the House of Commons attempted to obligate the excise directly for the 'arrears of the inferior officers and common soldiers' and to secure, and eventually redeem, the debentures, or promissory notes that were to be issued to the soldiers when they disbanded.[42] These schemes failed because the soldiers recognized that once disbanded, they would forfeit their collective power and their arrears. Fairfax's march on London and the expulsion of the eleven Presbyterian leaders from the House of Commons cleared the way for the resumption of all tax collections with army support. The political struggles in the Long Parliament and the London Common Council were settled on the army's terms, enabling the financial machinery of the Commonwealth to resume operation.

The excise did not undergo major administrative or personnel changes after the 1647 crisis ended since its commissioners were generally sympathetic to the Independent political position of the New Model Army leadership. The commissioners possibly conducted the affairs of the excise system in a fiscally more prudent manner after the mid-1647 crisis, paying off many old debts and carefully monitoring new obligations to ensure the system's solvency. Towards those ends, in August 1647, the purged Parliament passed an ordinance 'for re-establishing the duty of the excise upon all commodities except flesh and salt in the kingdom'. The preamble shows Parliament's resolve to raise enough money to pay the army and illustrates the problems for tax collection in this troubled period.

> Being daily informed of the general opposition which is made against the collection of those duties of the excise . . . the many violences, injuries and abuses that are offered to the commissioners. . . . The Lords and Commons do therefore hereby declare, . . . in respect of the great debt . . . for which these continued receipts of the excise are engaged . . . must require obedience . . . unto the due payment. . . . The tumults and riots in opposition . . . being increased . . . the said Lords and Commons . . . deeply resent the great neglect of the authority of Parliament amongst the people and if they shall continue, . . . they shall be enforced . . . [with] exemplary punishment.[43]

The Long Parliament ordered sheriffs and constables to protect the excise collectors in their jurisdictions and asked General Fairfax to order the army to suppress riots, taxpayers' strikes, and tumults. Parliament responded to accusations that the excise officials had pocketed up to half of the receipts by noting that 'upon an exact examination it doth clearly appear . . . that until these late destructions and oppositions, the charge in collecting the excise hath never amounted . . . to full two shillings [in twenty]'. Further, the excise had raised £1,334,532 for public use since September 1643. However, since this £333,000 per year exceeded the revenue of the excise, on its future receipts there 'stands assigned, divers very great sums of money'.[44]

Parliament continued the excise on all commodities except flesh and salt from September 1647 to September 1650. It passed additional legislation protecting its tax collectors from all legal suits and actions with a general indemnity.[45] The declared accounts of the excise commissioners provide ample evidence to evaluate the results of these parliamentary efforts, as well as to evaluate the efficiency and financial importance of the excise. Table 7.1 summarizes the first declared account of the excise commissioners still in existence. It confirms the accuracy of the observation made in the House of Commons that the costs of excise administration were not greater than two shillings in the pound. The account for this period from 1647 to 1650 notes that there were earlier excise accounts made, indicating that Parliament's claim that £1.3 million had been raised by the excise for the support of the Westminster government was probably accurate. This earlier amount should eventually be counted as part of any estimate of the amount of money raised by the English governments with the excise during the civil wars.

Table 7.1: Declared Account of the Excise, 30 September 1647–29 September 1650[46]

Receipts and their sources	Amount (£)	%
a. Money collected in London	487,656	56.7
b. Money collected in counties	360,030	41.8
c. From sale of forfeited goods	7,297	0.8
d. From impost on gold and silver	5,688	0.7
Total	860,671	
Annual average	286,890	

Expenditures	Amount (£)	%
a. Pay of army and garrisons	294,521	35.2
b. Army supplies and services	229,671	27.4
c. Interest paid on secured debt	193,017	23.1
d. Excise salaries and costs	74,278	8.9
e. Paid to Navy Treasurer	32,616	3.9
f. Taken by soldiers illegally	12,949	1.5
Total	837,052	

The excise commissioners paid over 23 per cent of their expenditures for interest on the loans secured by the excise. This was essential for the credit of the parliamentary government and is a good example of what is sometimes called a secured debt. The English state continued to use anticipated excise receipts to secure and service its debt for the next three centuries. Furthermore, much of the debt secured on the excise in the 1640s evidently was paid off in the three years from September 1650 to September 1653, reducing interest and principal repayments in the later period to £152,381.[47] The administrative costs of the excise were just under 10 per cent of gross receipts, substantiating Parliament's claim in January 1647 that excise administration cost less than 'two shillings in twenty'.

The commissioners provided money to support the army for a wide variety of purposes on the order of warrants issued by the Committee of the Army or, after March 1649, the Council of State. The larger sums were usually payable to other treasuries or treasurers, like Sir John Wollaston, one of the Treasurers at War responsible for the payment of the army and Nicholas Loftus, Treasurer for Irish Causes. These men then dispensed the money in accordance with further warrants issued by parliamentary committees or the Council of State.[48] In this manner, £372,158 was provided for the army to the Treasurers at War from early 1645 until late 1651 from excise receipts.[49] Excise collectors in the counties also paid smaller sums directly to local garrisons and county committees, making the excise an essential part of war finance at both the national and local level.

In all, 62 per cent of excise cash receipts were provided to the army, in addition to the loans secured by anticipated excise revenues. From September 1647 to September 1650, £285,000 from the excise paid for essential services to the army such as 'money advanced for the Kentish horse . . . £600', the 'supplying of public stores of powder, match and bullet . . . £20,719', and 'for pay and relief of soldiers and wagoners of the train [of artillery] . . . £10,000'.[50] Many payments made after September 1647 were based on payment warrants issued by the Long Parliament's Army Committee in 1645 and 1646, reflecting both that large debts existed from before 1647 and that these old debts were being paid off along with the current expenditures for pay and supplies.

The excise commissioners' declared accounts list significant arrears that were considered to be due to the excise office. The account from which the data in Table 7.1 is drawn lists £132,331 as arrears carried forward from the missing account for the period October 1646 to September 1647. At the end of their account in September 1650, the excise commissioners indicated that the arrears had grown to £165,071. Of this later amount, £39,155 was owed by merchants or retailers to the excise collectors, while the excise officials throughout England owed the central excise office another £56,320. The central commissioners were responsible for the remaining £69,596, of which they eventually paid only £5,145.[51] There is no evidence in the later accounts about what happened to the £64,416 for which the commissioners were still accountable.

REPUBLICAN ADMINISTRATION

Thomas Foote and his associates weathered the political turbulence of the late 1640s, remaining in office until September 1650. The execution of the King and the creation of a republican Commonwealth cleared the way for the conquests of Ireland (1649–52), and Scotland (1650–2), and the first naval war against the Dutch (1652–4). The financial requirements of these wars increased the state's need for money, ensuring that the excise would be continued.

The Rump Parliament tried once more in 1649 to obligate the excise for £400,000 to pay for Cromwell's Irish campaign. However, the London

Common Council refused to loan the first £120,000 of this sum, indicating that the excise was no longer considered a sound security for loans due to the large amounts already charged to its future revenue. Consequently, the government had to turn to land sales (discussed in chapter five above) to raise the money needed to pay off old debt and to increase taxes to provide enough current income to pay its military forces.[52]

During 1649 and 1650, the Rump and its executive body, the Council of State, worked to re-establish government credit by paying off over £3 million in debt. Parliamentary acts in June and August 1649 transferred previously incurred obligations from the anticipated proceeds of the sale of bishops' lands to the revenue of the excise.[53] This transfer replaced the promise of near-term repayment with one of eventual payment of principal and periodic payment of 8 per cent interest. It was also an underhanded way to get around London's reluctance to loan further money secured by future excise receipts. In August 1649, another act reaffirmed the legality of the excise, its procedures, and the goods liable for taxation. Although no changes were made in administrative procedures, this act made it a crime for any law officer to fail to support excise agents and added a 2d in the pound gratuity for those local officials who aided in excise collection.[54]

Parliament made two further significant changes to the excise in 1650. New commissioners were appointed and were given the authority to farm out the collection of all or part of the excise. The 20 September act embodying these changes named George Snelling, Thomas Bulstrode, Thomas Foote, William Parker, Maurice Thomson, and Richard Downes as commissioners. Foote was the only London alderman in the group and was also the current Lord Mayor. He had served as an excise commissioner since 1643 and was the only commissioner retained in 1650 – Towse had died, and the others were replaced. The other new commissioners could be called a 'Cromwell crowd' because of their close ties to the New Model Army. The New England doctor Maurice Thomson and the wealthy merchant William Parker had not been members of the London's inner circle of merchants and financiers before 1640 and both had made fortunes supplying arms and supplies to the army.[55] The evidence is insufficient to support more than the observation that in 1650/1 major changes were made in the personnel of the excise commission and the Treasurers of War that seemed to indicate a shift in power further away from the older established London financial community and towards men who had been closely associated with Independency and Oliver Cromwell.[56] The sub-collectors, local excisemen, and clerks in the various excise offices did not change when this shift at the top occurred. This pattern of continuity within the bureaucracy in spite of change at the top continued throughout the rest of the century.[57]

The decision to allow tax farming of the excise was due probably to the belief that the arrears in collection could be reduced with a farm. Direct collection had resulted in up to a half of one year's revenue outstanding at any time. Since tax farmers would pay in advance for the excise farm, it was thought they would work harder to gather receipts and therefore to collect their profit. Farming the revenue would mean a lower net receipt for the state, but it could provide predictable payments to the government during the period of the contract. Such predictability in income would greatly facilitate orderly and accurate budgeting. Unlike the pre-1640s customs farmers, the excise tax farmers were not allowed to keep all receipts above the rent of the farm. The act retained the same audit procedures and commissioners' powers as before, while the poundage rate was reduced from 6d to 3d per pound.[58]

Partial farming of the excise probably increased the net revenue of the excise, as the data in Table 7.2 indicates. However, it did not end the existence of large arrears in tax collections.

Table 7.2: Declared Account of the Excise, 30 September 1650–29 September 1653[59]

Receipts and sources	Amount (£)	%
a. Money collected in London	552,143	47.6
b. Money collected in counties	348,114	30.0
c. Paid by excise farmers	221,448	19.1
d. From Treasurers at War	28,330	2.4
e. Profits of forfeitures	11,107	0.9
Total	1,161,142	
Annual average	387,047	

Expenditures	Amount (£)	%
a. Pay and services of army	749,861	67.0
b. Interest paid on secured debt	152,381	13.6
c. Estimated salaries and costs	121,920	10.9
d. Paid to bishops' land debt	61,986	5.5
e. Paid to Navy Treasurer	21,142	1.9
f. Paid to widows and maimed	11,107	0.9
Total	1,118,397	
Unaccounted for	42,745	

The excise commissioners made £214,367 (19 per cent) of their disbursements for interest and principal payment, contributing to the ability of the republic to raise short-term loans to pay for its military operations. The excise revenue also provided the money used to repay the loans originally secured on the anticipated proceeds from the sale of the bishops' land, undoubtedly contributing to the Commonwealth's public credit.

The administrative costs in Table 7.2 are estimates because the declared account is unclear as to their exact amount. This estimate is the only figure not explicitly listed in the declared account but it is in line with previous costs. Farming the excise may have lowered administrative costs. However, this is a more conservative estimate based on the roughly 10 per cent rate for administration mentioned by Parliament in 1647 and confirmed in the declared account for the period from September 1647 to September 1650.

An additional £133,904 was owed by, or 'depending on', taxpayers and sub-collectors to the London excise treasury. This sum cannot be considered income in this period and is not listed as such. By 1653 the arrears increased £38,429 from the £95,475 listed in the excise account ending in September 1650. The rate of growth in the arrears since that date compares favourably with the growth of arrears from 1647 to 1650, especially since the revenue in the later period was £272,000 (31 per cent) greater. Farming did not increase the rate of growth of the arrears and it seemed to have increased the net income of the excise, as annual average revenue grew from £286,000 to £387,000.[60]

From 1650 to 1653, the excise provided the Commonwealth's army with over £249,000 per year for pay and services. This money was essential for military operations since expeditionary forces were campaigning in Ireland and Scotland and required a steady stream of munitions, food, recruits, and clothes from England that could only be procured with cash.[61] The excise revenue also paid for pensions to widows and maimed soldiers, a practice that is certainly modern. In spite of the increased contributions of the excise, state debt increased in the 1650s, as the Commonwealth expanded its war efforts. The ability of the republican government to increase its debt reflects the fact that its tax system and financial management had secured its credit with lenders.

THE PROTECTORATE

The military coup that led to the Protectorate in the spring of 1653 brought in its train minor change in the excise commission in September. Thomas Bulstrode and William Parker were the only old commissioners to continue on a smaller three-person commission (Luke Hodges was the third member). A parliamentary act of 24 December 1653 reduced the commissioners' poundage rate from 3*d* to 1*d* in the pound, and forbade them from farming out the excise without the Protector's permission.[62] None the less, farming continued to be used for portions of the excise collection, in spite of its shortcomings, because the regularity of the farmers' payments greatly eased the government's budgeting problems.

Another act appointed a commission to inquire into the excise arrears and to punish tax evaders. This commission was to hear all complaints and could sequester the estates of anyone violating the excise ordinances.[63] These efforts to eliminate the arrears and increase the excise revenue had mixed results, as the declared account of the excise summarized in Table 7.3 indicates. The declared account in Table 7.3 ended in March 1654 and is the last one available until the declared account for the period beginning in March 1658.[64] Possibly this account ends in March 1654 because from that date the excise commissioners and farmers paid their receipts and farm rents directly into the Exchequer, which had been re-established as a central treasury by the Protectorate.

Table 7.3: Declared Account of the Excise, 30 September 1653–25 March 1654[65]

Receipts and sources	Amount (£)	%
a. Money collected in London	97,202	50.9
b. Money collected in counties	67,437	35.3
c. Money for confiscated goods	25,112	13.0
d. Profits of fines	1,275	0.7
Total	191,026	

Expenditures	Amount (£)	%
a. Paid to Navy Treasurer	130,586	67.5
b. Excise salaries and costs	20,295	10.5
c. Interest paid on secured debt	16,902	8.7
d. Paid for army uses	9,775	5.1
e. Salaries of navy office	7,730	4.0
f. Paid for wounded and sick	4,206	2.2
g. Paid former excise farmers	4,004	2.0
Total	193,498	

Tax farming was used for the collection of the excise levied on beer and ale, while the large excise on other commodities continued to be collected directly.[66] Beer production was a big industry in the larger towns like London and Bristol and, therefore, was easier to tax and more desirable for a tax farmer. The excise on many other items was much more difficult to gather because of the decentralized nature of English manufacturing and retailing. If the government wanted to continue to collect excise on many consumption items, it had to continue to operate its own excise system throughout England. This possibly accounts for the decision to continue direct collection alongside a tax farm.

The half-year account in Table 7.3 shows a decline in the portion of the expenditures made for payment of debt interest and principal. Administrative costs remained at their normal 10 per cent, while some of the navy's administrative costs were directly paid by the excise commissioners. The enormous naval expenses of the First Dutch War explain this shift. The majority of excise expenditure in 1653/4 supported the navy, while only a small 5 per cent of gross receipts was provided to support the army. Here again, we see evidence of English governments moving away from the idea of a dedicated revenue for a dedicated purpose and towards the modern idea of a central treasury. The costs of the Dutch war and the Scottish campaigns in the same period possibly encouraged this shift.[67]

The excise's gross receipts of £191,000 included direct and farmed taxes, showing an annual yield of £380,000, an amount only slightly smaller than the average annual revenue of £387,000 from 1650 to 1653. The First Dutch War did not adversely affect the gross revenues of the excise or customs. Indeed, the war may have caused an economic boom due to the greatly increased ship-building and provisioning requirements of the navy and the undiminished logistical needs of the army.

Arrears of collections declined to around £120,000 by March 1654, although the account is damaged and this figure is difficult to read. This is the cumulative figure for arrears, indicating by its small decline that excise taxes were possibly becoming more accepted.[68] Finally, the government continued to pay large amounts of money for the relief of sick, wounded, and maimed sailors and soldiers and their families. These payments continued during the Interregnum, accompanying the establishment of military hospitals in England and Ireland.[69]

In July 1654, Parliament passed an act for the consolidated payment of all major revenues except the assessment into one treasury of receipt, officially approving the re-establishment of the Exchequer that had taken place earlier in the year. Concurrently, Parliament passed acts ordering a committee to be established to investigate the financial obligations of the

Protectorate and to explain the procedures for taking the accounts of the soldiers to determine their pay arrears.[70] These acts showed the muddle into which the accounting of the Westminster government had fallen during the hectic days of the First Dutch War and the willingness of the Protectorate to honour previous 'public faith' obligations incurred since 1642. This effort was capped off with a parliamentary act in October 1654 ordering all persons who had collected money, arms, horses, or supplies for the service of the Long Parliament to 'deliver into the commissioners [of the Committee for Taking the Accounts] . . . a plain alphabetical list . . . of the persons . . . from whom, and the sums of money or other things they have taken' so that these obligations could be audited and substantiated debts paid.[71] Excise revenue paid off part of this accumulated state debt, as the summaries in Tables 7.1, 7.2 and 7.3 indicate. Continuation of the excise was due in part to the understanding by many people that they would never see the money owed to them by the state without the repeated levying of the tax.

Excise operations went on in much the same way during this period of transition to a single treasury of receipt. Annual acts continued the excise, while attempts were made to determine total government debt.[72] In December 1654, a report to Parliament estimated the debt and revenue of the Protectorate. As a result of this summary Parliament and the Protector agreed to the long-term levying of the excise, customs, and assessment.[73] This decision marked the acceptance of these regular taxes as a normal part of peacetime government revenue.

In this same report, an attempt was made to develop a budget and to convince the Protector to reduce the annual cost of the army in England by £138,547.[74] This procedure indicated the enduring desire of Members of Parliament to deal with the state's financial matters. Cromwell allowed some reduction in the army to be made in response to this budget proposal, but his government continued to maintain an army and navy whose combined costs approached £2 million per year.[75] Parliament's attempt to curtail the army and to assert its right to affect such matters of state was a confirmation of its increased role in the daily management of governmental affairs.

From 1654, excise receipts were paid into the Exchequer and the expenditures were accounted for with other Exchequer revenues and disbursements. Table 7.4 is a summary of the excise revenues, to include those of the farmers of the beer excise, which were paid into the Exchequer from 1654 to 1660. The gross receipts of the excise were at least 10–15 per cent more than these totals, since the commissioners and farmers deducted their costs, profit, and salaries before they paid the amounts listed below into the treasury.

Table 7.4: Net Excise Revenue, 28 October 1654 –4 July 1660[76]

Period	Direct excise (£)	Beer farm (£)
28 Oct 1654–26 Sept 1655	335,005	–
27 Sep 1655–27 Sept 1656	352,644	–
28 Sep 1656–25 Sept 1657	364,709	10,700
26 Sep 1657–28 Sept 1658	258,322	204,140
29 Sep 1658–27 Sept 1659	203,476	189,181
28 Sep 1659–4 Jul 1660	193,125	19,728
Total	1,707,281	+ 423,749
Grand total		= 2,131,030

Excise receipts provided an annual average net revenue to the Exchequer in this 68-month period of roughly £376,000. This amount compares favourably to the approximately £300,000 in average net excise revenue provided annually to the Westminster governments from 30 September 1647 to 25 March 1654. The fluctuations in the beer excise receipts in the table show that the rent for the beer excise farm was not fixed. The farmers were required to surrender profits above a certain level to the Exchequer, making the farm less lucrative to the farmers than the customs farm had been before 1640, when the farmers could keep all of the profit. The regular parliamentary involvement with the internal financial operations of the excise farm, and the fact that the state received the receipts that exceeded the rent, changed the concept of revenue farming into one that operated a great deal more like modern government's contracting-out procedures.[77] While the practice of farming of parts of the excise persisted until 1683, its procedures were basically established during the Interregnum and maintained at the Restoration, however grudgingly.[78]

The navy continued to receive the lion's share of the Exchequer revenue in the late 1650s, while the army received the majority of its financial support from the monthly assessments.[79] The excise had ceased to be a main source of money for the army, while still providing a large part of the state's total revenue.

Detailed evidence concerning the receipts and net revenue of the excise is available in the declared accounts of the excise for the period from 25 March 1658 to 18 August 1660. There is a gap in the existing accounts between August 1660 and November 1662, when the next account starts. The first of these accounts covers some of the time and revenues listed in Table 7.4, and the two accounts agree closely. These declared accounts and the accounts for the period after 1662 show that most of the excise procedures established in the 1640s and 1650s were continued by the Restoration governments.[80]

The various declared accounts of the excise commissioners for the period from September 1647 to August 1660 provide the evidence needed to make some general conclusions about the efficiency of the excise system during the civil wars and Interregnum. Total excise administrative costs were £292,161, or roughly 10 per cent of the gross receipts of £2.9 million. Another £68,836 was unaccounted for in the records provided to the auditors, bringing the cost of administration to 12.6 per cent if these sums ended up in the pockets of the commissioners and their staffs. The excise's administrative costs compared favourably with the 10–15 per cent of receipts spent on excise administration in the period from 1660 to 1688.[81] We lack the declared accounts to use as evidence for estimating the revenue and administrative costs for the three years before September 1647 and part of the late 1650s; however, the report made to the House of Commons in late 1647 noted that

Table 7.5: Excise Receipts and Expenditures, 25 March 1658–18 August 1660[82]

Receipts and sources	Amount (£)	%
a. Money collected in London	400,583	60.2
b. Money collected in counties	258,308	38.8
c. Fines and forfeitures	6,471	1.0
d. Miscellaneous	37	
Total	665,399	

Expenditures	Amount (£)	%
a. Paid into the Exchequer	474,245	73.3
b. Excise salaries and costs	75,668	11.7
c. Interest paid on secured debt	56,669	8.8
d. Repayments to retailers	20,584	3.2
e. Paid on special orders and warrants	19,043	3.0
Total	646,209	

Table 7.6: Estimated Excise Revenue, September 1643– July 1660

Period	Revenue (£)	Average per annum (£)
Sept 1643–Sept 1647[83]	1,334,532	334,000
Sept 1647–Sept 1650[84]	860,890	286,000
Sept 1650–Mar 1654[85]	1,352,073	387,000
Mar 1654–Jul 1660[86]	2,373,742	369,000
Total	5,921,237	
Annual average, Sept 1643– July 1660		493,000

administrative costs did not exceed 2*s* in the pound (or 10 per cent) and there is no evidence to contradict this report.[87]

The total revenue raised by excise taxes from 1643 to 1660 cannot be determined exactly because of the absence of the accounts for the first three years. Nevertheless, an approximate total of receipts can be made with reasonable accuracy thanks to the information in the excise ordinance of September 1647 about the amounts provided by the excise to that date. Additional large sums were secured by the anticipated excise revenue as well, and later paid off with sequestrations and the receipts from various land sales, but Table 7.6 (above) omits these later amounts.

THE RESTORATION AND CONTINUATION

The political confusion in 1659 and the Restoration in 1660 did not end the use of excise taxes in England. Future excise revenues estimated at over £400,000 were included in all financial schemes put forward to support the royal government in 1660, although excise receipts consistently fell short of that amount.[88] The continuation of the excise on liquor at the Restoration confirmed the shift in English attitudes about taxation in general and the excise in particular.[89] It was now held acceptable that nearly all members of society should pay some taxes, regardless of wealth. Charles II and his leading financial administrators felt that the excise was one of the best ways to make this happen, and the Cavalier Parliament was unable to develop an acceptable alternative in 1662.[90]

From 1660 to 1662, the excise was directly collected, rather than farmed. When farming was resumed in 1662, the personnel, procedures, and organization of the system remained largely unchanged.[91] Commissioners appointed by the government retained significant oversight powers, while the farmers had full administrative control of the London excise office. The excise was broken into a number of separate tax farms during the 1660s, with separate farmers collecting the taxes in the counties and in London. However, by the mid-1670s, the system was well on its way to consolidation under a single group of farmers, easing the return to complete direct collection in 1683.[92]

Excise taxes were retained after 1660 because the traditional ordinary revenues of the customs and royal demesne were insufficient to sustain the costs of government and the maintenance of permanent military forces in peacetime. The Royal Navy kept over sixty major warships on active service in the peacetime years of 1660 to 1664, while the King's standing army numbered over 17,000 men in his three kingdoms and Tangiers. A direct result of the Military Revolution in England was the wartime creation and the peacetime retention of excise taxation to support permanent military forces.

Parliament kept only the excise on alcoholic beverages in 1660. The costs of the Second Dutch War, however, made it necessary to increase the liquor excises and to add other items to the list of taxable goods. Excise receipts show only moderate results from these increases before 1670 because of the adverse effects which the London fire and the plague had on overall economic activity. Additional items were added to the rate book in the early 1670s in an attempt to bring the revenue up to its desired level. The prosperity of much of that decade further increased the annual yield of the excise taxes. The data in Table 7.7 reflects these points and provides a basis to evaluate the importance of excise receipts to total state revenue during the second half of the seventeenth century.

Table 7.7: Net Excise Receipts and Total State Revenue, March 1660–Michaelmas 1700[93]

Period	Total (£)	Excise (£)	%	Excise per annum (£)
Mar 1660–M 1664	5,208,842	1,358,475	26.1	302,000
M 1664–Ms 1669	9,251,201	1,394,625	15.1	293,000
Ms 1669–Ms 1674	9,005,725	2,236,773	24.8	447,000
Ms 1674–Ms 1679	8,261,103	2,721,303	32.9	544,000
Ms 1679–Ms 1684	7,286,176	2,418,914	33.2	483,000
Ms 1684–Ms 1688	7,701,732	1,837,983	23.9	459,000
Nov 1688–M 1691	8,613,190	2,429,750	28.2	769,000
M 1691–M 1695	19,643,620	3,915,411	19.9	978,000
M 1695–M 1700	24,301,914	5,759,988	23.7	1,152,000

M = Michaelmas, Ms = Midsummer

Excise receipts reflect the level of civilian consumption to a certain extent. During periods of peace (1678 to 1688), excise receipts made up over 30 per cent of total state revenue, indicating that civilian consumption was up and other taxes down. Excise taxes were dramatically expanded in wartime, leading to higher receipts, but the excise fell as a percentage of total state revenue as direct taxes, and especially the assessment or Land Tax, were raised. During wartime, however, excises were easy to increase quickly and thus were always an important part of war finance after 1642.

RETURN TO DIRECT COLLECTION

The gross yield of the excise grew steadily after 1674, with the end of the Second Dutch War. Even with the check to economic activity brought by the French war of 1677/8, gross and net receipts grew steadily, although Parliament allowed the rates on a number of additional items to lapse.[94] This upward trend in receipts prompted considerable interest in the resumption of direct collection, while the successful organization and centralization of excise administration made by the farmers in the 1670s made centralized government collection a feasible and profitable option.

Farming had replaced direct collection in 1662 because the royal government found it difficult to collect the excise taxes and because of the King's desperate need to get large cash advances from the farmers secured with the anticipated excise receipts. By 1674, the gross receipts of the excise had clearly begun to outrun the rents paid by the farmers, while the increasingly strong Treasury imposed modifications on the lease which limited the farmers' profits and forced them to pay their running cash balances into the Exchequer on a more frequent basis.[95] In 1677, the terms of the lease required the Treasurer of the Excise to make a independent quarterly report of the excise's gross receipts to the Treasury, making it more difficult for the farmers to reap large profits on the growing revenue.

The government's limitation of the excise farmers' gains caused the tax farmers to attempt to reduce administrative costs below the level necessary to provide sufficient personnel to operate the system efficiently throughout the country. This, in turn, limited the growth of gross revenue. These factors combined to convince the King and his Treasury officials to resume direct collection of the excise permanently in 1683.[96]

Commissioners of the state again collected the excise directly beginning in June 1683. Their declared accounts provide evidence about the wisdom of the King's decision to resume direct collection.

Table 7.8: Excise Receipts and Costs, 24 June 1683–24 June 1700[97]

Period	Gross (£)	Net (£)	Net per annum (£)	Costs (£)
1683–9	4,206,005	3,648,301	608,000	479,748
1689–95	6,629,840	6,002,018	1,000,000	461,414
1695–1700	4,652,394	4,269,073	711,000	438,142
Total	15,488,239	13,919,392		1,379,304
Average per annum			818,000	

The return to direct collection increased the net receipts of the excise to the Exchequer dramatically. The excise commissioners paid more than £600,000 per year into the Exchequer. This was 86.74 per cent of their gross excise receipts. The costs of administration averaged 11.4 per cent in the peacetime period of 1683 to 1688. When war came in 1689, Parliament levied excise duties on a number of new commodities and raised it on others already taxed. The gross receipts of the excise jumped dramatically to over £1.1 million annually from 1689 to 1695, while annual net receipts paid by the commissioners into the Exchequer increased over 60 per cent to £1 million. In this same period the costs of excise administration fell to 6.96 per cent of total receipts.

The methods used by the excise commissioners to collect and account for money in the 1680s and 1690s were not much different than those used by the excise commissioners of the 1640s. The excise bureaucracy was second only in size to the customs in the 1690s and by 1708 it had become the largest revenue establishment in Britain.[98]

The return to the direct collection of the excise was a triumphant vindication of Treasury policy. The successful experience with direct collection in the 1640s and 1650s played some part in the government's willingness to try to use direct collection again. After the disruptions of the Restoration, the excise farmers had reorganized the excise structure to a certain extent, passing on to the state's commissioners an efficient organization which gave the government unrestricted benefit of the excise yield.[99] The organization of the excise by 1683 was not much different than it had been in the civil wars, although Treasury control was significantly more effective than the Long Parliament's oversight. By 1688, gross excise yield reached £732,000, providing the financial resources needed to pay off war debts during periods of peace. While the excise would never raise enough money to pay for the current costs of warfare, it remained a 'stock of credit' for government borrowing, just as it had done in the 1640s.

IMPLICATIONS OF THE EXCISE

The retention of the excise, after 1660, reflected a major change in English attitudes about who should pay taxes in normal times and the role of the central government in local affairs. Before the mid-century financial revolution, tax theory had tended to hold that the wealthy should bear the financial burdens of the government, and the working poor should be spared.[100] The retention of an excise meant that this attitude had changed. The excise is a consumption tax levied on all members of society that is not set according to means or ability to pay.

Nearly continuous warfare in the British Isles from 1638 to 1660 made it necessary for English governments to maintain large armies as well as navies. Both Royalists and Parliamentarians adopted excise taxation in 1643 to try to pay for their armies. Excise revenues were insufficient for the support of the armies, and the steadily increasing costs of naval operations and warfare prevented the use of the customs for financial support of the army. When Charles II returned in 1660 there was no serious talk about the elimination of excise taxes. Charles II's wars again brought the English state to the brink of financial disaster by 1672. The periods of peace in Charles's reign, however, were not accompanied by total demobilization. The costs of the peacetime army and navy dwarfed total state expenditures from the peacetime years before 1638. Consequently, Parliament continued to employ excise taxes as one of the pillars of state finance.

As England assumed its role as a great power under William III, the excise played an important part in providing the money needed to fight the wars against France that continued for nearly twenty years. The excise provided 35.7 per cent of the state's revenue from 1689 to 1695, while the customs provided 21.5 per cent. These steady revenues, along with the Land Tax, made possible the credit operations so important to Dickson's financial revolution.[101] The French wars were funded to a significant degree with borrowed money, most of which was not paid back immediately, but instead became part of a long-term national debt.

The debt accumulated in the two long wars against France from 1689 to 1713 far exceeded the debts of the royal and republican governments of the mid-seventeenth century, but such debts had ceased to be the hindrance to government operations that they had been in the crises of 1640 to 1660. The development of a funded national debt was only possible because of the financial foundations laid in the 1640s with the establishment of the excise and the assessment. The excise, more than any other tax, was innovative and a true parliamentary tax. Its continuation marked the effective demise of the notion that the monarch could 'live of his own' in peacetime, and the semi-feudal ideas of government fiscal theory that accompanied that notion. The excise became the most important English tax in the eighteenth century for the same reasons that it had been of such use to the Parliamentarians in 1643.[102]

The third pillar of state finance that was developed by the Long Parliament was the assessment. It, like the excise, evolved in that Parliament's first fiscal crisis of the civil war. The story of the development of the assessment and its importance to war finance is told in the next chapter.

CHAPTER EIGHT

The Assessment

The assessment was the largest single source of income devised by John Pym and the Long Parliament for the support of the New Model Army. Like the excise, it was created during the greatest political and military crises facing the Parliamentarians in the period 1643 to 1645. Again like the excise, it was continued through the civil wars, Interregnum and Restoration, becoming eventually known as the Land Tax in the 1690s.[1]

In October 1642, the Battle of Edgehill destroyed many Parliamentarians' hopes that the creation of Essex's army 'would procure a peace without fighting'.[2] Parliament had failed to overawe Charles I and was forced to raise a second army to defend London. Charles made no sincere move to compromise after Edgehill, and the Roundheads made none to submit. With the prospect of prolonged civil war looming in the winter and spring of 1643, the Long Parliament attempted to establish its war effort on a firmer footing. The financial foundation of its cause had been the possession of London – the largest port, the centre of the customs revenue, and the chief financial market in Britain. The customs provided a steady revenue for the navy, but none of the money needed to support the Parliamentarian armies. During 1642, Parliament had resorted to voluntary and involuntary loans, locally assessed taxes, and fines on Royalists' property in areas under its control to pay for its forces.[3] In spite of these efforts, it was evident by early 1643 that these extraordinary sources of revenue were inadequate to meet the financial needs of the armies. Other regular sources of revenue, in addition to the customs, were needed.

Under the skilful leadership of John Pym, the Long Parliament established the basic components of a financial system that was to become the mainstay of English state finance.[4] The three regular revenues in this system were the customs, extended for another year in January 1643, the excise, created in July 1643, and the assessment. Parliament passed the first assessment ordinance in February 1643.[5] Within two years, the assessment became the largest source of parliamentary revenue and the primary source of money for the support of the army during the next seventeen years. As such, it also became an important part of the financial base for the credit operations of the Westminster governments.

WEEKLY ASSESSMENTS

The Lords and Commons realized, by February 1643, that a regular and national source of revenue was needed to support their forces. The two houses

> fully satisfied and resolved in their consciences, that they . . . [had] lawfully taken up arms, and may and ought to continue the same for the necessary defence of themselves . . . the only causes for which they have raised and do continue an army and forces, which cannot possibly be maintained . . . without the speedy raising of large and considerable sums of money. . . . Be it ordained . . . that for the intents and purposes aforesaid, the several and weekly sums mentioned shall be charged, rated, taxed, and levied.[6]

This ordinance was the first of many that created and progressively modified a tax assessed on cash, plate, rents, land, tithes, annuities, offices, and even cows.[7] The Parliamentarians modified this 'weekly assessment' to make it more effective as they became experienced in war finance and firmer in their resolve to defeat the King. The question as to whether changes in the nature of war and its financial demands forced the creation of a more centralized state, or vice versa, is clearly answered for seventeenth-century England by the way in which the creation of the assessment and excise tax systems were directly linked to the military events of 1643 to 1645. For the next decade, Parliament adjusted the ways in which these revenues were collected and administered. Ten years of continuous warfare on land and sea made it impossible for the English state to do without these steady sources of revenue.

Parliament levied its first weekly assessment as a fixed amount on the counties, rather than as a tax on individual wealth. The weekly assessment was a logical descendent of the Tudor subsidy and the ship-money tax of Charles I. Like the subsidy, it was locally assessed and collected. Like ship-money and unlike the subsidies, the assessment was established with fixed county and national quotas to be raised. Each county and major town received a fixed quota to raise for the assessment period. While previously, with the subsidy, the gentry increasingly had avoided paying the costs of the central government, under the quota system of the assessment responsibility for the collection of the full amount of parliamentary taxation came to rest firmly on the shoulders of local leaders.[8] This local control probably accounted in large part for the remarkably little opposition to the assessment's collection and for its extremely high efficiency.

The Long Parliament used the Caroline ship-money levy as a model for the first assessment's apportionment. The other major precedent was the £400,000 levy raised in 1640/1 to pay for the expenses of the Scottish Army in northern England and to fund the disbandment of the English army used in the Second Bishops' War. It is unclear how much of this quota tax was collected, but its nature as a national levy was clearly based on the Caroline ship-money tax and it was logically part of the precedent followed by the Parliamentarians when they instituted the weekly assessment.[9]

The weekly assessment of 1643 lacked an accurate means of valuing property. Therefore, there was no reliable correlation between a county's assessment quota and its ability to pay.[10] The first 'weekly assessment' was levied on Royalist-controlled counties as well as on those under Parliamentarian control.[11] Parliament expected it to raise £33,750 weekly, or £135,000 monthly, if all counties and cities paid their quotas. However, the counties controlled by the King certainly did not do so. The Parliamentarians must have realized that this would be the case. Their intent in assessing them anyway may have been to ensure that once those Royalist areas were secured by Parliamentarian forces they could be made to pay assessment arrears.[12] Perhaps also, since the Long Parliament claimed to be the sole legitimate English government, it may have felt that a failure to rate every county could have been seen as *de facto* recognition of another sovereign authority in England.

The February 1643 assessment ordinance was intended to operate for three months, unless the King disbanded his army. Cash was urgently needed and, therefore, Parliament rated London far in excess of 'the proportion of other counties [but] the same shall not hereafter be drawn into example or consequences to their prejudice'.[13] London was the best place to raise large amounts of cash quickly in 1643, and the City leaders were willing to contribute to the war effort disproportionately due to their alliance with John Pym, leader of the Parliamentarian war party. Parliament soon rebated London £3,000 of its £44,200 monthly assessment for the duration of the ordinance to pay the salaries of the watch and the soldiers raised and paid by London for the security of London and Westminster.[14]

One of the most important provisions of the weekly assessment ordinance was the stipulation that Parliament appointed county committees to operate the assessment procedures and its collection in the counties and cities.[15] The initial membership of these committees usually reflected the traditional leadership of the localities.[16] For example, Sir John Hotham, knight and baronet, and Sir William

Strickland, baronet, were two of the members of the committee for the East Riding of Yorkshire, while Sir Thomas Fairfax was one of the members of the committee for the city of York.[17] The committees were to meet 'with all convenient speed' to ensure that the first assessment payments were made by 1 March. Once the local committees were operating, men of national political or military importance seldom attended the meetings.

The county committees generally divided into subcommittees that were responsible for the administration of the hundreds or parishes of the counties and for the appointment of one or more 'persons as they shall think fit, within their respective divisions . . . to assess all and every person' chargeable by the ordinance. The committees were to appoint 'collectors for the money so assessed' to gather the weekly assessment, and 'pay the same to the Treasurer of the Army' at the Guildhall in London. The ordinance allowed collectors to pay their receipts to other persons or places upon specific order of their county committee.[18] This last provision proved to be a weakness of the system because it enabled committees to pay local garrisons or troops, creating a situation in which money was diverted from Parliament's main army.

The assessors rated the property, profits, and rents within their jurisdictional area. Property belonging to Members of Parliament was to be assessed by their peers.[19] Assessors next prepared a copy of their assessments within one week and gave it to the committee that appointed them. The committee approved or modified the rates and gave one copy 'subscribed with their or any two of their hands to the several collectors' within ten days, and sent another copy to the Treasurer of the Army in London. In this manner, the committees, collectors, and the Treasurer of the Army all knew the amounts to be collected and forwarded to the Guildhall.[20]

Sir Gilbert Gerrard, the Treasurer of the Army, was to give an 'acquaintance' or receipt to the collectors. They, in turn, were to take this receipt to John Trenchard and William Wheeler, members of the House of Commons, for entry into a receipt book kept to allow the House to know how much money was available for the forces.[21] In theory, parliamentary committees then could make a reasonably accurate financial appraisal of the money available as they decided how much to spend for arms or for new regiments.

Parliament anticipated local resistance to the administration and collection of the assessment. Consequently, they gave the county committees the power to procure the best administrative talent available and to ensure that those men selected performed their duties efficiently and honestly.

And if any assessor or collector shall refuse the said service, or prove negligent or faulty therein, the said committee . . . shall have power to commit such assessor or collector to prison, or to set fine upon him . . . and to nominate other assessors or collectors.[22]

Additionally, collectors had the legal authority and power to deal sharply and effectively with any

person or persons, . . . corporate or not . . . [who] shall refuse to pay the sum or sums upon him or them assessed. . . . It shall be lawful to, and for, the respective collectors . . . to levy all and every sum . . . by way of distress, and sale of the goods of the person . . . to break open any house. . . . To call to their assistance any of the Trained Bands, . . . or any of the other forces of or within the county.[23]

Well before the institution of the military rule of the major generals the English Parliamentarians resorted to the use of military force to ensure the operation of their tax systems. As parliamentary control spread, the opportunity increased for Parliamentarians to use force to punish their local rivals, whether Royalists or neutral.[24] It is little wonder that the gentry came to associate a standing army with tyranny, rather than with the concept of national defence. The February 1643 ordinance also rated aliens and recusants at double and provided a triple rate for any taxpayer who unjustly escaped a portion of his tax by misleading the assessor as to his true wealth.

The administrative machinery of the assessment was simple. At no time in the next seventeen years was a large bureaucracy created. Instead, the county committees of local leaders were the heart of the system. To defray administrative costs, the weekly assessment ordinance provided a commission of 3*d* for each pound paid to the treasurer at London's Guildhall. Two pence of this commission was allowed to the collectors and the remainder was paid to the assessors and others engaged in the local administration of the tax.[25] County committees had the discretion as to how this last pence was to be divided, although it proved to be too little recompense for the effort and trouble required in the collection of the revenue. Consequently, Parliament raised the remuneration of collectors, assessors, and treasurers in later assessment ordinances.

Weekly assessments should have provided over £97,000 per month from the Parliamentarian-controlled counties. Another £38,000 per month might eventually be raised in the Royalist-controlled areas. But unfortunately, even the counties loyal to the Westminster government failed to pay their total weekly assessments in the spring of 1643. Part of the problem was caused by confusion as to how taxpayers could appeal their rates if they felt unfairly assessed. Parliament resolved this difficulty with the passage of an explanatory ordinance, on 4 March, allowing an aggrieved taxpayer to appeal his rating to his county committee. The committee was to examine his claim and relieve him of part of his tax liability if warranted. This ordinance stipulated that the person making the appeal could not escape former tax obligations levied by Parliament in 1642.[26]

Another hindrance to the smooth collection of the weekly assessment was that Londoners did not receive their disproportionately heavy assessments with raptures of joy. A committee from the London Common Council took a message to the House of Commons making it clear that if Parliament expected a £60,000 loan for the pay of Essex's army, members of the Houses must subscribe to the loan, promise the repayment of the loan with the first receipts of the assessment and, after hostilities, disband the army well away from London.[27] Parliament agreed to these demands and, on 28 February, secured repayment of the loan with the anticipated assessment receipts. They also promised to repay the amount in three months with 8 per cent annual interest.[28]

In spite of these concessions, the Long Parliament had to pass another 'ordinance for the explanation of the weekly assessment in London' in April, pledging the 'public faith' for the repayment of £24,000 out of every £40,000 collected in London. This repayment was 'to be restored proportionately to the parties that shall advance the same'. This provision in effect made part of the assessment a forced loan rather than a tax. Such a step indicates that the collectors were having a difficult time bringing in London's heavier assessment. The problem of London's arrears would not be solved fully until after Pride's Purge.

As another concession to Londoner's sensibilities in 1643, the capital's assessments were to be paid to the City financiers John Wollaston, John Warner, John Towse, and Thomas Andrews, instead of to the Treasurer of the Army.[29] These London aldermen later became the Treasurers at War in March 1645 and after that date managed the central affairs of the assessment system until 1651. Their assumption of control of the London assessments occurred at the same time as other London aldermen took over the customs, giving a closely knit group of London financiers control of, and the administrative profits from, a large portion of the Parliamentarian state's revenue.[30] The assessment treasurers received the assessments at the Guildhall alongside Gilbert Gerrard, the Treasurer of the Army. They entered the amount of their receipts in the parliamentary account book kept by John Trenchard and William Wheeler.

Parliament also found it difficult to collect the weekly assessment in most counties. Part of the problem was that a number of Members of

Parliament were reluctant to leave London and return to their localities to perform their duties as members of their county committees. The leaders remaining in the counties were often reluctant to institute the assessment process without the Members of Parliament at home to share the burden and, perhaps, the odium of the tax. Two weeks after the assessment was to have begun, the House of Commons had to order the parliamentary members of county committees to take copies of the ordinances into their counties and to have their servants pick up the rating books for their assessment at Haberdashers' Hall to take to the local committees.[31] As late as 24 March, Bedford and Hampshire still had not received their rate books nor put the assessment into operation.[32]

The assessment system began to produce a trickle of revenue in March and April, enabling the Treasurer of the Army to pay £3,000 to Mr White, the financial agent for the force commanded by Lord Fairfax.[33] Parliament also asked for a £60,000 loan from the London Common Council, and received the first third of it by mid-March. However, the subscriptions for the loan came in much slower than expected, forcing Wollaston and his associates to advance the remaining £40,000, secured by the 'public faith', once they were appointed to serve as Treasurers at War.[34]

Parliament never collected the weekly assessment with any regularity in London or the counties. Some of the weekly assessment's greatest weaknesses beyond its novelty were the small sums involved for each taxpayer each week, the lack of Parliamentarian control over many of the counties, taxpayer resistance to any direct tax, and the reluctance of many local leaders to implement an unpopular measure as unpaid agents. Most noticeably, London's assessments fell rapidly into arrears. The House of Commons passed resolutions encouraging assessment committees to hasten collections and to pay their rapidly accruing arrears. Such pleading did not improve the situation.[35] Parliament even empowered the committee at Haberdashers' Hall, which had originally been established to raise loans for the support of its armies, 'to send for committees, collectors, and assessors, and to require an account of them what proceedings they had made in the service upon the weekly assessment', while concurrently requiring London's trained bands to send musketeers with collectors to the houses of people who refused to pay their taxes.[36]

These measures did little to hasten collections. None the less, in May and again in July, Parliament extended the weekly assessment another two months. If the weekly assessment had been successfully collected, the Westminster government could have secured loans upon its anticipated receipts. Most of the money borrowed in 1643 and 1644, however, was secured by anticipated excise revenue. For example, from October 1643 to March 1644, at least £90,000 was advanced by the excise commissioners for the pay and supply of Parliamentarian armies, while only £60,000 was secured by assessment receipts.[37] Mrs Everett Green, the editor of the *Calendar of the Committee for Advances of Money*, concludes that the total receipts of the weekly assessments of 1643 and 1644 were only £260,000 of the £1,700,000 anticipated.[38] If she is correct, this ratio is an abysmal record for the first year of the assessment.

It is exceedingly difficult to determine the exact yield of the weekly assessment because a large part of the cash received locally was never forwarded to London. Since the parliamentary ordinances had authorized local committees to apply their revenue towards the pay of local garrisons, many of the committees did just that.[39] The simultaneous existence of the weekly assessment and the more traditional subsidy called 'the Ordinance of the Twentieth Part', which Parliament passed in May 1643, also make it difficult to confirm Mrs Green's estimate. Certainly, the weekly assessments were not fully paid and required a great deal of enforcement, refinement, and rationalization before the assessment could become the most productive wartime revenue of the English state.

Parliament's second renewal of the weekly assessment continued the local procedures. London was not assessed in the August ordinance, and Westminster and Middlesex were rated at only £750 per week.[40] This was either an oversight or a concession to London. The August ordinance ensured that the tax on land let at 'rack rent' was to be paid by the landlord, while that on land let at 'easy rent' was the responsibility of the tenant. Otherwise, few changes were made in the assessment procedures until March 1644.

During the autumn of 1643, the need for regularly paid armies became increasingly evident as thousands of soldiers deserted the Parliamentarian cause due to lack of pay. William Waller's defeat at Roundway Down and the close-run affair of the relief of Gloucester showed the Long Parliament's military weaknesses. Scottish accession to the Parliamentarian cause and the formation of the Committee for Both Kingdoms in 1643/4 barely balanced the fall of Bristol and most of the west to Prince Rupert's Royalist army. In response to these events, the Long Parliament resolved to raise new soldiers for its Western Army and to provide a more regular financial basis for the support of its forces. A grand committee of the House of Commons resolved to raise a £20,000 loan from the excise for the recruitment of its main army and to provide a separate £20,000 monthly assessment for its financial support.[41]

REGIONAL ARMIES AND MONTHLY ASSESSMENTS

The first 'monthly assessment' ordinance was read in the Commons on 13 December 1643, and finally passed on 26 March 1644. This ordinance provided for revenue to be committed directly to the army being raised by the Earl of Essex, establishing its strength at 7,500 infantry and 3,000 cavalry. Only £8,059 of the £30,500 needed monthly for this army's support was to be raised by this monthly assessment. The ordinance set London's, Westminster's, and Southwark's monthly assessment at £6,992 and Middlesex's at £1,097.[42] The excise was expected to provide £20,444 and the Treasury of the twentieth subsidy was to raise the remaining £2,000 needed monthly to support this army.

This assessment for Essex's force was one of several passed in the winter of 1643/4 that placed financial responsibility for a specific army upon the region that it defended. Similar ordinances included one passed on 2 January for the 'recruitment and regulating the forces of the Eastern Association under the Earl of Manchester' and the 27 February ordinance empowering Thomas Fairfax to impress soldiers for the defence of Yorkshire.[43]

Essex failed to recruit his army to full strength, but he did enlist enough men to resume operations against Charles in the spring.[44] His subsequent failure to operate cooperatively with William Waller's army and his disastrous defeat at Lostwithiel, in August 1644, drove home the point that disjointed military commands and financial systems endangered the Parliamentarian cause. The lost opportunity for a decisive victory at the Second Battle of Newbury and the acrimonious dispute between Cromwell and the Earl of Manchester in late 1644 seemed to support Charles I's view that his enemies would fall out among themselves.[45] Parliament did not renew the March ordinance for the support of the Western Army when it expired in July 1644. Its importance to financial history is that it was a monthly rather than a weekly assessment, specifically earmarked for the support of one army. It was the prototype for the monthly assessment passed in 1645 to support the New Model Army.

The 1644 assessments that the Long Parliament enacted to support the regional armies are difficult to evaluate as national taxes. The only assessment ordinance passed in 1644 which could be called national was one enacted in October to provide money for the support of the British armies in Ireland, and it was collected on a very irregular basis.[46] The excise and customs continued to carry the lion's share of the Long Parliament's financial burdens for the army and navy respectively, but the financial needs of the new armies and growing fleet rapidly exceeded these resources. The use of regional associations and armies proved admirable for local defence but inappropriate for coordinated offensive action against the King's forces. The command relationships of the Parliamentarian armies were badly snarled by this proliferation of regional authorities as well. Only the Self-Denying Ordinance could cut this Gordian knot.

The Self-Denying Ordinance was first introduced in December 1644. After a long political struggle the Lords accepted this tremendous limitation of their traditional military role in April 1645.[47] The ordinance stipulated that no Member of Parliament could hold a commission in the armed forces. Therefore, all members of the House of Lords were automatically removed from their army commands and members of the House of Commons had to resign either their military positions or their seats in the House. The intent was to end the internal bickering among the officers in the armies' high commands, and to get on with the war against the King with forces commanded by men who were willing to fight for a complete Parliamentarian victory.

THE NEW MODEL ORDINANCE

The Long Parliament sought to get a handle on its army's financial situation by also reorganizing its forces in 1645. The Self-Denying Ordinance was accompanied by a series of other measures, passed between January and April 1645, creating the New Model Army, appointing Sir Thomas Fairfax as the Lord General of all forces, and providing for the financial support of the new unified army establishment.[48] The Committee of Both Kingdoms – the closest thing to an executive that the Parliamentarians had – presented a report to the House of Commons in January 1645 calling for the audit of the soldiers' accounts and recommending that the Treasurer of the Army, Gilbert Gerrard, give debentures to the troops for their pay arrears. The House accepted this proposal and resolved that the New Model Army should consist of 6,000 horse, 1,000 dragoons, and 14,400 foot soldiers. The pay of this army totalled £44,952 per month, at 8*d* per day per foot soldier, and 2*s* per day for each horseman.[49] The ordinance creating the New Model Army also provided for the levy of a monthly assessment for its support. This levy was to fall only on those counties and towns then under Parliamentarian control. Table 8.1 lists the counties assessed and their monthly assessment.

Table 8.1: Monthly Assessment Rate, February 1645[50]

County or town	Amount (£)	County or town	Amount (£)
London and Middlesex	8,059.75	Kent	7,070
Essex	6,760	Surrey	2,000
Suffolk	7,070	Sussex	3,927.75
Norfolk	7,070	Derby	516
Norwich	366	Rutland	184
Lincoln	2,070	Warwick	300
Hertford	2,432.5	Leicester	250
Isle of Ely	728.6	Northampton	550
Cambridge	2,171.4	Bedford	1,000
Huntington	1,020		
Total			53,546

This assessment was to be in force from 1 February 1645 to 30 November 1645, giving creditors the security of over £500,000 for collateral for money they advanced against anticipated assessment receipts. The ordinance included remedies for problems that had emerged in the collection of the previous assessments. For example, the county committees appointed by this ordinance were to meet together within eight days to implement the assessment and 'afterward, seven of them at least, shall twice every week at least, meet . . . and appoint for the more speedy execution of this ordinance'.[51] Parliament recognized that the county committees were the key instrument of parliamentary administration and, therefore, they needed to meet regularly. The ordinance expanded the membership of the committees, making it easier to get sufficient participation to carry out daily business. County committees were given the power to issue warrants to whomever they thought fit to serve as assessors. The rates set by the assessors were to be based on every person having any real property or personal property, according to the 'most equal and usual rates'.[52] These provisions were major concessions to the principle of local control of tax assessment.

The New Model Ordinance provided for a national army and a national tax. It repealed the previous ordinances assessing regional associations of counties, although their arrears were still considered due. Collectors were to pay the receipts of the assessment monthly to the London treasurers. Furthermore, the rates were more proportionate to the counties' abilities to pay – especially for London and Middlesex. The ordinance did not assess those parts of England still under Royalist control, making it more feasible to anticipate future receipts reliably.

The measure also mandated that assessors provide a copy of their assessments within six days to the county committee that had appointed them. The committee reviewed, signed, and sealed copies of this assessment, providing one copy to the collectors, one to the treasurers at the London Guildhall, and a third copy to the parliamentary Committee for the Accounts of the Kingdom.[53] This committee had the power to administer oaths to the representatives of the county committees who brought the copies of the assessment to London in a manner similar to former Exchequer procedures.

The county committees continued to appoint the collectors, who were allowed 1 d per pound for the costs of collections and another ½d per pound for the payment of their clerks. 'If any question or difference' was to arise about the assessment rates or its collection, county committees had the power to resolve the conflict and to use force to ensure that the assessments were paid. Aggrieved taxpayers could still appeal their rates to their county committee and the county committee was the final arbiter in the appeal.[54]

Parliament also improved the assessment's accounting procedures considerably in 1645. County committees were required to provide Parliament with details of their proceedings. No place or person was exempt from the rates, and the treasurers provided the collectors with receipts for the money sent to London. Thousands of these receipts, beginning in 1645, survive in the Public Record Office, testifying to the successful operation of the system and substantiating the view that the majority of the monthly assessments reached the Treasurers at War in the Guildhall.[55]

The Westminster government moved quickly to raise an £80,000 loan in anticipation of the receipts of the February 1645 monthly assessment to pay for the New Model Army's recruitment. London's leading financiers and merchants, as well as many Members of Parliament, subscribed money to make up this loan, and £83,610 was quickly provided to the Treasurers at War.[56] The London Common Council extracted the following concessions during the negotiations for this loan.

> Those persons that shall advance . . . shall have the nominations of the treasurers for the receiving all the monies to be gathered upon the whole ordinance. . . . These treasurers shall have a salary of three pence in the pound . . . 400 pounds per annum for one who shall be appointed by Parliament to keep a clerk upon all receipts of the country.[57]

The ordinances, including the loan agreement passed on 28 March 1645, provided a more efficient financial system. This system raised the majority of the large amounts of money needed to support the New Model Army during the First Civil War. Henceforth, the collection of the assessment became increasingly reliable and well accounted for by the eight Treasurers at War.

The Treasurers at War included four London aldermen, Sir John Wollaston, Thomas Andrews, John Warner, and Thomas Adams, and four merchants, Abraham Chamberlain, George Witham, Francis Allen, and John Dethicke. All of these men except Allen had been prominent in London financial and commercial affairs before 1642. Six of them became aldermen before or during the 1640s, and their political affiliations were definitely Parliamentarian.[58] During the political struggles in London, from 1647 to 1649, Adams and Chamberlain were probably political Presbyterians. Adams was not reappointed as a Treasurer of War in 1647, and neither was reappointed in 1649. Towse died in 1645 and Warner, a political Independent, was still serving as a treasurer and as the army's pick for Lord Mayor in 1648. Dethicke, Andrews, and Wollaston were Independents who retained their Treasurers at War positions through 1651. Witham's political affiliation is uncertain. He was not reappointed in 1647 or 1649, and Allen, 'who combined political and commercial interests in the city with considerable financial expertise', was closely associated with Cromwell. Allen served as a treasurer until 1651 and as a member of the Rump Parliament and the Commonwealth's Council of State.[59] Because many of these men were Independents, the central treasury of the assessment remained generally in the same hands from 1645 to 1651.

The Treasurers at War declared accounts for their service have survived and provide detailed information about the operation and success of the assessment as a national direct tax.[60] These men operated the London Guildhall office and treasury of the assessment, assisted by a number of clerks and deputies and Sir Gilbert Gerrard, Treasurer of the Army. A parliamentary committee determined how the revenue was to be spent and issued payment warrants to the Treasurers at War telling them to whom the money should be paid.[61]

The Committee for Taking the Accounts of the Kingdom, established in February 1644, improved the House of Common's control of the assessment system since the New Model Ordinance required the county assessment committees to give an account of their tax collection to this parliamentary committee regularly. Many of these reports from the county committees are in the State Papers, showing the successful implementation of central control of the assessment.[62] This system continued through the Interregnum, with the Protector and his Council replacing the parliamentary oversight committees after 1653. Such close parliamentary involvement with the affairs of the assessment was a harbinger of future parliamentary control upon which historians have commented as a characteristic of the English financial revolution in the 1690s.[63]

THE OPERATION OF THE ASSESSMENT

The county collectors gathered the monthly assessments successfully from 1 February 1645 to October 1646, providing receipts to the London

Guildhall treasury of £934,363 of the £1,070,720 assessed in the twenty-month period (an 87 per cent collection rate).[64] This was a much greater rate of return than that provided to the central treasury by the weekly assessments. One reason for this increase was that the county collectors only received their 1½d per pound allowance when the money arrived at the Guildhall, encouraging the remittance of money to London. The punitive provisions of the ordinances, backed by military power, and the growing Parliamentarian resolve to win the First Civil War shown by the Self-Denying Ordinance also encouraged the payment and aggressive collection of the tax. The control of the central assessment treasury by skilled London financiers helped by providing an efficient accounting system operated by men who had a lot to gain if the system worked well.

The Treasurers at War received an additional £146,000 in loans in 1645, providing the cash needed to equip the New Model Army for the campaign that led to its decisive victory at Naseby.[65] These loans were secured by the anticipated assessment receipts and were to be paid off with 8 per cent interest. The London treasurers received assessment receipts of over £46,000 per month, a tremendous increase from the roughly £34,000 per month that Gilbert Gerrard had received for the armies from all sources from August 1642 to March 1645.[66] This improvement in the amount and percentage of assessments collected reflected the growing tide of Parliamentarian victory in 1645 and 1646, a trend allowing county committees greater safety from Royalists and an expansion of the taxable areas held by parliamentary troops.

Charles I's defeat and capture in 1646 did not resolve the military and constitutional conflicts facing England. In addition, warfare continued in Ireland as the Westminster government fought to maintain its toeholds in Leinster and Ulster. In 1647, the Long Parliament planned to crush the Irish rebellion with many of the regiments of the New Model Army and to disband the rest of the army. However, the Parliamentarians were divided over the questions of what to do with the King, the government, the church, and the army. While these issues were decided, the monthly assessment was continued to pay the army.

The Treasurers at War managed the assessment revenue system and acted as the disbursing agents for the army. Their declared accounts provide, therefore, a great deal of information about both the assessment and the money spent on the Parliamentarian armies. While it would seem that such a dual role as tax collectors and disbursing officers might have offered increased opportunity for fraud, there is no evidence that the Treasurers at War took improper advantage of their situation. They certainly were well paid, but their actions were carefully monitored by parliamentary committees with both executive and audit powers.

The evidence of the declared accounts indicates that the assessment was the most efficient and least costly of all the revenue systems and schemes of the civil wars and Interregnum. Table 8.2 lists the receipts and expenditures made by the Treasurers of War. These figures are corroborated by the declared accounts of the other treasuries and financial officials involved.

Table 8.2: The Declared Account of the Treasurers at War, 1 February 1645–25 December 1651 [67]

I. Assessment receipts:

Period	Assessed (£)	Received (£)	%
1 Feb 1645–1 Oct 1646	1,070,720	934,363	87
25 Mar 1647–25 Mar 1649	1,440,000	1,135,567	78
26 Mar 1649–25 Dec 1651	3,150,000	3,158,941	100
Total	5,660,720	5,228,871	92

II. Other receipts and sources

a. Loans and advances	476,720
b. Other treasuries[68]	1,794,554
c. Fines	1,128
d. Collected and spent in counties	119,872
Total	2,392,274
Total received by Treasurers at War	7,621,145

III. Expenditures	Amount (£)	%
a. Pay of army	6,675,183	87.6
b. Army incidental charges	315,400	4.1
c. Repaid to other treasuries	270,426	3.5
d. Loans repaid and interest	251,600	3.3
e. Salaries and collection costs	108,738	1.4
Total	7,621,347	

The monthly assessment system was comparatively inexpensive to operate. It provided a very large revenue, and was collected with fair regularity, except during the crisis period of 1647 and 1648, when only 78 per cent of the taxes assessed were collected. In this five-year period 74 per cent of the £6,990,583 the Treasurers at War provided to the army for all purposes came from the assessments. Only 2 per cent of over £5.2 million in assessment receipts were spent on administering the assessment system, to include £28,134 paid to collectors for bringing the money to London. The declared account lists only £27,012 as paid by county collectors to local garrisons. Garrisons and regiments of the New Model Army, scattered throughout England in this period, were paid a total of £3,247,059 by bills of exchange, warrants, and specie provided by the London-based Treasurers at War.[69]

The Treasurers at War advanced £125,891 from their own funds for the support of the army, and received total reimbursement with 8 per cent annual interest. Their advances paid for the refit of Fairfax's army in December 1645 and helped support the Scottish army during its successful siege of Newcastle. The eight treasurers received an average of £7,747 in fees and salaries per year, from February 1645 to December 1651. This was a handsome profit, but not excessive considering the services they provided as tax collectors and disbursing agents.[70] Their control of the army financial system and assessment revenue gave the London financial community a tremendous influence on parliamentary fiscal policy and increased lenders' faith in the willingness of the Westminster government to repay its growing financial obligations. As a result, from 1644 to 1649, over £3 million in debt was accumulated by the state (excluding Royalist debt). This was eventually paid off through the sale of property rather than settled by default (see chapter four).

Englishmen paid a high percentage of their monthly assessments for several reasons. Firstly, the Long Parliament's assessment ordinances gave county committees a number of instruments of coercion, from fines to confiscation, backed by armed force, that they could use against recalcitrant taxpayers. Secondly, in counties where Parliamentarian sympathies were strong, people may have paid their assessments more willingly to support the cause because they were assured that the less-well-affected members of their community were also paying their fair share. Finally, until the autumn of 1646, many men hoped that the tax burden would be greatly eased by peace and that the arrears due to the forces would be paid off through the proceeds of the confiscation of Royalists' property.

PEACE, CRISES AND WAR

Peace in England in 1646 did not bring an end to taxes nor to the war in Ireland. Worse, Parliament's failure to reach a settlement with the King and the Independent–Presbyterian struggle in the Houses of Parliament undermined many people's willingness to pay taxes and split the county committees, preventing them from using coercion to enforce taxation. Hence, the monthly assessment collections fell off. While the apparent end of civil war prompted many Englishmen to stop paying their monthly assessment, Parliament worsened the fiscal situation by allowing the assessment authorization to lapse in October, although the arrears had started to grow months earlier in January 1646. By early 1647, assessment collections were £310,000 behind and the army's pay was £330,000 in arrears.[71] Consequently, the army was forced to take free quarter, while the timely renewal of the assessment was prevented by the growing split between the parliamentary Presbyterians and Independents. Attempts in mid-1647 to disband most of the army without satisfaction of the soldiers' arrears and to send the remaining foot regiments to Ireland sparked the army's first coup against the Long Parliament.[72] Because of its attempt to avoid its financial obligations to its soldiers in 1647, Parliament forfeited the trust and loyalty of the officers and men, creating a situation in which the army became the instrument of those who desired a radical restructuring of church and state.

In the meantime, another monthly assessment ordinance for £60,000 was passed in June 1647, continuing the methods and personnel of previous measures. This assessment was to last from 25 March 1647 to 25 March 1648 for the 'due paying of such forces under the command of Sir Thomas Fairfax . . . in such manner as the subjects . . . may no more be impoverished by free quarter. . . . And for the effectual and more vigorous carrying on the war of Ireland.'[73] The measure assessed all English and Welsh counties and lowered the rates of the Parliamentarian areas that previous ordinances had taxed.[74] In September, Parliament again appointed Wollaston and his associates as Treasurers at War and selected a new Committee of the Army, composed of members of both Houses, to oversee and authorize the expenditures of the assessment receipts. All free quarter taken since March 1647 was to be credited to the provider as taxes paid, and the assessment receipts were to be used only for the support of the forces commanded by Sir Thomas Fairfax.

Assessments, however, remained largely unpaid throughout 1647 due to the political turmoil. In desperation, another ordinance in December promised anyone who paid his past six months' assessment credit for the past nine months' taxes. Further, part of his taxes would be used to pay local garrisons and prevent the further taking of free quarter by the soldiers.[75] The accounts of the soldiers were taken in this period, with deductions made for the free quarter, clothes, and pay that had been provided previously. Debentures were printed and issued to the soldiers for their net arrears. These debentures were listed in a register as they were issued and the public faith of the nation pledged for their redemption.[76] This procedure was to be used regularly thereafter, but the outbreak of the Second Civil War in April 1648 abruptly ended the disbandment of the army and postponed the reckoning of the soldiers' accounts until 1649.

Assessment receipts and soldiers' pay remained in arrears into 1649. The New Model Army's 1648 victories over the Scots and Royalists, along with Pride's Purge in December, set the stage for the trial and execution of the King and the establishment of the republican Commonwealth in early 1649. Once the political issues were forcibly resolved, assessment collection again was enforced and the arrears collected. The Independent's victory brought coercion by the county committees back into play with a vengeance, accounting for the resumption of tax collections and the collection of arrears. The financial state of the assessment was evaluated in a report to the Commons in October 1648.

Obligations secured by assessment receipts exceeded the arrears of past assessments by at least £132,000 for the period from August 1647 to October 1648. This account omits debt and pay arrears secured on the assessment from before August 1647. Once the army's grandees had effective control of the government the Rump passed a special additional assessment on London designed to recoup the arrears of the City. Such

Table 8.3: State of the Assessment, August 1647–October 1648[77]

Item	Amount (£)
a. Total charge for fifteen months	899,964
b. Arrears of assessments	314,351
c. London's arrears only	41,103
d. Unpaid warrants on assessment	116,672
e. Free quarter and army debt (est)	110,000
f. Army pay arrears since January 1648	120,000
g. Total debt and arrears on assessment	346,672

measures were essential if the war in Ireland was to be carried on successfully.

As Table 8.3 indicates, these arrears were obligated to redeem an immense pile of government debt. In addition to the £120,000 owed to the soldiers since January, £1.5 million was owed to them and the navy's seamen for their services since 1642. An additional £1.5 million or so was owed by the government to contractors and suppliers for munitions, clothes, food, and ships. These debts were secured by the customs, excise, assessment, Irish lands, and the anticipated revenues of property sales and Royalist fines.

REPUBLICAN MANAGEMENT

The Rump Parliament moved a long way towards the resolution of its inherited financial problems by passing an ordinance for a £90,000 monthly assessment in April 1649. The monthly assessments were continued by all English parliaments until 1662. The first two and a half years of the Commonwealth were marked by well-managed and regularly paid assessments. From March 1649 to December 1651, £3,150,000 in monthly assessments were levied (see Table 8.2). The amounts assessed per month varied from £60,000 to £120,000, depending on the needs of the army for pay and supplies.[78] While Parliament hoped to lower the rates, it was careful to raise enough money to pay for the costs of its army's conquests of Ireland and Scotland largely out of current tax receipts.[79] The punitive provisions of the assessment acts were increased, with the county committees able to imprison people refusing to pay taxes and to sequester and sell their estates.

The outbreak of the First Dutch War in 1652, along with the continued occupations of Ireland and Scotland by large armies thereafter, necessitated the continuation of the assessment at the higher rate of £120,000 per month. This rate seems to have reached the limit of England's ability to pay, since only £1.5 million of the £1.8 million assessed from December 1651 to June 1653 was collected (an 84 per cent collection rate).[80] Table 8.4 provides a summary of this accounting period and makes it clear how important the assessment was to the Commonwealth's war efforts.

Although only 84 per cent of the rated amount was collected when the monthly assessment was raised to £120,000, the assessment remained the army's major source of funds and its receipts helped pay the expanding naval costs during the Dutch war as well. The costs of administering the assessment

Table 8.4: Declared Account of the Treasurers at War, 26 December 1651–24 June 1653[81]

Receipts and sources	Amount (£)	% of Total
a. Assessment receipts	1,512,059	85
b. From other treasuries	249,723	14
c. From individuals	11,944	0.6
Total	1,773,726	

Expenditures		
a. Army pay	1,442,335	81.3
b. Paid to Navy Treasurer	200,000	11.2
c. Paid to next Treasurers	90,779	5.1
d. Paid for supplies, services	30,322	1.7
e. Administration costs	5,482	0.3
f. Treasurers at War salaries	4,730	0.2
Total	1,773,648	

system fell to just under 0.6 per cent of total revenues after 1651, in part because the Treasurers at War were paid a fixed salary rather than a poundage rate of 3*d* per pound.[82] County collectors and committees still got 2*d* per pound for their pains. This amount was deducted at the county level and cost an estimated £12,600 during this period.[83] Total administrative costs for the assessment system were easily below 3 per cent of revenue, and remained so until the end of the Interregnum. Local control of the assessment process and collection remained central to efforts to keep administrative costs low and to encourage the county committees and local collectors to operate the system efficiently. These features were retained into the eighteenth century in the assessment and collection of the Land Tax, allowing regional variations and economic conditions to be taken into account.[84]

Sir John Wollaston and his associates retired from the assessment management in December 1651. William Leman and John Blackwell took their place. Blackwell and Leman were close associates of Oliver Cromwell, with Blackwell having served as a captain in Cromwell's cavalry regiment in 1645, before becoming a deputy Treasurer at War in 1646. Blackwell was part of the Independent minority in London during the struggles of 1647/8, and he became the senior deputy Treasurer at War in 1649. Leman was an obscure back-bench MP and 'a middle-level administrator'.[85]

Blackwell and Leman were joined as Treasurers at War in April 1653 by Captain Richard Deane, reflecting both the professionalization of English financial administration and the treasurers' connection to the army. Gerald Aylmer correctly observes that the Treasurers at War 'did handle millions of pounds with exemplary honesty. That they took advantage of their influential position to get priority for the settlement of their own just claims for arrears, is true; but it would have been unnatural if they had not done so. . . . Fortunate is the regime which can command such servants as this.'[86] The declared accounts and other records confirm Aylmer's conclusion.

John Blackwell served as a Treasurer at War until 1659, when the returning Rump deposed him. Blackwell, Leman, and Deane handled £5.5 million from June 1653 to December 1659. The assessment was the Protectorate's largest single source of money in that period. The monthly assessment rate was reduced from £120,000 (June 1653 to September 1654), to £90,000 (September to December 1654), to £60,000 (December 1654 to June 1657), to £35,000 per month (June 1657 to December 1659), with a total of £5.8 million assessed.[87] The decline in rates reflected the return of peace in 1654 only to a limited extent. Cromwell and his Council were reluctant to maintain taxes at such a high level. Consequently, they lowered the monthly assessment to £35,000 in 1657, in spite of the Spanish war then ongoing. Their failure to maintain the assessment at £60,000 per month was the single most important financial cause for the rapid accumulation of English state debt from 1657 to 1659. This accumulation was itself a major cause of the political and fiscal crises in 1659 that led to the demise of the Protectorate and, eventually, the return of Charles II.[88]

Table 8.5: Declared Account of the Treasurers at War, 25 June 1653–2 February 1659[89]

Receipts	Amount (£)	% of Total
a. Assessment receipts	5,164,519	94
b. From other treasurers	235,837	4.2
c. From the Exchequer	93,778	1.7
Total	5,494,134	

Expenditures		
a. Paid to the army	4,767,352	86.7
b. Paid to Navy Treasurer	726,233	13.2
c. Paid to Thomas Perry	438	0.1
Total	5,494,023	

Roughly 85 per cent of the monthly assessments were collected within this period and over £202,000 of the assessment receipts listed in Table 8.5 were paid to the Treasurers at War by county collectors for the arrears of assessments from previous assessment periods. Thus, from December 1651 to June 1653, over 94 per cent of the monthly assessments of £1.8 million was eventually collected. A similar pattern occurred for the assessments from 1653 to 1659, with £40,154 in arrears collected after February 1659.[90] The Treasurers at War remained the administrators of the army's treasury and most of their expenditures were for army purposes. During the Dutch war, however, they provided £726,333 to Richard Hutchinson for the navy's support.[91] The declared account for this period does not list the salaries and costs of administration explicitly, but the Treasurers' salaries were reduced to £2,400 per year in 1653 and totalled £15,600.[92] The poundage rate of 2d per pound for the county committees and collectors should have totalled roughly £43,000, bringing administrative costs to about £58,000, or 1.1 per cent of gross receipts.

During 1654, Parliament ordered the receipts of the excise, customs, and all revenues except the assessment to be paid into the revived Exchequer. Most of the receipts of the assessment remained committed to the army and the Treasurers at War administered them separately from the Exchequer. The Treasurers at War were professional administrators politically linked to the army and Cromwell. The local administration of the assessment remained largely unchanged during the 1650s.

The declared accounts of the Treasurers at War document the importance of the monthly assessment to the fiscal system of all English governments during the civil wars and Interregnum. Monthly assessment revenues totalled over £11.9 million from 1645 to 1659. An additional £1.94 million was raised by the English from Irish assessments in this period as well, although all of this money was spent to support the English troops occupying Ireland.[93] These receipts provided the largest single component of England's revenue in this period and the vast majority of the money used to support the professional armies deployed in England, Ireland, Scotland, Jamaica, and Dunkirk. By 1652, after the Commonwealth had sold all available property to settle the debts it inherited from the Long Parliament, the English state could never again rely on the sale of capital assets to fund military operations. This made future parliamentary participation in the financial affairs of England essential if the state was to continue to sustain the high costs of modern warfare.

RESTORATION AND BEYOND

The monthly assessments were continued after the Restoration in 1660, providing over £798,000 for the pay and arrears of the Royal Army from 1660 to April 1662.[94] The history of the development of the assessment system from 1643 to 1662 confirms Michael Braddick's recent conclusion about the revolution in English finance in the seventeenth century.

> The driving force behind innovation appears to have been warfare, although patterns of expenditure are even less easy to recover than patterns of income. War – and the debts arising from war – helped push the budget into recurring deficit between 1590 and 1610, and the strains of war contributed significantly to the resort to parliament in the 1620s and in 1639–40. The demands of civil war led to unprecedented levels of taxation, levels sustained subsequently. . . . The basis of successful military action was taxation.[95]

Most importantly, the assessments remained the pattern for English direct taxation during the later seventeenth century, until replaced by the Land Tax of 1692/3 which was directly modelled on the earlier assessments.[96] Chandaman provides, again, the evidence for an evaluation of the importance of this component of the English government's financial system from 1660 to 1688. In this case, Chandaman's figures include all 'direct taxes' levied by Parliament in these years, although the monthly assessments were far and away the most important of these.

Table 8.6: Direct Tax Receipts as Part of Total State Revenue, July 1660–Michaelmas 1700[97]

Period	Total (£)	Direct taxes (£)	%	Per annum (£)
July 1660–M 1664	5,208,842	1,703,030	32.7	425,000
M 1664–M 1669	9,251,201	5,055,888	54.6	1,012,000
M 1669–M 1674	9,005,725	1,446,965	16.1	289,000
M 1674–M 1679	8,261,103	1,307,520	15.8	261,000
M 1679–M 1684	7,286,176	521,417	7.1	104,000
M 1684–M 1688	7,701,732	10,331	0.1	2,500
M 1688–M 1691	8,613,190	3,171,739	36.8	1,057,000
M 1691–M 1695	19,643,620	7,059,064	35.9	1,765,000
M 1695–M 1700	24,301,914	7,289,303	30.0	1,458,000

M = Michaelmas

During the war years of 1665 to 1667 the assessments and poll taxes provided over half of the receipts of the Exchequer. Assessments remained an efficient way to collect state revenue because of their low administrative costs and high predictability. The assessment bureaucracy at both the central and local level remained simple and inexpensive throughout the period. But the assessment had a greater financial impact on the lives of Englishmen than any other tax, including the excise, during wartime. Its central office personnel and the county assessors and collectors became professionals who displayed a high degree of honesty in their work.

Although all parliaments after 1660 tried hard to avoid the imposition of assessment taxes, the nation's military costs forced them to regularly resort to such taxes. A steady series of assessments and poll taxes were used to pay for the costs of disbanding most of Cromwell's army in 1660 and 1661. Similar direct taxes were enacted during the Second and Third Dutch Wars (1665–7 and 1672–4) to pay the enormous costs of the Royal Navy and the smaller Royal Army. Nearly continuous warfare for the twenty-five years after 1688 made it essential for Parliament to continue the assessment, in the form of the Land Tax, alongside the excise and customs into the next century.

Although the monthly assessment was created only because of the need to support the New Model Army, an army designed with the best organizational and tactical innovations of the European Military Revolution in mind, it was continued regularly thereafter. The special relationship of this tax to 'Cromwell's Army' highlights the connection between war and English government fiscal innovation. The tactical and technical changes characteristic of the Military Revolution in England directly led to the administrative and fiscal changes known as the Financial Revolution. Both the army and the assessment system survived the seventeenth century and remained essential elements underpinning England's rise to the status of a great world power by 1714.

CHAPTER NINE

Final Reckoning: the Impact of Seventeenth-century Warfare on the English State

The most obvious impact of three decades of warfare on the English state in the mid-seventeenth century was the dramatic increase in the amounts of money required to sustain the large naval and military forces which the Westminster governments raised to fight their wars. As a result, taxation increased in an exponential fashion as the English governments collected immense sums of money. In turn, the need for heavy taxation over a long period of time forced the English to abandon many of their fiscal ideas and practices and to replace them with financial techniques and concepts of a particularly modern form.

Beginning in 1643, the Long Parliament's need to fund its armies and navy forced it to adopt new forms of regular taxation and to create the administrative systems necessary to collect, account for, and disburse the growing state revenue. The development of these taxes and the bureaucracies that managed them were central elements in the story of England's rise as a great power.[1] Over the next fifty years, the central government increased in size, competency, and impact on daily life. The steady flow of taxes to the English state provided the collateral for the expansion and elaboration of government credit operations, enabling the state to develop new ways to borrow large amounts of money to meet the spiralling costs of war. During the 1640s another very important development occurred. Parliament began to accept responsibility for the state's fiscal affairs and obligations, a major step in the process which culminated with the establishment of a funded, long-term national debt in the 1690s. These developments, from 1643 to 1700, constituted a 'revolution' in English financial affairs.

The English financial revolution began forty years before the Glorious Revolution and was a precursor rather than a result of that political event; John Brewer maintains it was the latter.[2] The military and financial developments of the mid-century were the seismic fault line between semi-feudal and modern England. During this period, the Long Parliament scrapped the remaining feudal dues and fiscal prerogatives of the Crown, while establishing the professional army and navy. The monarch's use of non-parliamentary impositions and his ability to increase the customs rates disappeared. The customs itself became a parliamentary-controlled tax, although it was still granted for the monarch's lifetime until 1689. The English adopted the odious excise taxes which they had previously looked down upon as 'Dutch' or foreign and as a mark of servitude. After 1643, all Englishmen paid some taxes, regardless of their economic status. Direct taxes, most notably the monthly assessment, were levied with increasing regularity, even in peacetime, with parliamentary approval. The Long Parliament's three main taxes of the civil wars – customs, excise, and assessment – were retained as the major sources of revenue by the parliaments after 1660. They continued to serve into the next century as the triangular base of the English state's fiscal system.

A SUMMARY OF THE EVIDENCE

The costs of sustaining prolonged warfare and maintaining a professional navy and army in peacetime and war forced the English to abandon long-held theories of taxation. By 1640, it was clear that the King could no longer 'live of his own' from the profits of the customs, his demesne lands and feudal dues. Beginning in the 1640s, Parliament grudgingly, but steadily, assumed responsibility for the fiscal needs of the state. After the restoration of the monarchy, in 1660, Parliament's awareness of its duty to provide additional revenue to the government for the support of the nation's military forces and foreign policy continued to grow.[3] The financial settlement of 1660 provided the King with too little peacetime income for the operation of his household and government. None the less, Parliament's decision that year to provide the king with a steady income raised by the customs and excise was due to the unwilling recognition by the Cavalier Parliament of its obligation to provide the monarch with adequate resources to operate the government.[4]

Because the full £1.2 million per year settled upon by the Cavalier Parliament as the Crown's revenue in 1660 could not be raised with the taxes initially allocated, Parliament decided to enact additional excise taxes on top of the grants of the customs and liquor excise it had already made. Perhaps more significant, as a sign of its growing sense of fiscal obligation, Parliament granted the King large amounts of money annually in direct taxes, such as the poll tax, the window tax and monthly assessments. These direct taxes were granted during the peacetime years of 1660 to 1664 as well as during the Second Dutch War (1665–7). For example, in the 102–month period from 24 June 1660 to 26 December 1668, 106 monthly assessments were granted.[5] By 1663, the monthly assessment was the most regularly imposed extraordinary tax, and contemporaries were already calling it the 'Land Tax'.[6]

The mid-century military and political struggles also increased parliamentary interest and direct participation in state financial management. As early as the 1620s, Charles I's parliaments had attempted to tie appropriations to specific expenditures. The King easily evaded these early attempts to affect policy through the power of the purse because no parliamentary organizations existed when the houses were not in session. However, these attempts by the Caroline parliaments to become involved in the financial administration of the realm were harbingers of more direct involvement by Parliament with the nation's financial affairs beginning in the 1640s.

During the wars of the 1640s, the Long Parliament established an increasingly effective network of committees to raise and spend money for its forces and to audit its various treasuries and the pay accounts of its soldiers and sailors.[7] The Committee for Taking the Accounts of the Kingdom and the Committee of Both Kingdoms were two of the more famous of these audit and executive committees. These groups long pre-dated the parliamentary Committee for the Inspection of Accounts of the 1690s which W.A. Shaw maintains was such an important part of Parliament's assumption of responsibility for the financial management of the English state.[8] In the 1640s, as later in the 1690s, Parliament managed its war effort through an interlocking series of parliamentary revenue, expenditure, and administrative committees. The continuous sessions of the Long Parliament made such oversight by legislative committees possible. When the King returned in 1660 it seemed that parliamentary oversight would end, and strictly speaking it did for a short period of time. But the King had to develop an alternative way to provide central supervision over the spending departments that had developed during the Military Revolution. The development of a strengthened Treasury was the result.

The Treasury began to assume many of the functions of the parliamentary audit committees by 1665, using Exchequer audit procedures as a means to account for the expenditure of the state's money.[9] While Treasury 'supremacy' took some years to establish during the reign of Charles II, it clearly was a recognition of the need to have professional administrators in control of the financial operations of the spending and revenue departments. The history of English government in the late seventeenth century is characterized by the steady growth of the Treasury's effective control of the state's revenues and expenditures. Concurrently, the personnel who managed many of the state's financial bureaucracies were progressively brought under effective central control. The state's continuing need for strong military forces drove this process of bureaucratic evolution and growth.

A trend towards the professionalization of the English bureaucracy accelerated when the tenure terms of the major officers of the Treasury, the Navy Board, the Mint, and the Ordnance Office were changed from 'tenure for life' to 'tenure at royal pleasure', thus making it easier for the Crown to remove dishonest or inefficient officers. This shift in tenure started in the Navy Board in 1635 and was adopted in these other bureaucracies starting in 1668.[10] It was no accident that the departments most involved with the operation and support of the professional navy were the first to have the terms of their officers' tenure changed.

Many of the financial practices employed to raise money on credit which played a large role in Dickson's financial revolution of the 1690s developed in the forty-five years before 1688. For example, the practice of registering and paying off debt in the order in which it was incurred is evident in the Navy Treasurer's declared accounts of the early 1650s. The Navy Treasurer routinely discharged older debts before paying off newer charges, consequently sustaining the financial credit of the Navy Office.[11] The Ordnance Office used a similar method of dealing with departmental debt in the 1660s and 1670s, managing a floating debt to suppliers of up to £268,000. The Ordnance Office steadily paid off earlier debt, even as it accumulated new debt in the war years of those two decades.[12]

The use of Exchequer 'Sol' tallies and the adoption of Treasury Orders as credit instruments in 1665 were additional steps forward in the revolution in state financial affairs of the seventeenth century. Under the Treasury Order system, the Treasury registered loans made to the government in anticipation of tax revenues in the order in which they were made and paid them off in the chronological order of their registration, with interest. While use of this form of short-term credit was set back by the Stop of the Exchequer in 1672, it was continued by the

Treasury under Lord Treasurer Danby (1673–8) and by the Treasury Commission installed in 1679.[13]

English theories about who should pay taxes also changed dramatically in the 1640s.[14] The Elizabethan notion that the poor and working poor should pay little or no taxes was sacrificed to the need of John Pym and his fellow Parliamentarians to find a way to finance their armed forces once their one-shot fiscal remedies had run their predictable course in 1643. The institution of excise taxes in that year made all Englishmen taxpayers.[15] As the women's lament best expressed it,

> Excise on ale, excise on salt, excise on cloth, excise on malt;
> Excise on what so ere you call't, and fear not.
> All linen fine or course must pay
> excise or else they'll take it away.[16]

The Cavalier Parliament retained the excise taxes on liquor in 1660. Excise taxes continue to this day to serve as a major fiscal prop of the English state.[17] Remarkably little resistance was offered to excise taxation after the 1640s, especially after the Long Parliament removed meat and fish from the list of rated items in 1647. After 1660, excise taxes were considered the easiest form of taxation to impose because of the relatively small amount of resistance they engendered.[18] The abandonment of the fiscal paternalism of the Tudors and the early Stuarts is one of the marks of the great divide between the medieval and modern fiscal orders in English history. This change was caused directly by the English state's need to support permanent military forces.

The retention of direct taxes in peacetime – and especially of the monthly assessments – after 1660, and the evolution of the assessments into the Land Tax of the eighteenth century was another mark of the emergence of modern English fiscal theory.[19] Starting in the 1640s, the English aristocracy regularly paid taxes on their landed wealth through the assessment tax. While it is true that the landed classes paid less in proportion to the middle and working classes in peacetime, when the excise taxes were normally higher than the assessments, the gentry taxed itself heavily during wartime through its parliamentary institutions.[20] In return, parliamentary assessment acts gave the gentry control of the local government machinery which levied and collected the assessment and, later, the Land Tax in the counties. This local control of the rating for the assessments was similar to the self-rating processes of the Tudor subsidies. However, the Long Parliament's practice of assigning to each county a fixed quota of assessment revenue to raise, prevented tax receipts from declining over time as subsidy revenues had done before 1640.[21]

The Glorious Revolution was a further dramatic step forward in the administrative and theoretical trends in English fiscal theory and practice.[22] It opened the way for the complete acceptance by Parliament, in the 1690s, of its responsibility for the state's financial obligations, as well as for its increasing share in the political management of the nation. Parliament henceforth approved the budgets of the navy, army, and Ordnance Office annually. The legislative body assumed responsibility for providing the appropriations needed to raise the immense amounts of money required to support military forces. Resistance to the growing fiscal power of the English state became ineffective once this had occurred, helping to explain why there was so little resistance to taxation in England even though the nation was possibly the most heavily taxed state in Western Europe in the late seventeenth and early eighteenth centuries.[23] Parliament's assumption of the responsibility for the state's financial affairs was accompanied by a major increase in its political power, soon leading to the development of cabinet government.

The development of English parliamentary government was a crucial step in the financial revolution. Political developments in this direction were evident in some early aspects of Parliamentarian administration in the 1640s. Parliamentary government was, in part, a logical descendant of the executive and financial committees of the Long Parliament and the elective Councils of State of the Commonwealth. This heritage further demonstrates the reciprocal effects of the changes that occurred in military, political, and administrative practices during the Military Revolution in England in the half century after 1640.

The evidence for these seventeenth-century revolutions in English military and financial affairs can be summarized statistically and graphically. The revolution in military affairs came first, as the Parliamentarians struggled to field and sustain the military forces needed to protect their steadily expanding interests in Britain and the growing world economy.

THE NAVY

The development of the Royal Navy demonstrates the relationship between military growth and government change well, since it was the first line of defence and the essential means for England to project military power throughout the world. The complexity, size, cost, and killing power of the ships of the line of the battlefleet grew considerably in the half century after 1640, as the European maritime powers engaged in a naval arms race. During the first half of the century, warships had displaced roughly 500 to 800 tons and carried between twenty and fifty cannon, with only a handful of costly three-decked 'first-rates' carrying over ninety guns in the fleet. By the Second Dutch War the proportion of larger warships in the fleet was increasing steadily, until by 1688 only ships weighing over 1,000 tons and mounting fifty or more guns were considered suitable for the line of battle used in 'line ahead' tactics. Because larger 'battleships' became the standard vessels of the major naval powers, English fleet size seemed to stabilize at around 120 of this type.[24] However, this statistic is misleading about fleet size since it counts only the three largest categories or 'rates' of the navy.

The number of major vessels in the navy grew dramatically in response to war, first from 1642 to 1674, and then from 1688 to 1697. The Royal Navy maintained 30 state-owned warships in the period 1600 to 1635,[25] and over 40 warships in the 1640s.[26] The fleet increased to over 200 purpose-built warships in the 1650s, due to the First Dutch War.[27] The fleet then fluctuated between 80 and 100 major combatant vessels (sixth-rates and larger) maintained on active peacetime duty until 1688.[28] Because so much of the navy's purpose and efforts were dedicated to protecting English commerce and destroying that of England's enemies, the vessels of the fourth- through sixth-rates were just as important to English naval power and success as were the 'ships of the line' of the first- through third-rates. The Royal Navy actually sent over 300 major combatant vessels to sea against the French in 1690, and at least that many out again during the War of the Spanish Succession (1702–13).[29] A large percentage of the fourth- and fifth-rate ships used as cruisers in the 1690s would have been suitable for service in the front line in the major sea battles of the First Dutch War.

The growth in the annual costs of the English navy during the seventeenth century is another reliable guide to the magnitude of the Military Revolution at sea. Table 9.1 lists the average annual expenditures made for the support of the navy and Ordnance Office, indicating the trend of these costs. The table identifies the major transition points in the navy's history by reflecting the remarkable changes in total expenditures which occurred in response to sustained periods of naval warfare. The increase in costs during the first half of the century took place with a background inflation of roughly 20–35 per cent. However, from 1650 to 1700 the value of money stabilized and inflation ceased, making the level of naval expenditures an even more useful measure for the growth of English naval efforts.[30]

Table 9.1: Naval Expenditures, 1600–99[31]

Period		Naval cost (£)	Per annum (£)
1600–9	W/P	678,405	67,000
1610–19	P	591,630	59,000
1620–9	P/W	1,214,925	121,000
1630–9	P	1,436,770	143,000
1640–50	W	2,901,802	290,000
1651–60	W	6,302,671	663,000
1660–9	P/W	6,610,620	661,000
1670–9	P	6,061,678	606,000
1680–9	P	5,013,843	501,000
1690–9	W	17,632,863	1,763,000

P = peacetime, W = wartime

The changes in the annual average naval and ordnance expenditures directly reflect the periods of peace and war in the first half of the century. Naval expenditures declined slightly in real and notional terms after the end of the Elizabethan wars against Spain and the Irish in 1604. Annual average naval expenditures were remarkably steady until the Spanish and French wars of 1625 to 1630, when they again shot up. Average expenditures again fell in the period from 1630 to 1635, but then grew dramatically as Charles I used ship-money and Exchequer receipts to pay for a permanent and increasingly professional navy from 1635 to 1639.[32] England's need to support the continuous deployment of naval forces in British waters and overseas from 1640 to 1660 drove naval costs to unheard-of levels, as one would expect. Figure 9.1 indicates the importance of the 1640s and 1650s to these developments.

Significantly, after 1660 naval expenditures remained very high even in the peacetime decade of the 1680s, as Charles II and James II continued to support one of the three largest navies in Europe and to use it as an instrument of foreign policy in Northern and Southern Europe.[33] The explosion of expenditures in the last decade reflects directly the cost of the worldwide war fought against France.

The English navy had become a major permanent fighting force well before 1688, as the sustained rate of financial investment indicates. David Baugh was absolutely right when he concluded that

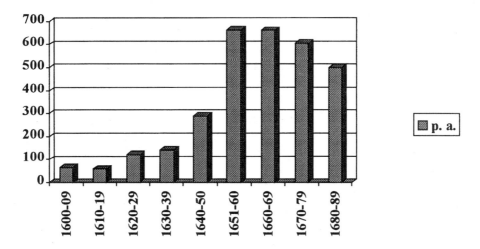

Figure 9.1: Annual Average Naval Costs, 1600–89 (£000s)

'developing these English sinews of power was mainly the work of six decades, roughly from 1650 to about 1710', and that, in his view, 'Brewer's *Sinews of Power* does not pay sufficient attention to the manner in which the English State developed between 1660 and 1688.'[34] The development of the small Channel fleet of Charles I into the 'blue water navy' used by William III was accomplished in the 1650s. The financial and logistical support of the steadily expanding fleet required the development of the administrative structure described in chapters two and three. The financial sinews to sustain the naval force and its administrative structures could only be provided by a state fiscal system which underwent a financial revolution from 1640 to 1700.

THE ARMY

The development of the English army followed a different course than that of the navy, due in large part to the geographic realities facing the island state. The New Model Army was the first standing peacetime army in English history. English armies before 1645 were organized, equipped and deployed in a manner similar to the best continental military practice, but they were not retained in peacetime. Consequently, the militia's trained bands provided the organizations through which much of the continental Military Revolution reached England.[35] In addition, significant numbers of English, Scottish, and Irish mercenaries provided a source of up-to-date military experience for English and Scottish armies when they returned to Britain to fight the Bishops' Wars and the Civil Wars.[36]

Peacetime army strength in Britain became significant for the first time in the 1650s. The garrisons in Ireland, England, and Scotland totalled more than 50,000 men during the Protectorate. Although most of these forces were disbanded in 1660, 10,000–20,000 men were retained in the garrisons of the three kingdoms, Dunkirk, and Tangiers.[37] The Royal Army saw little action from 1660 to 1689; however, Charles II and especially James II steadily increased its strength so that it numbered 40,000 men in England alone in 1688. Once William III was in command, the army expanded dramatically, maintaining a strength of at least 80,000 men during the War of the League of Augsburg (1689–97). In addition, in the 1690s the English Exchequer spent millions in support of allied armies and paid for tens of thousands of continental mercenaries to augment the English armies in Ireland and the Netherlands.

The different natures of land and sea warfare account for the relative simplicity of the army's administration system. Companies and regiments of soldiers could be fed and housed locally as long as their pay arrived in a timely manner. Even when pay was not forthcoming, as was often the case during the 1640s, the troops could be billeted in the homes of the local population and fed through the process known as free quarter. After 1649, English armies were comparatively well paid, eliminating some of the worst abuses. However, it was necessary to develop well-funded and carefully managed logistical systems when army expeditionary forces were sent overseas. This was successfully done in the Elizabethan wars, and then again during Cromwell's conquests of Ireland and Scotland.[38] In each of these cases, the Westminster government found ways to raise the steady stream of money needed to sustain the army's logistical system. In each case, the state's debt grew rapidly.

The amounts of money spent by English governments for the support of their land forces during the first century of the English Military Revolution provide clear evidence about the timing of the creation of the professional English Army and its relationship to the mid-century wars. Table 9.2 lists the amounts spent on the army from 1600 to 1700. As mentioned earlier, price-inflation of roughly 20–35 per cent occurred in the first half of the century, while the period after 1650 was characterized by generally stable prices.

Table 9.2: Expenditures for English Armies, 1600–1700[39]

Period		Total army costs (£)	Average per annum (£)
1600–9	W/P	1,778,561	177,000
1610–19	P	613,161	61,000
1620–9	P/W	965,914	96,000
1630–9	P	534,611	53,000
1640–51	W	9,369,354	803,000
1652–60	W	7,714,223	771,000
1660–70[40]	P	3,253,540	325,000
1670–80[41]	P	3,945,209	394,000
1680–8[42]	P	3,538,567	416,000
1689–Sep 1700	W/P	15,053,082	1,281,000

P = peacetime, W = wartime

Elizabethan wartime expenditures are reflected in the relatively high expenditures of the first decade. Her land forces routinely cost more than her navy. The virtual disbandment of these forces, except for a garrison in Ireland and a few key places in Britain, such as Berwick, allowed James I to reduce his annual army costs to less than £62,000 for the ten years after 1609. The 50 per cent increase in annual costs in the 1620s was due to the money spent on Vere's expedition in 1620/1, Mansfeld's ill-fated expedition in 1624/5, and the forces sent on the Cadiz fiasco. Table 9.2 does not list all of the military expenditures of the seventeenth century. County governments spent significant amounts to support their trained bands and militias. Local governments also spent additional large sums for coat-and-conduct money during the wars of the 1620s and the two Bishops' Wars. One of the results of the mid-century wars was that the central government shouldered a far greater proportion of such military costs after 1645. Figure 9.2 illustrates the trend that in the periods of peace after 1660, the average annual amounts spent on the English Army remained significantly higher than those of the peacetime years before 1640.

Charles I reduced army costs in 1629, spending less per year during the 1630s than was spent at any comparable time in the century. Had he used the equivalent of the ship-money tax on his army, the results of the Bishops' Wars and the political crisis of 1640/1 may well have been quite different. The amounts used to finance the army in the 1640s and 1650s

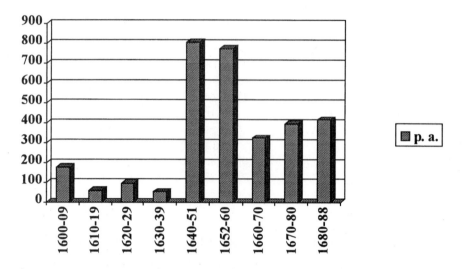

Figure 9.2: Annual Average Army Costs, 1600–88 (£000s)

reflect only the money spent on the main Parliamentarian armies. These sums exclude the large amounts directed to Royalist forces and the troops serving in Ireland before 1649, and the £3 million in pay arrears accumulated in this twenty-year period and paid off at a discount with the sale of confiscated lands in England and Ireland from 1649 to 1656.[43] None the less, the amounts devoted to the Parliamentarian armies were staggering, especially when compared to the spending in all previous periods. These expenditures were sustained in every year of the period, forcing the Westminster governments to adopt permanent excise and assessment taxes.

The importance of the mid-century wars to the development of the English fiscal state is evident when one looks at the percentage of total annual state expenditure dedicated to the navy, army, and Ordnance. The trend in the percentage of military spending in relation to total spending is more important than the exact amounts used in any single period.

It is not surprising that the percentage of total expenditure devoted to the support of military forces rose dramatically in wartime: that had been the pattern for several centuries at least. As Figure 9.3 indicates,[44] during the last three years of Elizabeth I's Spanish war over 69 per cent of total expenditures were made in support of her armies in Ireland and the Low Countries and for her navy, albeit on a smaller scale. Similarly, military

Table 9.3: Military Expenditures as Part of Total Expenditures, 1 January 1600–September 1699[45]

Period		Total state expenditure (£)	Military (£)	Military %	Average annual military expenditure (£)
1600–4	W	2,366,444	1,672,545	70.7	334,509
1605–9	P	2,571,959	752,330	29.2	150,466
1610–14	P	2,931,725	735,672	25.0	147,134
1615–19	P	2,112,393	431,596	20.4	86,319
1620–4	P	1,869,831	430,388	23.0	86,077
1625–9	W	3,356,683	1,405,989	41.9	281,197
1630–4	P	2,155,890	735,865	34.1	147,173
1635–9	P	3,106,807	1,299,369	41.8	259,873
1640	W	899,519	658,766	73.2	658,766
1642–60	W	34,352,545	29,173,019	84.9	1,535,422
1660–4[46]	P	5,706,492	3,650,814	63.9	730,162
1664–9	W	9,398,653	6,254,184	66.5	1,250,836
1670–4	P	10,216,899	5,081,023	49.7	1,016,204
1674–9	P	9,046,627	5,102,760	56.4	1,020,552
1679–84	P	6,605,992	3,667,730	55.5	733,546
1684–8	P	7,421,940	4,197,341	56.6	1,049,335
1688–97	W	49,823,023	36,272,274	72.8	4,030,252
1697–9	P	11,387,663	4,562,756	40.1	1,937,913

P = peacetime, W = wartime

costs consumed over 40 per cent of total expenditures in Charles I's naval wars of 1625 to 1630 against Spain and France.

What is clear from Table 9.3 and Figure 9.3 is that from 1640 to 1660 the English civil wars and Anglo-Dutch wars drove military costs to levels never seen before. Westminster governments in this period committed over 88 per cent of their revenues to support the New Model Army and the Commonwealth Navy. The mid-century wars were a watershed for two major reasons. The military forces became permanent and increasingly professional. The proportion of total expenditures made in peacetime costs did not fall again to the levels of the twenty years of peace from 1605 to 1624.

Military outlays constituted over 50 per cent of the peacetime expenditures from 1674 to 1688, compared to roughly 25 per cent of

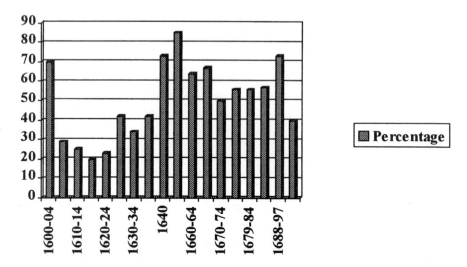

Figure 9.3: Military Expenditures as a Percentage of Total State Expenditures, 1600–97

state outlays during the long Jacobean peace. Inflation does not account for the doubling of the percentage of total peacetime disbursements made in support of English armies and fleets; the highest estimate for price-inflation from 1600 to 1650 is roughly 50 per cent.[47] The growth in notional military expenditures in peacetime rose over 600 per cent, from the £117,000 spent annually from 1605 to 1624 to the £864,000 spent annually from 1674 to 1688.

Wartime costs of English military forces skyrocketed as well. The Parliamentarian and Interregnum governments spent an average of £1.5 million annually from 1642 to 1660 in support of their navy and armies. William III's governments spent an average of £4 million annually, an amount 166 per cent greater than that spent in the mid-century wars. From 1650 to 1700, average notional costs equalled real costs. This level of spending would have been unsustainable if the Parliamentarians had not initiated a financial revolution in 1643.

Military costs grew during both wartime and peacetime, reflecting the establishment of the standing army and navy. The most important period in this process of military modernization was from 1640 to 1660. How to pay for these permanent military forces became the primary financial question for the remainder of the seventeenth century.

THE FINANCIAL REVOLUTION

Elizabeth I and James I relied on the traditional fiscal methods of the demesne state to pay for their government's expenses. The customs duties, the revenues of the Crown lands, and feudal dues were the major branches of 'ordinary' peacetime revenue. Elizabeth was able to make ends meet and to save money from her demense revenue in most years before 1685. However, Elizabeth's ordinary revenue did not cover the expenses of the Spanish and Irish wars from 1585 to 1603. Consequently, the Virgin Queen turned to selling large blocks of royal lands and to asking for parliamentary subsidies. These 'extraordinary' revenues partially filled the gap between peacetime income and wartime expenses. None the less, Elizabeth bequeathed at least £300,000 in debt to her successor, along with a much reduced royal demesne due to the sale of over £565,000 in Crown lands during her reign.[48] Most of these sales of land occurred in the last five years of her wars against Spain and the Irish. These sales were necessary because the traditional financial structure of Tudor England was unable to cope with the high costs of sustained warfare.

James I was able to decrease his military expenditures rapidly by cutting the forces and laying up most of his warships. If James had been forced to fight a major war, his finances would have collapsed. As it was, by 1621 he had accumulated over £829,000 in debt because his ordinary expenditures routinely exceeded the peacetime revenues of the customs, demesne lands and feudal dues.[49] Much greater royal living expenses and the costs of gifts to favourites pushed expenses to a level at which the balance of ordinary revenue was routinely less than peacetime expenditure. The failure to negotiate 'the Great Contract' with Parliament in 1610 ended one of the few attempts made by English governments before 1643 to reform the obviously inadequate financial structure of early Stuart England.[50]

The predictable breakdown in the English state's financial affairs took place during Charles I's wars against Spain and France, from 1625 to 1630. Sizeable parliamentary grants of subsidies proved to be inadequate to cover the costs of an increasingly expensive navy and the expeditionary forces that were launched in that war. The real and notional value of parliamentary subsidies fell steadily, and the King and Parliament failed to work out adequate means to replace obsolete and inadequate fiscal practices.[51] Much of the long political crisis between Charles and his parliaments was directly linked to the failure to develop new means to pay for war.[52] While such struggles were central to many of the seventeenth-century conflicts between European rulers and their estates as well, in England's case the estates won after expensive and bloody civil wars.

The Long Parliament's adoption of new forms of taxation and new credit methods initiated the English financial revolution. The Parliamentarians' need to support standing military forces during the First Civil War forced them to make radical changes in English financial practices and theories. The spiralling costs of the parliamentary armies and navy were met in large part through the revenue raised by the excise and assessments, especially after 1649. The Long Parliament's development of excise and assessment taxes to accompany the customs proved financially and militarily decisive. However, the dramatic increase in naval costs in the 1650s, due to the First Dutch War, greatly strained the revenue provided by the three regular revenues. By 1659, due to the decrease in assessment rates by the Protectorate, a major fiscal crisis had developed, helping in part to bring about the Restoration.

The Restoration Parliament continued the financial methods of the Interregnum. It continued the assessments to pay off nearly £800,000 in army pay arrears in 1660/1.[53] It also adopted a permanent excise on liquor which was continued for the rest of the century as one of the major sources, along with the customs, of the state's peacetime revenue. Thereafter, English state finance mostly relied on the three regular parliamentary taxes to support wartime expenses. Additionally, the customs, excise, and frequent resort to assessments (known after 1692 as the Land Tax) provided the majority of the state's peacetime revenue from 1660 to 1700.[54]

The importance of the customs, excise, and assessments to the English state's fiscal operations is shown clearly by the data in Table 9.4. Customs receipts grew steadily as a component of total state revenue from 1600 to 1640. This reflected the revised Books of Rates adopted by the Crown to take into account the rising value of goods imported and exported and the changes in the type of imports and exports. This trend also reflected the decreasing value of subsidies and of the income from the royal demesne. During the mid-century wars, direct and indirect taxes provided between 66 and 76 per cent of the money raised by the Long Parliament and Interregnum governments. This large percentage of wartime revenue provided by current taxation is remarkably similar to the proportion of wartime costs provided by current taxes from 1689 to 1697. The English habit of paying for a large portion of the costs of war with wartime taxation clearly was established in the mid-century wars. In turn, the increased level of taxation made possible the elaboration of new credit methods by the government to raise loans during the wars.

Feudal dues, demesne income, and parliamentary subsidies declined dramatically as a percentage of total state revenue well before 1640.

Table 9.4: The Major Components of Total English State Revenue, 1603–1700[55]

Period		a. Total revenue	b. Customs (£)	c. Excise (£)	d. Assessment	b,c,d, as % of a
1603–5	P	1,319,234	291,260	–	–	22
1606–10	P	2,775,666	691,804	–	–	24
1611–15	P	2,813,786	1,024,032	–	–	36
1616–20	P	1,834,362	816,853	–	–	44
1621–5	P	2,166,988	1,043,083	–	–	48
1626–30	W	3,140,241	1,129,380	–	–	36
1631–5	P	2,285,131	1,088,881	–	–	48
1636–40	P/W	3,541,981	1,781,277	–	750,613	71
1643–50	W	13,299,645	1,485,191	2,195,203	5,228,871	67
1650–9	W	18,565,731	3,777,864	3,720,910	6,676,578	76
1660–4	P	5,208,842	1,346,797	1,358,475	1,703,030	85
1665–9	W	9,251,201	1,550,817	1,394,625	5,055,888	86
1670–4	P	9,005,725	2,433,992	2,236,773	1,446,965	68
1675–9	P	8,261,103	2,883,907	2,721,303	1,307,520	84
1680–4	P	7,286,176	2,845,797	2,418,914	521,417	79
1685–8	P	7,701,732	3,472,165	1,837,983	10,331	69
1689–91	W	8,613,190	1,919,514	2,429,750	3,171,739	87
1692–5	W	19,643,620	3,335,538	3,915,411	7,059,064	72
1696–1700	P	24,301,914	5,742,898	5,759,988	7,289,303	77

P = peacetime, W = wartime

For example, subsidies fell from 32 per cent of total Exchequer receipts in 1603 to 17 per cent in 1628.[56] In both of these years England was at war. The sale of Crown lands progressed steadily from the end of Elizabeth's reign through Charles I's and resumed with a vengeance during the Interregnum. As a result, royal land rents no longer played an important part in the Crown's fiscal operations. However, all forms of confiscatory receipts and the proceeds from royal and episcopal land sales provided the central government with less than £8.8 million of its receipts from 1642 to 1660, or roughly 28 per cent of the total revenue of £31.8 million of the Westminster governments in that period. The inadequacy and exhaustion of such sources of income was obvious by 1652. English governments never again could turn to such fiscal expedients to raise money. This was an important step towards modern financial practices and one important cause of the rise of parliamentary power and participation in state affairs.

The importance of excise taxes is clearly evident in Table 9.4. From 1660 to 1688, excise receipts ranked second only to customs income as a proportion of peacetime revenue. During wartime, excise receipts exceeded those of the customs but fell behind assessment receipts. By 1660 the excise had become a key part of the public credit. Without permanent continuation of this parliamentary tax on consumption, the creation of a long-term national debt in the 1690s would have been very difficult because there would have been insufficient peacetime tax revenue to service it.

Assessment taxes were the state's single most important wartime revenue in the seventeenth century. For example, assessment receipts provided 37 per cent of the total revenue of the central treasuries from 1642 to 1660, by itself more than all the money received from fines, land sales, and confiscations. Total assessment receipts also exceeded total customs and excise income by £720,000 in this period. During the civil wars and Interregnum, the assessment tax was remarkably efficient, with less than 5 per cent of gross receipts spent for collection costs. This compares favourably with the collection costs of the customs and excise which ran between 10 and 12 per cent of gross receipts.[57] The assessment was the most dependable of parliamentary taxes as well, since it was set as a county quota. By the 1690s, when it evolved into the Land Tax, it provided a predictable flow of money to support English wartime military and financial operations and it had become an essential part of the collateral for short- and long-term state debt.

While poll taxes, annuities, and lotteries were resorted to by English governments from 1660 to 1700 to provide some of the financial sinews of power, the three regular taxes of the Interregnum – that is the customs, excise, and assessment – proved to be the most reliable and acceptable ways to raise money well into the eighteenth century.[58] They provided the 'stock of credit' necessary for the successful schemes finally employed to convert large amounts of short-term credit instruments of the 1690s and the early 1700s into the long-term national debt.[59]

Debt management evolved steadily from 1640 to the 1690s. Even in the 1690s, government borrowing methods were far from neat or pretty. Government short-term borrowing exceeded £3 million per year from 1688 to 1697 and Exchequer tallies and bills were being discounted at over 30 per cent by 1697.[60] This evidence further undermines the notion that England magically became the smoothly running modern fiscal state with the creation of the Bank of England in the 1690s. It confirms the picture of financial continuity for the period from 1643 to 1699 which the analyses of the customs, excise and assessment in chapters six through eight demonstrate. For these reasons, as well as for their importance to the funding of the English Military Revolution, the development and elaboration of these regular parliamentary taxes, accompanied by increased parliamentary interest in, and commitment to, public financial solvency deserves the title of an English Financial Revolution.

Conclusion

Cicero correctly noted that the 'sinews of war are infinite money'. Charles Davenant echoed this view in 1695 when he wrote the following:

> Now the whole art of war is in a manner reduced to money; and nowadays that prince who can best find money to feed, clothe, and pay his army, not he that hath the most valiant troops, is surest to success and conquest.[1]

Louis XIV would have agreed with this view.

Only those states which found effective ways to raise large amounts of money for long periods of time have succeeded in prolonged warfare. This was an essential part of the Military Revolution. England experienced a series of interrelated developments in military technology and government financial administration in the relatively short period of time from 1639 to 1674, which revolutionized the way the English state fought and sustained warfare. Tactical and strategic innovations and the need to conduct continuous warfare exerted pressure on related financial and administrative operations as well as on each other. These financial and military revolutions marked a major turning point in British history; they initiated a cumulative, self-sustaining advance in military and government technologies whose repercussions have been felt in all aspects of British life. These advances have, in turn, provoked and promoted a large complex of economic, political, and cultural changes which have influenced the rate and course of British military history since 1674. The Military and Financial Revolutions that England successfully navigated during the seventeenth century provided the island state with the means to defend its growing empire and to protect its vital interests as a world power.

Notes

INTRODUCTION

1. J.P. Kenyon, *The Civil Wars of England* (New York, Alfred Knopf, 1988), p. 2.

CHAPTER ONE

1. I am deeply indebted to Professors Geoffrey Parker, Jeremy Black, Cliff Rogers, Linda Frey, and Fred Kagan for their help with this chapter. They stimulated a great deal of thought and pointed out a number of shortcomings in the early drafts with their perceptive comments.
2. N.A.M. Rodger, *The Safeguard of the Sea, A Naval History of Britain, 660–1649* (New York, HarperCollins, 1997), pp. 347–78.
3. Richard W. Stewart, *The Ordnance Office, A Case Study in Bureaucracy* (Woodbridge, Suffolk, Boydell Press, 1996), pp. 141–9.
4. Rodger, *Safeguard of the Sea*, pp. 370–2.
5. Republished most recently as M. Roberts, 'The Military Revolution, 1560–1660', in C.J. Rogers (ed.), *The Military Revolution Debate: Readings on the Military Transformation of Early Modern Europe* (Oxford, Westview Press, 1995), pp. 13–35.
6. Ibid., p. 13.
7. Ibid., pp. 13–29.
8. G. Parker, 'The "Military Revolution", 1560–1660 – A Myth?', originally published in *Journal of Modern History*, 48 (1976), and reprinted in Rogers (ed.), *The Military Revolution Debate*, pp. 37–49.
9. J.R. Hale, 'Armies, Navies and the Art of War', in G.R. Elton (ed.), *The Reformation, 1520–1559* (Cambridge, Cambridge University Press, 1990), p. 540.
10. Ibid., p. 541.
11. G. Parker, *The Military Revolution: Military Innovation and the Rise of the West, 1500–1800* (Cambridge, Cambridge University Press, 1988, second edition 1996), chapter four, 'The military revolution abroad', pp. 115–45.
12. J. Black, *European Warfare, 1660–1815* (New Haven, Yale University Press, 1994), pp. 5–6.
13. J. Black, 'A Military Revolution?', in Rogers (ed.), *The Military Revolution Debate*, p. 110.
14. Ibid., p. 111.
15. Ibid., p. 111 and Black, *European Warfare*, p. 7.
16. Rogers, 'Military Revolutions of the Hundred Years' War', in *The Military Revolution Debate*, p. 56.
17. Ibid., p. 57 and pp. 76–7.
18. Parker, 'In Defense of the Military Revolution', in Rogers (ed.), *The Military Revolution Debate*, p. 345, quotes the 'doyen of historians of technology' in a way that makes this long-term view of history of Parker's clear. Lynn White observed the following: 'The early sixteenth century in Europe witnessed two revolutions, both of which altered habits of

the previous thousand years and each of which, by the late 1500s, had crystallized into patterns that remained nearly intact until the end of the nineteenth century. One was the Protestant Reformation. . . . The other was a sudden and profound change in military technology.' Parker's reference is Lynn White, Jr., *Medieval Religion and Technology, Collected Essays* (Berkeley, CA, University of California Press, 1986), p. 149.

19. Roberts, 'Military Revolution, 1560–1660', in Rogers (ed.), *The Military Revolution Debate*, p. 13.
20. Rogers, 'Military Revolutions of the Hundred Years' War', in *The Military Revolution Debate*, p. 76, where he strongly implies that for the reversal to be a revolution it must take place in no more than a single generation.
21. J.R. Hale, 'International Relations in the West: Diplomacy and War', in G.R. Potter (ed.), *The Renaissance* (Cambridge, Cambridge University Press, 1957), pp. 263–4.
22. Roberts, 'Military Revolution', in Rogers (ed.), *The Military Revolution Debate*, pp. 13–14; G. Parker (ed.), *The Cambridge Illustrated History of Warfare* (Cambridge, Cambridge University Press, 1995).
23. M. Prestwich, *Armies and Warfare in the Middle Ages: The English Experience* (New Haven, CT, Yale University Press, 1996), pp. 334–46.
24. Ibid., pp. 342–3.
25. S. Adams, 'Tactics or Politics? "The Military Revolution" and the Habsburg Hegemony, 1525–1648', in Rogers (ed.), *The Military Revolution Debate*, pp. 258–61.
26. Roberts, 'Military Revolution, 1560–1660', in Rogers (ed.), *The Military Revolution Debate*, p. 13.
27. Black, *European Warfare*, chapters four and five especially.
28. Parker, *The Military Revolution*, especially the chapters 'Victory at Sea' and 'The Military Revolution Abroad'; and Parker, 'In Defense of the Military Revolution', in Rogers (ed.), *The Military Revolution Debate*, pp. 337–56.
29. J. Black, *A Military Revolution? Military Change and European Society, 1550–1800* (Atlantic Highlands, NJ, Humanities Press International, 1991), p. 34.
30. Black, *European Warfare*, pp. 119–47; Black, *A Military Revolution?*, pp. 52–65.
31. For example of recent research derived from the Military Revolution concept see R. Bonney (ed.), *Economic Systems and State Finance* (Oxford, Clarendon Press, 1995) and D. Croxton, 'A Territorial Imperative? The Military Revolution and Peacemaking in the Thirty Years' War', *War in History* 5 (1998), 253–79.
32. For Landes's original words see D. Landes, *Unbound Prometheus* (Cambridge, Cambridge University Press, 1975), pp. 1–5.
33. J. Brewer, *Sinews of Power: War, Money and the English State, 1688–1783* (New York, Alfred A. Knopf, 1989), p. 7.
34. Ibid., pp. 9–14.
35. G. Parker, 'The Dreadnought Revolution of Tudor England', *Mariner's Mirror*, 82 (1996), 273.
36. J.B. Black, *The Reign of Elizabeth, 1558–1603* (Oxford, Clarendon Press, 1959), pp. 333–460 for her continental diplomacy and military efforts, pp. 477–92 for the two major Irish revolts and the English suppression of them; R.W. Stewart, 'The "Irish Road": Military Supply and Arms for Elizabeth's Army during the O'Neill Rebellion in Ireland, 1598–1601', in M. Fissel (ed.), *War and Government in Britain, 1598–1650* (Manchester, Manchester University Press, 1991), pp. 16–37; R.B. Wernham, *The Return of the Armadas* (Oxford, Clarendon Press, 1994).
37. For an estimate of the number of men levied for the land forces see L. Boynton, *The Elizabethan Militia, 1558–1638* (London, Routledge and Kegan Paul, 1967), p. 166; for the expenditures see P. Kennedy, *The Rise and Fall of English Naval Mastery* (New Jersey, Ashfield Press, 1983 edn), p. 26.

Notes

38. R.B. Wernham, *After the Armada: Elizabethan England and the Struggle for Western Europe, 1588–1595* (Oxford, Clarendon Press, 1984); C. Falls, *Elizabeth's Irish Wars* (Syracuse, Syracuse University Press, 1997).

39. Boynton, *Elizabethan Militia*, chapters four and five; C.G. Cruickshank, *Elizabeth's Army* (Oxford, Clarendon Press, 1966); Anthony Fletcher, *The Reform in the Provinces, The Government of Stuart England* (New Haven, CT, Yale University Press, 1986), pp. 282–316 – see chapter four of this work for a discussion of how the English militia was transformed from a medieval to a modern force from 1573 to 1638.

40. Boynton, *The Elizabethan Militia*, pp. 171–2, 212–20 and 237–8; Keith Roberts, 'Musters and May Games: The Effect of Changing Military Theory in the English Militia', *Cromwelliana* (1991), 5–9, discusses the influence of continental military ideas and technology on the organization and equipment of the trained bands in the early Stuart period. Organization and armaments of the English militia were most affected, while the militia generally did not reach continental standards in tactical expertise. Also see Geoffrey Parker's review in the 14 June 1996 *Times Literary Supplement* (p. 26) of D. Eltis, *The Military Revolution in Sixteenth-century Europe* (London, Tauris Academic Studies, 1995).

41. Eltis, *The Military Revolution in Sixteenth-century Europe*, pp. 107–11.

42. M. Duffy (ed.), *The Military Revolution and the State, 1500–1800* (Exeter, University of Exeter Studies in History, No. 1, 1980), pp. 1–3 for the general Military Revolution debate, and pp. 49–85 for Duffy's chapter entitled 'The Foundations of British Naval Power', in which he concludes that the revolution in naval affairs started in the republican period of 1649 to 1660 (p. 51). For discussions of the revolution in English army affairs see J. Adair, in the Foreword of C.H. Firth, *Cromwell's Army* (London, Greenhill Press, 1992), p. xi; and see J. Childs, *The Army of Charles II* (London, Routledge and Kegan Paul, 1976), pp. 1–16.

43. Brewer, *Sinews of Power*, p. 250.

44. P.G.M. Dickson, *The Financial Revolution in England: A Study in the Development of Public Credit, 1688–1756* (London, Macmillan, 1967), p. 9.

45. D.C. Chandaman, *The English Public Revenue, 1660–1688* (Oxford, Clarendon Press, 1975); H. Roseveare, *The Financial Revolution, 1660–1760* (New York, Longmans, 1991); M.J. Braddick, *Parliamentary Taxation in Seventeenth-century England* (Woodbridge, Suffolk, Royal Historical Society, 1994); M.J. Braddick, *The Nerves of State, Taxation and the Financing of the English State, 1558–1714* (Manchester, Manchester University Press, 1996); Braddick, 'The English Government, War, Trade, and Settlement, 1625–1688', in Nicholas Canny (ed.), *The Origins of Empire* (Oxford, Oxford University Press, 1998); J. S. Wheeler, 'English Naval Finance, 1650–1660', *The Historical Journal*, 39 (1996), 457–66.

46. M.J. Braddick, 'An English Military Revolution?', *The Historical Journal*, 36 (1993), 965–75.

47. Ibid., p. 965.

48. Ibid., p. 975.

49. G. Parker, *The Dutch Revolt* (New York, Viking–Penguin Inc., 1985 edn), pp. 218–24.

50. Cruickshank, *Elizabeth's Army*, pp. 14–15.

51. G. Mattingly, *The Defeat of the Spanish Armada* (Harmondsworth, Middlesex, Penguin, 1959); Wernham, *After the Armada*; M. Howard, *The British Way of War, A Reappraisal* (London, Jonathan Cape, 1975), pp. 8–11; Kennedy, *The Rise and Fall of English Naval Mastery*, p. 27.

52. Boynton, *Elizabethan Militia*, p. 166.

53. C. Brady, 'The Captain's Games: Army and Society in Elizabethan Ireland', in T. Bartlett and K. Jeffery (eds), *A Military History of Ireland* (Cambridge, Cambridge

University Press, 1996), pp. 144–7; Black, *The Reign of Elizabeth*, pp. 488–9; R. Stewart, 'The "Irish Road"', in Fissel (ed.), *War and Government*, p. 21; Falls, *Elizabeth's Irish Wars*, p. 47.

54. Cruickshank, *Elizabeth's Army*, p. 15, for the numbers sent to France and for the attrition rate.

55. Stewart, 'The "Irish Road"', in Fissel (ed.), *War and Government*, pp. 19–20 for costs; Cruickshank, *Elizabeth's Army*, pp. 51–4 for the organization of the English army units along modern continental forms. F.C. Dietz, 'The Exchequer in Elizabeth's Reign', *Smith College Studies in History*, 8 (1923), 6–104 provides figures which total £1,216,720 for the Exchequer expenditures in cash for the navy from 1585 to 1603 and £3,645,998 for the Ordnance Office and the support of land forces in the same period.

56. F.C. Dietz, 'The Receipts and Issues of the Exchequer during the Reigns of James I and Charles I', *Smith College Studies in History*, 13 (1928), 158–61.

57. Dietz, 'The Exchequer in Elizabeth's Reign', 71.

58. S.R. Gardiner, *History of England, from the Accession of James I to the Outbreak of the Civil War, 1603–1642* (10 vols, London, Longmans, Green and Co., 1883–8), ii, pp. 1–16; Conrad Russell, *The Crisis of Parliaments: English History 1509–1660* (Oxford, Oxford University Press, 1971), pp. 244–51.

59. G. Parker, *The Thirty Years' War* (London, Routledge and Kegan Paul, 1984).

60. Firth, *Cromwell's Army*, pp. 2–3.

61. Gardiner, *History of England*, iii, pp. 358–64; Russell, *Crisis of Parliaments*, p. 291.

62. Boynton, *The Elizabethan Militia*, pp. 243–70.

63. Mark Fissel, *The Bishops' Wars: Charles I's Campaigns Against Scotland, 1638–1640* (Cambridge, Cambridge University Press, 1994).

64. L. Stone, *The Causes of the English Revolution* (New York, Harper and Row, 1972). Stone notes that the English government collapsed in 1640. The fundamental cause of this collapse was the government's obsolete fiscal and military systems.

65. Public Record Office, Exchequer E351/302, 304–6, Treasurers at War declared accounts, 1645 to 1659 (hereafter cited as PRO, E . . . ; State Papers 25/118; SP63/281; SP28/139, part 22; K.S. Bottigheimer, *English Money and Irish Land* (Oxford, Clarendon Press, 1971), pp. 55–7; J. Ohlmeyer, *Ireland from Independence to Occupation, 1641–1660* (Cambridge, Cambridge University Press, 1995). For casualties see W. Petty, *The Political Anatomy of Ireland, 1672* (London, D. Brown, 1691), pp. 17–21.

66. C. Carlton, *Going to the Wars: The Experience of the British Civil Wars, 1638–1651* (London, Routledge, 1992), pp. 203–5.

67. Firth, *Cromwell's Army*, pp. 22–4.

68. I. Gentles, *The New Model Army In England, Ireland and Scotland, 1645–1653* (Oxford, Blackwell, 1992); B. Capp, *Cromwell's Navy: The Fleet and the English Revolution, 1648–1660* (Oxford, Clarendon Press, 1989).

69. H.M.C. Reece, 'The Military Presence in England, 1647–1660' (Oxford, Ph.D. unpublished dissertation, 1981), p. 287 for army strength; see chapter four below for the army's growth and administration; M. Oppenheim, *A History of the Administration of the Royal Navy* (Ann Arbor, MI, Cushing-Malloy Inc., 1961 edn of 1896 book), pp. 330–7 for number of ships. A total of 207 warships were added to the navy in the period 1649–1660: see Bodleian Library, Rawlinson MS A 223, fo. 130; also see chapter three below.

70. See chapter seven for the excise and chapter eight for the assessment.

71. J.S. Wheeler, 'English Naval Finance, 1649–1660', *The Historical Journal*, 39 (1996), 457–66.

72. Childs, *The Army of Charles II*, pp. 14–18, 198, 203–4.
73. R. Cust, *The Forced Loan and English Politics, 1626–1628* (Oxford, Oxford University Press, 1987).
74. R.D. Richards, 'The Stop of the Exchequer', *Economic History*, Series ii (1930–3), 45–62; G.O. Nichols, 'English Government Borrowing, 1660–1688', *The Journal of British Studies*, 10 (1971), 100–1.
75. J.D. Davies, *Gentlemen and Tarpaulins: The Officers and Men of the Restoration Navy* (Oxford, Clarendon Press, 1991), p. 228.
76. Kennedy, *The Rise and Fall of English Naval Mastery*, pp. 57–62.
77. Ibid., pp. 189–95.
78. S. Hornstein, *The Restoration Navy and English Foreign Trade, 1674–1688: A Study in the Peacetime Use of Seapower* (Aldershot, Scolar Press, 1991), pp. 109–10.
79. D.W. Jones, ·*War and Economy in the Age of William III and Marlborough* (Oxford, Blackwell, 1988), p. 29.
80. Nichols, 'English Government Borrowing', pp. 82–4, 104.
81. British Library, Additional MS 10119, fo. 173 for the army costs and see chapter four below; PRO, E351/2306–21, declared accounts of the Navy Treasurers, 1689 to 1699. Additional amounts were spent by the Ordnance Office on both services.

CHAPTER TWO

1. Rodger, *Safeguard of the Sea*, pp. 221–37; Kennedy, *The Rise and Fall of British Naval Mastery*, p. 24; C.S.L. Davies, 'The Administration of the Royal Navy Under Henry VIII: The Origins of the Navy Board', *English Historical Review*, 80 (April 1965), 268–88; D. Loades, 'From King's Ships to the Royal Navy, 1500–1642', in J.R. Hill (ed.), *The Oxford Illustrated History of the Royal Navy* (Oxford, Oxford University Press, 1995), pp. 24–30; D. Loades, *The Tudor Navy: An Administrative, Political, and Military History* (Cambridge, Scolar Press, 1992), pp. 1–10, 102–8; Oppenheim, *A History of the Administration of the Royal Navy*, pp. 1–44 for the earlier period; ibid., pp. 45–99 for Henry VIII's contributions. Oppenheim's book is a classic still used for statistical information by historians such as Kennedy, *The Rise and Fall of English Navy*, J. Glete, *Navies and Nations* (Stockholm, Almquest and Wiksell Inc., 1993), Capp, *Cromwell's Navy: The Fleet and the English Revolution, 1648–1660*, and K.R. Andrews, *Ships, Money and Politics: Seafaring and Naval Enterprise in the Reign of Charles I* (Cambridge, Cambridge University Press, 1991). Glete's work provides the best summary of statistics for Western European navies.
2. The term 'Sinews of power' is used in Brewer's brilliant book, *The Sinews of Power*; there is also an interesting and useful article with a similar title by G.V. Scammell, 'The Sinews of War: Manning and Provisioning English Fighting Ships, *c.* 1550–1650', *Mariner's Mirror*, 73 (August 1987), 351–69. The two works are quite different.
3. Oppenheim, *Administration*, pp. 49–52. The largest single building programme under Henry VIII was in 1544–6, when eighteen warships were built.
4. Parker, *The Cambridge Illustrated History of Warfare*, pp. 120–32; Parker, 'The Dreadnought Revolution of Tudor England', pp. 270–2; Oppenheim, *Administration*, pp. 28, 37–41, 52–60; Davies, 'Administration of the Royal Navy under Henry VIII', p. 268.
5. Loades, *Tudor Navy*, pp. 81–94.
6. Ibid., pp. 81–97; Loades, 'From King's Ships to the Royal Navy, 1500–1642', in Hill (ed.), *Oxford Illustrated History of the Royal Navy*, pp. 28–34; Rodger, *The Safeguard of the Sea*, pp. 221–8.

7. W. Beveridge et al., *Prices and Wages in England* (London, Longmans, Green and Co., 1939), pp. 503–7; Loades, *Tudor Navy*, pp. 161–71.

8. Davies, 'Administration of the Royal Navy under Henry VIII', pp. 277–9.

9. Loades, 'From the King's Ships to the Royal Navy, 1500–1642', in Hill (ed.), *Oxford Illustrated History of the Royal Navy*, pp. 32–3. Loades concludes that this reduction did not indicate a decline in the repair or maintenance budget, but he does not discuss the effects of the inflation of the late sixteenth and early seventeenth centuries.

10. Kennedy, *English Naval Mastery*, pp. 26–8. Kennedy indicates that Elizabeth spent roughly £4.5 million on the wars in France and the Netherlands and less than £1 million on her naval efforts. There is an interesting debate about the 'British way of war' between Michael Howard and B.H. Liddell Hart. Liddell Hart, like Raleigh and Drake, thought that England should pursue a maritime strategy, and except for the period 1914 to 1918 it has. He believes England must, and did historically, avoid committing large resources to a land war in the main theatre in Europe. Howard recognizes that England cannot allow a single power in Europe to dominate the North Sea and Channel ports. Thus she has often sent major land forces to the main area of operations on the continent. Howard reasons that Elizabeth pursued, and had to pursue, such a continental strategy. Mattingly, *The Spanish Armada*, concludes that Elizabeth I's war against Spain was the first of the modern wars fought by the English to maintain a balance of power in Western Europe. This issue is central to English naval history and diplomacy from 1570 to 1990.

11. Parker, 'The Dreadnought Revolution of Tudor England', pp. 271–2 and 283–4.

12. Oppenheim, *Administration*, p. 164.

13. The naval expenditures in Table 2.1 include the cash issued to the Navy Treasurer, the Surveyor of Victuals, and the Ordnance Office. Sources: Dietz, 'The Exchequer in Elizabeth's Reign', 96–104 for the total cash issues for the period 1566 to 1602 – the year ran from September to September for the Exchequer accounts; Dietz, 'The Receipts and Issues of the Exchequer during the Reigns of James I and Charles I', for the issues in the period 1603–5; for the period 1600 to 1605, PRO, Audit Office 1/1690/36–7, AO1/1691/38–41 and E351/2242–5, declared accounts of the Navy Treasurers, 1600 to 1605. The Navy Treasurers' accounts run from 1 January to 31 December each year. The two different accounting years are close enough to indicate trends only. The amounts for the different periods are, therefore, not absolute, but representative of the amounts issued. Also see Oppenheim, *Administration*, p. 161. Oppenheim's figures are generally close to those in the other sources, but his work is far less valuable as a source for financial data than are the declared accounts in the PRO and Dietz's Exchequer records. An additional £30,000 per year was provided to support Elizabeth's court and government through the assignment of tallies. The assignment by tallies showed up first in Dietz's Exchequer accounts in the account for 1572, and continued from then to the end of his Elizabethan account. Most of the tallies were issued for the support of the royal household. The tallies were instruments committing a specified source of revenue to pay for part of the expenses of a certain department. The tallies were presented by the recipient to the treasurer or collector of the specified revenue in exchange for cash. The treasurer then presented the tally to the Exchequer as partial payment of his tax receipts. The Exchequer issues in the tables in this chapter are for cash issues only.

14. Andrews, *Ships, Money and Politics*, pp. 140–2.

15. D.H. Fischer, *The Great Wave: Price Revolutions and the Rhythm of History* (Oxford, Oxford University Press, 1996), p. 90. The graph shows a 200 per cent or more rate of inflation from 1510 to 1590, indicating that seamen's victualling rates slightly exceeded the general rate of price-inflation.

16. Oppenheim, *Administration*, pp. 102 for 1546–7, pp. 161–3 for 1588, p. 160 for the 1596 Cadiz expedition.

17. Ibid., p. 183 and pp. 144–8 for Hawkin's accomplishments. See Oppenheim's biographical assessment of Hawkins, appendix C, for excellent insights into the way in which most Tudor governments were dishonest by modern English standards. He concludes that Hawkins delivered good services where they most counted, in the fighting ships.

18. Rodger, *Safeguard of the Sea*, pp. 366–70; Oppenheim, *Administration*, pp. 188–99; Dietz, 'The Receipts and Issues of the Exchequer during the Reigns of James I and Charles I', pp. 160–6. This figure includes the cash issued by the Exchequer to the Navy Treasurer, the Surveyor of Victuals, and the Ordnance Office for all purposes from 1605 to 1609. It excludes the value of tallies issued since Dietz's account records the specific purposes for the £918,651 in tallies issued from 1603 to 1625.

19. G.E. Aylmer, 'Attempts at Administrative Reform, 1625–40', *English Historical Review*, 72 (April 1957), 234–5.

20. Ibid., pp. 234–5; Oppenheim, *Administration*, p. 195.

21. Aylmer, 'Administrative Reform', pp. 234–36.

22. See Table 2.1. Also, see A. Thrush, 'Naval Finance and the Origins and Development of Ship Money', in M. Fissel (ed.), *War and Government in Britain, 1598–1650*, pp. 135–7.

23. Dietz, 'The Receipts and Issues of the Exchequer during the Reigns of James I and Charles I', pp. 160–6 for total Exchequer cash issues and for the £918,651 in assignment of anticipated revenue by tallies; PRO, AO1/1690/36–7, AO1/1691/38–41 for the declared accounts of the Navy Treasurers, 1 January 1600 to 31 December 1603; E351/2242–62 for the declared accounts of the Navy Treasurers, 1604–24; Oppenheim, *Administration*, p. 161 for victualling costs for 1600–3 and p. 197 for victualling costs 1604–24.

24. Fischer, *The Great Wave*, p. 90, figure 2.13 and p. 92, figure 2.14 for inflation in the trend of prices of consumables from 1450 to 1650. Inflation is extremely hard to measure in early modern Europe. Fischer shows the trends. He also shows, on pp. 102–3, figures 2.18 and 2.19, that prices fell in real terms from roughly 1650 to 1738. There is solid agreement as to the existence of significant price-inflation from 1550 to about 1650, although not to its causes. Another good source on price-inflation of early modern England is R.B. Outhwaite, *Inflation in Tudor and Early Stuart England* (London, Macmillan, 1969).

25. Rodger, *Safeguard of the Sea*, pp. 364–8; Oppenheim, *Administration*, p. 145.

26. Glete, *Navies and Nations*, i: 162–3, Table 21.8, lists the growth of the Danish, English, French, Dutch and Swedish navies from 1590 to 1650. By 1620, the Dutch war fleet had 56 major warships, versus 29 English warships. In the 1620s, the size of the French navy exploded, rising from 3 to 57 warships in 1630.

27. Dietz, 'The Receipts and Issues of the Exchequer during the Reigns of James I and Charles I', pp. 135–45.

28. Oppenheim, *Administration*, p. 161 for the amounts spent on the navy from 1559 to 1602; ibid., p. 194 for the debt James inherited.

29. He also spent £505,026 on the defence of the Palatinate from 1620 to 1623, with nothing to show for it. B[ritish] L[ibrary], Add[itional] MS 10119, Montague Revenue Accounts, fo. 3.

30. L.C. Martin, 'John Crane (1576–1660) of Loughton, Bucks., Surveyor General of All Victuals for Ships, 1635–1642', *Mariner's Mirror*, 70 (May 1984), 143–8. Sir Allen Apsley, Victualler from 1612, died in 1630 while owed possibly as much as £100,000; Sampson Darrell, Victualler from 1630, resigned in 1634 because it cost him more to

feed the seamen than he was allowed; John Crane, Surveyor of Victuals from 1635 to 1642 was owed roughly £27,500 when he fled to Oxford to join Charles I, in spite of the fact that the *per diem* victualling rate was raised from 6½*d* in harbour and 7*d* at sea to 7½*d* and 8*d* respectively.

31. A. Thrush, 'The Ordnance Office and the Navy, 1625–40', *Mariner's Mirror*, 77 (November 1991), 339–54; Stewart, *English Ordnance Office*, pp. 142–6.

32. Andrews, *Ships, Money and Politics*, pp. 7–8.

33. C. Holmes, 'Parliament, Liberty, Taxation, and Property', in J.H. Hexter (ed.), *Parliament and Liberty from the Reign of Elizabeth to the English Civil War* (Stanford, CA, Stanford University Press, 1992), pp. 123–44.

34. Ibid.

35. Oppenheim, *Administration*, p. 251; Kennedy, *Naval Mastery*, p. 40, says there were 100 ships with only 2 royal vessels in the Cadiz expedition. Oppenheim is using PRO, SP 67/47. Kennedy uses C.D. Penn, *The Navy Under the Early Stuarts* (London, Cornmarket Press, 1970 edn).

36. Kennedy, *Naval Mastery*, p. 40; R.W. Stewart, 'Arms and Expenditure: The Ordnance Office and the assaults on Cadiz (1625) and the Isle of Rhe (1627)', in Fissel (ed.), *War and Government*, pp. 112–3 and 119–21.

37. For the amounts of money see PRO, E351/2263. This was an increase of eight-fold from the £26,092 he spent in 1624 (PRO, E351/2262); Oppenheim, *Administration*, pp. 219–25; Rodger, *Safeguard of the Sea*, pp. 358–63.

38. Kennedy, *Naval Mastery*, p. 40; Stewart, 'Arms and Expenditures', pp. 121–8.

39. E. Clarendon, *History of the Rebellion* (London, Printed at the Theater, 1733 edn), i: pp. 38–42.

40. Oppenheim, *Administration*, p. 221.

41. PRO, E351/2428, declared account of Sir Allen Apsley, 1 January through 31 December 1628.

42. PRO, E351/2429, declared account of Sir Allen Apsley for 1629 and E351/2430 for 1630, Apsley's final account listing his great indebtedness. Oppenheim, *Administration*, p. 233 for his 1629 petition.

43. PRO, E351/2431 for 1630; E351/2432 for 1631; there is no account surviving for 1632; E351/2433 for 1633; E351/2434 for 1634; E351/2435 for the first five months of 1635; and E351/2436 for May to September 1635.

44. PRO, E351/2437–47 for Crane's declared accounts for his seven years as Surveyor of Victuals.

45. Oppenheim, *Administration*, 281–2. They were appointed at the pleasure of the King, instead of for life.

46. PRO, E351/2448–58, the declared accounts for the Surveyors of Victuals, 1660–78 list the money clearly as received from the Navy Treasurer; E351/2285–96, Navy Treasurers' declared accounts, 1643–60 make it clear that the treasurer paid the victuallers; E351/2297–333, the declared accounts of the treasurers from 1660 to 1700 make it clear that the Navy Treasurer was paying the victualler or the contractors who undertook victualling.

47. BL, Egerton MS 2541, fos. 119–125.

48. Dietz, 'The Receipts and Issues of the Exchequer during the Reigns of James I and Charles I', pp. 164–6 for Exchequer issues to the navy and Ordnance. Assignment by means of tallies totalled over £1.3 million, but a large portion of these tallies were really royal debt and unredeemed because the tax revenues were over-obligated in the late 1630s; PRO, E351/2263–83, AO1/1705/85–8, AO1/1706/89 for the declared accounts of Navy Treasurers for 1625 through 1642; Bodl. Rawlinson MS A223, fos. 75–7 and T[homason] T[racts], E405(8), pp. 7–9 for 1643–4 costs; PRO, E351/2428–47 for the

declared accounts of the victuallers for 1628–42, and Oppenheim, *Administration*, p. 294 for victualling costs for 1625–7.

49. The total issues for the period 1635–9 by the Exchequer were £3,106,807, according to Dietz's reckoning. I have added the £702,698 raised by the ship-money tax and disbursed by the Navy Treasurer to the Exchequer issues to provide a clearer picture of government expenditures, since ship-money was paid directly to the Navy Treasurer. See Table 2.4 for the ship-money receipts.

50. I have added the ship-money received by the Navy Treasurer to the totals issued by the Exchequer to the Navy Treasurer and the Ordnance Office.

51. The Ordnance Office provided arms, cannon and munitions to the land forces as well as to the navy, but it is impossible to separate the amounts in Dietz. See Dietz, 'The Receipts and Issues of the Exchequer during the Reigns of James I and Charles I', fn. 102, p. 171 for the breakdown of money expended in 1640 for the war in the north.

52. Gardiner, *History of England*, viii: p. 82.

53. J.V. Beckett, 'Land Tax or Excise: The Levying of Taxation in Seventeenth- and Eighteenth-Century England', *English Historical Review*, 100 (April 1985), 285.

54. Thrush, 'Ship Money', in Fissel (ed.), *War and Government*, p. 141; he cites BL, Harleian MS 703, fos. 129 v–130.

55. Kevin Sharpe, *The Personal Rule of Charles I* (New Haven, CT, Yale University Press, 1992), pp. 567–96 for a superb discussion of the difficulties involved with the rating and collection of ship-money, and for its financial success.

56. BL, Add. MS 10119, Montague Revenue Accounts, fo. 5. A single subsidy in Elizabeth's reign produced over £100,000, while a single subsidy in James I's reign brought in about £70,000 in money whose real value was eroded by severe price-inflation.

57. Beckett, 'Land Tax or Excise', p. 287.

58. Andrews, *Ships, Money and Politics*, p. 147.

59. PRO, E351/2275, Navy Treasurer's declared account, 1635; Gardiner, *History of England*, viii: p. 376 for the total assessment and the plans for its implementation; Andrews, *Ships, Money and Politics*, pp. 139–49, for a brilliant analysis of the politics and strategy of ship-money; Thrush, 'Ship Money', in Fissel (ed.), *War and Government*, pp. 133–4.

60. PRO, E351/2275.

61. BL, Add. MS 9301, fo. 53.

62. Gardiner, *History of England*, viii: pp. 279–81.

63. BL, Lansdowne MS 232, fos. 34–6 for the assessments of all counties for the years 1635 to 1639.

64. BL, Lansdowne MS 232, fo. 34.

65. PRO, E351/2275, 2276, 2278, 2280, 2282 show how much the Navy Treasurer received from the Sheriffs and how much he spent directly on the navy. Dietz, 'The Receipts and Issues of the Exchequer during the Reigns of James I and Charles I', p. 149. In 1636 the only payment of ship-money into the Exchequer by the Sheriffs or Navy Treasurer took place. This was a repayment by the Navy Treasurer for money provided to the ship-money fleet by the Exchequer in the previous year. M.D. Gordon, 'The Collection of Ship-money in the Reign of Charles I', *Transactions of the Royal Historical Society*, 4 (1910), 141–62, provides slightly different figures for the yield of ship-money. She confused the amount levied with the actual receipt, and confused the payments with receipts as well. The Navy Treasurer's (Russell's) receipts of ship-money from the Sheriffs are clear in his declared accounts, as are his disbursements. But her article is useful if interpreted correctly along with the declared accounts of Russell.

66. PRO, E351/2275 declared account for 1635; E351/2276 for 1636; E351/2278 for 1637; E351/2280 for 1638; E351/2282 for 1639; and *Calendar of State Papers, Domestic,*

1640, pp. 350 and 645 for the assessment and collection of 1640. The amounts received by the Navy Treasurer in 1635 were from the assessment of 1634, 1636 for those of 1635, etc. There is no declared account of the Navy Treasurer for 1640.

67. Dietz, 'The Receipts and Issues of the Exchequer during the Reigns of James I and Charles I', p. 152 for Exchequer receipts of 1636; PRO E351/2276 and 2277 for the Navy Treasurer's declared accounts for 1636, listing the money the treasurer received from ship-money and the Exchequer and disbursed for the navy; E351/2437–8 for the victualler's declared accounts.

68. Rodger, *Safeguard of the Sea*, pp. 384–6.

69. Ibid., pp. 382–3; Sharpe, *The Personal Rule of Charles I*, pp. 596–8.

70. BL, Add. MS 9301, Navy Papers, 1618–37, fos. 53–4 for 1635 summer guard of 34 ships and 4,130 men at sea, with 8 ships and 1,602 men in port.

71. F.E. Dyer, 'The Ship-Money Fleet', *Mariner's Mirror*, 23 (April 1937), 199–209.

72. BL, Add. MS 9301, fo. 67.

73. O. Murray, 'The Admiralty II', *Mariner's Mirror*, 23 (April 1937), 145–6 for some financial difficulties associated with the ship-money fleets.

74. Gardiner, *History of England*, viii: pp. 202–22. Gardiner is very critical, justifiably, of Charles's propensity to ask too much, offer too little. Andrews, *Ships, Money and Politics*, chapter six gives Charles credit for conceiving of how to use the ship-money fleets diplomatically, and concludes that Charles's diplomacy broke down because he could not afford war (p. 156).

75. Fissel, *Bishops' Wars*, pp. 3–6. Fissel opens by claiming that Charles's 'maladministration of the institutions at his disposal, rather than structural failure within the institutions themselves, . . . precipitated failure in a war that was entirely of the King's choosing' (p. 1). This is true to a point. Charles was bankrupt and unable to pay his troops, to arm them, or to supply them adequately with food. His armies in these two wars were untrained because he could not afford to raise them early enough to have them properly drilled, nor could he afford to pay for a sufficient cadre of drill masters. These failures were due to a lack of funds and the absence of professional military institutions in England needed to face a Scottish army modelled much more closely on modern continental practice in the 1630s.

76. Fissel, *Bishops' Wars*, p. 24 for a discussion of the condition of the army in 1639 and pp. 116–17, 141 for the army's condition in 1640.

77. *CSPD, 1640*, p. 645.

78. The Exchequer provided £22,430 in 1640 to the Navy Treasurer and £71,194 for the fleet operating in the north in 1639–40. (Dietz, 'The Receipts and Issues of the Exchequer during the Reigns of James I and Charles I', p. 168 and fn. 102, p. 171). PRO, E351/2445, the Surveyor of Victuals' declared account for 1640 lists £29,467 as spent for victualling, and E351/2446, declared account for victualler in 1641, lists £22,561 as spent in 1641. There is no Exchequer account for 1641.

79. BL, Add. MS 9301, fo. 53; Glete, *Navies and Nations*, i: pp. 129 and 162–3 says there were forty-one warships in the fleet in 1635 and forty-three in 1640.

80. BL, Add. MS 9300 for debt in 1641; see PRO, E351/2284, for debt in 1642; Bodl., Rawlinson MS A223, fos. 12–13 for the debt for 1641–3.

81. Russell, *The Crisis of Parliaments*, p. 352.

82. Rodger, *Safeguard of the Sea*, pp. 413–16.

83. Ibid., pp. 416–24; Oppenheim, *Administration*, pp. 287–8; W.B. Cogar, 'The Politics of Naval Administration, 1649–1660' (Oxford, unpublished Ph.D. dissertation, 1983), pp. 9–21.

84. A.C. Dewar, 'The Naval Administration of the Interregnum, 1641–59', *Mariner's Mirror*, 12 (October 1926), 409–15; D.E. Kennedy, 'The Establishment and Settlement of Parliament's Admiralty, 1642–8', *Mariner's Mirror*, 48 (November 1962), 276–81.

85. Bodl., Rawlinson MS A223, is the Navy Commissioners' letter book containing their estimates for the cost of the winter and summer fleets from 1642 to 1654.

86. Oppenheim, *Administration*, p. 403, quoted by Rodger, *Safeguard of the Sea*, p. 422.

87. Cogar, 'Politics of Naval Administration', p. 16. There were six salaried Navy Commissioners appointed in 1642: Richard Crandley, John Morris, Roger Tweedy, John Hollond, William Batten, and Phineas Pett.

88. PRO, E351/2447, victuallers' declared account for 1642; Bodl., Rawlinson MS A223, fo. 75 for 1643; C[ommons] J[ournal], vi: 14–15, for Vane's accounts 8 August 1643 to 12 May 1645; PRO, E351/2284, Navy Treasurer's declared account for 1642; E351/2285, treasurer's declared account for 13 May 1645 to 31 December 1646; E351/2286 and 2287 for 1 January 1647 to 12 May 1649; TT, E405(8), Giles Green, *A Declaration . . . of the Committee of the Navy*, (London, 1 September 1647), p. 8 for 1642; Green's figures for the years 1643–6 are corroborated by the Rawlinson MS A223 and the declared accounts of the Navy Treasurers, PRO, E351/2285. His figures for 1642 are the best available in all of the sources used in this book.

89. Bodl., Rawlinson MS A223, fos. 6, 45–8, 75–7, and 97.

90. M.L. Baumber, 'The Navy and the Civil War in Ireland, 1643–46', *Mariner's Mirror*, 75 (August 1989), 265–9.

91. PRO, E351/2287, the declared account ending in May 1649, lists £233,220 as the amount 'depending and owing' to various suppliers for services and goods actually delivered.

92. Oppenheim, *Administration*, pp. 255 and 263. Andrew Thrush, 'In Pursuit of the Frigate', *Historical Research*, 64 (1991), 29–45. Glete, *Navies and Nations*, Table 21.9 indicates that the average size of English warships fell from 880 tons in 1640 to 680 tons in 1650. J.R. Jones, *The Anglo-Dutch Wars of the Seventeenth Century* (London, Longmans, 1996), pp. 40–2, indicates that the ships built in the 1640s and 50s were mostly 38- to 42-gun frigates, mounting two tiers of guns with about 19 guns per side. Oppenheim, *Administration*, p. 255 for the 1640s ships and pp. 330–7 for the 1650s fleet.

93. Glete, *Navies and Nations*, i: pp. 162–3, Table 21.8 lists the size of the war fleets of England (72), The United Provinces (62), Denmark (43), Sweden (42), and France (32).

94. TT, E405(8), Green, *Vindication . . . of Committee of the Navy*, pp. 8–10; CJ, vi: 14–15 for August 1643 to May 1645, and PRO E351/2285–7 for the period from May 1645 to May 1649.

95. Bodl., Rawlinson MS A223, fo. 6.

96. Bodl., Rawlinson MS A223, fo. 75 for 1643, fos. 80–1 and 85 for 1647–8. These numbers are slightly different from those in R. Harding, *The Evolution of the Sailing Navy, 1509–1815* (New York, St Martin's Press, 1995), p. 152. He takes his data concerning the size of fleets and their composition from Glete, *Navies and Nations*. Glete uses Oppenheim, *Administration*, for the English fleet statistics up to the year 1660. The Navy Commissioners' data is found in Bodl., Rawlinson MS A223, which is the best source for such data.

97. G. Holmes, *Augustan England: Profession, State and Society, 1680–1730* (London, George Allen and Unwin, 1982), p. 239 defines a state servant as someone 'whose vocational justification lay entirely in serving the state's needs, as opposed to private needs'.

98. Bodl., Rawlinson MS A223, fos. 100–2 and 108–9 for 1650–1; Rawlinson MS A225, fos. 99–100 for 1651; Rawlinson MS A226 for 1652; BL, Add. MS 10,119, fo. 12b for 1658; Add. MS 9302, fo. 14 for 1660; Glete, *Navies and Nations*, i: p. 129 agrees with these numbers, and uses Oppenheim, *Administration*, as his source. Jones, *Anglo-Dutch Wars*, p. 38 notes this trend to the exclusion of hired merchant ships in the battlefleets.

99. TT, E405(8), Green, *Vindication of . . . Committee of Navy*, pp. 9–10; Bodl., Rawlinson MS A223, fos. 45–8 and 80–1.

CHAPTER THREE

1. R.C. Anderson, 'The Royalists at Sea, 1649', *Mariner's Mirror*, 14 (1928), 320–30; J. Ohlmeyer, 'Irish Privateers during the Civil War, 1642–1650', *Mariner's Mirror*, 75 (May 1990), 119–34.
2. Bodl., Rawlinson MSS A223–A225 are the Navy Commissioners' letter books for 1649–53, providing a detailed account of their activities; J.S. Wheeler, 'Prelude to Power: The Crisis of 1649 and the Foundation of English Naval Power', *Mariner's Mirror*, 81 (May 1995), 148–55.
3. Bodl., Rawlinson MSS A224–A227 are records of the proceedings of the Admiralty Committee from March 1649 to the summer of 1653. They contain thousands of copies of warrants and orders sent to the Commissioners, the Treasurer, and Generals at Sea.
4. R.C. Anderson, 'Operations of the English Fleet, 1648–52', *English Historical Review*, 31 (1916), 406–28; Capp, *Cromwell's Navy*, pp. 1–11, 42–72 for the Navy 'New-Modelled'; P. Lefevre, 'Sir George Ayscue, Commonwealth and Protectorate Admiral', *Mariner's Mirror*, 68 (1982), 189–200; J.R. Powell, 'The Expedition of Blake and Montague in 1655', *Mariner's Mirror*, 52 (1966), 341–67; W.B. Cogar, 'The Politics of Naval Administration, 1649–1660' (Oxford, unpublished Ph.D. dissertation, 1983), p. 288.
5. M. Baumber, *General at Sea Robert Blake: Robert Blake and the Seventeenth-Century Revolution in Naval Warfare* (London, John Murray, 1989).
6. Bodl., Rawlinson MS A223, fos. 100–3 for 1650, fo. 113 for fleet operating off Portugal in 1651; C.R. Boxer, 'Blake and the Brazil Fleet, 1650', *Mariner's Mirror*, 36 (1950), 212–33 for Blake's sustained operations off Lisbon.
7. Bodl., Rawlinson MS A223, fo. 112 for cost of ten frigates; Oppenheim, *Administration*, p. 330 for the number of ships built in 1649 and 1650.
8. Blake's extended blockade of Lisbon was sustained by one of the first examples of 'under way replenishment' in history. J. Black, *Cambridge Illustrated Atlas of Warfare: Renaissance to Revolution, 1492–1792* (Cambridge, Cambridge University Press, 1996), p. 88, incorrectly states that the first example of 'revictualling at sea was first employed in 1705 to support an English fleet maintaining watch on Brest'. John Ehrman, *The Navy in the War of William III, 1689–1697* (Cambridge, Cambridge University Press, 1953), describes how the English used fifty or more hired merchant ships to supply their fleets at sea in William's war. The English also maintained a two-month blockade of the Dutch coast in the First Dutch War, according to Jones, *Anglo-Dutch Wars*, pp. 55–65.
9. Wheeler, 'Prelude to Power', pp. 150–1.
10. *CSPD, 1649–50*, pp. xxii–xxiii; N.A.M. Rodger, 'Guns and Sails in English Colonization', in N. Canny (ed.), *The Origins of Empire* (Oxford, Oxford University Press, 1998), p. 96.
11. PRO, E351/2288–96, declared accounts of the Navy Treasurers Sir Henry Vane, Jr and Richard Hutchinson, May 1649 to 7 July 1660.
12. Fischer, *The Great Wave*, pp. 90, 92, 102 for the general inflation rate; Oppenheim, *Administration*, pp. 142–3 for victualling rates and 314 for seamen's wages.
13. The move away from the use of a mixed fleet of private and state-owned ships is shown clearly in Bodl. Rawlinson MS A223, fos. 1–110. The Navy Commissioners list the

fleets deployed from 1643 through 1650 according to state's ships and merchant ships. The latter category begins a steady decline in proportion of the battle fleet in the mid-1640s. By the early 1650s, the commissioners have ceased to differentiate between the categories.

14. Bodl., Rawlinson MS A223, fo. 130, for the total number of sailors sent out in the summer of 1654; Oppenheim, *Administration*, pp. 330–7 for the size of Cromwell's fleet.

15. PRO, E351/2290–3, and 2296 list the amounts paid by the Treasurers at War to the Navy Treasurer from 1652 to 1655, and in 1660 – 11 per cent of the navy's funds was provided from the assessment 1655 to 1660; Bodl., Rawlinson MS A208, the Treasurers at War account book listing the payment of assessment receipts to the Navy Treasurer, 1655–9.

16. *CSPD, 1652–3*, p. 44.

17. Bodl., Rawlinson MS A227, fos. 53, 54, 59, 63–6, 74, 76 for the directions and orders for the use of replenishment hoys and ships to support over eighty warships at sea with food, water, and munitions.

18. Kennedy, *Naval Mastery*, pp. 54–7; C.R. Boxer, *The Anglo-Dutch Wars of the Seventeenth Century* (London, HMSO, 1974), p. 15.

19. Jones, *Anglo-Dutch Wars*, p. 30.

20. J.S. Wheeler, 'English Financial Operations During the First Dutch War, 1652–54', *The Journal of European Economic History*, 23 (Autumn, 1994), 329–43.

21. Bodl., Rawlinson MS A227, fo. 45.

22. *CSPD, 1652–3*, pp. 19, 29, 42–3.

23. Ibid., pp. 8, 56, and 100; Rodger, 'Guns and Sails in English Colonization', in Canny (ed.), *Origins of Empire*, pp. 95–7.

24. The declared accounts for the Ordnance Office run from 1642 to 1651 and then there is a gap until the resumption of an independent Ordnance Office in 1660. The money spent for munitions and ordnance is accounted for in the Navy Treasurer's declared accounts in the 1650s.

25. Clarendon, *History*, vi: p. 94.

26. Kennedy, *Naval Mastery*, p. 45; Jones, *Anglo-Dutch Wars*, p. 51 is also confused on this matter.

27. *CJ*, vi: 14–15, Vane's account for 8 August 1643 to 12 May 1645; PRO, E351/2285–7, declared accounts of Navy Treasurer Henry Vane, 13 May 1645 to 12 May 1649. No other such receipts from Royalists are listed in these accounts for this period. See above discussion for the sources of money for this period.

28. PRO, E351/2288–96, Navy Treasurers' declared accounts; E401/1930–2, Exchequer Receipt Books, November 1654 to July 1660; E401/1933, Exchequer Receipt Book, July 1660–September 1661; R.D. Richards, 'The Exchequer in Cromwellian Times', *Economic History* (January 1931), 213–33 has slightly different totals, and only covers the period to April 1660.

29. PRO, E401/1930–2. The taxes and fees were English customs (£1.72 million), Irish customs farm (£17,500), excise to include farm of beer excise (£2.134 million), postal farm (£47,521), new building tax (£39,650), probate of wills (£35,542), assessment (£10,720), wine licences (£2,520), alum farm (£2,000), rents (£6,460), subsidy arrears (£2,035), tax on sea coals (£1,838), sheriffs' profits (£3,551), and lady day (£631), for a total of £4,023,532.

30. PRO, E401/1930, fos. 199, 204, 212, 216, 219; PRO, E401/1931, fos. 18, 23, 29, 35, 41, 47, 55, 60, 76, 81, 88, 98, 110, 116, 123, 134, and 183.

31. For these totals see the weekly amounts in PRO, E401/1930–2. This includes £183,565 that was sent to the Exchequer from the county receiver generals that possibly could

be considered fines or rents from Royalists and Catholics, £69,878 from delinquent fines and sequestrations, £33,498 from the sale of delinquent estates, £18,375 from the sale of dean and chapter lands, £22,234 from fines and alienations, £1,537 from fee farm rents, £13,541 from Goldsmiths' Hall treasury, and £33,683 from Vyner and Richards, for a total of £376,311. H.J. Habakkuk, 'Public Finance and the Sale of Confiscated Property during the Interregnum', *Economic History Review*, 15 (1962), 83–7.

32. Bodl., Rawlinson A187, fo. 223, for a record of a letter from a Navy Commissioner to the Committee of the Navy asking it to order the Navy Treasurer to issue 'some considerable sum of money for payment of 2 or 3 months' bills in course'; J.S. Wheeler, 'Navy Finance, 1649–1660', *Historical Journal*, 39 (June 1996), 457–66; PRO E351/2287 for 1649 and E351/2294 for 1656. These declared accounts provide the amounts owed to individual contractors and merchants at the end of each account. They include the date the debt was incurred and the amount still owed in the period the account covers.

33. *CSPD, 1651–2*, p. 357.

34. PRO, E351/2288–96, each of the Navy Treasurer's declared accounts lists the amounts owed to the victuallers at the end of the account, under the years in which the warrants for contract were issued. Also, unpaid obligations for supplies and services were listed under the amount 'depending' (owed) in the current accounting year. The total of the current year's depending amount was the 'new debt'.

35. PRO, E351/2294, declared account for 1656. Ninety per cent of the £238,302 in debt accrued in 1654 was paid off by the end of 1656; Wheeler, 'Navy Finance, 1649–1660'.

36. Chandaman, *English Public Revenue*, pp. 285–8. Use of Sol and Pro tallies as credit instruments in the 1660s mean that 'beyond the possibility of doubt . . . in the Restoration period, by a procedure as yet unknown to Exchequer historians, not only the Pro tally but the ordinary Sol tally of receipt was in fact being employed on a large scale for purposes of payment', p. 288.

37. PRO, SP28/259–60, for examples of the records of the Committee for the Accounts that contain thousands of warrants used in this manner. The Treasurers at War used warrants in a similar manner, but their declared accounts do not contain the same kind of information provided by the declared accounts of the Navy Treasurer about the retirement of debt each year from 1650 to 1660.

38. PRO, E351/2295 for 1657 and E351/2296 for January 1658 to July 1660.

39. PRO, E351/2296.

40. Capp, *Cromwell's Navy*, p. 374 maintains that the fleet and dockyards were paid off in 1660–1, but he says nothing about the debt owed to suppliers and contractors.

41. Ibid., pp. 331–68 for the navy's role in politics, 1659–60.

42. BL, Add. MS 9302, fo. 14 lists 109 warships in rates one through six, while Bodl. Rawlinson MS A181, fo. 407 lists 139 warships in rates one through six and 22 support vessels.

43. Harding, *The Evolution of the Sailing Navy, 1509–1815*, p. 62 for first half of quote and p. 79 for second part. This book better supports the view that there was a revolution in naval affairs in the 1650s.

44. Brewer, *The Sinews of Power*, p. 7.

45. Black, *European Warfare, 1660–1815*, pp. 7–9.

46. Glete, *Navies and Nations*, pp. 178–9 for first Glete quote and p. 6 for the second quote and for Glete's general observations on the process.

47. Parker, *Military Revolution* (1996 edn), pp. 83 and 100–2.

48. Ehrman, *The Navy in the War of William III*, p. 135, points out that these instructions

were reaffirmed by the Lord Admiral, James, Duke of York in 1661 and that the articles of 1652 were 'based on ordinances of the House of Commons of 1649'.

49. Capp, *Cromwell's Navy*, p. 331.
50. BL, Add. MS 9300, fo. 413 for size of fleet in 1661; See G. Robinson, 'Admiralty and Naval Affairs, May 1660 to 1674', *Mariner's Mirror*, 36 (January 1950), 12–40 for an abstract of a seventeenth-century record book 'Admiralty and Naval Affairs, 31 May 1660–March 1674'. This document is similar in a number of ways to the style and content of the Add. MS 9302.
51. Jones, *Anglo-Dutch Wars*, p. 50, considers the changes made in the crisis of 1652–3 to be of 'absolutely fundamental importance. . . . To continue until the mutinies of 1797 with only minor modifications'; Capp, *Cromwell's Navy*, pp. 371–3, although Capp says the changes were sweeping, he goes on to prove that the changes in personnel, organization, and procedure were not sweeping; Robinson, 'Admiralty Affairs', p. 13, the Navy Commissioners were continued in their places. The victualler, Denis Gauden, had been a victual contractor in the 1650s, and the Admiralty and Navy Board, originally part of the Commonwealth's Council of State, and then of the Protector's Council, continued as part of the Royal Council.
52. Capp, *Cromwell's Navy*, pp. 379–91; Jones, *Anglo-Dutch Wars*, pp. 53–5.
53. Harding, *The Evolution of the Sailing Navy*, pp. 87–91; Holmes, *Augustan England*, p. 240 says that by 1680 the sea service was regarded as a lifetime's vocation. Further, he does not believe that the professional navy officer corps came into existence before this date, even though he acknowledges that Charles I's ship-money fleets began the peacetime opportunity for 'semi-permanent' employment.
54. Harding, *The Evolution of the Sailing Navy*, p. 99. Harding concludes that the navy, from 1660 to 1685, was 'large, well supported by maritime industries and seafaring communities, and increasingly well organized, but it lacked the basic financial strength for full mobilization over a long period'.
55. PRO, AO1/1845/67, declared accounts of the Ordnance Office, 23 June 1662 to 13 October 1670; Chandaman, *English Public Revenue*, pp. 350–7 for September 1670 to April 1680.
56. Fischer, *The Great Wave*, pp. 102–6.
57. PRO, E351/2297–312, and AO1/1711/107, AO1/1712/108 and 110, AO1/1713/111–112 Navy Treasurers' declared accounts from 6 July 1660 to 31 January 1680; BL, Add. MS 9302, fo. 186 lists the expenditures for the navy from July 1660 to 1674. My totals, which come from the treasurers' declared accounts, and Add. MS 9302 agree very closely, within 3 per cent. For example, the MS total for the period ending June 1661 is £269,335 and that for 1674 is £1,306,510. When one uses the declared accounts, it is important to separate the actual disbursements from money carried forward in hand and from the old and new debt. It is necessary to add the new debt in each account to the disbursements, since the debt was incurred for goods and services purchased for the navy in the account period. The total amount of navy debt is listed at the end of each account as money 'depending' and then is carried forward to the next account and listed again as a charge.
58. W.A. Shaw, 'The Beginning of the National Debt', in T.F. Tout and James Tait (eds), *Historical Essays by Members of the Owens College, Manchester* (London, Longmans, 1902), p. 99, 393–4 and 398–400 for actual revenue, 1661–7; G. Holmes, *The Making of a Great Power* (London, Longmans, 1986), pp. 88–90; Roseveare, *The Financial Revolution*, pp. 13–14; Chandaman, *English Public Revenue*, chapters one, two, and three provide detailed descriptions of the customs, the excise, and the hearth tax; Braddick does so as well in *The Nerves of State*.

59. PRO, E351/2297–2303 for each year's new debt, amount of old debt paid off, and total debt at the end. Large amounts of Exchequer tallies were also issued in payment for services and supplies, and would have been counted as navy debt in the 1650s. These tallies made the real debt of the navy much higher, but there is no way to find out how much was obligated in this manner.

60. Chandaman, *English Public Revenue*, p. 328.

61. Ibid., pp. 216–17.

62. Nicols, 'English Government Borrowing, 1660–1688', pp. 97–9.

63. Chandaman, *English Public Revenue*, p. 216.

64. Shaw, 'The Beginning of the National Debt', in Tout and Tait (eds), *Historical Essays*, pp. 400–3 and 418–20.

65. Ibid., pp. 399–400; Chandaman, *English Public Revenue*, p. 328.

66. Holmes, *The Making of a Great Power*, pp. 88–92.

67. BL, Add. MS 9302, fo. 133B for size of the fleet in 1662; Egerton MS 2543, fos. 155–6 for 1664, fo. 182 for August 1666; Add. MS 9302, fos. 152B for 1664, fo. 156 for December 1665.

68. W.L. Clowes, *The Royal Navy* (London, 1897), pp. 42–5.

69. Ibid., p. 51.

70. PRO, E351/2306–34, declared accounts for the entire period are used.

71. Capp, *Cromwell's Navy*, p. 385–6; Harding, *Evolution of the Sailing Navy*, pp. 97–9.

72. Glete, *Navies and Nations*, pp. 190–2.

73. PRO, E351/2314, Navy Treasurer's declared account for 1 January–29 June 1681, lists the amounts of debt still owed for every year since 1661.

74. Ibid., the declared account also lists the names of the people owed these amounts. Roseveare, *Financial Revolution*, pp. 21–3.

75. Roseveare, *Financial Revolution*, pp. 19–25; Dickson, *Financial Revolution*, p. 44.

76. Roseveare, *Financial Revolution*, pp. 20–5; Richards, 'The "Stop of the Exchequer"', 48–9.

77. Ehrman, *The Navy in the War of William III*, p. 162.

78. PRO, E351/2315–21.

79. PRO, E351/2322–34, for the declared accounts from 1689 to 31 December 1699.

80. Holmes, *The Making of a Great Power*, pp. 62–6, 91–2.

81. Harding, *Evolution of the Sailing Navy*, p. 102.

82. Ibid., pp. 99–102.

83. Glete, *Navies and Nations*, Table 22:21, p. 226; D.W. Jones, *War and Economics in the Age of William III and Marlborough* (Oxford, Blackwell, 1988), p. 29.

84. BL, Add. MS 10119, fo. 173.

85. Chandaman, *English Public Revenue*, pp. 1–3; Roseveare, *Financial Revolution*, pp. 3–5, 30–2.

86. PRO, E351/2322–34, declared accounts of the Navy Treasurer, April 1689 to 31 December 1699.

87. PRO, E351/2333.

88. PRO, E351/2322–34.

89. PRO, E351/2323 and 2324.

90. PRO, E351/2334, see the foot of the account.

91. Dickson, *Financial Revolution*, p. 46; Holmes, *The Making of a Great Power*, p. 197 for a brief list of other schemes.

92. Dickson, *Financial Revolution*, p. 42.

93. Holmes, *Augustan England*, pp. 240–1, 246–9, 276–7.

94. Outhwaite, *Inflation in Tudor and Early Stuart England*, p. 10; Fischer, *The Great Wave*, pp. 102–11.

CHAPTER FOUR

1. Childs, *The Army of Charles II*, p. 1 maintains that the army formed in 1661 was the first English standing army.
2. Cruickshank, *Elizabeth's Army*, pp. 14, and 51–4; Eltis, *The Military Revolution in Sixteenth-century Europe*, chapter five, 'The English Military Development'.
3. C. Barnett, *Britain and Her Army, 1509–1970* (Harmondsworth, England, Penguin Books, 1970), pp. 53–6; J.W. Fortescue, *A History of the British Army* (London, Macmillan, 1910), i: pp. 141–71.
4. Falls, *Elizabeth's Irish Wars* (1997 edn), pp. 252–67.
5. R.W. Stewart, 'The "Irish Road": Military Supply and arms for Elizabeth's Army During the O'Neill Rebellion in Ireland, 1598–1601', in Fissel (ed.), *War and Government in Britain, 1598–1650*, pp. 1–37; Cruickshank, *Elizabeth's Army*, pp. 90, 143–4, 148, 181–2, 199, and 206; Brady, 'The Captains' Games: Army and Society in Elizabethan Ireland', in *Military History of Ireland*, pp. 144–51; Dietz, 'The Exchequer in Elizabeth's Reign', 65–118.
6. Cruickshank, *Elizabeth's Army*, pp. 252 for casualty rate, and 281–2 for corruption and inefficiency.
7. Kennedy, *The Rise and Fall of British Naval Mastery*, p. 40.
8. Mattingly, *The Armada*, pp. vi and 401; Wernham, *After the Armada*, pp. vii–xi.
9. Fletcher, *Reform in the Provinces*, chapter nine, 'The Militia', is a superb source concerning the Stuart militia and its capabilities; Boynton, *The Elizabethan Militia 1558–1638*, pp. 126–206; Fortescue's *History of the British Army* ignores the contributions of the Stuart militia to English military skills in the early seventeenth century.
10. Eltis, *The Military Revolution in Sixteenth-century Europe*, chapter five, 'English Military Development'; M.J.D. Cockle (ed.), *Bibliography of Military Books Before 1642* (London, Simpkin, Marshall, Hamilton, Kent & Co., 1900, 1975 edn).
11. Fletcher, *Reform in the Provinces*, pp. 282–99.
12. Dietz, 'The Exchequer in Elizabeth's Reign', pp. 103–4; Dietz, 'The Receipts and Issues of the Exchequer during the Reigns of James I and Charles I', pp. 158–67. The land forces' totals exclude the money provided to the navy and Ordnance but include the money provided for the garrisons and forces in Ireland and on the continent.
13. Dietz's accounts end Michaelmas (September) each year.
14. This period excludes the Exchequer amounts issued for the military and the total issued for the year ending Michaelmas 1619, since Dietz shows only the total issued for that year. He does not provide a total issue amount for 1618. The individual issues totalled £378,245. BL, Add. MS 10119, fos. 1–2 lists the issues for 1618 as £418,835. This manuscript also lists individual items of issues that agree exactly with the amounts shown in Dietz's tables. The manuscript adds some items missing from Dietz's record as well, coming up with totals for issues (£418,835) and receipts (£488,200). Gardiner, *History of England*, x: Appendix 1, gives the issues and receipts for 1619 as £442,360 and £487,984 respectively and £490,141 for the issues in 1623. He cites BL, Lansdowne MS 164, fos. 505–7 and MS 169, fo. 135.
15. Dietz, 'The Exchequer in Elizabeth's Reign', p. 158. In most years the majority of the money spent by the Ordnance Office was used in support of the navy, but in the years in which there was a major land operation, a great deal of the Ordnance expenses were for support of the train of artillery which accompanied the army and for the arms and munitions needed by the soldiers.
16. Ibid., pp. 158–67.
17. In the five years of the period from 1615 through 1619 for which Dietz has data,

annual average cash issues were £422,000, while in the period of 1620 to 1624, annual cash issues fell to £373,000. This decline was due to the decrease in royal revenue caused by the severe economic depression in the early 1620s. See Godfrey Davies, *The Early Stuarts, 1603–1660* (Oxford, Clarendon Press, 1959 edn), pp. 291–3 and 331; Alan G.R. Smith, *The Emergence of a Nation State, the Commonwealth of England, 1529–1660* (New York, Longmans, 1984), pp. 173–4.

18. Fletcher, *Reform in the Provinces*, pp. 285–301

19. T.G. Barnes, *Somerset 1625–1640: A County's Government During the 'Personal Rule'* (Cambridge, MA, Harvard University Press, 1961), see chapter nine for the short-lived success and long-term difficulties of the 'Perfect Militia' project.

20. There is no direct evidence to prove this beyond a doubt. However, all accounts of the Bishops' Wars and the civil war describe how the local leaders formed companies that conformed to modern organization, and these units seemed to be able to do some elementary military evolution when they were deployed. See J. Jones, 'The War in the North: The Northern Parliamentary Army in the English Civil War, 1642–1645' (unpublished Ph.D. dissertation, North York, Ontario, York University, 1991), p. 23 for evidence of the Yorkshire trained bands in the Bishops' Wars, and the entire work for an example of how forces and officers were recruited and selected.

21. Fletcher, *Reform in the Provinces*, pp. 288–92; Eltis, *Military Revolution in Sixteenth-century Europe*, pp. 99–100.

22. Gardiner, *History of the Great Civil War*, i: pp. 57–60 for the trained bands at Turnham Common in November 1642, a stand-off that Gardiner correctly compares to the Battle of Valmy in the French Revolution, and pp. 202–9 for the London trained bands' critical role in the relief of Gloucester in September 1643; BL., TT, 669, fo. 6 lists the officers and units of the six regiments of the London trained bands in 1642.

23. Gardiner, *History of the Great Civil War*, pp. 254–9.

24. Sharpe, *The Personal Rule of Charles I*, pp. 8–15, 105–20.

25. Fletcher, *Reform in the Provinces*, pp. 287, 301 and 303–5.

26. Ibid., pp. 289–91 and 301.

27. Gardiner, *History of England*, viii: pp. 384–5; Fissel, *The Bishops' Wars*, pp. 10–24.

28. Sharpe, *The Personal Rule of Charles I*, pp. 802–13; Kenyon, *The Civil Wars of England*, pp. 16–18; D. Stevenson, *The Scottish Revolution 1637–44, The Triumph of the Covenanters* (New York, St Martin's Press, 1973), pp. 141–51.

29. Stevenson, *The Scottish Revolution*, p. 189; Gardiner, *History of England*, viii: pp. 387–90.

30. Dietz, 'The Receipts and Issues of the Exchequer during the Reigns of James I and Charles I', pp. 162–6.

31. This period includes the ship-money receipts that the Sheriffs paid directly to the Navy Treasurer, Sir William Russell, from 1635 to 1640. For ship-money see chapter one and PRO, E351/2275, 2276, 2278, 2280, 2282 for collections in the years 1635–9, and *CSPD, 1640*, pp. 350 and 645 for 1640's collection.

32. *CSPD, 1640*, pp. 330 and 373.

33. Gardiner, *History of England*, viii: pp. 384–5; Fissel, *Bishops' Wars*, p. 111.

34. PRO, E351/292 for Uvedale's declared account for 1639–40 and E351/298 for Vernon's declared account.

35. PRO, E351/293 for Uvedale's declared account for 16 February to 10 November 1640 and E351/299 for Vernon's account for 2 June to 31 August 1640.

36. Dietz, 'The Receipts and Issues of the Exchequer during the Reigns of James I and Charles I', p. 171, fn. 102.

37. Ibid., 171, fn. 102; PRO, E351/294, declared account of William Payton, Treasurer at War in Ireland, 8 January 1640 to 24 July 1641; *CSPD, 1640*, p. 373, in June 1640 it was estimated that this force, with artillery train, would cost £262,796 per year.

38. Wheeler, 'Four Armies in Ireland', in Ohlmeyer (ed.), *Ireland from Independence to Occupation, 1641–1660*, pp. 44–5.

39. Hugh Hazlett, 'The Financing of British Armies in Ireland, 1641–1649', *Irish Historical Studies* (1938), 37, estimates that over £2 million was provided to the British Protestant forces in Ireland from England by 1649. However, he is mistaken. The assessments passed by the Westminster Parliament for the support of the British armies in Ireland from 1644 to 1647 were not effectively collected until 1649. Therefore, it is doubtful that the £980,000 Hazlett credits from this source of revenue reached Ireland. Most of the £292,000 raised by the Adventurers for Irish lands was spent by Parliament in support of its armies in England from 1642 to 1646. See PRO, E101/67/11A for the Treasurers at War ledger accounts for assessments collected from February 1645 to March 1649. This source indicates that £351,157 was collected from the assessment for Ireland from 1647 to 1649. There is no record of exactly how much was sent to Ireland, but given the conflict between Parliament and the New Model Army over pay and service in Ireland in 1647, it is unlikely that much of this was sent over. Also see Wheeler, 'Four Armies', in Ohlmeyer (ed.), *Ireland from Independence to Occupation*, pp. 59–61, for the financial condition of Parliament's armies in Ireland in 1647–9.

40. C.H. Firth and R.S. Rait (eds.), *Acts and Ordinances of the Interregnum, 1642–1660* (London, HMSO, 1911), i: pp. 1–4, 5, and 6 for the ordinances concerning the militia and the forces for Ireland.

41. I. Roy, 'The Royalist Army in the First Civil War' (Oxford, unpublished Ph.D. dissertation, 1963), pp. 101 and 162–3.

42. Kenyon, *The Civil Wars of England*, p. 30.

43. Roy, 'The Royalist Army', pp. 110–14, 144, 160–76, and 185.

44. R. Hutton, *The Royalist War Effort 1642–1646* (New York, Longmans, 1982), pp. 21–3, 29, 120–42.

45. Roy, 'The Royalist Army', p. 5, where Ian Roy concludes correctly that 'in general material shortages were not a continuing or critical factor in the defeat of the Royalist army. Lack of money, provisions and arms at Oxford may, however, have weakened the authority of the high command, which controlled the central magazines. . . . The political divisions were more decisive in ensuring that the Royalist army resisted reform in 1644 and was unable to make better use of its still formidable strength in the following year.'

46. Hutton, *Royalist War Effort*, p. 30; J. Engberg, 'Royalist Finances During the English First Civil War, 1642–46', *Scandinavian Economic History Review*, 14 (1966), 73–96.

47. Engberg, 'Royalist Finances', pp. 74–84.

48. Ibid., pp. 80–9.

49. See chapters five, six, seven, and eight for a discussion of how the Westminster government adapted its financial systems to the military needs and experiences of the civil wars.

50. I. Roy, 'The Royalist Council of War, 1642–46', *Bulletin of the Institute of Historical Research*, 35 (1962), 150–68. The Royalist war council gave the Royalists the opportunity to create a far more effective and centralized strategic planning and command structure than the Parliamentarians possessed in 1643. However, Charles's methods of dealing with people and issues quickly undermined the potential of this body.

51. Hutton, *The Royalist War Effort*, pp. 125–6.

52. G. Davies, 'The Parliamentary Army under the Earl of Essex, 1642–45', *English Historical Review*, 49 (1934), 33–6; Firth, *Cromwell's Army*, pp. 17–20; Kenyon, *The Civil Wars of England*, pp. 48–9.

53. Davies, 'The Parliamentary Army under the Earl of Essex', pp. 33–6; Kenyon, *The Civil Wars of England*, pp. 53–9.

54. A military participation ratio is the comparison of the number of soldiers employed in a nation's military forces compared to its total population. It is always a very rough figure at best for early modern Europe because we have only very inexact population figures.

55. Firth, *Cromwell's Army*, pp. 22–4 for England, Stevenson, *The Scottish Revolution* for Scotland; Wheeler, 'Four Armies in Ireland', in Ohlmeyer (ed.), *Ireland from Independence to Occupation*, pp. 50–1; Gentles, *The New Model Army*, chapter eleven for Ireland; J.S. Wheeler, *The Cromwellian Conquest of Ireland* (Dublin, Gill and Macmillan, 1999) for estimates of the size of the forces on both sides in Ireland in 1652.

56. For population see E.A. Wrigley and R.S. Schofield, *The Population History of England, 1541–1871* (London, Edward Arnold, 1981), p. 575 for England and Wales (5.5 million); Ohlmeyer, *Ireland from Independence to Occupation*, p. 13 estimates Ireland's population at 2.1 million, a number from T.W. Moody, F.X. Martin, and F.J. Byrne (eds), *A New History of Ireland*, vol. iii, *Early Modern Ireland, 1534–1691* (Oxford, Clarendon Press, 1976), p. 389.

57. Parker, 'The Military Revolution Reassessed', in Rogers (ed.), *The Military Revolution Debate*; Parker and R. Loeber, 'The Military Revolution in Seventeenth-century Ireland', in Ohlmeyer (ed.), *Ireland From Independence to Occupation*.

58. Gentles, *New Model Army*, p. 544, fn. 163; Bodl., Carte MS 26, fo. 225, Letter of Ormond to the Confederate commissioners in Kilkenny, 17 October 1649, commenting about Cromwell needing to leave strong garrisons in places like Wexford; TT, E533(27), *Several Proceedings . . . of Parliament*, 30 November to 7 December 1649, pp. 120–1 for a list of garrisons in Leinster and Munster.

59. See Hutton, *The Royalist War Effort*, pp. 49–83 and 111–42 for this process of displacement and professionalization in the Royalist armies in England; Gentles, *New Model Army*, pp. 1–27 for the similar process in the main Parliamentarian armies in 1644–5; and Jones, 'The War in the North', for an excellent assessment of the changing nature of the officer corps.

60. E.M. Furgol, 'Scotland Turned Sweden: The Scottish Covenanters and the Military Revolution, 1638–1651', in J. Morrill (ed.), *The Scottish National Covenant in its British Context* (Edinburgh, Edinburgh University Press, 1990); Gentles, *New Model Army*, p. 390.

61. See chapter five for a discussion of Parliamentarian finance and revenue collection schemes in the period 1642–9.

62. Gardiner, *History of the Civil War*, i: pp. 361–3 for Cropredy Bridge in June 1644, and ii: pp. 13–19 for Essex's defeat at Lostwithiel in August and September 1644; Kenyon, *The Civil Wars of England*, chapter six is appropriately titled 'Deadlock: 1644'.

63. Firth and Rait, *Acts and Ordinances*, i: pp. 614–25 for New Model Ordinance; i: pp. 630–46 for assessment to support the Scots' army; i: p. 650 for an impressment ordinance; i: p. 653 for ordinance allowing Fairfax to appoint his own officers; i: p. 660 for the ordinance making Thomas Fairfax the Commander-in-Chief of all parliamentary armies; i: p. 664 for the 'Self-Denying Ordinance' removing all Members of Parliament from the army.

64. See chapter eight, 'The Assessment', for a detailed account of the development and administration of the assessment.

65. W.A. Shaw, *Calendar of Treasury Books, Introduction to Volumes XI–XVII Covering the Years 1695–1702* (London, HMSO, 1934), pp. ccxxii– ccxxiii and clv–clvi.

66. Braddick, *The Nerves of State*, p. 10.

67. *CJ*, vi: pp. 3–14, Account given to the House for the period of August 1642 to March 1645, by Treasurer of the Army Sir Gilbert Gerrard, on 9 September 1648. The monthly and annual averages are determined by dividing the total by thirty-one, the

number of calendar months in the period. Gerrard's account fills a large gap in the declared accounts for the army's pay.

68. PRO, E351/302, declared account of Sir John Wollaston, Sir Thomas Adams, Sir John Dethicke, George Witham, John Warner, Abraham Chamberlain, Thomas Andrews and Francis Allen. The declared account cleared in the Exchequer on 13 March 1660. The amount listed is the net amount given to the armed forces or paid for the administration and support of the forces. The treasurers handled more money than shown in this table.

69. PRO, E351/304, declared account of John Blackwell and William Leman.

70. PRO, E351/305, declared account of John Blackwell and Richard Deane for the period 24 June 1653 to 2 February 1660, for money received from the assessments, given 13 August 1662; E351/306, declared account of Blackwell and Deane, for the period 25 July 1653 to 24 December 1657, for money received from the Exchequer, given August 1662; E351/307, declared account of Blackwell and Deane, for the period 25 December 1657 to 19 February 1660, for money from the Exchequer, given August 1662.

71. See Tables 4.1 and 4.2.

72. See Table 3.1.

73. See chapter five for a discussion of land sales and debentures in England; Ian Gentles, 'The Arrears of Pay of the Parliamentary Army at the End of the First Civil War', *Bulletin of the Institute of Historical Research*, 48 (1975), 53–5 estimates the arrears of all soldiers, including the main armies and garrisons at £2.8 million by January 1648. Only half of this amount was satisfied by giving the soldiers debentures that could be used to purchase Royalist property; Gentles, 'The Sales of Crown Lands during the English Revolution', *Economic History Review*, 26 (1973), 614–35; another £1.5 million was owed to the soldiers of the Commonwealth's army in Ireland by 1653 and was satisfied, at least in part, by the confiscation and exchange of Irish Catholics' lands for the soldiers arrears. See Bottigheimer, *English Money and Irish Land*, pp. 134–8.

74. *CJ*, viii, pp. 176–7 (for soldiers' arrears of wages of £835,000) and p. 243 (for sailors' arrears of wages of £428,952).

75. See chapter five for an analysis of government revenue during the revolution.

76. C. Holmes, *The Eastern Association in the English Civil War* (Cambridge, Cambridge University Press, 1974); Jones, 'The War in the North', pp. 125–7, 246 ; PRO, SP28/139/1&2 for the accounts of John Weaver, treasurer of the Eastern Association.

77. Firth and Rait, *Acts and Ordinances*, i: pp. 656–60.

78. Ibid., pp. 656–7; PRO, SP28/350/5, a book for the advance of an £80,000 loan in London to pay for the equipment of the New Model Army in February 1645; SP28/350/2A for the loan of £200,000 raised for pay and support of the forces in Ireland.

79. See chapter seven, 'The Excise', and chapter eight, 'The Assessment', for a full discussion of the changes made to financial administration in 1645 to increase the confidence of lenders and suppliers; PRO, SP28/140/3 for a ledger book record of munitions and supplies provided to the New Model Army from February 1645 to early 1649.

80. PRO, SP28/135, the record book of Sussex listing £21,585 spent by the county for local garrisons to 9 September 1645. This is one example of hundreds of similar records of payments to local garrisons by county committees.

81. PRO, SP28/140/6 & 7 contain hundreds of accounts taken by the Committee for the Taking of Accounts. These records indicate the length of service of the individual soldiers, how much they earned in that time, and the amounts deducted for pay they had received, free quarter taken, and clothes issued to them as part of their pay. See

also SP28/139 for accounts of soldiers sent to Ireland in 1649 which list the quantity and value of clothing sent to them and counted as part of their pay.

82. PRO, SP28/237, for example, contains a bundle of loose free quarter tickets given out for lodging by troops in 1643 and 1644. The tickets were used to substantiate a claim for repayment made to the Committee for Taking the Accounts of the Soldiers by a London householder named Thomas Marsh.

83. Gentles, *The New Model Army*, chapters eleven and twelve, for the conquests of Ireland and Scotland by English expeditionary forces that were sustained largely by shipments of food, money, munitions, and clothing from England.

84. M. Van Creveld, *Supplying War: Logistics from Wallenstein to Patton* (Cambridge, Cambridge University Press, 1977), p. 25.

85. PRO, E351/302, 304 etc., for the names of these London aldermen and merchants and for the explanation of their salaries and poundage rates.

86. PRO, SP28/58–62 for thousands of pay warrants issued by Fairfax, Cromwell, Fleetwood, and the Committee of the Army to the Treasurers at War from 1645 to 1652; SP28/8/1–3 for thousands of similar warrants issued by the Earl of Essex to Gilbert Gerrard for the pay of his army in 1643.

87. PRO, SP28/120–5 contain thousands of muster rolls. These rolls list the men by name and the muster master signed the list to verify its authenticity. SP28/120 contains the rolls for regiments mustered in 1642 in Ireland; SP28/121 contains English musters of 1644 and 1645, and SP28/124 contains records of musters held from 1646 through 1648.

88. Cruickshank, *Elizabeth's Army*, pp. 143–7 for the corrupt Elizabethan system and p. 153 for dead pays.

89. Jones, 'War in the North', pp. 147 and 167–8; H.M.L. Reece, 'The Military Presence in England, 1649–1660' (Oxford, unpublished Ph.D. dissertation, 1981), pp. 41 and 48–9. Reece concludes that the rank and file were not alienated from their officers, even in 1659–60 and that fraud and maladministration were rare.

90. PRO, SP28/132 for an example of a regimental record. SP28/135–6 contain dozens of such accounts.

91. PRO, SP25/118, a ledger of the accounts of Cromwell's expeditionary force to Ireland in 1649–50 lists the regiments, the food and clothes provided and the amounts deducted from the soldiers' pay.

92. PRO, SP28/137–9 for regimental accounts listing pay, free quarter taken, and the value of clothing and food issued in lieu of pay.

93. PRO, SP28/131/4–9, for example, list the contracts for £83,129 worth of clothes and supplies provided in 1647 to the parliamentary forces in Ireland by a consortium of London contractors; SP28/139/9 lists merchants working in partnership with John Davies to supply Ireland.

94. PRO, SP28/58 for examples of warrants for 1648–9; E351/304–7 for the Treasurers at War declared accounts which discuss the warrants on which they based their disbursements; AO1/1846–51 for Ordnance Office declared accounts which show that the same procedures were used in the 1660s, 1670s, and 1680s.

95. *CJ*, v: pp. 125–6, Mr Scawen reported to the House that the assessments were £310,360 in arrears, and Fairfax's field army was owed £331,000 in back pay. The Northern Army and the dozens of garrisons in England also were owed an unspecified amount.

96. *CJ*, iv: pp. 429–31 for the 26,124 men in Parliament's pay in Ireland. Their cost was estimated at £48,961 per month, and £293,768 for six months; see *CJ*, iv: pp. 654–5 for the Scots' army in England. It was estimated to number 21,000 men in August 1646. The Westminster Parliament had promised to pay them £31,000 per month in 1644. The Scots acknowledged that the English had paid them £464,063 in cash and £219,937 worth of free quarter since October 1643, while the English claimed to have paid

£1,462,769. This last amount included all local taxes, free quarter, thefts, and levies by the Scots on Newcastle coal shipments. Eventually the English agreed to pay them another £400,000 in late 1646 for them to surrender the King and return to Scotland (*CJ*, v: pp. 13–15). The first £200,000 was shipped by wagon to Newcastle in January 1647. These payments to the Scots are not included in the amounts in Table 4.3.

97. *CJ*, v: pp. 90, 107, 128–9, 137–40, 155. The officers going to Ireland were to receive their future pay in confiscated Irish land, after the £330,000 owed to the Irish Adventurers was settled in land (*CJ*, v: p. 140). The six weeks of pay arrears offered to those soldiers who were to be disbanded was not offered until April 1647, and by then the army was alienated from Parliament (*CJ*, v: pp. 155–8).

98. Gentles, *The New Model Army*, pp. 140–89 for the best account of this crisis and the army's occupation of London. Gentles notes that the soldiers would have settled for four months' pay arrears in cash in April 1647 (p. 165).

99. Reece, 'Military Presence in England, 1649–1660', p. 287 for the number of soldiers in England, 1647–60.

100. BL, Add. MS 10119, fo. 12b for the forces and Egerton MS 2542, fos. 307–9. The navy was estimated to cost another £916,000 (fo. 309) and the civil government £223,404.

101. BL, Egerton MS 2542, fos. 300–19 an estimate for 1660, 'the year ensuing', lists anticipated revenues for England, Ireland, and Scotland as £1,536,841, and issues of £2,885,540; Add. MS 10119, fos. 12b–14, in April 1659, Scawen estimated the annual income of England, Ireland, and Scotland in 1659 as £1,868,722 and expenditures as £2,201,540; Add. MS 11597, fos. 5–7, has another version of Scawen's 16 April 1659 report from the Committee for Inspecting the Accounts and Revenues of the Commonwealth. This account estimates the revenue of the Commonwealth at £1,868,717, with total issues of £2,201,540.

102. BL, Egerton MS 2542, fo. 321.

103. PRO, E351/308, declared account of James Nelthorpe and John Lawson for disbanding the forces, 2 February 1660 to 21 April 1662; E351/309, declared account of John Baynes for money paid for disbanding the regiments in Scotland; E351/310, declared account of Nelthorpe and Lawson for 27 August 1660 to 21 April 1662.

104. For estimates of the debts of the army in 1660 see *CJ*, viii: pp. 176–7, 182, 190, 196, and 243; *CSPD, 1659–60*, pp. 32, 383, and 494; BL, Add. MS 11597, fos. 5–9; Egerton MS 2542, fo. 321.

105. Childs, *The Army of Charles II*, pp. 8–10.

106. Ibid., pp. 198–207; PRO, AO1/308/1203–4 for the declared accounts of the army paymaster at Dunkirk in 1661 and 1662. The accounts list the seven regiments stationed there.

107. Childs, *The Army of Charles II*, pp. 1–10.

108. J.C. Beckett, 'The Irish Armed Forces, 1660–1685', in J. Bossy and Peter Jupp (eds), *Essays Presented to Michael Roberts* (Belfast, Blackstaff Press, 1976), pp. 41–53.

109. PRO, E351/59–71, declared accounts of Sir Stephen Fox from January 1661 to September 1671, and from September 1672 to December 1675; E351/72–3, declared accounts of Samuel Kindon from 1 January 1677 to December 1678; E351/74–6, declared accounts of Sir Stephen Fox from 1 January 1679 to 31 December 1681. AO1/50–3 for paymaster declared accounts, January 1675 through December 1687. There are no declared accounts for September 1671 to September 1672, so I used Chandaman, *English Public Revenue*, Appendix 3, 'Exchequer Receipts and Issues', p. 355 for September 1671 to September 1672. This table excludes the money disbursed by the Ordnance Office.

110. PRO, AO1/312/1237–8, declared accounts of the treasurers for raising and disbanding the expeditionary forces of 1677/8.

111. PRO, E351/59 lists amounts spent on the barracks and stables in Horse Guards, St James's, and Whitehall in the period from 1664 to 1666.
112. Beckett, 'Irish Armed Forces, 1660–1685', in Bossy and Jupp (eds), *Essays Presented to Michael Roberts*, pp. 41 and 52–3.
113. Fischer, *The Great Wave*, pp. 96–106.
114. Chandaman, *The English Public Revenue 1660–1688*, pp. 339–66. The military totals include the forces in English pay in England, Tangiers, Dunkirk, and the American colonies. The latter were minuscule.
115. Chandaman, *The English Public Revenue*, pp. 362–3 for the Exchequer issues; BL, Add. MS 10119, fo. 58 and Add. MS 11597, fo. 46 for the money spent for the army in the same period.
116. Chandaman, *The English Public Revenue*, pp. 339–66. Also, see Tables 2.4 and 2.5.
117. Childs, *The Army of Charles II*, p. 204.
118. Ibid., p. 207.
119. Ibid., pp. 183–95.
120. Ibid., p. 195.
121. PRO, AO1/312/1237–8, declared accounts of the paymaster of the expedition and of the treasurer for the disbandment of the army.
122. Gordon, *The History of Our National Debts and Taxes from the year MDCLXXXVIII to the present year MDCCLI* (London, M. Cooper of Paternoster Row, 1751), p. 88; BL, Add. MS 10119, fo. 173 for the costs of all forces, closely agrees with *The History of Our National Debts*, p. 88. The totals for the entire period are very close, but the amounts for individual years vary.
123. PRO, AO1/54–6, Paymasters' declared accounts, 1 January 1688 to 24 December 1700.
124. PRO, AO1/313/1246–50, AO1/314/1251–2, and AO1/315/1253–5, declared accounts of the Paymasters for the forces in Ireland, November 1689 to 29 September 1701. Less than £300,000 of this came from Irish revenues.
125. C. Carlton, 'The Impact of the Fighting', in John Morrill (ed.), *The Impact of the English Civil War* (London, Collins and Brown, 1991), p. 20.
126. Shaw (ed.), *Calendar of Treasury Books, Introduction to Volumes XI–XVII*, pp. ccxi–ccxiii.
127. J. Childs, *The British Army of William III and the Glorious Revolution* (Manchester, Manchester University Press, 1987).
128. BL, Egerton MS 2543, fo. 295.
129. Beckett, 'Land Tax or Excise', pp. 285–308.

CHAPTER FIVE

1. R. Ashton, 'Deficit Finance in the Reign of James I', *Economic History Review*, second series, 10 (1957), 17.
2. Outhwaite, *Inflation in Tudor and Early Stuart England*, pp. 10–15; Fischer, *The Great Wave*, pp. 85–91.
3. Braddick, *The Nerves of State*, pp. 91–5.
4. Smith, *The Emergence of a Nation State*, pp. 236–9. From 1593 to 1601, Elizabeth received ten subsidies from her parliaments; for the debt in 1603 see D. Thomas, 'Financial and Administrative Developments', in H. Tomlinson (ed.), *Before the English Civil War* (New York, St Martin's Press, 1984), p. 103; and Gardiner, *History of England*, i: pp.186, 293–4.
5. Thomas, 'Financial and Administrative Developments', in Tomlinson (ed.), *Before the English Civil War*, p. 116.

6. Ibid., pp. 103–6; Ashton, 'Deficit Finance in the Reign of James I', pp. 20–4.

7. Ashton, 'Deficit Finance in the Reign of James I', pp. 21–2, Ashton cites the figure for the value of land sales as £1.1 million by 1610, but Dietz, 'Receipts and Issues of the Exchequer during the Reigns of James I and Charles I', lists the receipts from land sales as £409,577 for the seven years 1603–10. The first two Stuarts eventually sold at least £1,238,509 worth of lands.

8. Ashton, 'Deficit Finance in the Reign of James I', p. 22.

9. Ibid., p. 23; Gardiner, *History of England*, ii: pp. 64–5, 68–9; ibid., iii: pp. 198–9.

10. Dietz, 'The Receipts and Issues of the Exchequer during the Reigns of James I and Charles I', pp. 135–70. Dietz's data for the years 1621, 1623, 1627, 1628, where he had figures for issues for only half a year each, have been supplemented with data from Gardiner, *History of England*, x: p. 222 for data for 1619 and 1623, and BL, Add. MS 10119, fo. 1 for 1623. Dietz's receipt data for 1623, 1627 and 1628 were for full years and the revised figures are lower than his receipts in each case. The ship-money receipts and expenditures for the years 1635 through 1640 have been added since these give a fuller picture of government revenue and expenditure. Ship-money receipts and issues were a little over £750,000. See chapter two for ship-money.

11. Dietz, 'The Receipts and Issues of the Exchequer during the Reigns of James I and Charles I', pp. 135–53 for the itemized cash receipts and pp. 159–71 for the itemized cash issues.

12. Ibid., pp. 120–2.

13. Smith, *The Emergence of a Nation State*, p. 270.

14. Ibid., pp. 271–6.

15. Dietz, 'The Receipts and Issues of the Exchequer during the Reigns of James I and Charles I', pp. 159–71. The cash spent on the royal family, household, and jewels from 1606 to 1625 was at least £2,916,966 (*c.* £145,000 per annum), while from 1626 to 1640 it totalled £1,341,186 (*c.* £89,000 per annum). This excludes tally anticipations.

16. Braddick, *The Nerves of State*, pp. 95–9.

17. See chapter eight, 'The Assessment'.

18. Beckett, 'Land Tax or Excise', pp. 285–308.

19. Cust, *The Forced Loan and English Politics, 1626–1628*; Sharpe, *The Personal Rule of Charles I*, pp. 15–23.

20. Fissel, *The Bishops' Wars*, pp. 139–51.

21. Sharpe, *The Personal Rule of Charles I*, chapters XVI and XVII.

22. *CJ*, ii: p. 668.

23. *CSPD, 1640*, p. 373 for the estimate of the cost of an army of 11,000 men for Ireland, for one year; Firth, *Cromwell's Army*, pp. 21–4. Essex's army's authorized strength was 24,000 infantry and 5,000 cavalry, although it only reached 20,000 men in September 1642. The English and Scottish forces in Ireland in the summer of 1643 cost at least £525,000, although Parliament provided not much more than £360,000 to these forces in the entire period before 1649. See PRO SP28/139, parts 7 and 22 for Adam Loftus's accounts for Ireland, 1641–52.

24. Bottigheimer, *English Money and Irish Land*, pp. 55–7.

25. G. Aylmer, *The State's Servants: The Civil Service of the English Republic, 1649–1660* (London, Routledge and Kegan Paul, 1973), p. 28.

26. Gardiner, *History of England*, x: p. 214, for the first casualty of the civil wars; Andrews, *Ships, Money and Politics*, pp. 184–7, for the decisive and dramatic way in which the fleet was kept safely in Parliament's camp in June and July 1642.

27. Gardiner, *History of the Civil War*, i: Map of England and Wales, September 1643, shows

graphically how important the fleet was to the maintenance of Parliamentarian garrisons in Plymouth, Dartmouth, Lyme Regis, Poole, Pembroke, and Hull.

28. Bodl., Rawlinson MS A223, fo. 16 for 1642, fos. 12–16 for the debt in 1643, and fos. 75–6 for 1643 estimates of total naval costs; PRO, E351/643 for 1643 customs revenue. The 1 August 1642 ordinance extending the customs for another year states that the navy's debt was £200,000, but it lumps together the debt of over £100,000 and the estimated cost of the forthcoming winter guard of 1642–3 (Firth and Rait, *Acts and Ordinances*, i: p. 16). Only £145,000 was provided to the Navy Treasurer by the customs in 1643. See chapter six, 'The Customs', for a full account of the customs system.

29. Aylmer, *State's Servants*, p. 24; G. Aylmer, *The King's Servants: The Civil Service of Charles I, 1625–1642* (New York, Columbia University Press, 1961), pp. 182–203, notes that the Exchequer had been a target of parliamentary criticism throughout the reigns of James I and Charles I; Fissel, *The Bishops' Wars*, pp. 137–51, makes the point that the Exchequer procedures and mechanisms were too slow, cumbersome, and inefficient to support the financial operations of warfare in 1639–40.

30. Deitz, 'The Receipts and Issues of the Exchequer during the Reigns of James I and Charles I', pp. 120–3.

31. PRO, E401/1928, Exchequer Receipt Book, April 1643 to March 1644; E401/1929, Receipt Book, 1644. The books are incomplete and were poorly maintained. There is an entry that indicates that £11,952 of this £79,000 was not received until the period September 1645 to March 1646 (fo. 64).

32. Firth and Rait, *Acts and Ordinances*, i: p. 6; Gardiner, *History of England*, x: p. 201.

33. PRO, SP28/131, part 5 for Londoners' advance of £54,474; SP28/334, account book of Richard Wither for the West Division of Surrey, 1642–8, fos. 3–7 lists £1,511 as raised on the ordinance for horse and plate in the West Division alone.

34. *CJ*, ii: pp. 598, 601, 606; Firth and Rait, *Acts and Ordinances*, iii: act of 4 June 1642.

35. Gardiner, *History of England*, x: p. 215; W.C. Abbott (ed.), *The Writings and Speeches of Oliver Cromwell* (Oxford, Clarendon Press, 1937, 1988 edn) i: pp. 164–5. The Irish Adventurers were people who had subscribed money for the support of the Protestant armies fighting in Ireland since October 1641 to suppress the Catholic rebellion. The subscribers were promised forfeited Irish land in exchange for their contributions by Acts of Parliament passed in March 1642 – 2½ million acres of land were promised, and the goal was to raise £1 million. Only £306,278 was raised in this manner in the 1640s; Bottigheimer, *English Money and Irish Land*, pp. 54–5. Eventually, the Westminster governments spent far more than this in the conquest of Ireland. For example, £83,129 worth of arms and supplies were provided to the forces in Ireland in 1647 (PRO, SP28/131/parts 1–4) and Adam Loftus, treasurer for Irish causes, paid out £366,717 by 1652 (PRO, SP28/139/part 22).

36. *CSPD, 1640*, p. 373, has an estimate of £262,796 as the cost for one year for 10,000 foot and 1,000 horse in Ireland.

37. Firth, *Cromwell's Army*, pp. 22–4. Essex's notional strength was 24,000 foot and 5,000 horse, but he had only 20,000 men at Edgehill in October 1642.

38. Firth and Rait, *Acts and Ordinances*, i: pp. 45–64 for a series of ordinances enacted from 29 November 1642 to 17 January 1643, extending the Twentieth Part and establishing county committees for local coordination of the war effort.

39. W.O. Scroggs, 'English finance under the Long Parliament', *Quarterly Journal of Economics*, 21 (May 1907), 464–7.

40. Gardiner, *History of the Civil War*, i: p. 72. Gardiner cites BL, Add. MS 18777, Yonge's Diary, fo. 82.

41. M.A.E. Green (ed.), *The Calendar of the Proceedings of the Committee for the Advance of Money* (London, HMSO, 1888), i.

42. PRO, SP28/258/4, John Weaver's account to the Committee for Taking Accounts, 1650.

43. Firth and Rait, *Acts and Ordinances*, i: pp. 49, 51, 53, 61, 64, 160, 757.

44. Holmes, *The Eastern Association*.

45. Ibid., pp. 146–8.

46. The best way to understand the importance of county and regional forces to the parliamentary war effort is to read the superb county histories that exist. The war in each county differed significantly, depending on whether it was completely Royalist or Parliamentarian controlled, or a disputed county. Generalizations about finance, government, and warfare thus must be taken as approximations. Some of the best histories of counties in the mid-seventeenth century include, E. Broxap, *The Great Civil War in Lancashire, 1642–1651* (Manchester, Manchester University Press, 1973 edn of 1910 work); A. Hughes, *Politics, Society and Civil War in Warwickshire, 1620–1660* (Cambridge, Cambridge University Press, 1987); A. Fletcher, *A County Committee in Peace and War: Sussex, 1600–1660* (London, Longmans, 1975); and J.S. Morrill, *Cheshire 1630–1660* (Oxford, Oxford University Press, 1974). For a very good analysis of how the war and upheavals of the 1640s and 1650s affected county and local government see Fletcher, *Reform in the Provinces*.

47. PRO, SP28/350/4.

48. Firth and Rait, *Acts and Ordinances*, i: pp. 106, 129, 136, 157, 176, 247, 254, 299 for the parliamentary ordinances expanding the process of sequestrations. See J.W. Pringle, 'The Committee for Compounding with Delinquents, 1643–1654: A Study of Parliamentary Finance' (University of Illinois, unpublished Ph.D. dissertation, 1961), for an excellent discussion of the creation of the sequestration process and its evolution to compounding.

49. PRO, E351/440, for declared account of Richard Waring, Michael Herring and his widow Elizabeth Herring for the period 1643–53; see PRO, E351/439 for the Sequestrations declared account of James Leech and Richard Sherwin for the sequestration income, 1653–5.

50. PRO, E351/439, the declared account of James Leech and Richard Sherwin, lists £166,625 as received in 1653–5; PRO, E351/440, the declared account of Richard Waring and Michael Herring, lists £377,535 as received in fines and rents from 1643 to 1653. Rough averaging is not of much use in this case, since there is no evidence indicating receipts were steady. The adoption of compounding by Royalist delinquents undoubtedly dried up the capital base on which sequestration rents were collected.

51. PRO, SP28/350/10, account of Fauconberge, Receiver General for this amount; also see PRO, E351/453, declared account of William Gibbs and Francis Allen, which lists £64,677 as the rent received from episcopal lands from 1646 to 1656. The sale of these lands began in late 1646. The Bishop of Durham's rents for the period 1643 to 1656 totalled £21,373, according to the account of Gilbert Marshall and Adam Smith found in PRO, SP28/289; Dietz, 'The Receipts and Issues of the Exchequer during the Reigns of James I and Charles I', pp. 135–53, documents a steady decline in receipts from the royal estates from 1603 to 1640. The cash received from the receiver generals for Crown estates was about £50,000 per year from 1603 to 1611, £31,000 per annum from 1612 to 1624, and about £12,000 per annum from 1625 to 1640.

52. Aylmer, *State's Servants*, p. 24. There is no certain explanation for why the Exchequer was not used. Probably the desire by the City for positive control of the revenues securing their loans was the major reason.

53. L. Glow, 'The Committee of Safety', *English Historical Review*, 80 (1965), 289–313.

54. Kenyon, *The Civil Wars of England*, pp. 49–88.

55. Firth, *Cromwell's Army*, pp. 22–3.
56. Ibid., p. 22. Firth estimates that 60–70,000 men were raised on each side in the First Civil War; £262,000 was needed for the pay alone of 11,000 men. *CSPD, 1640*, p. 373.
57. See chapter seven for the excise and chapter eight for the assessment.
58. See chapter seven for citation of sources for these figures.
59. James Pringle, 'The Committee for Compounding', pp. 29–41 for this evolution.
60. Ibid., pp. 41–3.
61. *CSPD, 1649–50*, p. x; see PRO, E351/440, for declared account of Richard Waring and Michael Herring. Of their total receipts of £1,663,739, they spent or charged only £50,400 for administrative-type expenses. This cost was just 3 per cent of total revenue.
62. Gardiner, *History of the Civil War*, i: pp. 338–62; ii: pp. 42–65; Kenyon, *The Civil Wars of England*, chapter six, 'Deadlock, 1644'; Gentles, *New Model Army*, pp. 3–6.
63. Gentles, *New Model Army*, p. 3.
64. For estimates of troop strength see Abbott (ed.), *Writings and Speeches of Oliver Cromwell*, i: pp. 322–3 and Firth, *Cromwell's Army*, pp. 22–5. For a well-supported estimate of the proportion of pay received by the troops in 1644 see Holmes, *Eastern Association*, pp. 146–8.
65. Gardiner, *History of the Civil War*, i: p. 72 estimated the annual charge of Parliament's armies in England as £1 million and the navy's charge as £400,000. The 21,000 men of the New Model Army were estimated to cost £44,952 per month, and there were thirteen lunar pay months in a year, for an annual total of £584,389 (*CSPD, 1644–5*, p. 232). The Scots' army in England was promised £30,000 per month by Parliament, although that was only a fortnight's pay for the 21,000 men in that army (*CSPD, 1644–5*, p. 72). For a discussion of the military situation and the anti-Catholic troop strength in Ireland in 1644 see Wheeler, 'Four armies in Ireland', in Ohlmeyer (ed.), *Ireland from Independence to Occupation*, pp. 50–2. There were 18–25,000 troops in Parliament's pay in Ireland in 1644. Eleven thousand men were estimated by the Council in 1640 to cost £262,796 annually in Ireland, multiplied by two = £525,592.
66. The sources of revenue used to support the armies provided the following estimated receipts in this two-year period: sequestrations £260,306, weekly assessments £129,819, King's revenue at £45,000 per year = £90,000, advances on the excise £325,000 approximately, compositions by delinquents £68,000. See the pages above for sources for each of these. Local sequestrations and county and regional association assessment and tax collections are excluded, since we do not have the evidence to determine them. Holmes, *Eastern Association*, pp. 146–8 has, however, shown that the regional forces were irregularly paid.
67. Firth and Rait, *Acts and Ordinances*, i: pp. 614–25.
68. Ibid., pp. 531–4 for the rate; *CSPD, 1644–5*, p. 233, where the contested counties were to 'maintain their own garrisons and forces as far as they are able'.
69. Firth and Rait, *Acts and Ordinances*, i: pp. 630–5.
70. Scroggs, 'English Finance under the Long Parliament', p. 476.
71. Firth and Rait, *Acts and Ordinances*, i: pp. 656–9.
72. PRO, SP28/350/5, Book of Advance of £80,000, March 1645.
73. PRO, E101/67/11A, fos. 112–14. Only £59,081 of the New Model assessment of £534,360 was not collected in the first ten months (11 per cent uncollected), and £31,957 of the £194,685 (16 per cent) due on the Scottish Army assessment was not collected. This is a much higher collection rate than that of the weekly assessments which provided only £129,819 to the London treasury in 1644 (PRO, SP28/350/4).
74. Firth and Rait, *Acts and Ordinances*, i: pp. 660 and 664.
75. Gentles, 'The Sales of Crown Lands during the English Revolution', p. 615.

76. Gentles, 'The Arrears of Pay of the Parliamentary Army', pp. 54–5.
77. Firth and Rait, *Acts and Ordinances*, i: p. 879 for dissolution of bishoprics; i: pp. 884, 907 and 920 for ordinances dealing with the sale of episcopal lands.
78. PRO, SP28/350/2 for an account book of the subscription for the loan and a list of the disbursements of £200,013 by Richard Glyde, Treasurer at Weavers' Hall.
79. G.B. Tatham, 'The Sale of Episcopal Lands during the Civil Wars and Commonwealth', *English Historical Review*, 23 (1908), 91–108. The first recorded sale was on 5 July 1647. Tatham has evaluated the indentures for sale and has calculated that £77,046 was realized in 1647; £208,925 in 1648; £177,330 in 1649; £95,000 in 1650; £36,413 in 1651; £35,397 in 1652; £10,538 in 1653; £9,463 in 1654; £3,853 in 1655; and £8,631 in 1656–9 (p. 108).
80. Habakkuk, 'Public Finance', pp. 70–1. Doubling was not popular with the state's creditors, but it did give them some repayment of their debt.
81. Bodl., Rawlinson MS B239, a ledger book, 'Conveyance for Bishops Lands', with 635 entries listing the sales of the bishops' lands. All but £10,000 realized from these sales came in by early 1653. The last dated entry was for 27 January 1655, but fourteen entries totalling £784 were made after that date. The total listed is £675,603 5*s* 11½*d*. Habakkuk, 'Public Finance', pp. 74–5, has argued convincingly that £320,000 of this was raised by doubling. He relies on Tatham, 'The Sale of Episcopal Lands', pp. 91–108, for his data. But he disagrees with Tatham's conclusion that much of the receipts from the sales were in cash. Habakkuk concludes that the total debt reduced by doubling and cash on these sales was £676,387. No one has convincingly challenged Habakkuk on this amount. In 1659, the surviving treasurers for the sale of bishops' lands, William Gibbs and Francis Ash, provided a declared account showing that another £64,677 in rents and profits was received by them and paid by them for the costs of the sales (clerks, surveyors, annuities, fees, etc.). Their declared account is PRO, E351/453. Therefore, £676,000 is a reasonable amount for the proceeds of the sale of episcopal lands.
82. Abbott (ed.), *Writings and Speeches of Oliver Cromwell*, i: pp. 420–4 provides a copy of the agreement between the Westminster and Edinburgh governments for the surrender of the King to the English and the withdrawal of the Scottish Army from northern England. The English sent £200,000 in coin to the Scots in two shipments.
83. Gentles, *New Model Army*, pp. 141–50 for the specific causes of the struggle. Chapter six, 'The Political Wars, 1646–8', is the clearest and fullest account of the 1647 crisis. I. Gentles, 'The Struggle for London in the Second Civil War', *Historical Journal*, 26 (June 1983), 277–305, is the best account of the conclusion of the struggle between the New Model and its Independent allies against the Presbyterian–Royalist coalition in the City in 1648–9.
84. *CJ*, v: pp. 56–7 for the January situation; p. 155 for the offer of six weeks' arrears; p. 183 for the order to disband on 1 June.
85. Eventually, two months' arrears and one month's advance was offered for troops going to Ireland, but all the foot regiments of the New Model were to be broken up. B. Whitelocke, *Memorials of the English Affairs* (London, Nathaniel Ponder, 1682), pp. 244–5, 248, 250; *CJ* v: p. 268; Gentles, *New Model Army*, pp. 149, 190–7.
86. Whitelocke, *Memorials of the English Affairs*, p. 242 for the excise riots; *CJ*, v: p. 298 for London's September 1647 assessment arrears.
87. Firth and Rait, *Acts and Ordinances*, i: pp. 958, 1018.
88. *CJ*, v: pp. 396, 400.
89. Ibid., p. 306.
90. Ibid., p. 395.
91. For a superb account of the Northern Army under Lord Ferdinando Fairfax, Sir Thomas's father, see Jones, 'The War in the North'.

92. Gentles, *New Model Army*, pp. 228–34 for the reduction and reorganization of the military establishment.
93. *CJ*, v: p. 459. There were thirty 'loose companies' in garrisons, and Parliament estimated that they and Fairfax's army would cost £60,000 per month. This excludes the cost of ordnance, ammunition and the routine replacement of broken or worn weapons.
94. *CJ*, iv: pp. 429–31 lists Parliament's Irish forces as 26,124 men, excluding the Scottish garrisons in Ulster.
95. Gentles, *New Model Army*, pp. 246–65.
96. *CJ*, vi: p. 158.
97. Ibid., pp. 138–9.
98. Aylmer, *State's Servants*, p. 320.
99. *CSPD, 1649–50*, p. 516 for arrears; PRO, SP25/118, fos. 1–6 for the pay of April to July 1649. See Wheeler, 'Logistics and Supply in Cromwell's Conquest of Ireland', in Fissel (ed.), *War and Government*, pp. 38–56.
100. Tatham, 'The Sale of Episcopal Lands', p. 108.
101. Firth and Rait, *Acts and Ordinances*, ii: p. 81 for the abolition of cathedral chapters and p. 140 for the act authorizing the sale of the lands in June.
102. PRO, E134/357, declared account of the treasurers for the sale, John Estwicke and William Hobson.
103. Habakkuk, 'Public Finance', pp. 75–6.
104. Firth and Rait, *Acts and Ordinances*, ii: pp. 160, 168, 200.
105. Gentles, 'The Sale of the Crown Lands during the English Revolution', pp. 614–17.
106. PRO, E351/603 for the declared account of the treasurers for the sale; H.J. Habakkuk, 'The Parliamentary Army and the Crown Lands', *Welsh History Review* (1960), 403–26 provides a case study of how the soldiers often banded together in a regimental association to concentrate enough money to buy the land. It is clear that the officers, who were owed the most money individually, gained the most from the sales. The private soldiers often sold their debentures for 20 to 50 per cent of their value; see S.J. Madge, *The Doomsday of Crown Lands* (London, Routledge and Sons, 1938). Habakkuk makes a good argument, which is supported by the evidence, that Madge missed the point that this land was paid for with debentures, rather than cash. Madge maintains that £1,464,409 was realized from the sale of the Crown lands. See Habakkuk, 'Public Finance', p. 73.
107. Habakkuk, 'Public Finance', p. 77.
108. PRO, SP28/350/9 for the warrants for the expenditures of the receipts. The warrants were endorsed and cashed; SP28/271–8 for more warrants of money spent by the treasurers for the sale.
109. Gentles, *New Model Army*, chapter eleven for the Irish war from 1649 to 1652 and chapter twelve for the Scottish war of 1650 to 1651.
110. For the navy see J.S. Wheeler, 'Prelude to Power: the Crisis of 1649 and the Foundation of English Naval Power', *Mariner's Mirror*, 81 (May 1995), 148–55, and Anderson, 'Operations of the English Fleet, 1648–52'.
111. Firth and Rait, *Acts and Ordinances*, ii: pp. 358 and 412 for sale of fee farm rents and p. 456 for the assessment.
112. PRO, E351/602, declared account of John Dethicke, treasurer for the sale. £239,206 of the proceeds were paid in new cash purchases, with the remainder purchased through the doubling process. See Habakkuk, 'Public Finance', p. 76. The cash disbursements of the trustees are in PRO, SP28/286 and 300.
113. PRO, E351/602, discharges.
114. J.S. Wheeler, 'The Logistics of the Cromwellian Conquest of Scotland, 1650–1651', *War and Society*, 10 (May 1992), 1–18.

115. PRO, E351/438, the declared account of John Dethicke, John Wollaston, Thomas Andrews, Francis Allen, 1651–2. The treasurers paid £262,108 to the Navy Treasurer and £181,309 to the Treasurers at War for the army.
116. Habakkuk, 'Public Finance', p. 81.
117. *CJ*, vi: pp. 14–15, Sir Henry Vane, Navy Treasurer account, 8 August 1642–12 May 1645; PRO E351/2284–96, declared accounts of the Navy Treasurer, 1643–60; E364/129, the declared account of Thomas Smith and John Hill, Collectors of Prize Goods, 27 February 1645 to 16 April 1649 (£123,202); E401/1930–3, Exchequer Receipt Books; BL, Add. MS 32471 Public Revenue Accounts, 1655–7; M.P. Ashley, *The Financial and Commercial Policy of Cromwellian England* (London, Humphrey Milford, 1934), pp. 84–5.
118. PRO, E401/1930, fos. 199–219; E401/1931, fos. 18–29, 35–51, 55–60, 76–88, 98, 110–16, 123, 134, 183. The money was received from the goldsmiths who had received the 'Mexico coins' and converted them to English money which they paid to the Exchequer.
119. Bottigheimer, *English Money and Irish Land*, pp. 55–7, 134–7; PRO, E351/438 for delinquent estates; E351/439–43 for sequestrations and delinquent estates; E351/453 for episcopal land sales; E351/602 for fee farm rents; E351/603 for sale of the King's goods; E351/604 for royal forests; E364/129 for prize goods accounts.
120. PRO, SP63/281, fo. 309.

Chapter Six

1. Ashton, 'Deficit Finance in the Reign of James I', pp. 15–17.
2. Braddick, *The Nerves of State*; Braddick, *Parliamentary Taxation in Seventeenth-Century England*; Chandaman, *The English Public Revenue*.
3. Braddick, *The Nerves of State*, pp. 56–65; Braddick, 'Government, War, Trade and Settlement', in Canny (ed.), *The Origins of Empire*, pp. 291–6.
4. Smith, *The Emergence of a Nation State*, p. 256 for the decrease of subsidies and p. 436 for price-inflation data; Fischer, *The Great Wave*, pp. 70–91.
5. PRO, E351/600, the declared account of Thomas Gardiner, treasurer for the sale of £176,644 worth of Crown land in Elizabeth's reign; Dietz, 'The Receipts and Issues of the Exchequer during the Reigns of James I and Charles I', pp. 135–53, lists receipts of £1.2 million from the sale of royal lands from 1603 to 1640.
6. N.S.B. Gras, 'Tudor "Book of Rates": A Chapter in the History of the English Customs', *Quarterly Journal of Economics*, 26 (1911–12), 210–22.
7. A.P. Newton, 'The Establishment of the Great Farm of the English Customs', *Transactions of the Royal Historical Society*, fourth series, 1 (May 1918), 129–55.
8. C. Coleman and D. Starkey (eds), *Revolutions Reassessed* (Oxford, Clarendon Press, 1986), chapter one for the 'Tudor revolution' in government and Coleman's chapter 'Reorganization of the Exchequer of Receipt', pp. 163–98 for the reforms made in Elizabeth's reign.
9. F.C. Dietz, 'Elizabethan Customs Administration', *Economic History Review*, 45 (1930), 35–8.
10. A 'farm' is an agreement in which the farmer of the revenue being leased undertook to pay a fixed amount of money for the expected annual receipts of the tax. This rent of the farm was less than the farmer or government expected the tax revenue to produce. The farmer provided management and financial service to the government, gaining in return the receipt over his rent.

11. Newton, 'The Great Farm of the 'Customs', pp. 136–8.
12. Dietz, 'Elizabethan Customs Administration', pp. 43–6.
13. Ibid., pp. 51–3.
14. Ibid., p. 53.
15. Braddick, *The Nerves of State*, pp. 53–5.
16. Newton, 'The Great Farm of the Customs', p. 143; Dietz, 'Elizabethan Customs Administration', pp. 55–6.
17. Dietz, 'Elizabethan Customs Administration', pp. 56–7.
18. Ibid., p. 57; R. Ashton, 'Revenue Farming under the Early Stuarts', *Economic History Review*, second series, 8 (1956), 310–11.
19. Newton, 'The Great Farm of the Customs', pp. 148–151.
20. Ibid., pp. 151–2.
21. Ashton, 'Revenue Farming under the Early Stuarts', pp. 310–11; R. Ashton, 'The Disbursing Official under the Early Stuarts: The Cases of Sir William Russell and Philip Burlamachi', *Bulletin of the Institute of Historical Research*, 30 (1957), 162; Ashton, 'Deficit Finance in the Reign of James I', pp. 15–6; R. Ashton, *The Crown and the Money Market, 1603–1640* (Oxford, Clarendon Press, 1960), pp. 19–24.
22. Newton, 'The Great Farm of the Customs', pp. 151–2.
23. Ashton, 'Deficit Finance in the Reign of James I', pp. 21–4.
24. J.R. Tanner, *English Constitutional Conflicts of the Seventeenth Century, 1603–1689* (Cambridge, Cambridge University Press, 1971), pp. 42–4. For a more detailed discussion of the customs see H. Atton and H. Holland, *The King's Customs* (London, John Murray, 1908); E. Hughes, *Studies in Administration and Finance, 1558–1825* (Manchester, Manchester University Press, 1934); W. Kennedy, *English Taxation, 1640–1799* (London, G. Bell and Sons, 1913, 1964 edn).
25. Ashton, *The Crown and the Money Market*, pp. 35–7.
26. Smith, *Emergence of a Nation State*, pp. 255–7.
27. Kennedy, *English Taxation*, p. 55.
28. Ibid.
29. Davies, *The Early Stuarts, 1603–1660*, pp. 81–3; Ashton, *The Crown and the Money Market*, p. 39.
30. Dietz, 'The Receipts and Issues of the Exchequer during the Reigns of James I and Charles I', pp. 135–53. These include the receipts from the Great Farm of the customs and a number of smaller customs and impositions that were farmed and directly collected in this period. These are cash receipts only. Further large amounts were paid by the customs farmers in the form of tallies in anticipation of receipts, ibid., pp. 120–4.
31. Chandaman, *The English Public Revenue*, pp. 287–9.
32. For the data on amounts see Dietz, 'Receipts and Issues of the Exchequer', pp. 135–53, and for their sources, see pp. 120–4; for the use of short-term credit and tallies see Ashton, 'Revenue Farming under the Early Stuarts', pp. 311–13, and especially fn. 1, p. 312.
33. Ashton, 'Revenue Farming under the Early Stuarts', pp. 310–22; V. Pearl, *London and the Outbreak of the Puritan Revolution* (London, Oxford University Press, 1961), pp. 72, 78.
34. Ashton, 'Revenue Farming under the Early Stuarts'.
35. Pearl, *London and the Outbreak of the Puritan Revolution*, p. 321; Tanner, *English Constitutional Conflicts of the Seventeenth Century*, pp. 73–9 for more on the King's financial measures from 1629 to 1640.
36. Ashton, 'Revenue Farming under the Early Stuarts', p. 311.
37. C. Wilson, *England's Apprenticeship, 1603–1763* (London, Longmans, 1965), p. 98.
38. Ashton, *The Crown and the Money Market*, p. 46.

39. Firth and Rait, *Acts and Ordinances*, i: p. 16.
40. *CJ*, ii: pp. 668, 694, 699; Firth and Rait, *Acts and Ordinances*, i: pp. 16–19.
41. Ibid.
42. PRO, E190/46/1, Port Book of London, December 1650 to December 1651; E122/232/16, Port Book of Sandwich, December 1651 to December 1652. These books list the ship departing, its cargo, destination, and the status of its customs duty liability.
43. Firth and Rait, *Acts and Ordinances*, i: p. 17.
44. Ibid., pp. 19–20.
45. Ibid.
46. *CJ*, ii: p. 705.
47. Ibid., pp. 705–6, 709.
48. Ibid., p. 946; Pearl, *London and the Outbreak of the Puritan Revolution*, pp. 93, 187, 194n, 208n, 255n.
49. *CJ*, ii: p. 710.
50. Ibid., pp. 714–16.
51. Ibid., pp. 763, 806.
52. Ibid., pp. 900–1, 908, 919; TT, E85(9), *Special Passages*, 10–17 January 1643, pp. 292–3.
53. *CJ*, ii: p. 934.
54. Pearl, *London and the Outbreak of the Puritan Revolution*, appendix II, 'The New Men'.
55. *CJ*, ii: pp. 928–38.
56. Ibid., p. 940.
57. Ibid., pp. 937–40.
58. PRO, E351/643, the declared account of the Commissioners of the Customs; Ashley, *The Financial and Commercial Policy under the Cromwellian Protectorate* gives the amount of net receipts as £140,744, but the declared account lists £145,000 as the amount provided to the navy in this period.
59. Firth and Rait, *Acts and Ordinances*, iii: p. 4; *CJ*, iii: p. 94.
60. *CJ*, ii: p. 988; iii: p. 94; TT, E85(45), *Certain Informations*, 16–23 January 1643, pp. 4–5, 7; E86(3), *Special Passages*, 17–24 January 1643, p. 199; E86(5), *Weekly Intelligencer*, 17–24 January 1643, p. 27; E88(17), *Certain Informations*, 30 January–6 February 1643, p. 23.
61. *CJ*, iii: pp. 72, 243, 274.
62. Hughes, *Studies in Administration and Finance*, p. 139, points out also that farms tended to fail in times of crisis, as in 1640 and 1671.
63. *CJ*, ii: p. 889.
64. Ibid., p. 932.
65. *CJ*, iii: p. 94.
66. Firth and Rait, *Acts and Ordinances*, i: p. 104.
67. PRO, E351/644.
68. PRO, E351/644, fo. 3.
69. *CJ*, iii: p. 664.
70. Ibid., p. 670.
71. Ibid., p. 672.
72. Ibid., iv: p. 22.
73. Ibid., p. 40.
74. Ibid., pp. 49–50.
75. PRO, E351/645, fo. 1; E364/129 for a duplicate copy of their declared account; *CJ*, iv: pp. 50–1; Firth and Rait, *Acts and Ordinances*, i: p. 627, for the ordinance continuing the customs on 21 February 1645.
76. *Dictionary of National Biography*, xv: pp. 28–30 for Packe and a mention of Avery; Pearl, *London and the Outbreak of the Puritan Revolution*, pp. 121, 130.

77. *CJ*, iv: pp. 68–9; Firth and Rait, *Acts and Ordinances*, i: pp. 627–30.

78. PRO, E351/645–9, declared accounts of the customs commissioners for the five accounting periods from February 1645 to July 1649.

79. PRO, E351/649 lists this money as 'Depending on sundry person for several sums of money by them received for which they are to render an account.'

80. PRO, E351/650–9 are the accounts through 1659. Avery et al. paid £13,521 in the period 24 July 1649 to 24 June 1650 (E351/650, fo. 2) to the commissioners Tichborne et al. There are no other records of a payment by the Avery group.

81. Pearl, *London and the Outbreak of the Puritan Revolution*, pp. 121, 150, and fn. 45 above; V. Pearl, 'London's counter-revolution, 1647', in Gerald Aylmer (ed.), *The Interregnum: Quest for Settlement, 1646–1660* (Hamden, CT, University of Connecticut Press, 1972).

82. Aylmer, *State's Servants*, pp. 161–2; R. Ashton, *The English Civil War, Conservatism and Revolution, 1643–1660* (London, Weidenfeld and Nicolson, 1978), pp. 330, 337; Ashley, *Financial and Commercial Policy*, pp. 53, 102.

83. Thurloe, as quoted by Ashley, *Financial and Commercial Policy*, p. 42.

84. Aylmer, *State's Servants*, p. 161.

85. PRO, E351/650–6, declared accounts of the customs commissioners for the seven periods from July 1649 to March 1656.

86. From June 1654 until the end of the accounts, the customs commissioners paid £480,993 into the re-established Exchequer, rather than directly to the Treasurer of the Navy. See PRO, E351/655–6.

87. Firth and Rait, *Acts and Ordinances*, ii: pp. 205–7.

88. Ashley, *Financial and Commercial Policy*, pp. 52–4; Aylmer, *State's Servants*, pp. 161–4, for Thurloe's views.

89. Ashley, *Financial and Commercial Policy*, pp. 53–5.

90. Aylmer, *State's Servants*, p. 161.

91. PRO, E351/650 and E351/652. See the foot of each account for the accounting and payments.

92. PRO, E351/656. See the foot for the reckoning with Harvey and his associates.

93. Ashley, *Financial and Commercial Policy*, p. 59; Aylmer, *State's Servants*, p. 99.

94. Aylmer, *State's Servants*, pp. 206, 399.

95. Ibid., pp. 220–1.

96. Ibid., pp. 72–3, 367.

97. Ashley, *Financial and Commercial Policy*, p. 59.

98. PRO, E351/657–9. Portions of the accounts are badly damaged. Several of the amounts disbursed are illegible. These numbers are rounded to the nearest tens or hundreds as appropriate. The unaccounted for amount of £4,728 is due to the damage of the document and the need to round off numbers. Actually, less than this amount was unaccounted for in the declared account.

99. PRO, E351/658, for example; they paid £5,515 into the Exchequer at the end of the accounting year that ended in March 1658.

100. PRO, E351/660, fo. 1.

101. Pearl, *London and the Outbreak of the Puritan Revolution*, pp. 93, 252n for Wolstenholme; pp. 101, 194, and 205 for Harrison; pp. 194, 255n for Harby; pp. 7, 119, 121, 148, 194 and 266 for Crispe.

102. PRO, E351/660 for the declared account of Crispe, Harby, Harrison, and Wolstenholme for the period July 1660 to September 1662.

103. Ms is for Midsummer, M. is for Michaelmas. Chandaman, *English Public Revenue*, appendix 2, pp. 303–8 for customs receipts and pp. 348–57 for total receipts of taxes, from the declared accounts of the various tax collectors for 1660 to 1688; Gordon,

The History of Our National Debts and Taxes, p. 88; Jones, *War and Economy in the Age of William III and Marlborough*, Table 3.1. Jones's totals are within 2 per cent of the sums in *The History of Our National Debts*.

104. Atton and Holland, *The King's Customs*, pp. 102–53 for the period 1660–1707; Hughes, *Studies in Administration and Finance*, pp. 139–41, 153–5.
105. Chandaman, *English Public Revenue*, p. 303.
106. Newton, 'The Great Farm of the Customs', p. 155.
107. Chandaman, *English Public Revenue*, p. 333 for total revenue from 1660 to 1688; p. 304 for customs gross revenue from 1671 to 1688.
108. Shaw (ed.), *Calendar of Treasury Books, Introduction to Volumes XI–XVII*, introduction.

CHAPTER SEVEN

1. Braddick, *The Nerves of State*, pp. 99–101.
2. J. Brewer, 'The English State and Fiscal Appropriation, 1688–1789', *Politics and Society*, 16 (1988), 335–85.
3. Ashley, *Financial and Commercial Policy*, chapter seven for a brief discussion of the excise during the Protectorate; Braddick, *Parliamentary Taxation in Seventeenth-Century England*, chapter four for an excellent discussion of the history of the seventeenth-century excise; Hughes, *Studies in Administration and Finance*, chapter four, 'The development of the excise' is very useful; Kennedy, *English Taxation, 1640–1799*, chapter four for the excise, 1640–1713; B.R. Leftwich, *A History of the Excise* (London, Simpkin, Marshall, Hamilton and Kent, 1908), chapter two for the excise in the 1640s and 1650s.
4. Firth and Rait, *Acts and Ordinances*, i: pp. 202–7 and 272–8. Tobacco, wine, strong liquor, beer, ale, hard cider, imported drugs, mercury, silk, linen, paper, pottery, skins, and leather, and domestic woollen goods and soap were the major items rated in the original excise ordinance.
5. Braddick, *Parliamentary Taxation*, p. 168; Chandaman, *English Public Revenue*, pp. 38–75.
6. Beckett, 'Land Tax or Excise', pp. 286, 297, and 299.
7. Kennedy, *English Taxation*, p. 23, for the quote; Braddick, *Parliamentary Taxation*, observes that the excise was integral to the creation of a tax state (p. 223), and that the 'driving force behind innovation appears to have been warfare. . . . The demands of civil war led to unprecedented levels of taxation, levels sustained subsequently, and further dramatic changes proceeded from the wars of the 1690s', p. 5.
8. *CJ*, iii: p. 89 for the excise proposal, p. 94 for the sale of royal goods, p. 74 for forced loans, pp. 53–5 for sequestration of Royalists' estates; Gardiner, *History of the Civil War*, i: pp. 150–73 for the Royalist successes of the summer of 1643, and p. 179 for the passage of the excise and its obvious connection to the need to provide large sums of money regularly to support the Parliamentarian armies.
9. *CJ*, iii: p. 98.
10. Ibid., p. 115; PRO, SP28 is full of warrants used for everything from buying supplies for the Earl of Essex's army (SP28/58) to paying Waller's, Manchester's, and Fairfax's forces (SP28/260–4). The warrant procedure was used to issue instructions to the treasurers of various revenues, such as those for the sale of royal property, to issue money from their receipts for the armies and to pay old debts and current salaries (SP28/271–86). The warrants were endorsed by the recipient and served as a receipt to the treasurer to account for the money he had issued.

11. *CJ*, iii: pp. 149, 171.
12. J.H. Hexter, *The Reign of King Pym* (Cambridge, MA, Harvard University Press, 1941), p. 25; *CJ*, iii: pp. 170–9 for the efforts in the Commons to pass the ordinance; C.V. Wedgwood, *The King's War, 1641–7* (New York, Book of the Month Club, 1991), pp. 215–16, 222.
13. *CJ*, iii: p. 181.
14. Firth and Rait, *Acts and Ordinances*, i: p. 202.
15. Ibid., pp. 203 and 206.
16. Ibid., pp. 203–4.
17. Ibid., pp. 274–8.
18. Pearl, *London and the Outbreak of the Puritan Revolution*, pp. 315–16 for Foot; pp. 253n, 259n, and 321 for Kendrick; pp. 39–40 and 325 for Towse. Pearl called them 'new men' because they had not played important roles in London government until after 1640. However, they were financially successful merchants before they became aldermen. See ibid, p. 240.
19. Ibid., pp. 321–2 for Langham; pp. 314–15 for Cullam; pp. 238n, 240n, 243, and 313–15 for their political positions and their removal.
20. Ibid., pp. 240–4; Braddick, *The Nerves of State*, pp. 99–101; TT, E999(1), 'Excise anatomized', 1659; E813(16), Pyrenne on the excise; Braddick, 'Popular Politics and Public Policy: The Excise Riot at Smithfield in February 1647 and its Aftermath', *The Historical Journal*, 34 (1991), 597–626.
21. Firth and Rait, *Acts and Ordinances*, i: p. 203.
22. Ibid., pp. 204–5 and 274–80.
23. Ibid., pp. 205, 207–8.
24. Ibid., p. 207; *CJ*, iii: p. 239; Ashley, *Financial and Commercial Policy*, p. 63.
25. Firth and Rait, *Acts and Ordinances*, i: p. 274.
26. Ibid., pp. 279, 281–2.
27. *CJ*, iii: pp. 265, 273.
28. Ibid., pp. 265, 273–4, 296, 299, 310, 319, 340, 356, 362, 365, 368–71, 400–3, 409, 422, 442, 540, 600, 635, 638, 644, 650, 677, and 686.
29. Ibid., p. 256, for example when Parliament confiscated the property of fourteen members of the Long Parliament who had left London and gone to Oxford to join the King.
30. Ibid., p. 296.
31. Ibid., pp. 316, 319.
32. For September 1644 to September 1645 see *CJ*, iii: pp. 677, 686, 720, 731–3; *CJ*, iv: pp. 108–9, 126, 148–9, 180, 200, 202, 230, 252–3, 260, 281–2, 284, 294; for September 1645 to September 1646 see *CJ*, iv: pp. 299, 304, 315, 319–20, 332–4, 338, 342–3, 374–5, 384–6, 388, 401, 408–9, 454, 460–1, 478, 484, 567, 575, 608, 620, 625, 688.
33. *CJ*, v: p. 58. The £400,000 for the Scots is not included in the £686,000 mentioned above.
34. PRO, E351/1295, declared account of the excise commissioners, September 1647 to September 1650.
35. Firth and Rait, *Acts and Ordinances*, i: pp. 769–71 for the obligations to support Essex's army; PRO, E351/1295, fo. 12 for the interest paid by the excise commissioners from September 1647 to 1650.
36. Firth and Rait, *Acts and Ordinances*, i: pp. 769–71.
37. Ibid.
38. Ibid., pp. 501–2; PRO, E351/1295, fo. 15.
39. *CSPD, 1645–7*, p. 602, includes a report from the newspaper known as *Perfect Occurrences*, for the week of 15 to 22 October 1647, that the engagements for the excise were 'about £1,000,000'; see Gentles, *New Model Army*, pp. 40–189 for the

political crises and confrontations between the New Model Army and the Presbyterian majority in Parliament.

40. Aylmer, *State's Servants*, p. 328–9, for his thoughts on the difference in administrative outcome; Gentles, *New Model Army*, pp. 164–8. Gentles believes, rightly I think, that the Long Parliament could have paid off the army successfully in early 1647 with not much more than £100,000.
41. *CJ*, v: pp. 163–5.
42. Ibid., pp. 181, 190–1.
43. Firth and Rait, *Acts and Ordinances*, i: pp. 1004–5 for the quote; TT, E589(1), 'The Good Women's Cry Against the Excise', 4 January 1650, for an example of popular attitudes to the excise and the connection people made between the excise and the regicides and army officers in their protests.
44. Firth and Rait, *Acts and Ordinances*, i: p. 1006.
45. Ibid., i: pp. 1004–8, 'An Ordinance for Re-establishing the duty of Excise upon all commodities except Flesh and Salt made in the Kingdom', 8 August 1647.
46. PRO, E351/1295, declared account of the excise commissioners, 30 September 1647 to 29 September 1650.
47. PRO, E351/1296 and Table 7.2.
48. PRO, SP28 for thousands of examples of these warrants. Also, *CSPD, 1649–50* lists hundreds of such warrants.
49. PRO, E351/302, fos. 1–6, the declared account of the Treasurers at War for the period 1645 to 1651.
50. PRO, E351/1295, fo. 10. There are thirty-six separate expenditures listed in the account for military purposes, varying in amount from £50 to £43,320.
51. PRO, E351/1295, fos. 24–5.
52. *CJ*, vi: pp. 147, 181, 184; *CSPD, 1649–50*, p. 246.
53. Firth and Rait, *Acts and Ordinances*, ii: pp. 158, 237–9.
54. Ibid., pp. 229–30.
55. Aylmer, *State's Servants*, pp. 264 and 276.
56. PRO, E351/304 for the Treasurers at War and E351/1296 for the excise commission.
57. Braddick, *The Nerves of State*, p. 100.
58. Firth and Rait, *Acts and Ordinances*, ii: p. 423.
59. PRO, E351/1296, declared account of the excise commissioners for 30 September 1650 to 29 September 1653.
60. PRO, E351/1295 lists total cash revenue from 1647 to 1650 as £860,671 which averages out to £286,890 per year; E351/1296 lists gross cash revenue from the excise from 1650 to 1653 as £1,132,812, which is an average of £377,604 per year. This latter revenue figure excludes the £28,330 paid to the excise by the Treasurers at War since that money was raised by another income source.
61. Gentles, *New Model Army*, chapters eleven and twelve for the conquests of Ireland and Scotland and the importance of a steady stream of supplies.
62. Firth and Rait, *Acts and Ordinances*, ii: p. 823.
63. Ibid.
64. PRO, E351/1297 is the declared account for September 1653 to March 1654; E351/1298 is the account for March 1658 to March 1659; E351/1299 is the account for 25 March 1659 to 30 September 1659; E351/1301 is the account for 1 October 1659 to 28 February 1660; E351/1300 is the account for 1 March 1660 to 18 August 1660. The next account is E351/1302, which is the excise account for November 1662 to June 1665, followed by E351/1303 for June 1665 to 8 November 1666.
65. PRO, E351/1297, declared account of the excise commissioners for the period 30 September 1653 to 25 March 1654.

66. PRO, SP28/333, Exchequer Receipt Book, 1655 to 1658, lists the separate deposits from the farmers of the excise and the excise commissioners.
67. Firth and Rait, *Acts and Ordinances*, iii: pp. 89, 90. Parliament passed acts before 1654 authorizing the excise commissioners to pay money to the Navy Treasurer. After 1654, it became accepted practice.
68. Braddick, *Parliamentary Taxation*, pp. 225–7.
69. PRO, SP28/141 for the records of hospitals in England from 1643–51.
70. Firth and Rait, *Acts and Ordinances*, ii: pp. 711–12, 714.
71. Ibid., pp. 765–77.
72. Ibid., pp. 823, 845, 889; *CJ*, vii: p. 315.
73. BL, Add. MSS 28854 and 32471, and Lansdowne MS 232, fo. 50, are in general agreement as to the debt, revenue, and estimated expenditures. They are probably all copies of the same estimate provided to Parliament in December 1654. See Kennedy, *English Taxation*, p. 55, for his view that excise taxes had come to be viewed as ordinary revenue by the late 1650s.
74. BL, Add. MS 28854, fos. 1–3.
75. C.H. Firth, *Last Years of the Protectorate, 1656–1658* (London, Longmans, 1909), pp. 257–68.
76. PRO, E401/1930–2, Exchequer Receipt Books for the period of the table.
77. Hughes, *Studies in Administration and Finance*, pp. 153–4, attributes the final phase of this change in management of the farm to the 1670s.
78. Braddick, *Parliamentary Taxation*, pp. 202–3; Chandaman, *English Public Revenue*, pp. 37–40.
79. PRO, E351/305–7 for the army records; SP28/333 for the itemized Exchequer expenditures.
80. PRO, E351/1302–3 for the declared accounts of 1662 to 1665.
81. Chandaman, *English Public Revenue*, pp. 53–76.
82. PRO, E351/1298–1301, declared account of the excise commissioners, 25 March 1658 to 18 August 1660.
83. Ibid. for Gilbert Gerrard's report of the £1,334,532 raised on the excise in this period; *CSPD, 1649–50*, p. 357 contains a report which lists the gross receipts of the excise for the period 29 September 1646 to 29 September 1647 as £357,423. The net debt secured on the excise was reported to be £398,211 in January 1647. While the excise was used to raise £1.3 million in four years, nearly £400,000 of this was borrowed money secured by future revenues.
84. PRO, E351/1295.
85. PRO, E351/1296 and 1297, declared accounts of excise commissioners for this period.
86. PRO, E401/1930–2.
87. Firth and Rait, *Acts and Ordinances*, i: p. 1004.
88. W.A. Shaw (ed.), *Calendar of State Papers, Treasury Books, 1661–1667* (London, HMSO, 1904), pp. xxvi–xxxiv for excise receipts for the period 1661 to 1667.
89. Beckett, 'Land Tax or Excise', p. 305.
90. Braddick, *Parliamentary Taxation*, pp. 201–2, 223; Chandaman, *English Public Revenue*, p. 39, fn. 7.
91. Chandaman, *English Public Revenue*, pp. 39–55.
92. Ibid., pp. 56–62.
93. Ibid., Appendix 2, pp. 308–16 for the period 1660 to 1688; Gordon, *The History of Our National Debts and Taxes*, p. 88; Jones, *War and Economy in the Age of William III and Marlborough*, Table 3.1. Jones's figures agree closely with *The History of Our National Debts* and he uses Chandaman for the period 1660 to 1688.

94. Ibid., pp. 67–71.
95. Ibid., p. 63–4; H. Roseveare, *The Treasury, 1660–1870* (New York, Barnes and Noble, 1973).
96. Chandaman, *English Public Revenue*, pp. 70–5.
97. PRO, AO1/1073/693–7, excise accounts 24 June 1683 to 24 June 1689; AO1/1074/698–703, excise accounts, 24 June 1689 to 24 June 1696; AO1/1075/704–7, excise accounts, 24 June 1696 to 24 June 1700.
98. Brewer, 'The English State and Fiscal Appropriation, 1688–1789', p. 353.
99. Chandaman, *English Public Revenue*, p. 72.
100. Kennedy, *English Taxation, 1640–1799*, p. 28.
101. Beckett, 'Land Tax or Excise', p. 306.
102. Braddick, *The Nerves of State*, pp. 99–101; Brewer, 'The English State and Fiscal Appropriation, 1688–1789', pp. 340–50.

CHAPTER EIGHT

1. Braddick, *The Nerves of State*, pp. 97–9; Brewer, 'The English State and Fiscal Appropriation, 1688–1789', p. 341.
2. Clarendon, *History*, ii: pt 1, p. 58.
3. Firth and Rait, *Acts and Ordinances*, i: pp. 38–40, 61, 64, 69, 77.
4. Hexter, *The Reign of King Pym*, pp. 19–26, 31, 134–5; Chandaman, *The English Public Revenue*, pp. 140, 144, 146–8, 157; Dickson, *The Financial Revolution*, p. 9–11.
5. There is surprising little written about the assessment tax of the 1640s and 1650s beyond Braddick's excellent chapter on it in his *Parliamentary Taxation*; for the period 1660 to 1688 see Chandaman, *The English Public Revenue*, pp. 140–8, discusses the continuation of the assessment and its importance to English state finance in the period 1660 to 1688; Ashley, *Financial and Commercial Policy*, has a short chapter about the assessment of the 1650s. Aylmer, *State's Servants*, pp. 24, 26, 28–9, remarks on its importance and eventual efficiency.
6. Firth and Rait, *Acts and Ordinances*, i: p. 85.
7. Ibid., pp. 85–9; Aylmer, *State's Servants*, pp. 300–1.
8. Braddick, *Parliamentary Taxation*, pp. 134–40.
9. Braddick, *The Nerves of State*, pp. 95–6.
10. Ibid., pp. 144–7; W.R. Ward, *The English Land Tax in the Eighteenth Century* (Oxford, Oxford University Press, 1953), pp. 1–5; Deitz, *English Public Finance*, pp. 382–93; S.A. Dowell, *A History of Taxation and Taxes in England* (6 vols, London, F. Cass, 1888), pp. 4–6.
11. *CJ*, ii: p. 972; Firth and Rait, *Acts and Ordinances*, i: pp. 86–8.
12. *CJ*, iv: p. 253; Parliament decided to collect these arrears in 1645.
13. Firth and Rait, *Acts and Ordinances*, i: pp. 86–8.
14. Hexter, *The Reign of King Pym*, pp. 29, 95–6 for the relationship of the London Common Council and John Pym; Firth and Rait, *Acts and Ordinances*, i: 99–100; *CJ*, ii: pp. 972, 984, 999.
15. Firth and Rait, *Acts and Ordinances*, i: pp. 89–95.
16. Aylmer, *State's Servants*, pp. 311–12; Fletcher, *Reform in the Provinces*, pp. 11–19. Fletcher makes the point that it is dangerous to generalize about such appointments. He implies that Parliament was prepared to sacrifice ideological considerations for quiet acquiescence and administrative ability in its appointments for the county committees; D.H. Pennington and I. Roots (eds), *The Committee at Stafford, 1643–1645* (Manchester, Manchester University Press, 1957), pp. xxii–xxiii, point out that the traditional élite in Stafford soon became a minority on the Stafford committee.

17. Firth and Rait, *Acts and Ordinances*, i: p. 91.
18. Ibid., pp. 98–100; BL, Add. MS 37491, 'The Minute Book for the County Committee of Essex', fos. 1–5.
19. Firth and Rait, *Acts and Ordinances*, i: p. 100.
20. Ibid., p. 98; BL, Add. MS 37491.
21. Firth and Rait, *Acts and Ordinances*, i: p. 98.
22. Ibid., pp. 98–9.
23. Ibid., pp. 95–6.
24. D.H. Pennington, 'The rebels of 1642', in R.H. Parry (ed.), *The English Civil War and After* (Berkeley, University of California Press, 1970), p. 39; Pennington and Roots (eds), *The Committee at Stafford*, p. lix; Fletcher, *Reform in the Provinces*, pp. 13–18.
25. Firth and Rait, *Acts and Ordinances*, i: pp. 97–8.
26. Ibid., p. 100.
27. *CJ*, ii: p. 972.
28. Ibid., p. 983.
29. Firth and Rait, *Acts and Ordinances*, i: p. 128.
30. PRO, E351/302, fo. 1 for the assessment; E351/643, fo. 1 for the customs.
31. *CJ*, ii: pp. 1002–3.
32. Ibid., p. 16.
33. Ibid., p. 1.
34. Ibid., p. 29.
35. *CJ*, iii: pp. 28, 41, 62, 98, 102, 260, 276, 291, 308.
36. Ibid., pp. 22–3.
37. Ibid., pp. 273, 310, 314, 319, 356, 364–5, 368, 371, 401–9, 422, 442.
38. Quoted in Scroggs, 'English Finances under the Long Parliament', p. 427; *CJ*, iii: p. 260; several London companies were threatened with sequestration if they failed to pay their arrears; PRO, SP19/63 lists the arrears for London, as late as 1646, as £90,764, for the special assessment of November 1642.
39. PRO, SP28/246, the weekly assessment account of Coventry, for just one example of many in SP28.
40. Firth and Rait, *Acts and Ordinances*, i: p. 224.
41. *CJ*, iii: pp. 384, 400.
42. Ibid., p. 340; Firth and Rait, *Acts and Ordinances*, i: pp. 398–9.
43. Ibid., p. 368; *CJ*, iii: pp. 402, 470, 473–4.
44. Godfrey Davies, 'The Parliamentary Army under the Earl of Essex', *English Historical Review*, 49 (1934), 42–4.
45. Clarendon, *History*, ii: pt. 2, pp. 560–6; Wedgwood, *King's War*, pp. 359–70.
46. PRO, E101/67/11A, fos. 112–13.
47. Gentles, *New Model Army*, pp. 1–16, provides a superb account of the creation of the New Model Army and the passage of the Self-Denying Ordinance and the monthly assessment.
48. Firth and Rait, *Acts and Ordinances*, i: p. 580 (to bring in London's assessment arrears), 614 (New Model Army Ordinance), 650 (impressment of soldiers), 653 (horses for artillery train), 656 (loan for army), 660 (Fairfax's command), 664 (Self-Denying Ordinance).
49. *CJ*, iv: pp. 10, 16, 31; *CSPD, 1644–5*, pp. 232–3.
50. Firth and Rait, *Acts and Ordinances*, i: 614–26.
51. Ibid., p. 616.
52. Ibid.
53. Ibid., pp. 616–17.
54. Ibid., pp. 617–18.

55. PRO, SP28/294–7, 334, 337, and 340, to cite only some. The receipts were printed, with blanks left for the county collectors' names, the county names, the amounts, and the date of the ordinance under which the money was collected. The Treasurers at War signed most of the receipts. These receipts clearly indicate that the money was paid to the treasurers in London; E360/208 contains dozens of declared accounts of local collectors. These accounts indicate that the vast majority of the assessments collected after February 1645 were remitted to the Treasurers at War in the London Guildhall.

56. PRO, SP28/350, pt 5, 'Book of Advance of the Eighty Thousand Pound Loan', March 1645.

57. *CJ*, iv: pp. 52–71 for the negotiations for this loan and agreement.

58. Pearl, 'London's counter-revolution', p. 217, notes 7 and 8, pp. 31–2, 51, 55; Pearl, *London and the Outbreak of the Puritan Revolution*, pp. 292–3, 325–31, 126n, 149n, 243n, 259n.

59. PRO, E351/302; Pearl, *London and the Outbreak of the Puritan Revolution*, pp. 114n, 126n, 142–4, 239n, 268, 292–3 for Adams, 259n for Chamberlain, 253n, 325–7 for Dethicke, 309–11 and 321 for Andrews, 328–31 for Wollaston; B. Worden, *The Rump Parliament* (Cambridge, Cambridge University Press, 1977), p. 31 for the quote, pp. 270–1, 308, 315, and 340.

60. PRO, E351/302, these Treasurers at War declared account for the period 28 March 1645 to 25 December 1651. No declared account for the weekly assessment exists.

61. Firth and Rait, *Acts and Ordinances*, i: pp. 658–9; PRO, SP28/58, 62–5, and 90 contain thousands of such warrants, issued by this committee and later the Committee of Both Kingdoms, to the Treasurers at War.

62. PRO, SP28/251, accounts sent to the Committee of Accounts from Wales (1643–57), Berkshire, Buckinghamshire, Oxon (1645–6); SP28/253–8 for the committee's work and for reports sent to it from Sussex, Kent, and elsewhere.

63. Shaw (ed.), *Calendar of Treasury Books, Introduction to Volumes XI–XVII*, pp. ccxxi–ccxxii.

64. PRO, E351/302 for the receipts of February 1645 to October 1646. The anticipated yield is computed by multiplying twenty times the £53,536 assessed monthly in the New Model Ordinance; E101/67/11A shows the slightly smaller amount of £928,551 as collected. In contrast, SP28/350, pt 4 indicates that Gerrard had received only £129,819 from the assessments of the earlier period of March 1644 to February 1645.

65. *CJ*, iv: pp. 73, 77, 83, 90, 178, 200; PRO, E351/302, fo. 2.

66. *CJ*, v: pp. 12–14

67. PRO, E351/302 for the receipts and all expenditures, *CJ*, iv: p. 602; *CJ*, vi: pp. 273, 414; *CJ*, vii: p. 10; Firth and Rait, *Acts and Ordinances*, i: pp. 958, 1107 and ii: pp. 24, 54, 285, 290, 456, 511 for amounts assessed.

68. PRO, E351/302, lists money received from the composition fines of Royalists and rents of their land, money received from the sale of lands and money paid to the Treasurers at War from the excise commissioners (£372,158).

69. PRO, E351/302, fos. 7–11.

70. Ibid., fos. 2–3; *CJ*, iv: pp. 294–9, 306, 387–9.

71. *CJ*, v: p. 56, 125; Firth and Rait, *Acts and Ordinances*, i: p. 817.

72. *CJ*, v: 90–104 and 155 is the best place to follow the growing dispute between the Presbyterian majority and the Independents in Parliament and the army. Parliament offered only six weeks' arrears to the army in April and was reluctant to pass an act of indemnity protecting the soldiers from prosecution for acts committed in the civil war. One of the very best accounts of this important episode is in J.S. Morrill, 'Mutiny and Discontent in English Provincial Armies, 1645–47', *Past and Present*, 56 (1972), 49–74; another very good account is in Gentles, *New Model Army*, chapters six and seven.

73. Firth and Rait, *Acts and Ordinances*, i: pp. 958, 981.
74. Ibid., pp. 958–84. The sums are rounded off to nearest pound.
75. Ibid., p. 1048.
76. PRO, SP28/61/1 for debentures; SP28/132 and 133 for examples of the regimental accounts from which the information of the soldiers' accounts were taken; SP28/120–4 for examples of the periodic musters carried out to ensure that the soldiers were really in their units. *CJ*, v: pp. 399, 492, for the appointments of Mr Wilcox, Edward Shorter, and John Haddock to serve as auditors of the soldiers' accounts and agents to issue the debentures.
77. *CJ*, vi: 44–6.
78. Firth and Rait, *Acts and Ordinances*, ii: pp. 51–4 for the April 1649 act.
79. PRO, E351/302, lists the cash sent to support the conquests of Ireland and Scotland by the Treasurers of War. Most of this money came from tax receipts; SP25/118, for the record of how Cromwell's campaign in Ireland in 1649–51 was supported; Wheeler, 'Cromwell's conquest of Ireland', in Fissel (ed.), *War and Government*; Wheeler, 'Cromwell's conquest of Scotland'; Gentles, *New Model Army*, chapters eleven and twelve.
80. PRO, E351/304, fos. 1–3; *CJ*, vii: pp. 54, 142; Firth and Rait, *Acts and Ordinances*, ii: p. 653.
81. PRO, E351/304, declared account of the Treasurers at War, 26 December 1651 to 24 June 1653.
82. PRO, E351/304, fo. 4.
83. Firth and Rait, *Acts and Ordinances*, ii: p. 683.
84. Beckett, 'Land Tax or Excise'; Braddick, *Parliamentary Taxation*, pp. 289–91.
85. Aylmer, *State's Servants*, pp. 242–6.
86. Ibid., p. 245–6.
87. During 1654 and 1655, the two £60,000 assessments ran concurrently for a time. The monthly rates are in Firth and Rait and are summarized in Ashley, *Financial and Commercial Policy*, p. 77.
88. R. Hutton, *The Restoration: A Political and Religious History of England and Wales, 1658–1667* (Oxford, Oxford University Press, 1985).
89. Blackwell, Leman and Deane handled an additional £475,855 for the army. This money was paid to them from the Exchequer and a variety of other treasuries and was accounted for in two separate declared accounts (E351/306 and E351/307).
90. PRO, E351/308, the declared account for the period February 1659–April 1662.
91. Bodl., Rawlinson MS A208.
92. PRO, E351/308, fo. 1.
93. PRO, SP63/281, fos. 3–9.
94. PRO, E351/308, £454,000 for pay and arrears; E351/309, £28,898 for pay of troops in Scotland; E351/310, £341,000 for disbanding thirteen foot regiments and twelve horse regiments; Shaw (ed.), *Calendar of . . . Treasury Books, 1661–1667*, pp. vii–xii, underestimates the amount paid for arrears and overestimates the arrears due the troops being disbanded.
95. Braddick, *Parliamentary Taxation*, pp. 5 and 9.
96. Chandaman, *English Public Revenue*, pp. 175, 189–90, 195; W.A. Shaw, 'The Beginning of the National Debt', pp. 395–6.
97. Chandaman, *English Public Revenue*, pp. 326–9 for 1660–88; PRO, E351/308–10 to add to Chandaman's data the sums raised by special assessments in 1660 to 1662 to pay off the army before most of its regiments were disbanded. These assessments were the last ones not paid into the Exchequer.

CHAPTER NINE

1. M.J. Braddick, 'The English Government, War, Trade and Settlement', in Canny (ed.), *The Origins of Empire*, pp. 286–308; Braddick's *The Nerves of State*, pp. 6–16, drew my attention to J.A. Schumpeter's article 'The Crisis of the Tax State', *International Economic Papers*, 4 (1954), 5–38. The period from 1640 to 1697 clearly was a crisis for the English state which resulted in the abolition of the remnants of a feudal demesne state and the establishment of the English fiscal state.

2. Brewer, *Sinews of Power*, pp. 7–14.

3. D.A. Baugh, 'Maritime Strength and Atlantic Commerce: The Use of a Grand Marine Empire', in L. Stone (ed.), *An Imperial State at War: Britain from 1689 to 1815* (London, Routledge and Kegan Paul, 1994), pp. 190–2.

4. Braddick, *The Nerves of State*, pp. 6–16.

5. Braddick, *Parliamentary Taxation*, p. 158.

6. Beckett, 'Land Tax or Excise', p. 287; Brewer, 'The English State and Fiscal Appropriation, 1688–1789', p. 341; Braddick, *The Nerves of State*, pp. 97–8.

7. L. Glow, 'The Committee-men in the Long Parliament, August 1642–December 1643', *Historical Journal*, 8 (1965), 1–14; L. Glow, 'The Manipulation of Committees in the Long Parliament, 1641–1642', *Journal of British Studies*, 5 (1965), 31–52; Firth and Rait, *Acts and Ordinances*, i: pp. 381–6 for Committee of Both Kingdoms, 1644, and i: pp. 387–90 for the first Committee for Taking the Accounts of the Whole Kingdom.

8. Shaw, *Calendar of Treasury Books, Introduction to Volumes XI–XVII*, p. ccxxii.

9. D. Gill, 'The Treasury, 1660–1714', *English Historical Review* (1931), 600–31, for a superb summary of the evolution of treasury control from 1660 to 1714; Gill, "The Relationship Between the Treasury and the Excise Commissioners (1660–1714)', *The Cambridge Historical Journal*, 4 (1932–4), 94–9; Roseveare, *The Treasury, 1660–1870*, pp. 17–45. Roseveare correctly points out that Dickson's book, *The Financial Revolution*, pays too little attention to financial developments from 1660 to 1688. Dickson certainly is mistaken in stating (p. 351) 'that it was only after 1688 that Treasury Orders were printed'. Fn. 26 on Roseveare's p. 25.

10. J.C. Saintly, 'A Reform of Tenure of Offices during the Reign of Charles II', *Bulletin of the Institute of Historical Research*, 41 (1968), 150, 156–9, and 164.

11. PRO, E351/2287–96, the declared accounts of Richard Hutchinson, Navy Treasurer, 1650–60; Wheeler, 'Naval Finance, 1650–1660', pp. 457–66.

12. PRO, AO1/1846/71 through 1851/87, declared accounts of the Ordnance Office, November 1670 to June 1680.

13. Roseveare, *The Treasury, 1660–1870*, pp. 23–6; Chandaman, *English Public Revenue*, pp. 287–98; W.A. Shaw, 'The Treasury Order Book', *The Economic Journal*, 16 (1906), 3–40; Richards, 'The Stop of the Exchequer', pp. 45–62, for the best account of the nature and outcomes of the Stop. Richards proves that the Stop was not a general default, that it affected only ten bankers and that less than £1.3 million was involved, most of which was eventually repaid.

14. Braddick, *The Nerves of State*, pp. 115–19.

15. Firth and Rait, *Acts and Ordinances*, i: pp. 203–14, for the 22 July 1643 excise ordinance and the list of taxable goods; Ibid, i: pp. 273–83 for the September 1643 ordinance clarifying the rules for the excise.

16. TT, E586(1), 'The Good Women's Cries Against the Excise of All Their Commodities', (London, 4 January 1649), pp. 1–3.

17. Beckett, 'Land Tax or Excise', pp. 286 and 305.

18. Braddick, *Parliamentary Taxation*, pp. 168, 170, 174–9, 201, 225–6. Braddick makes the point that while there was a fair amount of resistance to the excise in the 1640s and 1650s, after 1660 resistance became insignificant.

19. Chandaman, *English Public Revenue*, pp. 194–5 for a concise discussion of the evolution of the assessment into the Land Tax in the early 1690s, and Table 2, p. 157, for a list of direct taxes in the early 1660s; Beckett, 'Land Tax or Excise', pp. 285–308.

20. The monthly assessments were £60–90,000 per month in the 1640s, rising to £120,000 in the early 1650s. Over 90 per cent of these assessed amounts were collected, the assessment receipts were three to four times greater than the excise or customs, as Table 9.2 below indicates; Jones, *War and Economics in the Age of William III and Marlborough*, pp. 67–8, shows the same situation in the 1690s.

21. Braddick, *Parliamentary Taxation*, p. 141; Braddick, *The Nerves of State*, pp. 91–9; Firth and Rait, *Acts and Ordinances*, i: pp. 614–26.

22. Jones, *War and Economics in the Age of William III and Marlborough*, p. 67.

23. P. Mathias and P. O'Brien, 'Taxation in Britain and France, 1715–1810. A Comparison of the Social and Economic Incidence of Taxes Collected for the Central Governments', *Journal of Economic History*, v (1976), p. 611.

24. D.A. Baugh, 'The Eighteenth-Century Navy as a National Institution, 1690–1815', in J.R. Hill (ed.), *The Oxford Illustrated History of the Royal Navy* (Oxford, Oxford University Press, 1995), p. 123; A. Caruana, *The History of English Sea Ordnance*, vol. one, *The Age of Evolution, 1523–1715* (Ashley Lodge, Sussex, Jean Boudriot Publications, 1994), pp. 87–9, for the list of the Royal Navy's ships in 1677, when there were seventy-seven ships of the first three rates in commission; p. 92 for the list of the additional thirty ships of these rates that were built from 1677 to 1680; pp. 102–4 for the 1687/8 list of the 100 warships of the navy that carried forty or more heavy cannon.

25. Glete, *Navies and Nations*, i: pp. 129, 162–3 and Table 21:8. For naval strength in the year 1635 see BL, Add. MS 9301, fo. 53; for strength in 1628 see BL, Add. MS 9301, fo. 98.

26. Bodl. Rawlinson MS A223, fos. 6, 45–8, 75–7, 80–1 85, 97; TT, E405(8), 'Giles Green report on the Customs and the Navy', 1642–5, pp. 8–10.

27. BL, Add. MS 9304, fos. 29 and 79; Add. MS 10119, fo. 12b; Add. MS 9305, fo. 140b; Add. MS 9302, fo. 14.

28. Bodl., Rawlinson A181, fo. 407 for 1660; BL, Egerton MS 2543, fos. 155–6 for 1664 and fos. 154, 182 for 1666; Bodl. Rawlinson MS A195, fo. 28 for 1666 and fo. 24 for 1669; Rawlinson A17, fo. 2 for 1678; Rawlinson A181, fo. 407 for 1679; Glete, *Navies and Nations*, i: pp. 220 for the 1690s.

29. Ehrman, *The Navy in the War of William III, 1689–1697*; Jones, *War and Economics in the Age of William III and Marlborough*, p. 29.

30. Fischer, *The Great Wave*, pp. 75–102; Outhwaite, *Inflation in Tudor and Early Stuart England*, p. 10; R.A. Doughty, 'Industrial Prices and Inflation in Southern England, 1401–1640', *Explorations in Economic History*, 12 (1975), 177–92.

31. Dietz, 'The Exchequer in Elizabeth's Reign', pp. 103–4; Dietz, 'The Receipts and Issues of the Exchequer during the Reigns of James I and Charles I', pp. 158–67; PRO, E351/2239–334, Navy Treasurers' declared accounts, 1600 to 1699; E351/2428–58, Surveyor of Victuals' declared accounts, 1628–42 and 1660–78; E351/2664, declared account of the Ordnance, 1641–52; AO1/1845–51, Ordnance Office declared accounts, 1662 to 1680; Chandaman, *English Public Revenue*, pp. 348–63; Gordon, *The History of Our National Debts and Taxes*, p. 88.

32. See chapter two for the annual costs of the navy and Ordnance Office during the period 1600 to 1648. See chapter three for the detailed naval costs for the period 1649 to 1699.

33. J.I. Israel, 'The Emerging Empire: The Continental Perspective, 1650–1713', in Canny (ed.), *The Origins of Empire*, pp. 423–44.

34. D.A. Baugh, 'Maritime Strength and Atlantic Commerce: The Uses of 'a Grand Marine Empire', in Stone (ed.), *An Imperial State at War*, p. 190 for the first quote and fn. 18, p. 216 for the second quote.

35. Fletcher, *Reform in the Provinces*, pp. 282–316.

36. Furgol, 'Scotland Turned Sweden: The Scottish Covenanters and the Military Revolution, 1638–1651', in J. Morrill (ed.), *The Scottish National Covenant in its British Context* (Edinburgh, Edinburgh University Press, 1990).

37. Childs, *The Army of Charles II*, pp. 13–19, 162–76. This includes the 7,500 men in Ireland, 2,500 in Scotland, 3–6,000 in London, and 1–4,000 in Tangiers. It excludes the brigades of roughly 3,000 men each in the French and Dutch armies.

38. Falls, *Elizabeth's Irish War*, Gentles, *New Model Army*, chapters eleven and twelve.

39. Dietz, 'The Exchequer in Elizabeth's Reign', pp. 103–4 for 1600 to 1603; Dietz, 'The Receipts and Issues of the Exchequer during the Reigns of James I and Charles I', pp. 158–67 for 1603 to 1639; PRO, E351/292–9, declared accounts of the Army Treasurers for 1639–41; PRO, E351/302, 304–7, Treasurers at War declared accounts, 1645–60; *CJ*, vi: pp. 13–14, for the Army Treasurer's account to the Commons for the period 1642 to February 1645; Chandaman, *English Public Revenue*, pp. 348–63 for 1660–88 and PRO, E351/309–10 for 1660–2; BL. Add. MS 10119, fo. 173 for costs of all forces, 1689–1700; PRO, E351/2306–24 Navy Treasurers' declared accounts for 1689–1700; Gordon, *The History of Our National Debts and Taxes*, p. 88, for the expenditures for 1688 to 1700. The last source and BL, Add. MSS 10119, fo. 173 are remarkably close. The accounting years vary. Exchequer years ran from Michaelmas to Michaelmas, while the Army Treasurers' declared accounts usually, but not always, ran from 1 January to 31 December.

40. These amounts are for the period Easter to Easter in each year.

41. Ibid.

42. From Easter 1680 to Michaelmas 1688.

43. See chapter five for the discussion of the sale of Crown and episcopal lands to raise money to pay off short-term debt.

44. Bonney (ed.), *Economic Systems and State Finance*, Part II, chapters six, seven, and eight.

45. PRO, E351/292–9, 302, 304–10 for the declared accounts of the Treasurers at War, 1639–62; Dietz, 'The Exchequer in Elizabeth's Reign', pp. 103–4 for 1600 to 1602; Dietz, 'The Receipts and Issues of the Exchequer during the Reigns of James I and Charles I', pp. 158–67 for 1603–40; Chandaman, *English Public Revenue*, pp. 348–63 for 1660–88; BL, Add. MS 10119, fo. 173 for 1688–99; Gordon, *The History of Our National Debt and Taxes*, p. 88 for 1688–99; *CJ*, vi: pp. 13–14 for 1643–5; PRO, E351/2239–334 for Navy Treasurers' declared accounts, 1602–99; PRO, E351/2664, Ordnance Office declared account, 1642–5; PRO, AO1/1845/67, Ordnance Office declared account, 1662–70. The accounting years vary.

46. PRO, E351/308–10, the figures in the declared accounts of the Treasurers at War for disbandment of the army, in the period 1660 to 1662, have been added to Chandaman's figures for total Exchequer issues and to the issues for the land forces.

47. Outhwaite, *Inflation in Tudor and Early Stuart England*, p. 10; Doughty, 'Industrial Prices and Inflation', pp. 177–92.

48. Dietz, 'The Exchequer in Elizabeth's Reign', pp. 80–9.

49. Ashton, 'Deficit Finance in the Reign of James I', pp. 15, and 23–4.

50. Ibid., p. 15 for Ashton's description of Stuart finance as 'medieval'; Gardiner, *History of England*, ii: pp. 63–87 for the Great Contract, which was James I's and the Commons' attempt to replace feudal impositions and fees with a regular parliamentary revenue.

51. Sharpe, *The Personal Rule*, pp. 9–23. See chapter six, 'The Customs', Table 6.1 for the decline in the value and proportion of subsidies as part of total state revenue from 1603 to 1640.

52. Sharpe, *The Personal Rule of Charles I*, pp. 105–30, 858–920.

53. PRO, E351/308–10, declared accounts of the Treasurers for Disbanding.

54. Chandaman, *English Public Revenue*, Appendix 3.

55. Dietz, 'The Receipts and Issues of the Exchequer during the Reigns of James I and Charles I', pp. 158–67; Chandaman, *English Public Revenue*, pp. 348–63; Gordon, *The History of Our National Debts and Taxes*, p. 88; BL, Add. MS 10119, fo. 173. Chapters six, seven, and eight for the revenues of the customs, excise, and assessment, 1642 to 1660. Chapters two, three, and four for the expenditures made for the military forces and Ordnance.

56. Dietz, 'The Receipts and Issues of the Exchequer during the Reigns of James I and Charles I', pp. 135–53. Chapter six, 'The Customs', Table 6.1.

57. Chapter six for the customs, seven for the excise and eight for the assessment systems and their operational costs.

58. Beckett, 'Land Tax or Excise', pp. 285–90.

59. Dickson, *The Financial Revolution*, pp. 42, 47–9, 57, 60–70, for Dickson's recognition of the importance of the three regular taxes and for his discussion of the efforts that were taken to convert over £9 million in short-term debt into long-term debt in 1710–12. The stock of the South Sea Company eventually absorbed £9.4 million in short-term debt (p. 71).

60. Ibid., pp. 344–7.

CONCLUSION

1. C. Davenant, *Essay on Ways and Means of Supplying the War* (1695), quoted in R.D. Heinl (ed.), *Dictionary of Military and Naval Quotations* (Annapolis, MD, United States Naval Institute, 1966), p. 115. Cicero, *Philippics*, v, *c.* AD, 60; quoted in Heinl, p. 115.

Bibliography

1. SECONDARY SOURCES:

Aiken, William, 'The Admiralty in Conflict and Commission, 1679–1684', in William Aiken and B.D. Henning (eds), *Conflict in Stuart England: Essays in Honor of William Notestein*, New York, Unwin, 1960

Alsop, J.D., 'Government Finance and the Community of the Exchequer', in C. Haigh (ed.), *The Reign of Elizabeth*, Athens, GA, University of Georgia Press, 1985

Anderson, R.C., 'Operations of the English Fleet, 1648–52', *English Historical Review* 31 (1916), 406–28

——, 'The Royalists at Sea', *Mariner's Mirror* 14 (1928), 320–30

Andrews, K.R., *Ships, Money and Politics: Seafaring and Naval Enterprise in the Reign of Charles I*, Cambridge, Cambridge University Press, 1991

Ashley, M.P., *The Financial and Commercial Policy of Cromwellian England*, London, Humphrey Milford, 1934

——, 'War in the Ordnance Office: The Essex Connection and Sir John Davies', *Historical Research* (1994), 337–45

Ashton, R., *The Crown and the Money Market, 1603–1640*, Oxford, Clarendon Press, 1960

——, 'Deficit Finance in the Reign of James I', *Economic History Review* 8 (1957), 310–22

——, 'The Disbursing Official Under the Early Stuarts: The case of William Russell and Philip Burlamachi', *Bulletin of the Institute of Historical Research* 30 (1957), 162–74

——, *The English Civil War, Conservatism and Revolution, 1643–1660*, London, Weidenfeld and Nicolson, 1978

——, 'Revenue Farming Under the Early Stuarts', *Economic History Review* 7 (1956), 310–28

Ashton, T.S. and R.S. Sayers (eds), *Papers in English Monetary History*, Oxford, Clarendon Press, 1953

Atkinson, C.T., 'The Cost of Queen Anne's Wars', *Journal of Army Historical Research* (1955)

Atton, Henry and Henry Holland, *The King's Customs*, London, John Murray, 1908

Aylmer, G.E., 'Attempts at Administrative Reform, 1625–1640', *English Historical Review* 72 (1957), 229–59

——, 'Crisis and Regrouping in the Political Elites: England from the 1630s to the 1660s', in J.G.A. Pocock (ed.), *Three British Revolutions: 1641, 1688, 1776*, Princeton, Princeton University Press, 1980

——, 'From Office-Holding to Civil Service: The Genesis of the Modern Bureaucracy', *Transactions of the Royal Historical Society*, fifth series, 30 (1980), 91–108

——, *The Interregnum: Quest for a Settlement, 1646–1660*, London, Routledge and Kegan Paul, 1972

——, *The King's Servants: The Civil Service of Charles I 1625–1642*, New York, Columbia University Press, 1961

——, *The State's Servants: The Civil Service of the English Republic 1649–1660*, London, Routledge and Kegan Paul, 1973

Barnes, T.G., *Somerset, 1625–1640*, Cambridge, MA, Harvard University Press, 1961

Barnett, C., *Britain and Her Army, 1509–1970*, London, Penguin, 1970

Bibliography

Bartlett, T. and K. Jeffrey (eds.), *A Military History of Ireland*, Cambridge, Cambridge University Press, 1996

Baumber, M.L., *General at Sea: Robert Blake and the Seventeenth-Century Revolution in Naval Warfare*, London, John Murray, 1989

——, 'The Navy and the Civil War in Ireland, 1643–46', *Mariner's Mirror* 75 (1989), 265–9

Baxter, S.B., *The Development of the Treasury, 1660–1702*, Cambridge, MA, Harvard University Press, 1957

Beckett, J.C. 'The Irish Armed Forces, 1660–1685', in J. Bossy and P. Jupp (eds), *Essays Presented to Michael Roberts*, Belfast, Blackstaff Press, 1976

Beckett, J.V., 'Land Tax or Excise: The Levying of Taxation in Seventeenth- and Eighteenth-Century England', *English Historical Review* 100 (April 1985), 285–308

Beresford, J., *The Godfather of Downing Street: Sir George Downing, 1623–1684*, London, Richard Cobden-Sanderson, 1925

Beveridge, W., et al., *Prices and Wages in England from the Twelfth to the Nineteenth Century*, London, Longmans, Green and Co., 1939

Black, J., *The Cambridge Illustrated Atlas of Warfare: Renaissance to Revolution, 1492–1792*, Cambridge, Cambridge University Press, 1996

——, *European Warfare, 1660–1815*, New Haven, Yale University Press, 1994

——, *A Military Revolution? Military Change and European Society, 1550–1800*, London, Macmillan, 1991

Black, J.B., *The Reign of Elizabeth, 1558–1603*, Oxford, Clarendon Press, 1959

Bonney, R., (ed.), *Economic Systems and State Finance*, Oxford, Clarendon Press, 1995

Bottigheimer, K., *English Money and Irish Land*, Oxford, Clarendon Press, 1971

Boxer, C.R., *The Anglo-Dutch Wars of the Seventeenth Century*, London, HMSO, 1974

——, 'Blake and the Brazil Fleets in 1650', *Mariner's Mirror* 36 (July 1950), 212–28

Boynton, L., *The Elizabethan Militia, 1558–1638*, London, Routledge and Kegan Paul, 1976

Braddick, M.J., 'An English Military Revolution?', *Historical Journal* 36 (1993), 965–75

——, *The Nerves of State, Taxation and National Finances, 1558–1714*, Manchester, Manchester University Press, 1996

——, *Parliamentary Taxation in Seventeenth-Century England*, Woodbridge, Suffolk, Royal Historical Society, 1994

——, 'Popular Politics and Public Policy: The Excise Riot at Smithfield in February 1647 and its Aftermath', *Historical Journal* 34 (1991), 597–616

Brenner, R., *Merchants and Revolution: Commercial Change, Political Conflict, and London's Overseas Traders, 1550–1653*, Cambridge, Cambridge University Press, 1993

Brewer, J., 'The English State and Fiscal Appropriation, 1688–1789', *Politics and Society* 16 (1988), 335–85

——, *Sinews of Power: War, Money and the English State, 1688–1783*, New York, Knopf, 1989

Brooks, C., 'Public Finance and Political Stability: The Administration of the Land Tax, 1688–1720', *Historical Journal* 17 (1974), 281–300

Broxap, E., *The Great Civil War in Lancashire, 1642–1651*, Manchester, Manchester University Press, 1973 edn of 1910 book

Brunton, D. and D.H. Pennington, *Members of the Long Parliament*, Cambridge, MA, Harvard University Press, 1954

Canny, N., *The Origins of Empire; British Overseas Enterprise to the Close of the Seventeenth Century*, Oxford, Oxford University Press, 1998

Capp, B., *Cromwell's Navy: The Fleet and the English Revolution, 1648–1660*, Oxford, Clarendon Press, 1989

Carlton, C., *Going to the Wars: The Experience of the British Civil Wars, 1638–1651*, London, Routledge, 1992

Carruthers, B.G., *City of Capital: Politics and Markets in the English Financial Revolution*, Princeton, NJ, Princeton University Press, 1996

Caruana, A., *The Age of Evolution, 1523–1715*, vol. one of *The History of the English Sea Ordnance*, Ashley Lodge, Sussex, Jean Boudriot Publications, 1994

Chandaman, C.D., *The English Public Revenue, 1660–1688*, Oxford, Clarendon Press, 1975

Childs, J., *The Army of Charles II*, London, Trinity Press, 1976

——, *The Army of James II and the Glorious Revolution*, Manchester, Manchester University Press, 1980

——, *The British Army of William III, 1689–1702*, Manchester, Manchester University Press, 1987

——, *The Nine Years War and the British Army, 1688–97*, Manchester, Manchester University Press, 1991

Clark, D.K., 'Edward Backwell as a Royal Agent', *Economic History Review* 9 (1938–9), 45–55

Clark, G.N., *War and Society in the Seventeenth Century*, Cambridge, Cambridge University Press, 1958

——, *The Later Stuarts, 1660–1714*, Oxford, Clarendon Press, 1956

Cockle, M.J.D. (ed.), *Bibliography of Military Books Before 1642*, London, Simpkin, Marshall, Hamilton, Kent and Co., 1900, 1975 edn

Cohen, K.S.H., 'The Naval Operations of the War of 1688–1697', *The Naval Review* 14 (1926), 431–6, 639–59

Coleman, C., 'Artifice or Accident? Reorganization of the Exchequer of Receipt', in Christopher Coleman and David Stanley (eds), *Revolutions Reassessed*, Oxford, Clarendon Press, 1986

Collins, J.B., *Fiscal Limits of Absolutism: Direct Taxation in Early Seventeenth-Century France*, Berkeley, University of California Press, 1988

Corvisier, A., *Armies and Societies in Europe, 1494–1789*, tr. Abigail Siddall, Bloomington, IN, Indiana University Press, 1979

Crews, C.C., 'The Last Period of the Great Farm of the Customs', *Bulletin of the Institute of Historical Research* 14 (1936–7), 118–22

Croxton, D., 'A Territorial Imperative? The Military Revolution; Strategy and Peacemaking in the Thirty Years' War', *War in History* 5 (1998), 253–79

Cruickshank, C.G., *Elizabeth's Army*, Oxford, Clarendon Press, 1966

Cust, R., *The Forced Loan and English Politics, 1626–8*, Oxford, Oxford University Press, 1987

Davies, C.S.L., 'The Administration of the Royal Navy Under Henry VIII: The Origins of the Navy Board', *English Historical Review* 80 (April 1965), 268–88

Davies, G., 'The Army of the Eastern Association', *English Historical Review* 46 (1931), 88–96

——, *The Early Stuarts, 1603–1660*, Oxford, Clarendon Press, 1959

——, 'The Parliamentary Army Under the Earl of Essex, 1642–1645', *English Historical Review* 49 (1934), 32–54

Davies, J.D., *Gentlemen and Tarpaulins*, Oxford, Clarendon Press, 1991

Dewar, A.C., 'The Naval Administration of the Interregnum', *Mariner's Mirror* 12 (October 1926), 406–30

Dickson, P.G.M., *The Financial Revolution in England*, London, Macmillan, 1967

Dietz, F.C., *English Public Finance, 1558–1641*, New York, The Century Co., 1932

——, 'Elizabethan Customs Administration', *Economic History Review* 45 (1930), 35–57

——, 'The Exchequer in Elizabeth's Reign', *Smith College Studies in History* 8 (1923), 65–118

——, 'The Receipts and Issues of the Exchequer during the Reigns of James I and Charles I', *Smith College Studies in History* 13 (July 1928), 117–71

Donagan, B., 'Halcyon Days and the Literature of War: England's Military Education Before 1642', *Past and Present* 147 (May 1995), 65–100

Bibliography

Doughty, R.A., 'Industrial Prices and Inflation in Southern England, 1401–1640', *Explorations in Economic History* 12 (1975), 177–192

Dowell, S., *A History of Taxation and Taxes in England From the Earliest Times to the Present Day*, 6 vols, London, F. Cass, 1888

Downing, B.M., *The Military Revolution and Political Change: Origins of Democracy and Autocracy in Early Modern Europe*, Princeton, Princeton University Press, 1990

Duffy, M. (ed.), *The Military Revolution and the State, 1500–1800*, Exeter, Exeter University Press, 1980

Dyer, F.E., 'The Ship-money Fleet', *Mariner's Mirror* 23 (1937), 198–209

Ehrman, J., *The Navy in the War of William III, 1689–1697: Its State and Direction*, Cambridge, Cambridge University Press, 1953

Eltis, D., *The Military Revolution in Sixteenth-Century Europe*, London, Tauris Academic Studies, 1995

Engberg, J., 'Royalist Finances During the English Civil War, 1642–1646', *The Scandinavian Economic History Review* 14 (1966), 73–96

Falls, C., *Elizabeth's Irish Wars*, London, Methuen and Co., 1970 and Syracuse, Syracuse University Press, 1997 edn.

Farnell, J.E., 'The Navigation Act of 1651, the First Dutch War, and the London Merchant Community', *Economic History Review* 16 (1964) 439–54

Firth, C.H., *Cromwell's Army*, London, Greenhill Books reprint, 1992

——, *The Last Years of the Protectorate, 1656–1658*, 2 vols, London, Longmans, 1909

——, 'The Raising of the Ironsides', *Transactions of the Royal Historical Society* 13 (1899), 17–73

——, 'Royalist and Cromwellian Armies in Flanders, 1657–1662', *Transactions of the Royal Historical Society*, second series, 17 (1903), 101–10

Fischer, D.H., *The Great Wave: Price Revolutions and the Rhythm of History*, Oxford, Oxford University Press, 1996

Fissel, M.C., *The Bishops' Wars: Charles I's Campaigns against Scotland, 1638–1640*, Cambridge, Cambridge University Press, 1994

——, 'Tradition and Invention in the Early Stuart Art of War', *Army Historical Research* 65 (1987), 133–47

——, (ed.), *War and Government in Britain, 1598–1650*, Manchester, Manchester University Press, 1991

Fletcher, A., *A County Committee in Peace and War: Sussex, 1600–1660*, London, Longmans, 1975

——, *Reform in the Provinces: The Government of Stuart England*, Yale, Yale University Press, 1986

Forster, G.C.F., 'Government in Provincial England Under the Later Stuarts', *Transactions of the Royal Historical Society*, fifth series, 33 (1983), 29–48.

Fortescue, J.W., *A History of the British Army*, vol. one, London, Macmillan, 1910

Fox, F., 'English Naval Shipbuilding Program of 1664', *Mariner's Mirror* 78 (1992), 277–92

Furgol, E.M., 'Scotland Turned Sweden: The Scottish Covenanters and the Military Revolution, 1638–1651', in J. Morrill (ed.), *The Scottish National Covenant in its British Context*, Edinburgh, Edinburgh University Press, 1990

Gardiner, S.R., *History of England from the Accession of James I to the Outbreak of the Civil War 1603–1642*, 10 vols, London, Longmans, Green, and Co., 1884

——, *History of the Great Civil War, 1642–1649*, 4 vols, London, Longmans, Green and Co., 1894

Gaunt, P., '"The Single Person's Confidants and Dependents"? Oliver Cromwell and his Protectoral Councillors', *Historical Journal* 32 (1989), 537–60

Gentles, I., *The New Model Army in England, Ireland and Scotland, 1645–1653*, Oxford, Blackwells, 1992

——, 'The Arrears of Pay of the Parliamentary Army at the End of the First Civil War', *Bulletin of the Institute of Historical Research* 48 (1975), 52–63

——, 'The Management of the Crown Lands, 1649–1660', *Agricultural History Review* 19 (1971), 25–41

——, 'The Sale of the Crown Lands in the English Revolution', *Economic History Review* 26 (1973), 614–35

——, 'The Struggle for London in the Second Civil War', *Historical Journal* 26 (1983), 277–305

Gill, D.M., 'The Relationship Between the Treasury and the Excise and Customs Commissioners (1660–1714)', *The Cambridge Historical Journal* 4 (1932–4) 94–9

——, 'The Treasury, 1660–1714', *English Historical Review* 46 (1931), 600–22

Glete, J., *Navies and Nations. Warships, Navies, and State Building in Europe and America, 1500–1860*, 2 vols, Stockholm, Almquist and Wiksell, 1993

Glow, L., 'The Committee-men in the Long Parliament, August 1642–December 1643', *Historical Journal* 8 (1965), 1–14

——, 'The Committee of Safety', *English Historical Review* 80 (1965), 289–313

——, 'The Manipulation of Committees in the Long Parliament, 1641–42', *Journal of British Studies* 5 (1965), 31–52

Gordon, G., *The History of Our National Debts and Taxes from the year MDCLXXXVIII to the present year MDCCLI*, London, M. Cooper of Paternoster Row, 1751

Gordon, M.D., 'The Collection of Ship-money in the Reign of Charles I', *Transactions of the Royal Historical Society* 4 (1910), 141–62

Gras, N.S.B., *The Early English Customs System: A Documentary Study of the Institutional and Economic History of the Customs from the Thirteenth to the Sixteenth Century*, Cambridge, MA, Harvard University Press, 1918

——, 'Tudor "Books of Rates": A Chapter in the History of the English Customs', *Quarterly Journal of Economics* 26 (1911–12), 766–75

Habakkuk, H.J., 'Landowners and the Civil War', *Economic History Review* 13 (1965), 130–51

——, 'The Land Settlement and the Restoration of Charles II', *Transactions of the Royal Historical Society* 28 (1978), 210–22

——, 'Parliamentary Army and the Crown Lands', *Welsh History Review* (1960), 403–26

——, 'Public Finance and the Sale of Confiscated Property during the Interregnum', *Economic History Review* 15 (1962), 70–88

Hale, J.R., 'Armies, Navies and the Art of War', in G.R. Elton (ed.), *The Reformation, 1520–1559*, Cambridge, Cambridge University Press, 1990

——, 'International Relations in the West: Diplomacy and War', in G.R. Potter (ed.), *The Renaissance*, Cambridge, Cambridge University Press, 1957

Hall, H., *A History of the Customs Revenue in England from the Earliest Times to the Year 1827*, 2 vols, London, Elliot Stock, 1885

Harding, R., *The Evolution of the Sailing Navy, 1509–1815*, New York, St Martin's Press, 1995

Harper, W.P., 'The Significance of the Farmers of the Customs in Public Finance in the Middle of the Seventeenth Century', *Economica* (1929), 61–70

Harris, G.L., 'Aids, Loans and Benevolences', *Historical Journal* 6 (1963), 1–19

Hart, M.C., *The Making of a Bourgeois State. War, Politics, and Finance during the Dutch Republic*, Manchester, Manchester University Press, 1993

Hazlett, H., 'The Financing of British Armies in Ireland, 1641–1649', *Irish Historical Studies* (1938), 21–41

Hexter, J.H., *The Reign of King Pym*, Cambridge, MA, Harvard University Press, 1941

Hill, J.R. (ed.), *The Oxford Illustrated History of the Royal Navy*, Oxford, Oxford University Press, 1995

Hirst, D., *Authority and Conflict: England 1603–1658*, Cambridge, Cambridge University Press, 1986

Bibliography

Holmes, C., *The Eastern Association in the English Civil War*, Cambridge, Cambridge University Press, 1974

——, 'Parliament, Liberty, Taxation, and Property', in J.H. Hexter (ed.), *Parliament and Liberty*, Stanford, Stanford University Press, 1992

Holmes, G., *The Making of a Great Power: Late Stuart and Early Georgian Britain, 1660–1722*, London, Longmans, 1986

——, *Augustan England: Profession, State and Society, 1680–1730*, London, George Allen and Unwin, 1982

Hoon, E.E., *The Organization of the English Customs System, 1696–1786*, New York, Greenwood reprint, 1968

Hornstein, S., *The Restoration Navy and English Foreign Trade, 1674–1688: A Study in the Peacetime Use of Seapower*, Aldershot, Scolar Press, 1991

Howard, M., *The British Way of Warfare: A Reappraisal*, London, Jonathan Cape, 1975

——, 'War and the nation-state', *Daedalus* 108 (1979)

Hoyle, R.W. (ed.), *The Estates of the English Crown, 1558–1640*, Cambridge, Cambridge University Press, 1992

Hughes, A., *Politics, Society and Civil War in Warwickshire, 1620–1660*, Cambridge, Cambridge University Press, 1987

——, 'Militancy and Localism: Warwickshire Politics and Westminster Politics, 1643–1647', *Transactions of the Royal Historical Society*, fifth series, 31 (1981), 51–68

Hughes, E., *Studies in Administration and Finance, 1558–1825*, Manchester, Manchester University Press, 1934

Hunt, P. and P.K. O'Brien, 'The Rise of the Fiscal State in England, 1485–1815', *Bulletin of the Institute of Historical Research* 66 (1993), 129–76

Hutton, R., *The British Republic, 1649–1660*, New York, St Martin's Press, 1990

——, *The Restoration: A Political and Religious History of England and Wales, 1658–1667*, Oxford, Oxford University Press, 1985

——, *The Royalist War Effort, 1642–1646*, New York, Longmans, 1982

John, A.H., 'War and the English Economy, 1700–1763', *Economic History Review* 7 (1955), 329–44

Jones, D.W., *War and Economy in the Age of William III and Marlborough*, Oxford, Blackwell, 1988

Jones, J.R., *The Anglo-Dutch Wars of the Seventeenth Century*, London, Longmans, 1996

——, *Country and Court: England, 1658–1714*, Cambridge, MA, Harvard University Press, 1978

——, *The Restored Monarchy 1660–1688*, Totowa, NJ, Rowman and Littlefield, 1979

Judges, A.V., 'Philip Burlamachi: A Financier of the Thirty Years' War', *Economica* 6 (1926), 265–300

Keeler, M.F., *The Long Parliament, 1640–41: A Biographical Study of its Members*, Philadelphia, PA, University of Pennsylvania Press, 1954

Kennedy, D.E., 'The Establishment and Settlement of Parliament's Admiralty, 1642–1648', *Mariner's Mirror* 48 (1962), 276–91

Kennedy, P., *The Rise and Fall of English Naval Mastery*, New Jersey, Ashfield Press, 1983 edn

Kennedy, W., *English Taxation, 1640–1799*, New York, Kelly reprint, 1964

Kenyon, J.P., *The Civil Wars of England*, New York, Alfred A. Knopf, 1988

Kerridge, E., *Trade and Banking in Early Modern England*, Manchester, Manchester University Press, 1988

Kishlansky, M., *The Rise of the New Model Army*, Binghamton, NY, Vail Ballou Press, 1979

——, 'The Sale of the Crown Lands and the Spirit of Revolution', *Economic History Review*, 29 (February 1976)

——, *The Tudor Navy: An Administrative, Political and Military History*, Cambridge, Scolar Press, 1992

Latham, R. (ed.), *Samuel Pepys and the Second Dutch War*, transcribed by W. Matthews and C. Knighton, Cambridge, Naval Records Society, 1995

Bibliography

Lefevre, P., 'Sir George Ayscue, Commonwealth and Protectorate Admiral', *Mariner's Mirror* 73 (1982), 189–200

Leftwich, B.R., *A History of the Excise*, London, Simpkin, Marshall, Hamilton and Kent, 1908

Levy, F.J., 'How Information Spread Among the Gentry, 1540–1640', *Journal of British Studies* 21 (1982), 20–4

Loades, D., 'From King's Ships to the Royal Navy, 1500–1642', in J.R. Hill (ed.), *The Oxford Illustrated History of the Royal Navy*, Oxford, Oxford University Press, 1995

——, *The Tudor Navy: An Administrative, Political, and Military History*, Cambridge, Scolar Press, 1992

Madge, S.J., *The Doomsday of the Crown Lands*, London, Routledge and Kegan Paul, 1938

Martin, L.C., 'John Crane (1576–1660) of Loughton Bucks, Surveyor General of all Victuals for Ships, 1635–1642', *Mariner's Mirror* 70 (1984), 143–8

Mathias, P. and P. O'Brien, 'Taxation in Britain and France, 1715–1810. A Comparison of the Social and Economic Incidence of Taxes Collected for the Central Governments', *Journal of European Economic History*, v (1976), 601–50

Mattingly, G., *The Defeat of the Spanish Armada*, Harmondsworth, Middlesex, Penguin, 1959 edn

May, J., 'Monck as a Naval Commander', *The Naval Review* 21 (1933), 322–39

Melton, F.T., *Sir Robert Clayton and the Origins of English Deposit Banking, 1658–1685*, Cambridge, Cambridge University Press, 1986

Morrill, J.S., 'The Army Revolt of 1647', *Britain and the Netherlands*, eds A.G. Duke and G.A. Tamse. Hague, Martinus Nijhoff, 1977

——, *Cheshire, 1630–1660: County Government and Society During the English Revolution*, Oxford, Oxford University Press, 1974

——, *The Impact of the English Civil Wars*, London, Collins and Brown, 1991

——, 'Mutiny and Discontent in English Provincial Armies, 1645–1647', *Past and Present 56* (1972), 49–74

——, (ed.), *Oliver Cromwell and the English Revolution*, New York, Longmans, 1990

——, *The Revolt of the Provinces: Conservatives and Radicals in The English Civil War, 1630–1650*, New York, Barnes and Noble, 1976

——, (ed.), *Revolution and Restoration: England in the 1650s*, London, Collins and Brown, 1992

Murray, A.L., 'The Scottish Treasury, 1667–1708', *The Scottish Historical Review* 14 (1966), 89–104

Murray, O.A.R., 'The Admiralty', *Mariner's Mirror* 23 (1937), 129–47

Newton, A.P., 'The Establishment of the Great Farm of the English Customs', *Transactions of the Royal Historical Society* 4 (1918), 129–55

Nichols, G.O., 'English Government Borrowing, 1660–1688', *Journal of British Studies* 10 (1971), 83–104

Nolan, J.S., 'The Militarization of the Elizabethan State', *Journal of Military History* 57 (1994), 391–420

North, D. and R.P. Thomas, 'An Economic Theory of the Growth of the West', *Economic History Review* 22 (1970), 1–17

Notestein, W., 'The Establishment of the Committee of Both Kingdoms', *American Historical Review* 17 (1911–12), 477–95

O'Brien, P.K., 'The Political Economy of British Taxation, 1660–1815', *Economic History Review* (1988)

——, 'Public Finance in the Wars with France, 1793–1815', in *Britain and the French Revolution, 1789–1815*, London, Macmillan Education, 1989

Ohlmeyer, J. (ed.), *Ireland from Independence to Occupation, 1641–1660*, Cambridge, Cambridge University Press, 1995

——, 'Irish Privateers during the Civil War, 1642–1650', *Mariner's Mirror* 76 (1990), 119–34

——, and J.P. Kenyon (eds), *The Civil Wars, A Military History of England, Scotland, and Ireland 1638–1660*, Oxford, Oxford University Press, 1998

Bibliography

Oppenheim, M., *A History of the Administration of the Royal Navy and of Merchant Shipping in Relation to the Navy: From 1509 to 1660*, Ann Arbor, MI, Cushing-Malloy, Inc, 1961

Outhwaite, R.B., *Inflation in Tudor and Early Stuart England*, London, Macmillan, 1969

——, 'Royal Borrowing in the Reign of Elizabeth I', *English Historical Review* 86 (1971), 251–63

Parker, G., *The Cambridge Illustrated History of Warfare*, Cambridge, Cambridge University Press, 1995

——, 'The Dreadnought Revolution in Tudor England', *Mariner's Mirror* 82 (1996), 269–300

——, *The Dutch Revolt*, New York, Viking, 1985 edn

——, *The Military Revolution: Military Innovation and the Rise of the West*, Cambridge, Cambridge University Press, 1988, second edn 1996

——, *The Thirty Years' War*, New York, The Military Heritage Press, 1987 edn

Pearl, V., *London and the Outbreak of the Puritan Revolution, 1625–1643*, London, Oxford University Press, 1961

——, 'Oliver St John and the 'Middle Group' in the Long Parliament, August 1643–May 1646', *English History Review* 81 (1966), 490–519

Pennington, D.H., 'The Accounts of the Kingdom, 1642–1649', in F.J. Fisher (ed.), *Essays in the Economic and Social History of Tudor and Stuart England*, Cambridge, Cambridge University Press, 1961

——, 'The Costs of the English Civil War', *History Today* (1958)

——, and I. Roots (eds), *The Committee at Stafford, 1643–1645*, Manchester, Manchester University Press, 1957

Perjes, G., 'Army Provisioning, Logistics and Strategy in the Second Half of the 17th Century', *Acta Historica Scientiarum Hungaricae* 16 (1970), 1–52

Porter, B.D., *War and the Rise of the State. The Military Foundations of Modern Politics*, New York, Free Press, 1994

Powell, J.R., 'Blake's Capture of the French Fleet Before Calais, 4 September 1652', *Mariner's Mirror* 48 (1962), 193–207

——, 'The Expedition of Blake and Montague in 1655', *Mariner's Mirror* 52 (1966), 341–67

Prestwich, M., *Armies and Warfare in the Middle Ages: The English Experience*, New Haven, CT, Yale University Press, 1996

Reid, W., 'Commonwealth Supply Departments within the Tower, and the Committee of London Merchants', *Guildhall Miscellany* 2 (1966), 319–51

Reitan, E.A., 'From Revenue to Civil List, 1689–1702: The Revolution Settlement and the Mixed and Balanced Constitution', *Historical Journal* 13 (1970), 571–88

Richards, R.D., 'The Exchequer Bill in the History of English Government Finance', *Economic History* 3 (1934), 193–211

——, 'The Exchequer in Cromwellian Times', *Economic History* (1931), 213–33

——, 'The Stop of the Exchequer', *Economic History* 2 (1930), 45–62

Richmond, H.W., *National Policy and Naval Strength*, London, Longmans, 1928

Roberts, K., 'Musters and May Games: The Effect of Changing Military Theory on the English Militia', *Cromwelliana* (1991) 5–9

Robinson, G., 'Admiralty and Naval Affairs, May 1660 to March 1674', *Mariner's Mirror* 36 (1950), 12–40

Rodger, N.A.M., *The Safeguard of the Sea, A Naval History of Britain, 660–1649*, New York, HarperCollins, 1997

Rogers, C.J. (ed.), *The Military Revolution Debate*, Oxford, Westview Press, 1995

Roseveare, H., *The Financial Revolution, 1660–1760*, New York, Longmans, 1991

——, *The Treasury, 1660–1870, The Foundation of Control*, London, Allen and Unwin, 1973

Roy, I., 'The Royalist Council of War, 1642–46', *Bulletin of the Institute of Historical Research* 35 (1962), 150–68

Russell, C., 'Charles I's Financial Estimate for 1642', *Bulletin of the Institute of Historical Research* 58 (1985), 110–20

——, *The Crisis of Parliaments: English History, 1509–1660*, Oxford, Oxford University Press, 1971

——, (ed.), *The Origins of the English Civil War*, New York, Barnes and Noble, 1973

Saintly, J.C., 'A Reform in the Tenure of Offices During the Reign of Charles II', *Bulletin of the Institute of Historical Research* 41 (1968), 150–71

——, 'The Tenure of Offices in the Exchequer', *English Historical Review* 316 (1965), 449–75

Scammell, G.V., 'The Sinews of War: Manning and Provisioning English Fighting Ships, 1550–1650', *Mariner's Mirror* 73 (1987), 351–67

Schumpeter, J.A., 'The Crisis of the Tax State', *International Economic Papers* 4 (1954), 5–38

Scott, W.R., *The Constitution and Finance of English, Scottish and Irish Joint-Stock Companies to 1720*, 3 vols, Cambridge, Cambridge University Press, 1910–12

Scroggs, W.O., 'English Finances under the Long Parliament', *Quarterly Journal of Economics* 21 (May 1907), 463–87

Sharpe, K., *The Personal Rule of Charles I*, New Haven, CT, Yale University Press, 1992

Shaw, J.J.S., 'The Commission of Sick and Wounded and Prisoners, 1664–1667', *Mariner's Mirror* 25 (1939), 306–27

Shaw, W.A., 'The Beginnings of the National Debt', in T.F. Tout and J. Tait (eds), *Historical Essays by Members of the Owens College, Manchester*, London, Longmans, 1902

——, 'The Treasury Order Book', *The Economic Journal* 16 (1906), 33–41

Smith, A.G.R., *The Emergence of a Nation State: The Commonwealth of England, 1529–1660*, New York, Longmans, 1984

Stewart, R.W., *The English Ordnance Office: A Case Study in Bureaucracy*, Woodbridge, Suffolk, Boydell Press, 1996

Stone, L. (ed.), *An Imperial State at War: Britain from 1689 to 1815*, London, Routledge and Kegan Paul, 1994

——, *Causes of the English Revolution, 1529–1642*, New York, Harper and Row, 1972

Tallett, F., *War and Society in Early Modern Europe, 1495–1715*, London, Routledge and Kegan Paul, 1992

Tanner, J.R., *English Constitutional Conflicts of the Seventeenth Century, 1603–1689*, Cambridge, Cambridge University Press, 1971

Tatham, G.B., 'The Sale of Episcopal Lands during the Civil Wars and Commonwealth', *English Historical Review* 23 (1908), 91–108

Taylor, A.H., 'The Battle of Sole Bay', *The Naval Review* 41 (1953), 405–15.

——, 'Pepys and His Thirty Ships of the Line', *The Naval Review* 43 (1955), 55–60

——, 'Tromp and the Spanish Fleet', *The Naval Review* 39 (1951), 23–5

Tedder, W.A., *The Navy of the Restoration: From the Death of Cromwell to the Treaty of Breda*, Cambridge, Cambridge University Press, 1916

Thirsk, J., 'Sale of Royalist Land During the Interregnum', *Economic History Review* 5 (1952), 188–207

Thomas, D., 'Financial and Administrative Developments', in H. Tomlinson (ed.), *Before the English Civil War*, New York, St Martin's, 1984

Thrush, A., 'In Pursuit of the Frigate', *Historical Research* 64 (1991), 29–45

——, 'Naval Finance and the Origins and Development of Ship Money', in M.C. Fissel (ed.), *War and Government*

——, 'The Ordnance Office and the Navy, 1625–40', *Mariner's Mirror* 90 (1975), 19–39

Tilly, C. (ed.), *The Formation of Nation States in Western Europe*, Princeton, Princeton University Press, 1975

——, *Coercion, Capital, and the European States, A.D. 910–1900*, Oxford, Blackwell, 1990

Tomlinson, H.C., 'Financial and Administrative Developments in England, 1660–1688', in J.R. Jones (ed.), *The Restored Monarchy, 1660–1688*

——, *Guns and Government: The Ordnance Office under the Later Stuarts*, London, Royal Historical Society, 1979

——, 'The Ordnance Office and the Navy, 1660–1714', *English Historical Review* 90 (1975), 19–39

Underdown, D., *Somerset in the English Civil Wars and Interregnum*, Hamden, NJ, Archon Press, 1972

Ward, M.F.B., 'The Strategy of the Anglo-Dutch Wars of the Seventeenth Century', *The Naval Review* 18 (1930), 289–305, 431–7

Ward, W.R., 'The Administration of the Window and Assessed Taxes, 1696–1798', *English Historical Review* 67 (1952), 522–42

——, *English Land Tax in the Eighteenth Century*, Oxford, Oxford University Press, 1953

Webb, J.T., *Memorials of the Civil War in Herefordshire*, London, Longmans, Green and Co., 1879

Wedgwood, C.V., *The King's Peace, 1637–1641*, New York, Book of the Month Club edn, 1991

——, *The King's War, 1641–1647*, New York, Book of the Month Club edn, 1991

Wernham, R.B., *After the Armada: Elizabethan England and the Struggle for Western Europe, 1588–1595*, Oxford, Clarendon Press, 1984

——, *The Making of Elizabethan Foreign Policy, 1558–1603*, Berkeley, University of California Press, 1980

——, *The Return of the Armadas*, Oxford, Oxford University Press, 1994

Wilson, C., *England's Apprenticeship, 1603–1763*, London, Longmans, 1965

——, *Profit and Power: A Study of England and the Dutch Wars*, London, Longmans, Green and Co., 1957

Worden, B., *The Rump Parliament*, Cambridge, Cambridge University Press, 1977

Wrigley, E.A. and R.S. Schofield, *The Population History of England, 1541–1871*, London, Edward Arnold, 1981

2. PRINTED PRIMARY SOURCES:

Abbott, W.C. (ed.), *The Writings and Speeches of Oliver Cromwell*, 4 vols, Oxford, Clarendon Press, 1988

Cary, H. (ed.)., *Memorials of the Great Civil War from 1646 to 1652*, 2 vols, London, Henry Colbum, 1842

Clarendon, Edward, Earl of, *History of the Rebellion and Civil Wars in England*, 6 vols, Oxford, Clarendon, 1732 edn

Firth, C.H. and R.S. Rait (eds), *Acts and Ordinances of the Interregnum, 1642–1660*, 3 vols, London, HMSO, 1911

Journals of the House of Commons

Calendar of the Committee for the Advance of Money, 1642–1656, London, HMSO, 1888

Hamilton, W.D. (ed.), *Calendar of State Papers, Domestic Series, Charles I*, 25 vols, London, HMSO, 1891

Calendar of State Papers, Domestic, Commonwealth, 13 vols, London, HMSO, 1891

Calendar of State Papers, Ireland, 1633–1660, 3 vols, London, HMSO, 1901–3

Green, M.A.E. (ed.), *Calendar of the Proceedings of the Committee for Compounding, 1643–1660*, 5 vols, London, HMSO, 1889

Shaw, W.A. (ed.), *Calendar of Treasury Books, 1661–1667*, London, HMSO, 1904

——, *Calendar of Treasury Books, Introduction to Volumes XI–XVII*, London, HMSO, 1934

Thomason Tracts:

E85(9), *Special Passages*, 10–17 January 1643

E85(45), *Certain Informations*, 16–23 January 1643

E86(3), *Special Passages*, 17–24 January 1643

E86(5), *Weekly Intelligencer,* 17–24 January 1643
E88(17) *Certain Informations,* 30 January– 6 February 1643
E405(8), Giles Green, 'Vindication of the Navy Committee', London: 1 September 1647
E813(16) Pyrenne, 'the Excise', 1643
Whitelocke, Bulstrode, *Memorials of the English Affairs,* London, Nathaniel Ponder, 1682

3. MANUSCRIPT PRIMARY SOURCES:

a. In the Bodleian Library, Oxford:

Rawlinson MS A176 Papers of Col. Scott, Army and Navy, 1659–78; French fleet size
Rawlinson MS A181 Navy Costs, 1660–7 compared to 1652–60
Rawlinson MS A184 Pepysian MSS, 1670s
Rawlinson MS A185 Navy Papers, 1653–9
Rawlinson MS A186 Navy Papers, 1687–8
Rawlinson MS A187 Admiralty Letters, 1650s
Rawlinson MS A195 Pepys–Navy 1666 and Treasurer at War Accounts, 1645–51
Rawlinson MS A207 Navy Committee, 1650–3 Warrant Books
Rawlinson MS A208 Treasurers at War Account Book, Blackwell and Deane, 1653–9
Rawlinson MS A209 Navy Misc Papers
Rawlinson MS A223 Navy Commissioners' Record Book, 1643–54 (estimates)
Rawlinson MS A224 Admiralty Committee, 1647–50
Rawlinson MS A225 Proceedings of Admiralty Committee, 1650–1
Rawlinson MS A226 Ibid., 1651–2
Rawlinson MS A227 Ibid., 1652–3
Rawlinson MS A461 Debenture Book of Navy Treasurer, 1654
Rawlinson MS B239 Declared Account of Sale of Episcopal Lands
Rawlinson MS C389 Excise Book, Nov 1649–May 1652

Tanner MS 53, Letters between England and Ireland, 1652–4 (Thurloe and Henry Cromwell
Tanner MS 57, Correspondence, England–Ireland, 1648–9

b. In the British Library, London:

Additional MS 4107 Thurloe Correspondence
Additional MS 4156 Letters & Papers, Birch Collection, 1650s Revenue
Additional MS 4166 Thurloe Papers; letters to H. Cromwell
Additional MS 4761 Irish Establishment, 1629, 1660, 1663, 1666, 1669
Additional MS 5500–2 Prize Commissioners, 1649–1660
Additional MS 5755 Exchequer Revenue Offices, Misc. 16th and 17th c.
Additional MS 9294 Navy Papers, 1558–1636
Additional MS 9299 Navy Papers, 1606–1654
Additional MS 9300–6 Seventeenth-century Naval Papers, fleet data
Additional MS 10119 Montague Revenue Accounts, 1618–1701
Additional MS 11597 Scawen Revenue Papers, 1659, 1689
Additional MS 17019 Hyde Papers, Misc. vol. two
Additional MS 17503 List of the navy with cost estimates, 1642–7
Additional MS 18986 Navy Papers, 1644–99
Additional MS 20085 Monck Letters

Additional MS 22546 Navy Papers, 1643–77
Additional MS 22919 Downing's Letters, 1658–9
Additional MS 28053, Correspondence of Osborne, Duke of Leeds
Additional MS 28078, Misc. Treasury Papers, 17th century
Additional MS 28854 Revenue of Protectorate, 1654
Additional MS 28937 Ellis Papers, 1585, 1608–78
Additional MS 32093 Malet Collection, State Papers, 1646–58
Additional MS 32471 Public Revenue, Exchequer, Sept 1656–Sept 1657
Additional MS 33118 Irish Land Transactions, 1656–9
Additional MS 37491 Minute Book of Essex County Committee, 1643–50
Additional MS 63788A Misc. Warrants, 1640s and 1650s

Egerton MS 1048 Prize Goods, April 1649–March 1652
Egerton MS 2126 Fairfax and Fleetwood correspondences, 1649
Egerton MS 2539–43 Nicholas Papers, Public Revenue 1660, Fleet data
Egerton MS 2618 Letters and Papers, 1556–1753.
Egerton MS 2620 O. Cromwell letter to Fairfax, 9 May 1648
Egerton MS 2651 Muster Master Accounts, 1643 for Essex's army
Egerton MS 2978 List of Cromwell's Major Generals, 25 Oct 1655

Harleian MSS 6802–4 State Papers, Charles I; Army Petitions to Parliament
Harleian MS 6844 Military Papers 1704; Treasurer and Paymaster, 1689–96, Army
    establishment 1660; Army pay, 1688–92
Harleian MS 7649 Poems to Lady Newcastle

Lansdowne MS 164 Caesar papers, Exchequer
Lansdowne MS 165 Exchequer receipts and issues, 1609–17
Lansdowne MS 169 Exchequer papers, 1616
Lansdowne MS 232 Ship-money rates; 1654 revenue
Lansdowne MS 323 Tower records, 1703
Lansdowne MS 822 Letters to H. Cromwell in Ireland, 1657

Stowe MS 185 Fee Farm Accounts and letters; Monck proclamation; Whalley's Chester
    Account (£62,349)
Stowe MS 188 Hampden Letter
Stowe MS 322 Extracts from Statute Book, 16th & 17th cent, pop. est.

c. In the Pepys Library, Magdalene College, Cambridge:

Pepysian MS 1534 The state of the Royal Navy . . . 1684
Pepysian MS 2581 Navy White Book
Pepysian MS 2583 The Debt of the Navy, 1668
Pepysian MS 2589 The Navy 1660–8

d. In the Public Record Office, London:

ADM 2/1729 Admiralty Orders and Instructions 1656–7
ADM 7/777–8 Navy Ships' Log Books, 1648–55
ADM 7/827 Duke of York's instructions, 1660
ADM 17/111–12 Victualling, 1655–8
ADM 20/1 Carteret's account Book, Jul 1660–June 1661

AO1/50/24–7 Army Paymaster accounts, 1 Jan 1675–31 Dec 1677
AO1/51/29–34 Army Paymaster accounts, 31 Dec 1677–31 Dec 1680
AO1/52/35–7 Army Paymaster accounts, 1 Jan 1681–31 Dec 1683
AO1/53/38–42 Army Paymaster accounts, 1 Jan 1684–31 Dec 1687
AO1/54/43–6 Army Paymaster accounts, 1 Jan 1688–31 Mar 1692
AO1/55/47–9 Army Paymaster accounts, 1 Apr 1692–24 Dec 1699
AO1/56/50 Army Paymaster account, 24 Dec 1699–24 Dec 1700
AO1/308/1203–4 Paymaster accounts for Dunkirk, 1660–1662
AO1/312/1237–9 Accounts for recruiting and disbanding the 1677/8 expeditionary force
  to France
AO1/315/1256 Paymaster account of Artillery Train in Ireland, 1690–3
AO1/607/65 Customs account, 1659–62
AO1/848–9 Proceeds of the Sale of Dunkirk
AO1/866/1–2 Accounts for circulating Exchequer Bills, 1697–1701
AO1/867/13 Account for purchase and cancellation of Exchequer Bills
AO1/889/3 Excise Account, Mar 1654 to Mar 1655
AO1/890/5 Excise Account, Mar 1655 to Mar 1656
AO1/891/7 Excise Account, Mar 1656 to Mar 1657
AO1/891/9 Excise Account, Mar 1657 to Mar 1658
AO1/893/15 Excise Account, Feb 1661 to Sept 1662
AO1/1073/692–7 Excise Commissioners' accounts, 1683–9
AO1/1074/698–703 Excise Commissioners' accounts, 1689–96
AO1/1075/704–7 Excise Commissioners' accounts, 1696–1700
AO1/1690/36–7 Navy Treasurer accounts, 1600–1
AO1/1691/38–40 Navy Treasurer accounts, 1602–4
AO1/1705/85–8 Navy Treasurer accounts, 1639–41
AO1/1706/89 Navy Treasurer account, 1642
AO1/1708/95–7 Navy Treasurer accounts, 1653–4
AO1/1711/107 Navy Treasurer account, July 1667–Nov 1668
AO1/1712/108 Navy Treasurer account, Nov 1668– Dec 1669
AO1/1712/110 Navy Treasurer account, 1670
AO1/1713/111–13 Navy Treasurer accounts, 1 Jan 1671–31 Dec 1674
AO1/1845/67 Ordnance Office account, 1662–70
AO1/1846–51 Ordnance Office accounts, 1670–80

Exchequer Accounts:

E101/67/1 Accounts of Lord Davenport, Ireland
E101/67/11A Treasurers at War, Feb 1645–9
E101/612/65 Account of Navy Sick and Maimed, 1653–60 (£225,416)
E101/676/51 Assessments Levied, 1653–60; no receipts listed
E122/232/16 Customs Coast Book, Sandwich, 1651–2
E122/232/18 Ibid., Feversham, 1655–6
E190/46/1 Ibid., London, 1650–1
E351/2 Acts of Parliament
E351/4 Victualler's account Book, 1630
E351/5 Pay Claims Books, 1647–52 examinations listed
E351/6 Letter Book of accounts, Devon, 1643–8
E351/59–76 Army Paymasters' accounts, 1660–81
E351/289–90 Carteret's Accounts for Jersey, 1627–9
E351/291 Richard Slanning's account for Pendennis Castle, 1638–9

E351/292–3 Uvedale's accounts, Treasurer at War, 1639–40

E351/294 William Payton's Treas. at War, Ireland, 1640–1

E351/295 Patrick Ruthwen's account for Edinburgh Castle, 1640

E351/296–7 James Lecharte's account, Paymaster in North, 1639–40

E351/298–9 Paymaster Vernon's accounts for Hamilton's army 1639–40

E351/300 Nathaniel Steven's account, Garrison of Gloucester, 1645

E351/301 Justin Heard's account, Garrison of Plymouth, 1646–9

E351/302 Treasurers at War account, Mar 1645 to Dec 1651

E351/303 Robert Hammond's account, Wight, 1648–9 (King's jailer)

E351/304–7 Treasurers at War accounts, Dec 1651 to Feb 1659

E351/308 Assessment Account of James Nelthorpe and J. Lawson 1659–21 Apr 1662

E351/309 Paymaster account of John Baynes, 1659– 62

E351/310 Treasurers at War accounts of James Westham and John Lawson 27 Aug 1660–21 Apr 1662

E351/311–12 Viscount Mordant's account of Windsor, Sep 1660–Aug 1663

E351/438 Sale of Delinquent Estates account, John Dethicke

E351/439 Sequestrations accounts, 1653–5

E351/440 Rents and Profits of Delinquent Estates, 1643–53

E351/441–3 Account of seizure of Delinquent Properties

E351/453 Sale of Bishops' Lands account, 1646–56

E351/592 Committee of Advance account, 1653–4

E351/594 Jessop's accounts of money received on COS warrants

E351/600 Account of sale of land by Elizabeth I

E351/601 William Bennet's account, 1638

E351/602 Sale of fee farm rents accounts

E351/603 Sale of Late King's lands account, 1649–52

E351/604 Sale of Royal forests, 1650s

E351/604/26 Samuel Bond, Alienation fines

E351/605 Sherriffs' accounts, 1638–40

E351/606 William Burnett's account, 1638

E351/607 Missing from the PRO since 1967

E351/608 Badly damaged account, unusable

E351/609 Customs Farmers, Dec 1604–Dec 1605

E351/610 Customs Farmers' accounts, 1605–6

E351/611–13 Customs Farmers' accounts, 1609–12

E351/640 Beer Farm accounts, 1635–6

E351/643–60 Customs Commissioners' accounts, Jan 1643–Sept 1662

E351/1281 Account for 1714 Exchequer bill costs

E351/1282–94 Accounts for costs of circulating Exchequer Bills, 1697–1704

E351/1295–301 Excise Commissioners' accounts, 1647–60

E351/1302–3 Excise Farmers' accounts for London, Nov 1662– Nov 1666

E351/1307 Excise Farmer's account, London, 1671–4

E351/1308 Ibid., Middlesex, 1671–4

E351/2238 Navy Treasurer's account, Jan–Dec 1600

E351/2240–334 Navy Treasurers' accounts, 1 Jan 1602 to 31 Dec 1699

E351/2346 Navy Treasurer Walpole's account, 1711

E351/2428–47 Surveyor of Victual accounts, Jan 1628–Dec 1642

E351/2448–58 Ibid., 1660–Dec 1678

E351/2664 Ordnance Office account, 1642–51

E351/3273 Works and Buildings account, 1644–Mar 1645

E360/102 Assessments accounts, Lincoln, 1649–60

E360/128 Oxon Assessment account, 1646–60
E360/164/346–9 Sussex Assessment Book, 1647–61
E360/208 Accounts of Receivers-General, 1642–60
E364/129 Excise, customs, prize goods, accounts, 1644–59
E401/1406 Exchequer Receipts, Sept 1657–Mar 1658
E401/1928–33 Exchequer receipt books, 1643–4, 1654–61
E403/2608 Lord Protector's Privy Seal Book, Jul 1655–Apr 1659
E403/2700 Exchequer Order Book 1631–2
E403/2751–3 Exchequer Order Books, 1632–5
E404/157 Exchequer parchment warrants, 1655–9
E404/237–8 Treasurer orders and warrants, 1649–52 Fauconberge
E405/286–90 Exchequer Receipt Books, 1636–40, and 1658–61
E407/50 Receipts of Committee of Public Revenue, 1640s and 1650s
E407/80 Ibid.
E407/116–20 Exchequer papers, 1469–1676

State Papers (PRO)

SP 16/514 Navy Commissioners record, 1642–3
SP 25/118 Account Book of money spent for Cromwell's Ireland expedition
SP 28/1–356 Interregnum accounts, Misc., from 1640 to 1660
SP 63/281 Book account of money sent to Ireland, 1649–56

T 1/1 Treasury Books, 1650s
T 48/3–5 Misc. Accounts of Royal debt, Charles II to William III

WO 47/1–4 Journal Book of Ordnance Office, 1644–5, 1651–4, 1657
WO 49/83–5 Debenture Entry Book for Ordnance and supplies, 1644–8
WO 51/2 Entry Book for Bills for Provisions and Ordnance stores, 1655
WO 54/17–19 Ordnance Quarter Books, 1647–58
WO 55/462 Ordnance warrants for stores
WO 55/1666 Book listing stores returned to Ordnance by Ships' gunners

4. DISSERTATIONS AND THESES:

Ashley R., 'The Organization and Administration of the Tudor Office of Ordnance', M. Litt. thesis, Oxford, 1973
Cogar, W.B., 'The Politics of Naval Administration, 1649–1660', Ph.D. dissertation, Oxford, 1983
Hutton, R., 'Royalists' War Effort in Wales and the West Midlands, 1642–46', Ph.D. dissertation, Oxford, 1980
Jones, J., 'The War in the North: The Northern Parliamentarian Army in the English Civil War 1642–1645', Ph.D. dissertation, York University, Ontario, 1991
Reece, H.M.C., 'The Military Presence in England, 1674–1660', Ph.D. dissertation, Oxford, 1981
Roy, I., 'The Royalist Army in the First Civil War', Ph.D. dissertation, Oxford, 1963
Seim, J.E., 'Participation and Practice: County Administration in Staffordshire, 1649–1658', Ph.D. dissertation, Oxford, 1994
Smith, L., 'Scotland and Cromwell: Study in Early Modern Government', Ph.D. dissertation, Oxford, 1980

Index